SOCIETY FOR NEW TESTAMENT STUDIES
MONOGRAPH SERIES
General Editor: R. McL. Wilson, F.B.A.
Associate Editor: M. E. Thrall

43

PARADISE NOW AND NOT YET

Paradise Now and Not Yet

Studies in the role of the heavenly dimension in
Paul's thought with special reference to his
eschatology

ANDREW T. LINCOLN
Lecturer in New Testament
St John's College, Nottingham

CAMBRIDGE UNIVERSITY PRESS

CAMBRIDGE
LONDON · NEW YORK · NEW ROCHELLE
MELBOURNE · SYDNEY

Published by the Press Syndicate of the University of Cambridge
The Pitt Building, Trumpington Street, Cambridge, CB2 1RP
32 East 57th Street, New York, NY 10022, USA
296 Beaconsfield Parade, Middle Park, Melbourne 3206, Australia

First published 1981

Printed in Great Britain by
Redwood Burn Ltd
Trowbridge and Esher

British Library cataloguing in publication data
Lincoln, Andrew T
Paradise now and not yet. – (Society for New
Testament Studies. Monograph series; 43).
1. Bible. New Testament. Epistles of Paul
2. Mysticism – Biblical teaching
3. Heaven – Biblical teaching
I. Title   II. Series
248'.2   BS2655.M9   80-41024
ISBN 0 521 22944 8

CONTENTS

PREFACE

An earlier draft of this work was a doctoral dissertation accepted by the University of Cambridge early in 1975. In revising it for publication, I have attempted to take account of the most significant literature which has appeared since that time in this area of New Testament scholarship.

I am greatly indebted to Professor C. F. D. Moule of Ridley Hall, Cambridge, and formerly Lady Margaret's Professor of Divinity in the University of Cambridge who supervised my original research and who always made himself available to offer help and advice. My thanks go also to the editors of this monograph series, Professor R. McL. Wilson and Dr M. E. Thrall, for their very helpful comments. To my wife, Paula, belongs my deepest gratitude for her sacrifices in support of my work.

September, 1978

ABBREVIATIONS AND NOTE ON THE TEXT

ARW	*Archiv für Religionswissenschaft*
BASOR	*Bulletin of the American Schools of Oriental Research*
BJRL	*Bulletin of the John Rylands Library*
BS	*Bibliotheca Sacra*
CBQ	*Catholic Biblical Quarterly*
EQ	*Evangelical Quarterly*
ET	*Expository Times*
EvT	*Evangelische Theologie*
HTR	*Harvard Theological Review*
IEJ	*Israel Exploration Journal*
JAmAR	*Journal of the American Academy of Religion*
JBL	*Journal of Biblical Literature*
JSS	*Journal of Semitic Studies*
JThCh	*Journal for Theology and the Church*
JTS	*Journal of Theological Studies*
NEB	*New English Bible*
NT	*Novum Testamentum*
NTS	*New Testament Studies*
RB	*Revue Biblique*
RGG	*Die Religion in Geschichte und Gegenwart*
RV	*Revised Version*
SJT	*Scottish Journal of Theology*
ST	*Studia Theologica*
TDNT	*Theological Dictionary of the New Testament*
TLZ	*Theologische Literaturzeitung*
TQ	*Theologische Quartalschrift*
TZ	*Theologische Zeitschrift*
WTJ	*Westminster Theological Journal*
ZKTh	*Zeitschrift für Katholische Theologie*
ZNW	*Zeitschrift für die Neutestamentliche Wissenschaft*

| ZST | *Zeitschrift für Systematische Theologie* |
| ZThK | *Zeitschrift für Theologie und Kirche* |

Unless otherwise stated the United Bible Societies' second edition of the Greek New Testament Text has been employed; the translation of the Bible is the Revised Standard Version; the translation of the Qumran writings is that to be found in G. Vermes, *The Dead Sea Scrolls in English* (third edition, Harmondsworth, 1970); text and translation of Philo are those in the *Loeb Classical Library* (translated by F. H. Colson, G. H. Whitaker and R. Marcus) (London, 1940–61); and the translation of Plato is to be found in *Dialogues* (translated by B. Jowett) (fourth edition, Oxford, 1953).

INTRODUCTION

Questions of immanence and transcendence continue to occupy theologians, the concept of apocalyptic with its transcendent eschatology has been to the fore in Biblical studies and there has been a resurgence of quests for experience of transcendence in contemporary culture. It is not surprising that in this intellectual climate the tension between this-worldliness and other-worldliness should have remained a crucial problem for the Christian life-style. Interest in such broad contemporary issues provided the original context and the initial impulse for a study which might at first sight appear to be a rather obscure angle of approach to Pauline theology.

Before embarking on a consideration of the function of heaven in Paul's thought it is worth briefly placing this consideration in some relation to aspects of the thinking of recent decades about the heavenly dimension or transcendence. If there is an average reaction to the concept of heaven, perhaps it is similar to the anguished but naïve doubts of the squadron chaplain in Joseph Heller's *Catch-22*.

> Did it indeed seem probable . . . that the answers to the riddles of creation would be supplied by people too ignorant to understand the mechanics of rainfall? Had Almighty God, in all his infinite wisdom, really been afraid that men six thousand years ago would succeed in building a tower to heaven? Where the devil was heaven? Was it up? Down? There was no up or down in a finite but expanding universe in which even the vast, burning, dazzling, majestic sun was in a state of progressive decay that would eventually destroy the earth too.[1]

If there is an average belief about heaven among church-goers then it usually remains that which reduces heaven to the vague notion of some place or state to be entered at death. Such popular views are, of course, only part of a much more varied cultural and theological spectrum.

Religious interpreters have been following the swinging pendulum between immanent and transcendent emphases in our culture. While

Harvey Cox's *The Secular City*,[2] which came to terms with secular people's wholly terrestrial horizon and the disappearance of any supra-mundane reality, was being assimilated, the irony was that these same secular people were undergoing a profound disillusionment with the closed secular system in which they had shut themselves and were beginning to break out in all directions. There had been some truth to the assertion of the religious sociologist, Peter Berger, that the Christian in the modern academic world had felt like a witch doctor in a circle of logical positivists. But then more and more a whole spectrum of visions became available from a counter-culture virulently opposed to the technocratic society. One stream was militant in its declarations about overthrowing the system and bringing in a new public paradise, while others pursued their more 'private heavens', grasping after transcendence in a legion of diverse directions which included astrology, Zen Buddhism, meditation, the occult, drug trips and becoming a 'Jesus freak'. But both revolutionary and mystical streams were at one in their dream of a paradise. The song 'Woodstock' had the repeated line – 'We've got to get back to the garden' and Theodore Roszak could write: 'This . . . is the primary object of our counter-culture: to proclaim a new heaven and a new earth so vast, so marvellous that the inordinate claims of technical expertise must of necessity withdraw in the presence of such splendour to a subordinate and marginal status in the lives of men.'[3] The mood was for a return to Paradise and in the words of Julian Beck's Living Theatre it had to be 'Paradise Now'. Cox was not left behind and responded to the festive breakaway mood with his *The Feast of Fools*,[4] in which he attempted to go beyond both radical theology and the theology of hope in a theology of juxtaposition which relied much on the concepts of laughter, festival and fantasy and which pictured Christ as the Harlequin. These very concepts, play, hope and humour, were seen by Peter Berger in his *A Rumour of Angels*,[5] a discussion of the rediscovery of the supernatural, as some contemporary signals of transcendence.

The new quests for paradise inevitably produced disillusionment. Some involved in the cultural upsurge continued the search for various forms of transcendence, but others accepted their own versions of compromise with the technocratic and bourgeois mentality, while the increasing mood became one of austerity, gloom and doom in the face of world-scale prob-lems of the environment and natural resources. The feeling of a number of religious interpreters at this juncture was that what was needed to speak to this situation was a rediscovery of the Bible's apocalyptic themes which, while relating to the threat of global disaster, provide a transcendent perspective on history.[6]

Meanwhile the theological debate about transcendence continued. In the course of it the American New Testament scholar, N. Q. Hamilton, wrote *Jesus For A No-God World*.[7] He stated that it is the 'traditional heavenly – or otherworldly – association of God that is the greatest obstacle to the creation of an adequate theology for our time' and then attempted a reconstruction of the Biblical material which would lead away from apocalyptic and support his declared project of devising 'a form of Christianity without another world'.[8] Similarly British theologian, Alistair Kee, devised *The Way of Transcendence: Christian Faith Without Belief in God*[9] in which he claimed to have moved beyond the work of Ogden, Altizer and van Buren. Belief in God, Kee asserted, was a cultural impossibility but the 'way of transcendence', a life-style of freedom and suffering, was still a viable option. The 'infinite qualitative distinction' was thus seen as a 'way' rather than as a 'being'. Numerous attempts such as these to do theology without reference to any transcendent ontological reality called forth a protest by others, reflected in the Hartford Declaration which affirmed the transcendence and reality of God over against the secular assumptions behind much of the contemporary theological enterprise,[10] and fresh attempts to express the reality of divine transcendence.[11]

The discussion of this-worldliness and other-worldliness is of crucial importance for thinking about the church and its mission. W. H. Capps in *Time Invades the Cathedral: Tensions in the School of Hope*[12] illustrated this by outlining two 'religions of Christianity' which, he believed, stand in irreducible dialectical tension. On the one hand there exists a dominant other-worldly viewpoint in which individual salvation is fostered through hierarchical institutions and the vertical projection of this type of Christianity can be represented by cathedral imagery. On the other hand there is a this-worldly, corporate and horizontal viewpoint and the projection of this variety of Christianity is best symbolized by the ship. The 'cathedral' image pinpoints a view of the church in the classical nature-grace framework where a sense of other-worldliness, of being on the periphery of earthly life, is nourished, a view which could sometimes result in embarrassment at the humanists' charge of 'pie in the sky' escapism. More in line with modern thought has been the 'ship' model where the church is seen as a movement in history which in its demonstration of community shows itself to be the servant of God's concern for all humanity, not as a separate sphere related to the heavenly realm but simply as that part of the world that is discovering the servant life within the structures of society.

At the individual level there had been quite a transition from the tradition of piety, associated particularly with the Puritan heritage, which was distinguished by its assurance of heaven and awareness of heavenly things. Some Christians found new freedom, wholeness and motivation for cultural and political activities in the realization that Christ is the Lord of all of life, while others were still uneasy about how wholehearted affirmation of this life was to be reconciled with the Pauline passages which emphasize the believer's other-worldly orientation, a commonwealth in heaven, or issue commands to seek the things that are above. The latter were suspicious that not a little in the shift in the style of Christian commitment had been dictated by intellectual pressures and fashions.[13]

The issue of a transcendent dimension still plays a major role in the cultural and religious scene, is integral to contemporary theological debate and is crucial for determining the life-style of both the church and the individual Christian. And whether the talk is of paradise or apocalyptic, transcendence or other-worldliness, the concept of heaven is supremely relevant. Yet to move from these issues to the Biblical material about heaven and in particular to a detailed study of how the heavenly dimension functions in Paul's writings involves a gigantic leap. Those for whom the Bible functions in some way as canon do however look to its various strands of thought to inform their perspective on such issues. But particularly with the concept of heaven they immediately discover that the vehicle of revelation concerning the transcendental dimension is limited groping human language, full of symbols which point beyond themselves, language which uses categories of space and time in an attempt to witness to realities which it claims transcend space and time. There is also the obvious difficulty that the writers speak of concepts such as heaven in terms very much bound up with their own cosmological framework clearly different from that of the twentieth-century interpreter. The hermeneutical problem is stated in its classic form by Bultmann in his essay 'The New Testament and Mythology'.

> We no longer believe in the three-storied universe which the creeds take for granted . . . No one who is old enough to think for himself supposes that God lives in a local heaven. There is no longer any heaven in the traditional sense of the word . . . And if this is so, the story of Christ's . . . ascension into heaven is done with. We can no longer look for the return of the Son of Man on the clouds of heaven or hope that the faithful will meet him in the air (1 Thess. 4: 15ff).[14]

Volumes could be and have been written on this. Here is not the place to indulge in lengthy exposition or justification of a personal stance. As will become evident in the last chapter Paul's presentation of God's action in history for human salvation can be seen in terms of a cosmic drama. His depiction of this cosmic drama provides the concepts in which the modern interpreter needs to be 'remythologised'. It is not a question of whether

modern people will interpret their lives by symbols or myths but rather
the question is which symbols or myths they will accept or choose. Will it
be those rooted in the Biblical perspective or those originating in some
other world-view? If the vision involved in Pauline eschatology is not dis-
missed simply because it employs symbolic language to speak of transcendent realities, it may well be found to offer pointers to present-day concerns. Since much of the message of salvation in Paul's writings is presented
through the vehicle of the language of a cosmic drama and cannot be separated from it in the way one would separate a kernel from its husk, the
modern reader needs to become so much at home with this symbolic
language and its function that the message of salvation which the symbols
convey can have its intended effect.[15] This involves a continuing dialogue
where the reader questions the text about the function of its language and
symbols and then expects a response as the text is allowed to interact with
his or her own imagination and intellectual constructs. In this way the gulf
between ancient symbols and modern times can be bridged by what
Gadamer has called a fusion of horizons.[16] The initially strange world of
meaning of the text when appropriated through the fusion of horizons can
illuminate and expand the horizon of the modern reader. A. N. Wilder
writes of the power of Biblical archetypes to mould the imagination 'in
ways that relate to new language-situations and in ways that correct
inherited distortions'.[17]

Only two further elementary observations about the language of eschatology will be made here. First of all, this language involves both vertical
and horizontal referents, spatial and temporal categories. In other words
eschatology involves heaven as well as the Last Day. All too often in treatments of eschatology the latter pole is given all the attention and the
former is virtually ignored. Both sorts of language are to be given their full
weight. All too frequently also, and sometimes subconsciously, twentieth-
century presuppositions about space and time as a closed continuum have
been brought to bear on the New Testament so that anything which transcends space and time is automatically considered unreal. Far greater flexibility is needed in interpreting writings which are themselves rooted in the
belief that the God who created space and time is by no means limited by
his creation. Such flexibility will enable the reader to avoid the simplistic
approach of those who would reduce the possibility of definition to two
options by asserting that these eschatological realities are *either* in time *or*
timeless, they are *either* in space *or* spaceless.[18] Secondly, the key to this
flexibility in interpreting eschatological language is to be found in allowing
for both continuity and discontinuity. The model here must be the resurrection of Christ. In 1 Corinthians 15 Paul's analogy of the transformation

of the seed into the plant suggests that there can be both an element of identity and an element of difference in the relation of the present body to the resurrection body. Since for Paul what will happen to Christians is what has happened to Christ and the resurrected bodies of believers will be like that of Christ (cf. 1 Cor. 15: 20; Phil. 3: 20f), it is legitimate to infer a similar continuity and discontinuity in Paul's conception of what had happened to Christ's body in his resurrection. Paul's insistence in verse 38 of the analogy that 'God gives it a body as he has chosen' places the emphasis on discontinuity but in his argument 'the fundamental continuity is underlined by the fact that it is precisely the mortal, weak man who exists now who undergoes the transformation'.[19] Since, according to Paul in Romans 8, redemption will affect the cosmos in a similar way to the human body, it is also fruitful to apply this same interplay between continuity and discontinuity to the space-time continuum. Thus, contrary to Oscar Cullmann,[20] the age to come should not be viewed as simply continuous with time and in terms of endless time. Nor, contrary to Wilbur Smith in his book *The Biblical Doctrine of Heaven*,[21] should heaven be conceived simply as a place somewhere billions of miles away in this cosmos. On the other hand these eschatological concepts are not part of a Platonic ideal spiritual world and therefore completely a-temporal and a-spatial. It must be stressed again that the language of space and time is being employed for realities which transcend space and time and the paradox which arises from applying the language of continuity to the fact of discontinuity cannot be avoided.[22]

The only scholarly studies of recent date which focus specifically on the topic of heaven are H. Bietenhard, *Die himmlische Welt im Urchristentum und Spätjudentum*,[23] U. Simon, *Heaven in the Christian Tradition*[24] and C. Schoonhoven, *The Wrath of Heaven*.[25] The last work deals almost exclusively with the theme of evil and heaven. Bietenhard provides some valuable Jewish background and Simon some interesting, though often fanciful, insights but neither can be said to have given detailed NT studies but rather a broad overview of the theme arranged topically. The present study is limited to Paul and even then makes no claims to be exhaustive. It focuses on passages where the term οὐρανός or a functional equivalent plays a significant role in an extended discussion. This selectivity means that topics such as angels or principalities and powers which would have to be given fuller treatment in any comprehensive discussion of the heavenly dimension are mentioned only in passing. Few scholars would dispute that there is a tension between the present and the future in Paul's eschatology, but there is far less agreement about the precise nature of that tension. The relation of present and future elements in Paul has been investigated in studies of such concepts as resurrection, righteousness, the Spirit and inheritance, but no thorough study has been undertaken from the perspective of the spatial concept of heaven.[26] The focus of the exegetical and contextual studies which follow will therefore be on the relations between realized[27] and future, spatial and temporal elements in Paul's eschatology. This focus enables the work to contribute substantially to two further areas of debate in NT scholarship. The first is the matter of the relation of the New Testament, and here Paul in particular, to apocalyptic[28] and the second is the question of development in Paul's thought, particularly as this bears on judgment about the status of Colossians and Ephesians in the Pauline Corpus.

As the study progresses it will emerge that three main factors contribute to the general picture of the concept of heaven that it is possible to trace in Paul. The first is Paul's conceptual background and his knowledge of OT and other Jewish traditions about heaven. But then what had previously been just part of the conceptual world he had inherited became an integral element in the startlingly dramatic event of the apostle's meeting with the resurrected and exalted Christ and in his later visions and revelations of the heavenly Christ. The third main influential factor in Paul's thinking about heaven arises from his apostolic task of moulding the thought and practice of converts in the churches for which he felt responsible. He frequently had to deal with distorted views about salvation and the heavenly life which appeared in these churches and his task often involved clashes with opponents, interaction with what he considered to be unsatisfactory alternatives and rejection of false options. This study is therefore set firmly in the context of such apostolic work and sets out to determine how the concept of heaven functions in the particular settings of the various letters. Comparative history-of-religions investigation has been limited to material directly relevant to the passages being studied.

Chapter 1 treats the role of the reference to the heavenly Jerusalem in the polemic of Galatians, examining its implications for Paul's views about the history of salvation and the place of Jerusalem in the development of the early church. In chapter 2 Paul's description of Christ and believers as heavenly in 1 Corinthians 15 is considered as part of his discussion of the resurrection of the dead and related to the problems about heavenly existence and the body in the Corinthian church. Paul's assertions about the heavenly body and about being in Christ's presence after death in 2 Corinthians 4: 16ff and the mention of his rapture to the third heaven in 2 Corinthians 12 are examined in chapter 3 as part of his defence of his apostleship against mounting opposition led by agitators who had come to Corinth. The reference to the heavenly commonwealth in Philippians

3: 20f in the context of the polemic of that passage provides the focus for our fourth chapter, while chapter 5 – Colossians and heavenly-mindedness – discusses the prominence of the heavenly dimension in Colossians, concluding with a detailed evaluation of Colossians 3: 1–4. Chapter 6 deals with the passages concerning heaven in Ephesians and considers why this theme and realized eschatology in general are so pervasive in this letter.

The problem of the sequence of the Pauline letters is a complex one. I shall proceed in what I hold to be the most probable chronological order, considering it slightly more likely that Philippians comes from a Roman than from an Ephesian imprisonment. Colossians is held to be Pauline. Ephesians has been included both because it contains the most extensive treatment of the heavenly dimension in the Pauline Corpus and because, though there are more serious considerations against authenticity in other areas,[29] in regard to its treatment of heaven and eschatology, as the study will show, I find much greater continuity than discontinuity with the undisputed Pauline letters.

The broader questions in relation to Paul's thought are taken up again in the concluding chapter of the study. Heaven is related to the two age structure in Paul's eschatology and it is argued that Paul's spatial language about heaven in contexts of realized eschatology has closer ties with apocalyptic than has been recognized and that this has important implications for various theories about the development of eschatology within the Pauline Corpus. In addition, this chapter shows the role of the concept of heaven in Paul's view of salvation as cosmic in scope, in his perspective on the destiny of humanity and in the tension between this-worldliness and other-worldliness in his assertions about Christian existence.

From this sketch of the contents it should be clear that this study makes no grand claims to break totally new ground in the discipline of New Testament. It is hoped rather that its contribution will be seen to lie in its treatment of a neglected topic which has allowed a new approach, the possibility of looking at aspects of Pauline eschatology from a different angle. The study may also serve as a contribution to the initial stages of the hermeneutical process described earlier whereby an exploration of the Pauline vision of paradise now and not yet can lead to a recognition of the power of this language for moulding our own imagination and intellectual sensitivities.

1

GALATIANS AND THE HEAVENLY JERUSALEM

Paul's reference to ἡ ἄνω Ἰερουσαλήμ in Gal. 4: 26 turns his readers' attention to the heavenly dimension. Elsewhere in the NT the term ἄνω, most characteristic of the Fourth Gospel, is virtually synonymous with heaven and often its purely spatial and its more religious connotations cannot be separated. Here its attributive use is equivalent in meaning to ἐπουράνιος.

1. The polemical setting

In refuting the attacks of the proponents of 'another gospel' (1: 6f) who are intent on making capital out of the tensions which existed between the apostle to the Gentiles and the Jerusalem church, Paul in Galatians 1 and 2 sets out the origins of the gospel which he taught and reviews the history of his apostleship as it relates to the 'pillar apostles' of the Jerusalem church. In the central section of the letter in chapters 3 and 4 he takes up in a more systematic but nevertheless highly polemical fashion the main issues under debate. He gives his perspective on God's actions in the history of salvation and focuses on the question, 'Who are the true heirs of Abraham?' It is to this question that Paul returns in the pericope 4: 21 – 5: 1 which presents in a novel way the insistence throughout the letter that his is a gospel of grace and freedom. Paul believed this theme to be of vital importance in the Galatian situation where false teachers were attempting to draw away his converts. Who were these men?[1] Despite the various identifications that have been proposed[2] the evidence of the letter favours the traditional view of the Judaizers as Jewish Christians from Jerusalem who were concerned about what they considered to be Paul's liberalism with regard to the law.[3] In sketching the position of these opponents from Paul's passing comments it should be remembered that the characterization the apostle provides often operates in terms of pushing his opponents' arguments to their logical conclusion. He is passionately involved, and, as with many who argue presuppositionally, sometimes gives his opponents' position in its extreme form so that the sharpness of the antitheses - Christ or the law, freedom or slavery - which he believes to be involved will become apparent. The opponents obviously may not have been as consistent as he holds them to have been. Something of the force of this observation can be seen in the way Paul interprets Peter's drawing back from eating with Gentiles as *compelling* the Gentiles to live like Jews (2: 14).[4]

The Judaizers were clearly advocating that the Galatians accept circumcision (cf. 5: 2-12; 6: 12f, also 2: 3f) and follow the law (cf. 3: 2, 10ff; 4: 21; 5: 4). In so doing they claimed to represent the official position of the Jerusalem church. This hypothesis best fits the interplay in chapters 1 and 2. We may infer from Paul's anathema on even an angelic messenger if he were to bring 'another gospel' (1: 8, 9) that the agitators came claiming high qualifications. In 1: 22 - 2: 10 the apostle makes a point of denying that his gospel was dependent in any way on the Jerusalem apostles and claims that in fact the apostles themselves recognized his independent apostolic authority. It can only be supposed that this was intended to counter the attack of those who were alleging that because the Jerusalem apostles were the source of Paul's gospel he must follow their approach. In recounting the Antioch incident (2: 11-21) Paul obviously considered that it provided a close parallel to the issue and situation in the Galatian churches and in that incident the circumcision party feared by Peter are closely linked if not identified with τωας ἀπὸ Ἰακώβου (2: 12). It is likely that the Galatian agitators were just such strict law-abiding members of a group from the Jerusalem church associated with James.[5] As a pressure group within that church they took a more extreme line than James himself and yet were able to claim to be spokesmen for the mother-church and its apostles.[6] Paul's mention of the one who is troubling the church 'whoever he may be' (5: 10) could be a reference to his opponents' claim to represent those 'who are reputed to be pillars', especially James.[7]

The Judaizers insisted that if a Gentile wished to become a Christian he must also become a Jew and in this way Christianity would have had to remain a movement within Judaism. They seem to have attempted to put forward this position in its most attractive form by offering the Galatian converts a more complete version of the Christian message (cf. the use of ἐπιτελεῖν in 3: 3 where Paul asks his readers, 'Having started with the Spirit, are you now finishing up with the flesh?').

This view of the opposition provides the best explanation for the theological discussion of chapters 3 and 4 where Paul deals with the place of the law in the history of salvation in the context of addressing himself to the question about the true seed of Abraham. It could well be that σπέρμα Ἀβραάμ (3: 16) was a self-designation of the opponents[8] and that it was this which led Paul to emphasize that in fact the original promise was made to 'seed' in the singular and therefore should be seen as finding its fulfilment in Christ.[9] In any case it appears that the Judaizers promoted circumcision on the grounds that only those who submitted to this rite could enter fully into the elect community of the people of God and become the seed of Abraham. It is striking that in response to such propaganda the apostle in chapters 3 and 4 tries to make plain to the Galatians that they have already attained to the goals the agitators are holding before them and that they have done so simply by faith in Christ. Nothing needs to be added. Through faith they have received the blessing of Abraham which was demonstrated in their reception of the promise of the Spirit (3: 14). His opponents' claim to be the true seed of Abraham in addition to their concern for the law allows Paul to play off these factors against each other as he develops the inherent tension in Israel's history between the Abrahamic covenant of promise and the Mosaic covenant of law. He is able to point out to the Galatian Christians that in fact the law can add nothing to the status they have already attained through faith in the promise, for the law was intended for a very different purpose and for a limited period of time. Instead, through faith in Christ, they are already the seed of Abraham, heirs according to promise (3: 15-29). Even further, they have become not just sons of Abraham but sons of God himself (3: 26; 4: 6f). How can this require completion?

Into this view of Paul's polemic 4: 21 - 5: 1 with its references to the law, the promise, Abraham's descendants and Jerusalem fits beautifully. Chapters 5 and 6 can then be seen as Paul's attempt to make certain that he is not misunderstood either by the Galatian churches or by his opponents from the Jerusalem church and to demonstrate that in his preaching of freedom from the law he is not calling for moral licence but for that sort of responsible love which is in fact the fulfilment of the law (cf. 5: 13, 14).

2. Genesis and the two Jerusalems

In 4: 21 - 5: 1 Paul immediately takes the battle on to his opponents' ground. Those who want to be under the law should be consistent and hear what the law (i.e. the Pentateuch) says. Paul is thinking of a specific command from the law which the Galatians inclined to be swayed by the Judaizers' teaching need to obey. Thus the passage leads up to the quotation of that command in verse 30.[10] In order to show the Galatians that his application of this portion of the law to their situation is appropriate the apostle prepares the way by a midrash on and around the incident in Genesis from which this command is taken, a midrash which sees the incident from his new vantage point in the history of salvation. He points out that if the Galatians are so concerned about being sons of Abraham they should remember that in fact Abraham had two sons and there were two very different lines of descent from the patriarch. One son came by a slave and the other by a free woman. The distinction goes further, for the former can be said to have been born according to the flesh, the latter through promise. 'Flesh' here need not have the negative ethical overtones of a sphere of existence dominated by sin which it has elsewhere in the letter, notably in 5: 13ff. In this particular contrast it simply means by natural procreation, without the intervention of a divine promise (cf. the same argument as expounded by Paul in Rom. 9: 6-9).As Paul has already shown in chapter 3 this natural descent from Abraham is no longer a decisive factor for the continuity of the history of salvation, it is rather a matter of faith (cf. 3: 7, 14, 23ff).

Why does Paul introduce this midrash on this particular passage at this stage in his argument? At first sight the Genesis narrative does not appear especially promising for Paul's viewpoint and, as we shall see, the apostle has to do some manoeuvring in interpreting the text in order to reach the end he has in view. Both these factors may well indicate that the Sarah and Hagar narrative is not entirely Paul's own choice of text. Rather he felt it necessary to address it because it was being used by his opponents to their own advantage.[11] Once more, with his own midrash, the apostle is attempting to turn the tables on his opponents who would have made use of the straightforward implications of Genesis 15 and 16 that, while the descendants of Hagar and Ishmael were Gentiles, it was only the descendants of Sarah and Isaac who counted as the true seed, Jews who were to inherit the promises. It would be but a short step from this for the Judaizing opponents to point out that this line included Moses and the law and had its seat in Jerusalem. Any Gentiles who wished a share in the promise would therefore have to recognize the claims of the law, be circumcised and acknowledge Jerusalem as the authoritative centre of the renewed people of God.[12]

The Judaizers build effectively on the literal force of the text, but what method of interpretation allows Paul to outflank them, to invert this exegesis so that it is now the people of the law who are the descendants of Hagar and the offspring of Sarah are the minority of Jews and increasing preponderance of Gentiles who embrace the gospel by faith[13] and to move from Hagar and Sarah in Genesis 15 and 16 to the Jerusalem of his day and the heavenly Jerusalem? His own words on the matter are – ἅτινά ἐστιν ἀλληγορούμενα. ἀλληγορέω can mean to speak allegorically or to interpret allegorically. It is the former meaning which best fits this

context[14] and the present participle parallels the present tense used in
verse 30 – τί λέγει ἡ γραφή; In other words Paul believes that these things
in the Scriptures can in fact speak to those in the Galatian churches who
will listen (cf. verse 21); but as he uses them they speak allegorically.

The word 'allegorically' should not however be allowed to prejudice any
decision on Paul's technique here and we should certainly not import into
that word all the connotations that come to be attached to it on account
of the later exegetical techniques of the Alexandrian school. Paul's use of
the verb ἀλληγορέω was not meant to denote a hard and fast hermeneutical category. The verb is a fairly late Greek word first found in Philo,
cf. *De Cherub.* 25, and also in Joseph and Asenath I, 24 and so certainly
had not developed a rigid technical sense at the time of Paul's usage.[15]
Literally ἀλληγορέω need only mean 'to speak with another meaning' and
theoretically the means by which this was done could involve what we
would now term either analogy or typology or allegory. Thus Paul's use of
this particular verb cannot be decisive for indicating in any detail his
method of interpretation. Indeed there have been quite sharply varying
opinions ever since the time of Paul as to whether this passage is pure allegory or simply typology. H. J. Schoeps says that it 'is allegorical rather
than typological' and 'by its wilful distortions is sheer Hellenistic midrash
speculation against a rather obscure apocalyptic background'.[16] On the
other hand Antiochene scholarship, reacting to the abuse of allegory by
the early Fathers, refused to recognize any allegory in Paul, and
Chrysostom's comment that Paul used the word ἀλληγορέω in an unusual
sense, since what he had called an allegory was in fact a type, has been
echoed by more recent writers.[17]

If it is essential to typology that there be 'a real correspondence
between type and antitype' and 'this correspondence must be both historical (i.e. a correspondence of situation and event) and theological (i.e.
an embodiment of the same principle of God's working)'[18] and if Paul's
interpretation of the OT had simply included verses 22, 23, 28–30, then
there would be no difficulty whatsoever in recognizing the passage as
typology. Just as there were in OT history two sons of Abraham, one of
the flesh by a slave woman and the other by promise of a free woman, so
now in Paul's day there are also two sorts of descendants of Abraham,
those born according to the flesh and those born according to the Spirit.
Then as now the former persecuted the latter. However, as we have seen,
Paul finds himself up against the historical fact that it was the Jews who
were Isaac's seed and the Gentiles who were Ishmael's descendants, and
this produces a real tension between type and antitype in his midrash.[19]
In addition he wishes to make his application as pointed as possible for

the Galatian situation and to show that the passage has the law and Jerusalem in view. These factors force him to move out of the realm of straightforward typology. Even if one does not hold that the identification of Hagar with Sinai in verse 25 is based on onomatology or gematria, there is still a large element of contrived interpretation in the correspondence Paul makes between Hagar and Mt Sinai and the present Jerusalem. Even though it be asserted that the principle of bondage links the three concepts, it is this which Paul is trying to demonstrate in making the correspondence and it cannot be assumed as lying on the face of the OT texts and as therefore providing the basis for the correspondence. Furthermore there is no real historical correspondence between a woman and a covenant (verse 24) or a woman and a mountain (verse 25). It is true that Paul's method is very different from the sort of allegorization in which Philo indulges with regard to the same OT incident. Indeed Philo can explicitly say,

> When then you hear of Hagar as afflicted or evil-entreated by Sarah, do not suppose that you have here one of the usual accompaniments of women's jealousy. It is not women that are spoken of here; it is minds – on the one hand the mind which exercises itself in the preliminary learning, on the other, the mind which strives to win the palm of virtue and ceases not till it is won (*De Congress. quaer. Erud. grat.* 180).[20]

As compared to this, Paul's allegorizing does not attempt to develop philosophical principles and is rooted in the OT history, yet this does not justify a blurring of all distinctions whereby his interpretation is simply viewed as typology.[21]

Though the basic framework of Paul's treatment of the OT in Gal. 4: 21ff is typological, in his attempt to make its application specific he uses what we would now call allegory. Paul serves up a cake, the basic ingredients of which are typological but which has some allegorical icing.[22] What saves his allegorizing from becoming capricious is his deep concern with the history of salvation and his attempts even here to see Hagar, Sinai and Jerusalem in relation to the on-going process of God's redemptive activity. Similarly the reference to the Jerusalem above need not be considered simply as an arbitrary insertion but can be seen to be integral to the redemptive-historical context of Paul's thought. Yet the reason allegory can be a useful interpretative tool for the apostle is that the Genesis narrative does not function for him simply as part of the history of salvation but as sacred text which can be actualized in new contexts, a basic presupposition for midrash.[23] In fact his midrash has basic affinities with the handling of the sacred text in the synagogues. It moves from the Pentateuchal text (here the summary of the Genesis narrative in verses 21, 22) to an exposition (verses 23-9) which takes up terms from the narrative, particularly ἐλευθέρα and παιδίσκη but also υἱοί which becomes τέκνα in the midrash, and which introduces a citation from the prophets which has conceptual links with the Genesis narrative (verse 27), before returning to that narrative for its final textual citation and application (verse 30f).

3. The Development of the Argument about the Two Jerusalems

As Paul looks at God's dealings in history in covenantal terms Hagar and Sarah are seen as two covenants. According to the first part of the allegory one covenant is from Sinai and like the slave woman it bears children for slavery. So that there can be no mistake in the minds of those who would never have dreamed of associating Hagar with the law covenant from Sinai, Paul makes explicit that this is precisely the association he has in view.

The next clause (verse 25a) is notorious for its difficulties both of text and of meaning. We opt for the reading τὸ δὲ Ἀγὰρ Σινὰ ὄρος ἐστὶν ἐν τῇ Ἀραβίᾳ.[24] On this reading Paul is reversing the order of the previous verse in a summary statement which is meant at the same time to support the identification he has made and advance his argument. Many commentators have despaired of ever finding a satisfactory reason for the apostle's inclusion of such a statement. Deissmann's resort to gematria[25] is not only far fetched but also simply does not work. Not much more convincing is the etymological explanation which holds that Paul was indulging in a play on words and was linking Hagar with the Arabic word for stone or cliff (hadjar) which was also associated with Sinai in some way.[26] There are two explanations which are more likely. One sees the mention of Arabia as underlining the fact that Mt Sinai is situated outside the land of promise in a land of oppressed peoples who were often known as descendants of Hagar. In Baruch 3: 23 the Arabians are called 'sons of Hagar' (cf. also Ps. 83: 6f; 1 Chron. 5: 19). Paul may also have connected Sinai and the Arabian wilderness with the wilderness to which Hagar fled (cf. Gen. 16: 7, 14).[27] The other explanation treats the first δέ in verse 25 as resumptive and the second one as adversative and suggests that Paul is attempting to justify his identification of Sinai with the present Jerusalem despite the great difference in location between the two.[28]

In fact our own suggestion for the place of this verse in Paul's argument lies in a combination of these two possible explanations. The geographical reference ἐν τῇ Ἀραβίᾳ is meant both to strengthen the Hagar-Sinai correspondence and to build a bridge towards the Sinai-Jerusalem comparison which follows. To the Judaizers and their sympathizers in the Galatian churches it would have been by no means obvious, to say the least, that

Hagar corresponded to the Sinai covenant. In their view the law had been given at Sinai to the descendants of Abraham through Isaac and had nothing to do with Hagar. Thus the further statement with its geographical addition is meant to justify such an unexpected comparison. Hagar can be said to be Sinai because Sinai is in Arabia and Arabia has negative redemptive-historical connotations, since not only was it associated with the descendants of Hagar and Ishmael but was also outside Palestine, the land of promise. At the same time ἐν τῇ Ἀραβίᾳ followed by συστοιχεῖ δὲ forestalls objections to Paul's further unexpected comparison of Sinai to the present Jerusalem. How could he identify in his allegory two places geographically unconnected? That this could have been a consideration for Paul is supported by the fact that his one other reference to Arabia in this letter in 1: 17 is in a context which makes precisely the point that he could not have been dependent on Jerusalem because he was a great distance away in Arabia. Now in 4: 25 he is saying that Hagar is Mt Sinai in Arabia (with its special connotations mentioned above), nevertheless (despite being in Arabia) Sinai corresponds to the present Jerusalem because it bears children for slavery.[29]

The shorthand nature of Paul's development of his allegory becomes even more pronounced when we discover that on the other side of the comparison he simply states the last element – 'But the Jerusalem above is free, she is our mother.' He meant his readers to assume that Sarah was the other covenant. But which covenant? If he had spelled out this side of the allegory, would he have referred to the Abrahamic covenant of promise which came through Sarah and her son?[30] Or would he have identified Sarah with the new covenant in accordance with 2 Corinthians 3 where he contrasts the old Sinaitic covenant with the new covenant and its freedom?[31] The latter seems more likely. In which case Paul's thinking runs along very similar lines to that of the writer to the Hebrews who also links the new covenant with Mt Zion and the heavenly Jerusalem in a contrast with Mt Sinai (cf. Heb. 12: 18–24).

4. The present Jerusalem

The force of Paul's allegorical application is that 'the present Jerusalem' is to be characterized as in slavery on account of its ties to the Sinaitic law on which it prided itself. Jerusalem obviously refers to more than the geographical location. For Paul Jerusalem in its present state was the epitome of legalistic Judaism (cf. his remarks about Judaism and the tradition of the fathers in 1: 13ff) and therefore to be viewed as in bondage. His whole comparison with the slave woman Hagar, whose descendants were some of the traditional enemies of Israel, would have come as a stinging insult to

Jews proud of their Abrahamic descent who, like those depicted in the Gospel of John, might have boasted, 'We are descendants of Abraham and have never been in bondage to any one' (Jn 8: 33). The insult was increased by the association of Jerusalem with Arab territory (Sinai in Arabia corresponds to the present Jerusalem) which then as now would have enraged a patriotic Jew. But Paul's attack on Jerusalem and her children is of course not political or racial but from a religious viewpoint. Here he is at one with the gospel passages which depict Jesus' lament over and judgment on Jerusalem and her children (cf. Matt. 23: 31ff; Lk. 19: 41ff) and his knowledge of Jesus' struggle with the Jerusalem authorities and the end that he met at their hands must have influenced his negative evaluation of Jerusalem.

But the significance of the reference to the present Jerusalem and her children goes further. It was not only meant to designate Judaism on a broad scale but also, and more particularly, the Judaizers who were harassing the churches of Galatia and who were also slaves to the law.[32] It is striking that Paul develops his polemic in the terms he does. He is not content to talk in general terms about the law nor is he content simply to mention Israel or Judaism, as he does in 1: 13, 14. His polemic is aimed specifically at Jerusalem. It is this which makes his allegory so complicated. It is this also which indicates that his opponents are very much in his mind. We have noted their links with Jerusalem and the church there. It is very likely that Paul's reference to Jerusalem and his emphatic formulation in the next verse – 'But the Jerusalem above is free, she is our mother' – was provoked by the fact that one of the slogans of the Judaizers was Ἰερουσαλὴμ ἥτις ἐστιν μήτηρ ἡμῶν.[33] This would fit all the emphasis on Jerusalem in Paul's defence in 1: 13 - 2: 14. As Jewett comments, 'The fact that the agitators dwelt on Paul's alleged dependency on Jerusalem indicates they themselves had a Jerusalem-oriented viewpoint.'[34] It is also striking that Paul's contrast of his freedom in Christ with slavery in 2: 4 is in connection with false brethren in the Jerusalem church – οἵτινες παρεισῆλθον κατασκοπῆσαι τὴν ἐλευθερίαν ἡμῶν ... ἵνα ἡμᾶς καταδουλώσουσιν. Certainly the Judaizers attempted to use the authority and status of the Jerusalem church and its apostles against Paul. They would have claimed that not only they but also Paul were dependent on the Jerusalem church because of its status as the *mother*-church – hence Paul's disclaimer here as well as in chapters 1 and 2.

It is easy to see why the agitators would have given such primacy to Jerusalem in their thinking. First of all it would have had special significance for them as Jews, but even more so now as Jewish Christians. It was the place in which Jesus had been crucified and where as risen Lord he had appeared to his disciples. Just as the Jews expected the appearance of the Messiah in Jerusalem, so the early Christians expected his return there (cf. Luke 13: 35). In the meantime his disciples regarded themselves as οἱ ἅγιοι, the people of God, for whom the promises of the old covenant had been fulfilled and they assembled in the temple at Jerusalem as the appropriate place for their praise (cf. Luke 24: 52f). It was in Jerusalem that the Holy Spirit came on them at the feast of Pentecost and it was in Jerusalem that the first Christian community was formed and from Jerusalem that the gospel spread.[35] For these extreme Jewish Christians this sort of primacy of Jerusalem had taken on exaggerated proportions. Anything which did not emanate from and conform to the practice in the mother-church in Jerusalem, the city of the people of God, would automatically have been suspect to them. Their emphasis on the law and their misplaced claims for Jerusalem were such that Paul included these Judaizers in his category of the present Jerusalem and her children who are in slavery.

5. The heavenly Jerusalem – its background, meaning and eschatological reference

Paul makes his contrast to the present Jerusalem and her children in terms of ἡ ἄνω Ἰερουσαλήμ[36] and evidently felt that this terminology did not require the least explanation for his readers. He could introduce the concept of a heavenly Jerusalem quite casually and presuppose knowledge of it, which suggests that traditions about a heavenly Jerusalem were fairly widespread. Yet literary evidence for this concept in Jewish expectations is not as widespread as many commentators would have us suppose and is of a quite late date, though we can assume that it incorporates earlier tradition. In any case the predominant interest in Jerusalem in Jewish hopes lay in another direction.

As the apostle's supporting quotation in verse 27 indicates, the concept of a heavenly Jerusalem has its roots in OT prophecy with its hopes for a new eschatological Jerusalem. Yet passages such as Isa. 2; 54: 10–14; 60–2; Ezek. 40–8 and Zech. 12–14, while depicting a new and glorified Jerusalem as the centre of the world to which all nations will come in the last days, remain very much in continuity with Israel's national hopes which centre around the earthly Jerusalem. The vision of the new Jerusalem which seems most to transcend the bounds of the earthly is that contained in Isa. 65: 17–25 where Jerusalem is created as part of the new heavens and new earth, its inhabitants are described in terms which involve the miraculous and the depiction of its glory is mixed with motifs of paradise. Such a passage in particular can be seen as a starting-point for later development of a heavenly Jerusalem, a concept which as such does not occur in the OT.

In later Judaism too there are many traditions about a completely re-built and glorified earthly Jerusalem (cf. Tobit 13: 9ff; 14: 7; Jub. 4: 26; Sib. Or. V, 250ff; 414–433; Ps. Sol. 11: 8; Test. Levi 10: 5; Test. Dan 5: 7, 12). In 1 Enoch 90: 28f the old Jerusalem is taken away and the seer watches God bring a new one in which He will dwell, but this new Jeru-salem is not conceived of either as already pre-existent in heaven or as coming down from heaven at the last day.[37] There is evidence of similar expectations of a renewed Jerusalem in the Qumran literature (cf. 1QM XII, 13ff; 4Qp Isa.[a] I, 7, 11 and the Aramaic fragments 1Q32 which describe the new Jerusalem[38]). There can be little doubt that this rep-resents the predominant trend in Jewish eschatology and that, with all the speculative detail employed, nevertheless its hopes for the new age were firmly fixed on the earthly capital of an earthly state.[39]

Perhaps Rabbinic literature comes closest to a correspondence to the terminology used by Paul. The Rabbis knew of a 'Jerusalem that is above' (רושלם של מעלה') that was the counterpart of the Jerusalem below and also of a Jerusalem to come which they contrasted with the present Jeru-salem (cf. *B. Baba Bathra* 75*b*). Often this discussion of a heavenly Jeru-salem builds on Isa. 49: 16 and the fate of the heavenly city is seen to run parallel to that of the earthly, so that, for example, it can be stated that the Shekinah 'will not enter the heavenly city until the earthly city has been rebuilt'.[40] It is likely that this was viewed as an actual city built in heaven, but in the earlier rabbinic texts it was not an eschatological hope in that they did not suggest the Jerusalem above coming down from heaven at the end of history.[41]

Since this is so, Paul's concept of the heavenly Jerusalem has far more in common with the apocalyptic development of ideas about the new eschatological Jerusalem to be found in 2 Baruch and 4 Ezra, though it is difficult to tell how early the traditions incorporated in these writings from just after the time of Paul developed. In 4 Ezra the new Jerusalem will appear from heaven (10: 53f; 13: 35f) and be revealed along with paradise (7: 26). Meanwhile it is already visible to the seer (8: 52; 10: 25–27, 40ff). Significantly enough, in the revelation of the glory of the heavenly Jerusalem to the seer in the fourth vision (9: 26 – 10: 59) the earthly Jerusalem is depicted as a barren woman who through God's intervention is given a son, yet this son dies on his wedding night. On seeing the mother's anguish, the seer speaks of Sion, the mother of us all, who also is in great grief and affliction over her children. Later the woman's countenance is transfigured and the interpretation of the vision is then given in terms of the earthly and heavenly Jerusalems. To be precise, the writer does not actually speak of a heavenly Jerusalem here and perhaps it would be more accurate to speak of the woman as representing the city as God intended it to be in the beginning and as he will make it in the end. The son seems to represent the actual inhabitants of the city who share the nature of their mother but suffer destruction until they are reunited with her in the final transformation of the age to come. Although employed very differently, some of these traditional motifs are seen in Paul's treatment of Jerusalem in Galatians 4. In 2 Baruch also Jerusalem is to be restored and transformed in the age to come (cf. 6: 9; 32: 4), while at the same time this heavenly Jerusalem is seen as the pre-existent eternal home of the righteous (cf. 4: 2–7). As in a number of Rabbinic interpretations this passage uses Isa. 49: 16 as indicating a heavenly Jerusalem and is worth quoting in full as perhaps the clearest reference to the present existence of the Jerusalem above.

> Dost thou think that this is that city of which I said: 'On the palms of my hands have I graven thee'? This building now built in your midst is not that which is revealed with me, that which was prepared beforehand here from the time when I took counsel to make Paradise, and showed it to Adam before he sinned, but when he transgressed the commandment it was removed from him, as also Paradise. And after these things I showed it to my servant Abraham by night among the portions of the victims. And again I showed it to Moses on Mt. Sinai when I showed to him the likeness of the tabernacle and all its vessels. And now, behold, it is preserved with me, as also Paradise.[42]

Here the real Jerusalem is the heavenly, and this heavenly reality was shown only to a few most privileged people, the seer among them. It is to be assumed, though it is not stated in this section, that along with Paradise the heavenly Jerusalem will return at the end of time.

It seems very likely that the image of an eschatological heavenly Jerusalem was given an even stronger present reference at Qumran where it could be applied to the community itself. In 4Qp Isa[d]I, 1f the prophetic vision of a new and glorified Jerusalem from Isa. 54: 11, 12 is interpreted of 'the priests and the people who laid the foundations of the Council of the Community . . . the congregation of his elect, like a sapphire among stones'.[43] In 1QH VI, 24–33 the 'city' imagery used for the community is specifically that of Jerusalem and G. Jeremias has demonstrated in a comparison of the elements of this imagery with those found in the traditions of the eschatological and heavenly Jerusalems in Rev. 21, Heb. 11: 10,

Sib. Or. V, 250ff and Hermas, Vis. 3 and Sim. 9 that the Qumran passage is drawing on a similar tradition of the heavenly Jerusalem but boldly applying this to its own community.[44]

For Paul also the heavenly Jerusalem of the age to come is an already present reality, but his is a unique use of this concept. In both 4 Ezra and 2 Baruch the existence of the heavenly city, present with God and engraved on the palms of his hands, serves to guarantee the destiny and salvation of the earthly city. Here in Galatians 4 however there is no such suggestion as the apostle sets the heavenly Jerusalem over against the earthly in sharp contrast.[45] This negative evaluation of the present Jerusalem differs also from the positive relationship between the two cities found in the Rabbinic literature, where the heavenly city is the prototype or pattern of the earthly. Paul differs further in that he does not appear to hold that there is an actual city in heaven, for in seeing this city as the mother of all believers he relieves the concept of its purely material and national connotations.[46] On the other hand, because of its eschatological nature, Paul's notion of the heavenly Jerusalem must not be confused with any Platonic concept of 'the city whose home is in the ideal' (cf. *The Republic*, IX, 592).[47] In contrast to the Qumran passages Paul does not identify the heavenly Jerusalem with the present community of believers but maintains a distinction by viewing the Jerusalem above as the mother of believers.[48]

The mixed nature of the antithesis between the two Jerusalems has often been observed but should not for this reason be glossed over, for it is strikingly significant for any study of Paul's eschatology. The present Jerusalem is contrasted with the Jerusalem above, a temporally qualified concept being set over against a spatially qualified one. In this way the apostle has the best of both worlds, since

> by mixing the terms of the antithesis the characteristic of the one city implies the opposite trait in the other. Thus ἡ νῦν Ἰερουσαλήμ is 'present' but at the same time, being antithetical to ἡ ἄνω Ἰερουσαλήμ, it is by implication 'earthly'. Likewise ἡ ἄνω Ἰερουσαλήμ is 'heavenly', but being antithetical to ἡ νῦν Ἰερουσαλήμ it is also by implication 'future'.[49]

While it is true that the heavenly Jerusalem gains this eschatological perspective from the contrast, this should not be allowed to obscure the fact that the emphasis in Paul's statement is on *realized* eschatology.[50] As in the apocalyptic and Qumran references what is to be revealed at the end can be thought of as already existing and it is when his emphasis is on realized eschatology that the apostle exchanges temporal categories for spatial. This realized aspect of Paul's eschatology is underlined by the double use of the present tense (ἐστιν) – the heavenly Jerusalem *is* free, she *is* our mother. The heavenly city represents an order which is now being realized and the benefits of which can now be experienced by the believer. Paul modifies the concept he has taken over from Jewish apocalyptic tradition by employing it to describe the church's situation within the history of salvation as it now enjoys the anticipation of the eschaton by virtue of what Christ has accomplished.

The emphasis on realized eschatology comes in a setting where Paul has to stress in the face of Judaizing opposition that his readers' salvation is already complete. By faith the Galatians are already members of the heavenly Jerusalem. The enticement of a fuller gospel held out to them by those purporting to represent Jerusalem could add nothing to such a status. It could only detract, for if they succumbed they would thereby become enslaved to the law so characteristic of the earthly Jerusalem. The heavenly Jerusalem by contrast stands for the new order of salvation bound up with the new age which is accessible now to faith.[51] It is no longer the case that the inheritance promised to the descendants of Abraham is the land of Canaan with its centre in Jerusalem, but now this inheritance (cf. 3: 18, 29; 4: 1, 7, 30; 5: 21) comes to the sons of Abraham by faith and is the new age, the kingdom of God, with its focus as the heavenly Jerusalem. Whereas in 2 Baruch and 4 Ezra the heavenly Jerusalem guaranteed that in principle the earthly Jerusalem, whatever its present condition, would eventually fulfil its role in eschatological expectations, here in Galatians 4 there is no such hope for the present Jerusalem, for it is now classed as part of the old age and subject to the forces of that age, the law, sin and death. For Paul the element of continuity with the history of salvation under the old covenant lies not through Jerusalem as such but through Christ and those who by faith in him are children of Sarah through the promise (cf. verses 23, 28, 31).

6. The heavenly Jerusalem as mother

In the terms of Paul's allegory Sarah, the free woman, is the heavenly Jerusalem and this is why he can go on to state that ἡ ἄνω Ἰερουσαλήμ is both free and our mother. When Sarah is seen in the background of the latter description it compares remarkably with the apostle's description in Rom. 4: 16 of Abraham as 'the father of us all'.[52] It is noteworthy that in his allegory he concentrates on the feminine side of salvation history rather than on Abraham and the masculine side as earlier in the letter and, for example, in Romans 4 and 9.[53] A number of factors may have been involved in his use of the 'mother' image. If our earlier suggestion is correct that his opponents' propaganda made use of the traditional Jewish claim that Jerusalem was their mother, and Paul was intent on countering such a claim, then this would go a long way to explaining both why he starts out with the two women in the first place and why they lead up to the contrast between the two Jerusalems. In turning the tables on his opponents Paul is able at the same time to transform the traditional ways in which the concept of mother had been used in regard to Israel's history. He gives new content to the idea of Sarah as mother of Israel as she now becomes the prototype of the new covenant and its freedom and of the heavenly Jerusalem. Previously 'mother' had been applied to the earthly Jerusalem. It is described in this way in 2 Bar. 3: 1ff and 4 Ezra 10: 7, 17 and OT passages such as Isa. 50: 1; Jer. 50: 12 and Hos. 4: 5 probably paved the way for such a description. Ps. 87: 5 may have been particularly influential in this development – 'Of Zion it shall be said, "This one and that one was born in her".'

As the quotation of Isa. 54· 1 in verse 27 shows, Paul is quite consciously taking what had traditionally been applied to the earthly Jerusalem and claiming it for the heavenly.[54] This Isaiah passage is particularly appropriate for his purposes since it speaks of the future of Jerusalem in terms reminiscent of the Sarah–Hagar relationship. 'Rejoice, O barren one that dost not bear; break forth and shout, thou who art not in travail; for the desolate hath more children than she who hath a husband.' It is by no means a verse ripped out of context and applied arbitrarily. On the contrary, in the original context as the prophet looks to the eschatological fulfilment of God's promises to Israel, amid the numerous references to Abraham and Jacob and their offspring in Isa. 40–66, the theme of Jerusalem is especially prominent.[55] The prophecy considers how it is that the seed of Abraham, which should have been as numerous as the sand on the shore, has been reduced to a small remnant of exiles. God's answer is given in 48: 18, 19. If Israel had obeyed, then 'your offspring would have been like the sand, and your descendants like its grains'. Despite this God has not forgotten Jerusalem (49: 14ff) and the prophet brings consolation: 'Look to Abraham your father and to Sarah who bore you; for when he was but one I called him, and I blessed him and made him many. For the Lord will comfort Zion (51: 2, 3).' What God did for Abraham he will do for Zion (cf. 51: 1 – 52: 12) and this will come about through the vicarious suffering of his Servant who 'shall see his offspring' and 'make many to be accounted righteous' (53: 10, 11). Then the passage Paul quotes continues this theme, picturing Jerusalem in a way that recalls the earlier reference to Sarah in 51: 2. She was at first barren while Hagar had a son, yet through Isaac the descendants of Sarah were eventually to be as numerous as the stars (cf. Gen. 15: 5; 17: 16). Similarly God will have mercy on Jerusalem and restore her population in great numbers, so much so that the new Jerusalem will spread in all directions and 'your descendants will possess the nations and will people the desolate cities' (54: 1-3). Thus the children of the new Jerusalem would be more numerous than those of the old and mother Zion will stand amazed at their large number. 'Then you will say in your heart: Who has borne me these? I was bereaved and barren, exiled and put away, but who has brought up these? Behold, I was left alone; whence then have these come?' (49: 21). The abundance of children described could not have come simply from natural processes but must be ascribed to the activity of God. Those who receive this eschatological comfort are the offspring of Abraham (cf. 41: 8) and yet the prophet sees the multiplication of Jerusalem as involving the ingathering of non-Israelites (cf. 44: 5; 45: 22; 49: 6; 56: 6, 7; 60; 66: 18-21) and this whole multiplication of offspring as the fruit of the Spirit of God (cf. 44: 3-5).

It is important to note that all these themes from Isaiah also play a part in Paul's concept of the Jerusalem above. He sees them all as being fulfilled in what God has begun to accomplish through Christ. For him Isa. 54: 1 could not be applied to the present Jerusalem with its reliance on natural descent, but was only appropriate for describing the eschatological reality that had become present in Christ and the existence of those born according to the Spirit (verse 29). It could only describe a Jerusalem which was viewed not primarily as an ethnic centre for Jews or Jewish Christians, but where Isaiah's prophecies were being fulfilled and Jews and Gentiles were becoming one people. Thus Paul's concept of the heavenly Jerusalem must be understood in the framework of 3: 28 - 'there is neither Jew nor Greek ... for you are all one in Christ Jesus' and 6: 15, 16 where in the new creation neither circumcision nor uncircumcision count for anything, but all those who believe, not simply Jewish Christians, can in fact be called 'the Israel of God'.[56] Through Christ the heavenly Jerusalem is the origin of and belongs to the new people of God consisting of both Jews and Gentiles and in Paul's designation of it as μήτηρ ἡμῶν, ἡμῶν clearly has in view the community of believers, the church.

This church depends for its existence on the heavenly realm as is indicated by the heavenly Jerusalem's function as mother and the presupposition for such a concept must be that the one who is the church's Lord and the origin of its life is in heaven. The relation of the Jerusalem above to believers should be carefully noted, especially in the light of the application of similar imagery to the community at Qumran. The existence of the heavenly Jerusalem is at present lived out through the church, but the heavenly Jerusalem is not to be identified with the church as such. The ἡμῶν of verse 26 indicates believers who are on earth while the Jerusalem that is their mother is a heavenly phenomenon. Despite the Qumran precedent this verse provides no basis for the doctrines which became popular with the Church Fathers and which identified the church with the heavenly Jerusalem[57] or changed the relationship and viewed the earthly church as the mother of Christian believers.[58] The heavenly Jerusalem is rather to be viewed as the new age depicted in spatial terms and the anticipation of the full life of this new age is now present in the church. The emphasis is on realized eschatology and yet it is the very fact that the church is not made one with the Jerusalem above which indicates that for Paul the present existence and experience of the church remains anticipation. Though the church is not to be identified with the heavenly Jerusalem, it is clear that Paul conceives of the church in this passage as having a heavenly dimension.[59] Because he holds that Christ, the church's Lord, is in heaven he can describe the church as having its origin and centre of existence in the heavenly realm.[60]

7. The freedom of the heavenly Jerusalem

Most commentators who have written on this passage have felt it sufficient to make a few observations about the background of the idea of a heavenly Jerusalem but have largely neglected to consider its function in Paul's argument as 'mother' and especially as 'free'.

Since in his allegory Sarah, the free woman, stands for the heavenly Jerusalem, it too is said to be free and by the time he reaches the conclusion of verse 31 that believers are children of the free woman, in speaking of the free woman Paul has both Sarah and the heavenly Jerusalem in mind.[61] Through the allegory he has shown that the Galatian Christians are free. Chapter 5: 1 now concludes this section with an appeal to hold firmly to this freedom and not to submit again to a yoke of slavery. The Judaizers are clearly in view at this point in the conclusion, as they have been throughout the allegory. In line with the pattern we find elsewhere in Paul, the imperative to resist the advances of the agitators in Galatia rests on an indicative, on a statement of what Christ has accomplished – τῇ ἐλευθερίᾳ ἡμᾶς Χριστὸς ἠλευθέρωσεν. στήκετε οὖν . . .[62]

The passage contrasts the present Jerusalem with its enslaving emphasis on the law, an emphasis continuing in the message emanating from the present Jerusalem through the Judaizers, with the heavenly Jerusalem as the fountain of freedom and the true inheritance of the believer. It is Christ who has liberated the Galatians in order that they should enjoy this freedom of the Jerusalem above (cf. 5: 1), to which they have been called (5: 13). By linking it with the Jerusalem above Paul shows that freedom is a quality belonging to the new age. The spatial description of the new age underlines the fact that it is only the transcendent power of the new order which is able to free from the bondage of the powers of the old age. The law is one of those powers. Both 4: 9 and 5: 1 indicate that for the Galatians to turn to the law to complete their salvation would be the same as to return to their pagan past and its slavery. Christ has not done his work only for such an incongruity to occur. Redemption according to Paul involves not only liberation *from* the present evil age (1: 4) but also liberation *to* the life and freedom of the new age present as the heavenly Jerusalem (4: 26). The tour de force of Paul's allegory is that he is able to show that it is the very law which the Galatians are allowing to enslave them (4: 21) which should in fact speak to them of the freedom of the heavenly Jerusalem and those who belong to it. To understand this would be to be liberated specifically from any necessity for circumcision but also from the claims of the whole law, from which this one particular demand cannot be separated (cf. 5: 2, 3).

The believer is to live as the free citizen of a free city, and this freedom of the city is seen in terms of its ruler. It is Christ who has set people free for freedom (5: 1). The freedom that believers have can be said to be 'in Christ Jesus' (2: 4), and linking this section with Paul's earlier argument Christ is seen to be *the* seed of Abraham, *the* heir according to promise and thus *the* son of the free woman. He was born when the time had fully come in order to complete God's promised programme of liberation (cf. 4: 4f). From this vantage point any return to the law merits the apostle's strong warning in 5: 4 that this would be to sever oneself from Christ and fall away from God's grace. Instead of any such apostasy the freedom of the heavenly Jerusalem which centres in Christ is to be lived out through the power of the Spirit, for the children of the Jerusalem above are born according to the Spirit (4: 29) and are to walk by the Spirit (5: 16ff). If believers are led by the Spirit they cannot be under the law (5: 18) and in fact where the Spirit is producing his fruit the law becomes superfluous (5: 23).

In this way it is apparent from Paul's discussion in the rest of the letter that between the bondage of the present Jerusalem and the freedom of the Jerusalem above stand the cross of Jesus Christ, where liberation from the law and the powers of the present evil age was achieved, and the power of the Spirit, who makes this freedom of the heavenly Jerusalem operative in the lives of believers on earth as he unites them to the heavenly Christ.[63] The heavenly dimension is thus seen as having a dynamic effect on the lives of believers. It is because the heavenly Jerusalem, where Christ now rules, is itself free, that the existence of believers on earth can be a liberated one.

8. The clash between the representatives of the present Jerusalem and the representatives of the heavenly Jerusalem

Paul finds an additional element in the Genesis narrative which corresponds to the Galatian situation. Just as then he who was born according to the flesh, that is, Ishmael, persecuted him who was born according to the Spirit, that is, Isaac, so it is now in Galatia. It is usually held that the apostle's interpretation of the Genesis incident relies on rabbinic exegesis of the word מצחק in Gen. 21: 9 where this verb often translated as 'playing' is variously seen as immoral conduct or shooting arrows or quarrelling (cf. Gen. R. LIII, 11). The last of these explanations is developed in the Palestinian Targum on Gen. 22: 1 and it is probably its idea of Ishmael mocking Isaac's claim to inheritance which Paul had in mind.[64] Whatever the source of the apostle's interpretation of Gen. 21: 9, he clearly applies it to the clash he sees occurring in the situation of his own work. The rival groups are the same as those designated as children of the present Jerusalem and children of the Jerusalem above. The Spirit makes real to the latter their inheritance (cf. 3: 14; 4: 6, 7) and so can be seen both as the link with the heavenly Jerusalem and the guarantee of full inheritance of the heavenly dimension.[65] The former group should again be seen to include both Jews with their reliance on the law and the Judaizers in Galatia who are perpetuating this false emphasis. That Paul sees the Judaisers' emphasis on the law as belonging to the sphere of the flesh is shown in 3: 2, 3 where he asks the Galatians, 'Did you receive the Spirit by works of the law? . . . Having begun with the Spirit, are you now ending with the flesh?' and also by the parallel between 5: 16 and 5: 18 where in one case the Spirit-controlled life is contrasted to gratifying the desire of the flesh and in the other to being under the law. That the Judaizers are in view in this reference to those born according to the flesh is further indicated by the contrast between adherence to law and life in the Spirit elsewhere in the letter (cf. 3: 14, 18; 3: 23 – 4: 7; 5: 4, 5, 18, 24). Thus the persecution referred to in verse 29 must be seen as not only being perpetrated against the church by Judaism (cf. 1: 13, 23; 5: 11; 6: 12) but also as taking in the behaviour of the Judaizers in troubling the church and mocking or jeering at the believers' claim to be heirs by faith alone (cf 1: 7ff; 2: 4, 12f; 4: 17; 5: 7, 10, 12; 6: 17).[66]

Though the pericope closes with the summarizing remarks of 4: 31 and 5: 1, the OT quotation in 4: 30 is in fact the punchline of Paul's polemical midrash. After setting the stage for their application by means of his allegory he can now drive home the actual words of Scripture – 'But what does the Scripture say? "Cast out the slave and her son; for the son of the slave shall not inherit with the son of the free woman." '[67] Paul is using the quotation as a call for action based on a prophecy of what will in fact take place. Sarah's words in Gen. 21 were taken up into God's will and Paul is sure that similarly it is not God's will for the descendants of the slave woman, the representatives of the present Jerusalem, to share in the inheritance with the descendants of the free woman, the representatives of the Jerusalem above. The Jews who persecute the church and the Judaizers who are causing such trouble will by no means triumph, for through their reliance on the law for righteousness they are being and will be excluded from inheritance with the true people of God in the heavenly Jerusalem. Since the Scripture must be fulfilled, Paul sees the first part of the quotation as constituting a call for decisive resistance on the part of the Galatian believers. That this was his intention and that the Judaizers are in view is confirmed by his summing up of the message of the allegorical interpretation in 5: 1 where the call for action is stated explicitly – 'Stand fast therefore, and do not submit again to a yoke of slavery.'[68] Not only so, but this ties in remarkably with Paul's statement about the Judaizers' intentions in 4: 17, which immediately precedes this section of the argument. By casting doubts on whether the Galatians were really heirs and by telling them they needed circumcision and the law, the Judaizers were trying to shut out (ἐκκλείεσθαι) of the inheritance those whose claim was faith in Christ. But now once more Paul turns the tables. On the contrary, the Galatians who are the true heirs must be firm in their resolve to shut out or exclude these Judaizers – ἔκβαλε τὴν παιδίσκην καὶ τὸν υἱὸν αὐτῆς. Those who object that Paul would not expect the Galatians to do any such thing are ignoring further indications of the severity of his intentions elsewhere in the letter. In 1: 8, 9 he pronounces that the false teachers, whoever they may be, are to become ἀνάθεμα,[69] and while the 'bearing of judgment' in 5: 10 refers to God's judgment rather than man's, the reference to a little leaven leavening the whole lump in the preceding verse (5: 9), together with the apostle's call to his readers to take his standpoint in 5: 10a, constitutes an indirect appeal to take disciplinary measures. In the one place where Paul uses the same saying about the leaven (1 Cor. 5: 6), the saying is followed by the command – 'Cleanse out the old leaven' – and the whole context is one in which the apostle is pronouncing judgment and calling for ecclesiastical discipline (cf. 1 Cor. 5: 1–5, 13).

With its triumphant rhetorical flourish – 'But what does the Scripture say?' – 4:30 climaxes Paul's whole argument from Scripture and enables us to see the polemical reason for which he introduced his midrash in the first place. To the Galatians inclined to follow the Judaizers, he is saying, 'You want to be under the law, then why not hear what it says?' (verse 21). What does it say? 'Cast out the slave and her son' (verse 30). In other words: 'Send these Judaizers packing – back to Jerusalem, where they belong.'[70] Paul expects the Galatians to take measures to ensure that the community which belongs to the heavenly Jerusalem be kept free from the enslaving influence of the present Jerusalem. The present Jerusalem with its life lived under the law and according to the flesh cannot co-exist with the heavenly Jerusalem and its free life of the Spirit and of the new age.

9. Concluding observations on the significance of Paul's reference to the heavenly Jerusalem

What may have appeared to be rather an obscure reference to the heavenly dimension in the midst of a complicated passage in Galatians turns out to have great significance for an appreciation of Paul's eschatology, his view of salvation history, and his outlook on the nature of the church and developments in its early life. Three major points may be made.

First, Paul's use of ἄνω in conjunction with the concept of the holy city indicates clearly that language about the heavenly dimension is metaphorically qualified, employing earthly realities to point symbolically to realities which transcend time and space. Just as on account of the resurrection and the Damascus road appearance, Paul conceived of the heavenly Christ himself as having an independent reality, so for him the heavenly realm in which Christ rules, here viewed in terms of the holy city, was equally real and gave the church's life a transcendent point of reference as is reflected in his depiction of the heavenly realm as the mother of believers.

In both apocalyptic writings and Qumran the heavenly Jerusalem could be conceived of as already present and from his particular perspective on salvation Paul can also employ the image of the Jerusalem above to express a realized eschatology, but with a distinctive reference – the believer's present enjoyment of the benefits of the new age which Christ has made available. The image should not however leave the impression of the heavenly dimension as a static reality, for it signifies a reality which is, but which is also yet to come. For Paul the heavenly realm is part of the forward-moving history of salvation.[71] As such it has a dynamic effect on the believing community, as its mother providing life and as a realm of freedom making possible liberation from the bondage of the old age.

Secondly, reference to the heavenly realm is sparked off by the apostle's involvement in controversy, not a controversy about this realm itself but rather one in which claims to succession in the history of salvation are at stake. The contrast between the present Jerusalem and the Jerusalem above shows that Christ has made the decisive difference for Paul's perspective on salvation history and thus also for his evaluation of the place of Jerusalem in that history. As he compares the role of Jerusalem in the periods before and after Christ's death and resurrection, he sees both continuity and discontinuity. However, in reaction to the exaggerated claims of the Judaizers, Paul's contrast between the present Jerusalem and the heavenly Jerusalem clearly emphasizes the discontinuity. There are two factors in Paul's thinking about Christ which provide the necessary presuppositions for this perspective. The first is his knowledge of the rejection of Jesus by Jerusalem, especially by its religious authorities, which led to the crucifixion. The second is his belief that, through the resurrection and exaltation of Christ, the focus of salvation history has moved from the earthly to the heavenly realm. For him the hope of Israel lies not in Jerusalem but in Jesus Christ, the one who fulfils all that Jerusalem dimly foreshadowed in regard to the presence of God with his people.[72] Since Christ is in heaven (cf. for example Phil. 3: 20), all that the earthly Jerusalem promised can now be transferred to the reality of the heavenly dimension which Christ has opened up, in fact, to the heavenly Jerusalem. Thus there is an element of continuity in that the name Jerusalem is retained and the significance of that name for the fulfilment of God's promises to Israel still stands in the background, yet what God has accomplished in Christ has radically altered its meaning. The old category has been reinterpreted so that no longer in view is a restored national capital which will be the geographical centre for the ingathering of the nations in the Messianic era but Jerusalem can now designate instead the focal point of the heavenly existence of the new age.

These two views of Jerusalem represent the Jewish concept of salvation history, shared to a large extent by the Judaizers from Jerusalem, and Paul's new and more radical Christological perspective. Their emphasis is on the continuity of their hopes with the faith of their fathers, while Paul's whole argument is intended to demonstrate that any genuine claim to continuity with father Abraham must at the same time do justice to the decisive discontinuity, brought about by the fulfilment of the promises to Abraham in Christ.[73] Thus the true heirs of Abraham are no longer simply his physical offspring but those who by faith are incorporated into *the* offspring, Christ, and their true inheritance is no longer the earthly city but the heavenly Jerusalem of the new age whose life they already share.[74]

Thirdly, it has become clear that the relation of the church to the heavenly Jerusalem is not one of identification but that the heavenly realm must be seen as the source of both the church's life and its freedom. But if

Paul's mention of the present Jerusalem is not just a general concept standing for Judaism but is also directed at his Judaizing opponents' exaggerated
claims for Jerusalem's place in the early church, then the contrast between
the present and the heavenly Jerusalems carries further implications for
Paul's view of the church, implications which have generally been overlooked.

Instead of the earthly Jerusalem having such a dominant role in the life
of the early church that all other churches needed to come under the
authority of the Jerusalem church and conform to her practices, Paul's
negative evaluation of the present Jerusalem may indicate that he was by
no means convinced that Jerusalem was destined to remain the geographical and administrative centre of the church. On the contrary Paul's claim
over against the agitators from Jerusalem was that the Jerusalem church
had in fact renounced control over the Gentile churches (2: 9). But as it
took time for the first generation of Jewish Christians to recognize the
implications of Christ's death and resurrection for their attitude to the
temple and its worship, so it took time for the implications of what had
happened in Christ to be seen with regard to the role of Jerusalem. It was
Paul, the apostle to the Gentiles, who saw most clearly what was at stake.
He was convinced that believers need not look to the law-observing church
of Jerusalem as their mother-church. Their true mother and the guarantor
of their freedom is instead the heavenly Jerusalem. Christ, the church's
Lord, is in heaven and therefore the church is inextricably bound up with
the heavenly order and cannot be dependent on any earthly city, whether
it be Jerusalem, Antioch or Rome. No earthly centre is to be regarded any
longer as the official headquarters of the church. Rather the church is
thrown on to its relation to the heavenly realm and its glorified Lord for
its rule.[75] While Paul did not receive his authority from the Jerusalem
apostles, he recognized the importance of ensuring the continuity of his
message with theirs (cf. 2: 2), and while he did not view the Jerusalem
church as the centre of a hierarchical structure of authority, he did recognize various ties to that church. He would of course have granted that it
had a certain geographical and chronological primacy for the way in which
the gospel spread and the church developed (cf. Rom. 15: 19). The collection for the Jerusalem saints (cf. 2: 10; Rom. 15: 26ff) also provides
evidence that the apostle was eager to demonstrate the visible unity of the
churches he had founded with the Jerusalem church, but it involved no
recognition of the superiority or higher-ranking authority of the Jerusalem
church.[76]

The attitude expressed by Paul in the contrast of Gal. 4: 25, 26, by
decisively rejecting the view that the church remain a group within

Judaism centred in the earthly Jerusalem and by paving the way for the universal mission of a church looking to the Jerusalem above, urged the church forward in a period of great controversy. At the same time in its significance for the church's mission this notion of the Jerusalem above provided the fulfilment of Israel's eschatological hopes for Jerusalem noted earlier. The prophets, and in particular the prophecy of Isaiah which provides much of the background for Paul's thought here (cf. verse 27), saw the final salvation in terms of a 'centripetal' movement in which all the nations would be gathered to a renewed and glorified Jerusalem (e.g. Isa. 2: 2–4; 56: 6, 7; 66: 18–21). For Paul this prophetic motif is being fulfilled, for those Gentiles who are children of promise do come to a Jerusalem glorified by the presence of God but because of Christ's exaltation this Jerusalem is not on earth but has become the focal point of the heavenly dimension.

2

1 CORINTHIANS AND HEAVENLY EXISTENCE

In 1 Corinthians the heavenly dimension becomes explicitly prominent in Paul's discussion at chapter 15 when in verses 42-9 he describes both Christ and believers as heavenly. As he deals in a comprehensive way with the resurrection of the dead, he is able to set out his own perspective on heavenly life and the place of the body in Christian existence, two themes which are central not only to this chapter but also to an understanding of the diverse problems in the church at Corinth and the attitudes which gave rise to these problems.[1]

1. Heavenly existence in Corinth

It is generally agreed that the irony of the apostle's language in 1 Corinthians 4: 5, 8 reflects the 'over-realized' eschatology of many in Corinth. These Corinthians believed that the kingdom was already here and that they as the saints were already reigning and judging. Their life in the Spirit with its abundance of charismatic gifts seemed to them proof that they were already enjoying the eschatological blessings of freedom and fullness associated with the consummation. Some of Paul's attempts to correct this over-confidence can be seen in his emphasis on the suffering involved in his life as an apostle (4: 9f), his use of the race metaphor (9: 24f) and his reminder that the perfect is still future (13: 8-10, 12). The Corinthians, however, interpreted everything from their own perspective. The fact that their bodies had not changed simply showed that the body had no significant part to play in the life of God's kingdom. Such matters as the eating of meat offered to idols (chapters 8 and 10) and sexual activity (chapters 5-7) therefore had no integral relationship to the kingdom. Their disparagement of the body lent itself to both a libertinism ('all things are lawful' – 6: 12, including incest – 5: 1f and intercourse with prostitutes – 6: 15f) and an asceticism ('it is good for a man not to touch a woman' – 7: 1, which involved a disparagement of marriage). The Corinthians' views on the sacraments also seem to have been tied in with their claim to the possession of pneumatic existence in the kingdom, for they over-valued

33

baptism and the Lord's Supper, thinking that participation in these rites would secure them from all physical harm.[2] This is why the apostle plays down his baptismal ministry (1: 13f) and points out, in response to the Corinthian dismay that those who had eaten the sacramental meal could experience sickness and death, that the sacraments have as their reverse side the aspect of judgment (cf. 10: 1ff; 11: 29ff).

What is important for our study is the way in which the over-realized eschatology of the Corinthians was seen in terms of heavenly existence. In re-interpreting future apocalyptic expectations in terms of the present they saw themselves as living out the freedom and quality of life appropriate to angels in heaven. Not only did they believe that by speaking in tongues they were using the language of angels (13: 1) but a claim to angelic existence appears to have been behind the sexual asceticism reflected in chapter 7.[3] For those with an over-realized eschatology such an attitude could follow naturally from Jesus' teaching in Luke 20: 34ff – 'The sons of this age marry and are given in marriage but those who are accounted worthy to attain to that age and to the resurrection from the dead neither marry nor are given in marriage, for they cannot die any more, because they are equal to angels and are sons of God.' (Cf. also Matt. 22: 30; Mk. 12: 25 – 'they are like angels in heaven'.) If the Corinthians are already as the angels it is clear that there can be no more marital ties. Further, being as the angels would mean no more distinction between male and female which would account for the confusion about the role of women in the worship service, which Paul has to correct in 1 Corinthians 11 and 14.[4] It is possible that Paul's allusion to the Lord's Supper as 'spiritual' food and drink in 10: 3, 4 reflects a Corinthian belief that in partaking of the supper they were eating spiritual or heavenly food which provided immunity to death. The OT background to which Paul alludes mentions food from heaven (cf. Exod. 16: 4 and Ps. 78: 24, 25 where the manna from heaven is described as angels' food). In addition Adam's Paradisiac existence could be depicted in terms of the eating of angels' food (cf. Vita Adae et Evae 4: 2) and elsewhere in this letter 'spiritual' and 'heavenly' are virtually synonymous (cf. 15: 45-9). It is in the context of the Corinthians' claim to be ruling already that the apostle has to show that Christian existence at present involves suffering and that 'the church is *as yet before* the angels and that it is *not yet as* the angels' (4: 9).[5]

The Corinthians appear then to have held that they were as angels in their new eschatological existence. In this they went further than the Qumran community which saw itself as a still hidden paradise protected by God through angels (cf. 1QH VIII: 4-14) and also held that membership of the community involved membership of the heavenly world, joining with the Sons of Heaven (נ ישמים cf. 1QH III: 22; 1QS IV: 22; XI: 8),[6] but not yet becoming as them. The Corinthians saw their community with its pneumatic enthusiasm and freedom as the place where heavenly life could be found on earth. Käsemann rightly says of the church, 'the course of affairs in Corinth makes it clear that people lived on the assumption of the invasion of the earthly world by the heavenly' and 'in its eyes the only further significance of Christian existence on earth was to provide a temporal representation of heavenly being'.[7]

2. The Corinthians' views about the resurrection of the dead

It is not clear whether 1 Corinthians 15 is an answer to the oral or the written information that Paul had received about the situation in Corinth, but he certainly believed that the Corinthians had questions about the resurrection of believers and that some were going so far as to 'say that there is no resurrection of the dead' (verse 12). In the light of this reference and of the indications of the Corinthians' over-realized eschatology, various attempts have been made to reconstruct the view that some, though not all (τινες – verse 12), are likely to have held about the resurrection of the dead. Rather than examining these various options in detail,[8] we shall present our own reconstruction.

It seems highly likely that the Corinthians thought of the future in terms of continuing the reign they were already enjoying, so that when Christ returned they would simply continue to reign with him, though perhaps in a heightened and more extended fashion. It is to dispel such a misconception that Paul insists that σάρξ καὶ αἷμα cannot inherit the eschatological kingdom (verse 50), for the Corinthians' present bodies are not suited for the consummation realm of imperishability. As the Corinthians expected the parousia to occur imminently·they had made no provision in their thought for death or for what would happen to the body in this eventuality.[9] Considering themselves to be like the angels, they would certainly not have been expecting to die (cf. Lk. 20: 36) and the body was in any case of no great importance for many of them. Since they had allowed no room for death in their eschatology, it is clear that they would also have no place for the resurrection of the dead. Some obviously went further, not only believing the latter concept to be unnecessary but denying it as incompatible with their view of the spiritual nature of life in the kingdom.

Not being prepared for death, the Corinthians were troubled when it occurred and the letter reflects an undercurrent of concern about the dead. This can be seen especially in 11: 30f where Paul gives as one reason for the deaths in the community, which are perplexing the Corinthians, the judgment of God on their abuse of the Lord's Supper. He has already prepared the way for this assertion in 10: 8–10 where he states that even those who had spiritual food and drink under Moses were liable to the punishment of physical death. Indeed, earlier still, in 5: 5, Paul has stated that such a punishment could await the man the Corinthians are to put out of the community and yet in the process his spirit would be saved. In 15: 6 the apostle mentions that even some of the eye-witnesses of the resur-rected Christ have died and then in verse 18 plays on the same concern with his statement that Christians who have died have perished if there is no resurrection from the dead. Verse 20 should also be seen in the light of this concern, for 'Christ is not described as the first fruits of all Christians (although Paul no doubt believes that he is), but of those who have died; that is, the resurrection of Christ is related directly to the problem of the dead in Christ, not to the problem of everlasting life itself.'[10] The apostle insists that death is the *last* enemy to be destroyed (verse 26). Since this will not take place until Christ's coming (verse 23), one clear implication is that the Corinthians should not be surprised if believers die in the mean-time. Thus the whole discussion of the resurrection of the *dead* in chapter 15 speaks directly to the Corinthians' perplexity. Their confidence appar-ently extended only to those who were living. With regard to the problem-atic verse 29 it is likely that the Corinthians' confusion is at the root of the practice which has produced an even greater confusion among later com-mentators. One could guess that with their bewilderment about the fate of those who had died and their strong faith in the efficacy of baptism, some Corinthians were practising a baptism for the dead which they believed might still somehow ensure a place in the kingdom for deceased believers. An *ad hominem* argument by the apostle points out the futility of such a practice if the dead are not raised. In verses 30f Paul points out further that he himself could die at any time – he confronts death daily. Only if the dead are raised is it worthwhile facing such dangers. The last part of the chapter is also calculated to put all confusion to flight when in verse 51 he shows that those Corinthians who remain alive at the parousia will be in exactly the same position as the dead, about whom they are so per-plexed, in as far as *all* must be changed. Then in verses 54ff with ringing rhetoric the apostle mocks death.

We posit therefore a lack of provision by some of the Corinthians in their eschatology for the eventuality of death before the parousia and believe this to be preferable to the view which sees in their position a belief that the resurrection had already taken place spiritually, a belief condemned in 2 Tim. 2: 18.[11] The latter view would certainly suit the over-realized eschatology evidenced in 1 Cor. 4: 8, but, granted that Paul may indulge in exaggeration for the sake of his argument, the view he argues against is one which envisions no life after death (cf. verses 15–19, 29, 32) and this is surely the *prima facie* meaning of his presentation of the Corinthians' case in verse 12 – ἀνάστασις νεκρῶν οὐκ ἔστιν.[12] Paul understands them to be saying that there is no resurrection at all, that is, that the dead do not rise and the living do not need to since they enjoy the blessings of the kingdom already, rather than that there is no future resurrection but a present one which they are now enjoying. If they had believed themselves to be already raised in the spirit this would surely have carried with it a belief in continued spiritual existence despite bodily death, and there is no evidence that Paul thought himself to be combating such a belief.[13] Certainly the Corinthians believed they were already mature, wise and spiritual on the basis of their present experience of the Spirit, but rather than saying that they regarded this as a present resurrection, 'it would be better to say that they had concentrated on the "realized" and present aspects already promised by the Christian gospel and had in the main shut their eyes to the need for a future fulfilment'.[14] They held that heavenly existence had already been ushered in by Christ's exaltation, though there is no evidence that they considered that the resurrection had already fully taken place.

3. The significance of Christ's resurrection (15: 1–34)

Since the concept of the heavenly dimension is closely related to Christ's resurrection and to the spiritual body, it is indispensable to an understanding of how this concept functions in Paul's thought to follow the argument about resurrection existence which precedes its explicit discussion.

Highly skilled in debate, Paul begins to speak to the question of the resurrection of the dead in chapter 15 by underlining that which he and the Corinthians hold in common. Hence he reminds them of the basic gospel tradition which he had passed on to them, dwelling on Christ's resurrection and his appearances and making clear that this is the message of the whole church (verses 1–11). This provides the apostle with the basic premise for his whole argument. Everything he has to say about the resurrection of the dead rests on the fact that Christ rose from the dead. The Corinthians probably viewed Christ's resurrection as an enthronement ushering in his present kingdom and reign in which they were participating. As Paul goes on to show, they had failed to see the significance of what had happened to Christ for their own confusion about believers who had died, and had also failed to adjust their own notions of heavenly and spiritual existence to what had happened in the case of Christ. Since Christ actually died and was buried but was then raised from the dead, this guarantees the same destiny for the believing dead whom the Corinthians had buried, and since the possession of a risen body is integral to the heavenly life upon which Christ has entered, this must be the case for believers also.

For Paul the resurrection of Christ and the resurrection of believers are inseparably interwoven. To deny one is to deny the other, so that he can go as far as to say that if there is no future resurrection of the dead, then Christ was not raised, for Christ was also a dead man (verses 12–19 cf. verses 3, 4). As the firstfruits of the resurrection harvest, Christ's resurrection is a pledge of what is to come, it is the beginning of the one resurrection event (verse 20). Just as in Adam all die, so in Christ all will be made alive (verse 22). Yet there is a definite temporal sequence as the one event unfolds (verses 23–8). For those who had lost sight of any sequence Paul again emphasizes that the fullness of salvation is not yet a present possession, the reign of Christ and his followers is not yet complete. The fierce battle to make the powers recognize Christ's rule is still in progress and only when the last enemy, death, is destroyed and the second stage of the great resurrection event, the resurrection of those in Christ, takes place, will the end come. Then God will be all in all.

4. Celestial bodies (15: 35–41)

The second half of the chapter, verses 35–58, opens with two questions which Paul imagines an objector posing. The second defines the first more precisely, though it may be that the apostle tackles the second question about the nature of the resurrection body first in verses 35–49 and then in verses 50ff turns to deal with the first question as to how the event of the resurrection of the dead will take place.[15] By phrasing the second question in the way he does – ποίῳ δὲ σώματι ἔρχονται; Paul gets to the heart of the Corinthians' difficulty with the resurrection of the dead and indeed the heart of many of their problems, namely, the place of the body.[16] By phrasing it in this way he also prepares for his response in terms of more than one sort of body being imaginable. Indeed in verses 35–41 Paul provides examples of this basic principle from the natural world as he develops his main analogy of the sowing of a grain of corn. He asserts that not only do different kinds of earthly life have their own distinctive physical manifestation but that a further distinction can be made between earthly bodies as one class and heavenly bodies as another and that each category has its own type of glory. Even the heavenly category admits of further differentiation, for there is a difference in glory not only between the sun, the moon and the stars, but also between the various stars. The

whole point in developing the analogy in this way is to indicate the
immense variety in God's creation and that there is no type of life for
which God has not found appropriate glory or an appropriate body.

Since the thrust of the analogy prepares the way for the explicit teaching, a connection may be seen between Paul's use of the terms ἐπουράνιος
and δόξα in this context and in verses 42–9. In verses 40, 41 ἐπουράνιος is
used in a purely cosmological sense. It is a straightforward reference to the
heavenly bodies visible in the sky and not to angels or spiritual beings.[17]
Similarly δόξα here has the basic meaning of radiance, so that the glory of
the sun, moon and the individual stars is that brightness appropriate to
each. It is no accident that the same two terms occur as the apostle moves
into his more explicit assertions about the resurrection of the dead, and
that in that context they take on fuller eschatological connotations.[18] The
comparison between τὰ ἐπίγεια and τὰ ἐπουράνια in verse 40 anticipates
that between the earthly man and the heavenly man in the following discussion. As the analogy has shown, 'experience teaches that God finds a
suitable body for every type of earthly life and every type of heavenly
life'.[19] This is exactly what Paul goes on to claim in regard to believers.
Just as they have had a psychical earthly body so they will have a spiritual
heavenly body.

5. The contrast of psychical and spiritual bodies (15: 42–44*a*)

The concept of sowing continues into the next section of the apostle's
argument (verses 42–44*a*). The body is sown in one state and raised in
another, and these states are described by means of a fourfold antithetical
parallelism. The first three contrasting conditions lead up to the fourth
which is the most comprehensive, that between σῶμα ψυχικόν and σῶμα
πνευματικόν. This distinction, in turn, must be understood in the context
of its connection with the main comparison in this section, that between
the first and the last Adam. The body which is sown is characterized by
corruption, dishonour and weakness while that which is raised is described
in terms of imperishability, glory and power. δόξα no longer denotes
simply brightness as in verses 40, 41 but as in Jewish apocalyptic literature
such radiance of the stars is transferred to the eschatological state of the
righteous (cf. Dan. 12: 3; 2 Bar. 51: 10; 1 Enoch 62: 15; 105: 11, 12).
Because δόξα is also the form in which Paul conceives of the exalted state
of Christ, it is not surprising that this term should be used in describing
the state of those who participate in his resurrection (cf. also 1 Thess. 2: 2;
Rom. 8: 18, 21; Phil. 3: 21; Col. 3: 4). The series of antithetic characteristics sets the pre-eschatological state of the body over against the eschato-

logical and in this way forms part of Paul's continuing correction of those Corinthians who believed they already fully possessed the power and the glory of the age to come.

The two bodies which are contrasted are also designated as the 'psychical'[20] and the 'spiritual'. The psychical/spiritual distinction appears to be a distinction which was important in the Corinthian church. This is indicated by the fact that Paul uses ψυχικός only in 1 Corinthians and that whereas πνευματικός occurs once in Galatians, three times in Romans, twice in Colossians and three times in Ephesians, it is used no less than fifteen times in 1 Corinthians. In addition the apostle employs these terms with no explanation, evidently expecting his readers to be familiar with them.

No adequate comparative material has been found which establishes the exact origin of this ψυχικός/πνευματικός terminology. Some scholars have, however, viewed the antithesis as sure evidence of Gnostic background. This was due largely to the initial work of R. Reitzenstein.[21] It is true that parallels can be found in Gnostic thought, such as Hyp. Arch. 138: 13-15; Soph. J. C. 121: 4-6 and Hipp. Ref. V. xxvi. 8, 25, but the methodological question whether such parallels indicate that Gnosticism must be presupposed for the Corinthian situation is by no means settled,[22] so that for one writer to speak of 'the futility of trying to understand Paul's use of ψυχικός without the benefits of the gnostic parallels'[23] is certainly to overstate the case. Indeed other recent work has attempted to show that such parallels are by no means necessary for understanding Pauline usage.[24] Pearson has revived the suggestion made previously by Dupont that this terminological distinction developed out of the interpretation of Gen. 2: 7 in Hellenistic Judaism.[25] He sees in the distinction between the mortal soul and the immortal spirit reflected in the use of the Genesis passage in some references in Philo and the Wisdom of Solomon the germ of the contrast being made by Paul's opponents in Corinth. However, neither Philo nor the Wisdom of Solomon contains the specific ψυχικός/πνευματικός contrast or draws a fundamental anthropological distinction between ψυχή and πνεῦμα as the higher part of the soul.[26] It may well be that the NT parallels to Paul's usage are more significant. In Jude 19 those who are ψυχικόι are described as πνεῦμα μὴ ἔχοντες. In James 3: 15 'psychical' is used in the context of wisdom in contrast to that wisdom which comes from above. Wisdom in James functions in a manner often corresponding to the Pauline use of Spirit and of course when the 'psychical'/'spiritual' contrast is made in 1 Cor. 2 and 3, this is also in a wisdom context. Clearly this contrast and the pejorative use of ψυχικός are not unique to

Paul and particularly the reference in James lends weight to the view that their origin may be in Jewish Christian wisdom speculation. Pearson is on firmer ground when he points to the strand of Hellenistic Jewish exegesis that bases on Gen. 2: 7 the possibility of knowing God and his wisdom and suggests that Paul's opponents in Corinth were claiming that as πνευματικοί by a cultivation of wisdom they could rise above the earthly and 'psychical' level of existence and anticipate heavenly glory.[27] This sort of distinction between two types of humanity has some similarities with those in Philo between heavenly and earthly, perfect and children, contrasts which also appear in 1 Corinthians, and it is through possession of σοφία that one attains the former exalted status (cf. *Leg. Alleg.* I, 90–95; *De Mig. Abr.* 26–40; *Quaest. in Gen.* IV, 46).[28] In a Christian context πνεῦμα was seen to be most appropriate for describing experience of supernatural endowment and was set over against the ordinary endowment of ψυχή.[29] Paul, then, takes up this terminology current among the Corinthians and gives it his own connotations. Those in Corinth who regarded themselves as already possessors of the blessings of the eschatological kingdom thought of themselves as πνευματικοί (cf. 3: 1; 12: 1; 14: 37). They claimed a superior spiritual wisdom in contrast to those Christians who only had their ordinary ψυχή. To deflate such a boastful attitude Paul, in 1 Corinthians 2 and 3, takes up the term ψυχικός and uses it against the very people who considered themselves 'spiritual'. It becomes synonymous with σάρκινος and σαρκικός (1 Cor. 3: 1, 3) and designates one who simply cannot understand the things of God because he or she does not have the Spirit of God and whose activities are therefore on a merely human level (2: 13; 3: 3) and part of this age (2: 6). In contrast, the age to come, the blessedness of which is described in 2: 9, has already been revealed and opened up by the Spirit, so that the person who is truly πνευματικός belongs to the age to come. For Paul then the distinction is no longer merely describing an anthropological dualism but takes on its force from his eschatological perspective.

It is natural to see similar connotations involved when Paul applies the terms ψυχικός and πνευματικός to the body in 15: 44. Just as σάρξ in Paul can stand for ordinary human existence in this age and also take on a negative ethical nuance when this age is seen as evil through the disobedience' of Adam, so ψυχικός has a similarly nuanced meaning. In view in the verses under discussion is particularly the human body as it has become subject to sin and death, while in what follows the neutral sense comes to the fore. On the other hand πνευματικός is to be related to the Spirit and the life of the age to come. Hence the psychical body which is sown is that characterized by the old aeon, while it is raised as a spiritual body by virtue of the transformation it has undergone through the Spirit who characterizes the new aeon.

The conjunction of σῶμα with πνευματικόν was bound to be striking and even incongruous to the Corinthians who believed the new aeon and its Spirit to be fully present. The very thing they could not imagine, that the body should be an integral part of such an age, Paul asserts as essential to his perspective. They had to recognize that the Spirit who was presently at work in them would only at the resurrection fully dominate and control their lives and this would be in such a way that their bodies would become spiritual bodies no longer subject to the weakness and perishability of this age (cf. also Rom. 8: 11). Thus 'spiritual' in connection with body should not be confused with adjectives such as ethereal or immaterial.[30] Nor should it be understood as describing a substance, for just as the psychical body does not describe a body consisting of a psychical substance so neither does the spiritual body signify one made of a spiritual substance. Rather the all-important concept involved is that of domination by the Spirit.[31]

6. From the psychical to the spiritual order (15: 44*b*–46)

Verses 44*b*–46 form a new section in the apostle's discussion as he argues from the psychical body to the spiritual. The antithetic parallelism ceases and what were previously contrasting terms are now related by a different construction. The apodosis – ἔστιν καὶ πνευματικόν – leads on directly from the protasis – εἰ ἔστιν σῶμα ψυχικόν. Paul appeals to Scripture as the basis for this argument, and the peculiarity of his citation of Gen. 2: 7 has often been noted. In comparison with the LXX rendering the apostle adds πρῶτος before ἄνθρωπος and Ἀδάμ after it. This is clearly a modification designed to lead into his two Adams analogy and to stress the temporal sequence involved. What is even more noteworthy is that the latter part of verse 45 with its reference to the last Adam seems to be treated as part of the citation. There is no coordinating conjunction but the two clauses of verse 45 are nevertheless joined, so that the latter is parallel to the former and dependent on it for its verb – ἐγένετο. Not only so, but for this appeal to Scripture to be in any way effective it has to cover the two parts of verse 44*b* and this is only the case if ὁ ἔσχατος Ἀδάμ εἰς πνεῦμα ζωοποιοῦν is considered part of the quotation. It thus appears to be the apostle's own midrash pesher comment on Scripture which he equates with Scripture itself.[32]

By grounding his argument in this way Paul indicates that the first Adam is to be associated with the category of 'psychical' which has been under discussion, while the last Adam represents everything he has envisaged by the term 'spiritual'. It should immediately become clear that the reference of the term ψυχικός has widened, for it is no longer simply the body as it has fallen prey to sin which is in view but the appeal to Gen. 2: 7 shows that a reference to Adam by virtue of creation is now included. Just as Paul's use of σάρξ can involve a neutral or an ethically negative sense, so his use of ψυχικός here seems to be equally flexible. Only if this is the case can justice be done to the argument of verse 44b. It is not an *a fortiori* argument in the sense that if there is a psychical body subject to corruption then all the more must there be a spiritual body of glory. Nor is Paul saying that the spiritual body can somehow be directly inferred from the psychical body characterized by dishonour and death. If, however, by its close association with the ψυχή of Adam prior to the fall in verse 45, ψυχικός in verse 44b now has this broader reference, then instead the apostle is arguing typologically that there can be a direct inference from the psychical body of the first Adam at creation to the spiritual body of the last Adam.[33] Paul's expansion of the comparison to include the creation body would give his polemic at this point far greater force, for what he is now saying in verses 44b–46 is that from the beginning, from the creation, a different kind of body has been in view. The Corinthians should not view the idea of a bodily form appropriate to spiritual existence as something so novel and unimaginable, for in fact this has always been God's purpose. As Vos claims,

> The apostle was intent upon showing that in the plan of God from the outset provision was made for a higher kind of body ... The abnormal (body of sin) and the eschatological are not so logically correlated that the one can be postulated from the other. But the world of creation and the world to come *are* thus correlated, the one pointing forward to the other.[34]

Paul's argument therefore depends on a typological exegesis which sees the first Adam as prefiguring the last, and consequently the psychical body as pointing to the spiritual. The presupposition for such an argument seems to have been the view that there was an inherent eschatological structure to creation and that the eschatological prospect held out to the first Adam, which he forfeited by his disobedience, has been realized by the last Adam.

In this typological relationship between the two Adams verse 45 makes it clear that the first man Adam became a living soul (ψυχὴν ζῶσαν) and as such had a body appropriate to this quality of life. The last Adam however has a new quality of life, for as πνεῦμα ζῳοποιοῦν he is no longer merely alive and susceptible to death but rather has now become creatively life-giving. Paul emphasizes that Christ *became* life-giving Spirit, for the verb ἐγένετο belongs to both clauses, and it is clear from his whole discussion that this occurred at the resurrection (cf. also Rom. 1: 4). Verse 22 of this chapter underlines this, for in the Adam–Christ contrast there the being made alive (ζωοποιηθήσονται) which takes place in Christ is grounded in his resurrection. In Paul's view the resurrection brought about such a transformation for Christ that Christ and the Spirit can now be identified in terms of their activity and functions.

What started out as a comparison between two forms of bodily existence moved to a comparison between the two representatives of those forms and now proceeds to include the two world-orders which the first and last Adams exemplify. In other words, in verse 46 τὸ ψυχικόν and τὸ πνευματικόν should not be restricted simply to a reference to the body but have become descriptive of two contrasting orders of existence which have bodily expression. But why Paul's emphasis on temporal sequence? Some hold that here Paul is correcting a view similar to Philo's treatment of the heavenly and earthly men or the two men of Gen. 1: 27 and 2: 7.[35] While Philo does make such a distinction, Paul's explicit contrast is in different terms, ψυχικός/πνευματικός, and is not in fact between two men, cf. the neuters in verse 46. A more important objection to this hypothesis is that it is by no means clear that the chronological order was of particular interest to Philo in his distinction beyond the order involved in the Biblical text and the *logical* priority resulting from his Platonic view of ideas, cf. *De Op. Mundi* 69, 82, 134; *Leg. Alleg.* I, 31; II, 4.[36] What would be needed as a foil for the apostle's argument, if something specific was in mind, is a viewpoint which stressed the chronological order, possibly putting Philo's thought to its own use. Some have suggested Gnosticism as this viewpoint.[37] In Gnostic views of the 'Urmensch' in which psychical existence has fallen away from an original spiritual sphere, this sphere would of course be not only higher in the scale of being but also prior to the psychical. Yet when emphasis is laid on temporal priority in Gnostic thought, and, for example, a heavenly man belonging to the spiritual sphere is called the first man, cf. Soph. J. C. 94: 9–11; 96: 12; 98: 16; Pist. Soph. 185: 4; 208: 25; 215: 27, 29f, Hipp. Ref. V, vii, 30, 36; viii, 9f, it is not evident from such references that any special soteriological significance was seen in the temporal priority of a heavenly first man.[38] One is inclined to agree with Conzelmann that at this point there is not enough evidence to identify the view Paul is combating with a specific pattern of thought to be found in Philo or Gnosticism.[39] It could be that the Corinthians had put something similar to Philo's thought to their own use, as we have suggested earlier for the 'psychical'/'spiritual' terminology, and in a way which emphasized temporal priority. Whether this is the case or not, it still makes sense to see Paul arguing against what we know more generally of the Corinthians' viewpoint. On this interpretation the emphasis on temporal sequence is certainly polemical but no different from that set out in verses 23ff where Paul emphasizes that the history of salvation has a definite chronological structure. In both cases he is arguing against a viewpoint which is premature in its concept of salvation and of the eschatological kingdom because it has failed to grasp the divine timetable. Here in verse 46 this timetable for the whole of history is compressed into two general stages. First comes the psychical, the pre-eschatological era of the first Adam which is incomplete and provisional, then comes the spiritual, the eschatological era of the last Adam. To claim to be fully spiritual now is to forget this crucial order and so Paul has to underline it forcefully and spell out explicitly which comes first. 'Not the spiritual but the psychical is first, *then* the spiritual.' This does not require that the Corinthians had a view which claimed the exact opposite, that is, that the spiritual came first and then the psychical, but can simply be seen as the apostle's way of emphasizing his own particular sequence. It is significant that Paul does not feel any need to deny in an explicit fashion that τὸ ψυχικόν is second, he only denies that τὸ πνευματικόν is first. This is to expose the Corinthians' ignorance of the fact that before the spiritual could fully arrive they still had to reckon with the psychical order of existence. 'Taken in this way the verse becomes a polemic against an unrealistic spiritualizing of this present life, a blending of heaven and earth that does away with the earthiness of the latter.[40]

7. The heavenly nature of the second man (15: 47)

The terms γῆ and οὐρανός and their related adjectives now take over as parallels to what has previously been expressed in terms of ψυχικός and πνευματικός, as the language of Genesis 2: 7 is again employed to describe the first man – ὁ πρῶτος ἄνθρωπος ἐκ γῆς χοϊκός. The use of χοϊκός in particular seems to reflect the LXX χοῦν ἀπὸ τῆς γῆς. This description is then paralleled in the latter part of verse 47 which designates Christ as ὁ δεύτερος ἄνθρωπος ἐξ οὐρανοῦ. There is no parallel in this clause to χοϊκός which is to be seen as a duplication of ἐκ γῆς. This duplication however gives a most important clue for the meaning of the whole verse, for it emphasizes that ἐκ γῆς is to be taken qualitatively and thus also its parallel phrase ἐξ οὐρανοῦ. In other words, the first man is of the earth, earthly;[41] the second man is of heaven, that is, heavenly. It puts a very different complexion on this verse when we see that in the expression ὁ δεύτερος ἄνθρωπος ἐξ οὐρανοῦ, it is the last *two* and not the last three words which are the predicate.[42] Paul is saying that the second man is heavenly and not that the second is the man from heaven. Thus so much of the talk about 'a man from heaven' in connection with this verse really confuses the issue. Paul is not using the concept and phrase ἄνθρωπος ἐξ οὐρανοῦ.[43] This qualitative interpretation of ἐξ οὐρανοῦ is confirmed when we note that in verses 48, 49 ἐπουράνιος is used as its equivalent and applied to believers as well as to Christ, and this can hardly mean that believers have come from heaven. The verb to be supplied in the two clauses of verse 47 is not 'to come'.[44] The reference therefore is neither to a coming of Christ at the incarnation from a state of pre-existence[45] nor to Christ's second coming from heaven.[46] For Paul to talk about the heavenly origin of Christ's humanity by virtue of his pre-existence would be to contradict what he had said about the psychical being first and the spiritual second. If ἐξ οὐρανοῦ is to be taken qualitatively and if we take seriously Paul's language in Rom. 8: 3 which speaks of Christ's pre-resurrection life as ἐν ὁμοιώματι σαρκὸς ἁμαρτίας, then the phrase can only refer to the character of Christ's humanity by virtue of his resurrection. Just as the last Adam became life-giving Spirit through the resurrection, so it is because of the same event that the second man can be called heavenly. Even in his exalted heavenly state the focus is on Christ's humanity – he is ὁ δεύτερος ἄνθρωπος, indicating that in his resurrection existence he is the model for the new eschatological humanity.

In verses 47ff the terms 'earth' and 'heaven' are transformed by the apostle's eschatological perspective and by their connection with the heads of the two successive orders of existence, so that now these spatial terms can also characterize two created orders, two ages.[47] The category of the heavenly dimension is associated with Christ as the inaugurator of the resurrection life of the age to come. For Paul such a description of Christ is equivalent to saying that the resurrected Christ is characterized by the power of the Spirit, since in his mind the Spirit and the heavenly dimension are closely linked and with regard to both Christ's resurrection has paramount significance.

8. Background for Paul's conception of the second man as heavenly

It will have become evident from the exegesis of verse 47 and from the earlier discussion that we doubt that the Gnostic myth of a man from heaven who fell into matter has influenced Paul's thought about the second man being ἐξ οὐρανοῦ or that Philo's concept of the heavenly man provides his direct stimulus.[48] The Gnostic concept of the 'Urmensch' has in any case a number of varying referents, appears to build on Jewish speculations about the first man and did not exist as a self-contained myth. M. Black's verdict about the Gnostic notion of the heavenly Man, that 'there is no unequivocal evidence pointing to the existence of such a conception in pre-Christian sources, particularly within Judaism' still holds.[49] One of the passages in Philo with similar terminology to that of 1 Cor. 15: 47 is *Leg. Alleg.* I, 31f.

> There are two types of men; the one a heavenly man, the other an earthly. The heavenly man, being made after the image of God, is altogether without part or lot in corruptible and terrestrial substance; but the earthly one was compacted out of the matter scattered here and there, which Moses calls 'clay'. For this reason he says that the heavenly man was not moulded, but was stamped with the image of God; while the earthly is a moulded work of the Artificer, but not His offspring. We must account the man made out of the earth to be mind mingling with, but not yet blended with, body.

It is unlikely, however, that the Philonic concept of the heavenly man as reflected in such a passage was the immediate influence in the introduction of the terminology here in verse 47. As Scroggs points out, Philo does not 'ever compare the heavenly man with Adam, since the former is not a mythical figure but a platonic idea'.[50] It can be seen also that the two motifs are used for different purposes so that in Philo the heavenly and earthly men are not so much particular figures but 'are used to construct the ontology of every man'.[51] Scroggs's interpretation of Philo holds generally, though he has slightly overstated his case and exceptions can be found where 'Adam' is also used of every man (cf. *Leg. Alleg.* I, 90) and the heavenly man is regarded as the actual first man (cf. *Quis Rer. Div. Her.* 52).[52]

We should look then for other elements which may have been influential in Paul's depiction of the second man as heavenly and one factor in the background of this concept which has been neglected, perhaps because of the necessity of bringing the record of the Book of Acts into the picture, is Paul's own experience of the resurrected Christ. The evidence of Acts, though secondary, is still early and important. The dramatic event of Paul's encounter with Christ on the road to Damascus could not be forgotten and must have moulded his views of the exalted Christ. According to Luke's accounts the accompanying phenomena were associated with heaven, especially the great and blinding light, cf. Acts 9: 3 – φῶς ἐκ τοῦ οὐρανοῦ (cf. also 22: 6; 26: 13), so that in Acts 26: 19 Paul can be depicted as speaking of the whole event in terms of 'the heavenly vision' – οὐκ ἐγενόμην ἀπειθὴς τῇ οὐρανίῳ ὀπτασίᾳ. From this time on the heavenly nature of the resurrected Christ must have been indelibly stamped on his consciousness. This initial encounter and further early visions and revelations of his heavenly Lord (cf. 2 Cor. 12: 1f) helped to shape the apostle's Christology.

Since the second man who is heavenly is placed in an eschatological context and contrasted with the figure of the first man, we should look not only to Paul's own experience but also to the Jewish hopes, with which he is likely to have been familiar, about an exalted Adam, an eschatological figure who would be restored to glory and to the Paradise of the third heaven. It is a commonplace of Pauline studies that the first half of the contrast, people's relation to the first Adam as representative of the human race, who as created showed God's intended purpose for humanity and who in his fall brought about death and its spread to his descendants, has frequent antecedents in Jewish literature. But there is also reason to believe that the same background prepared the way for Paul's perspective on Christ as the last Adam, the second man, including the linking of this figure with angelic, heavenly existence. In the light of the Corinthians' concern with this type of existence and with being like the angels, it is not surprising that Paul should draw on such a tradition.

Jewish theologians often depicted the new existence of the age to come in terms of original existence restored (cf. Isa. 65: 17-25; 1 Enoch 45: 4, 5; 51; 58; 61-2; cf. also the Rabbinic sayings about the six things Adam lost at the fall, including his glory and life, which will be restored when Messiah comes, for example, Gen. R. XII. 6). Sometimes this relationship is reversed, so that what is believed will exist in the age to come is projected backwards to life before the fall. In this way the portrait of a glorified exalted Adam can function both as the ideal original person and the ideal eschatological person. Paradise is to be restored and in the Apocalypse of Moses in particular there is the promise of its restoration to Adam himself: 'yet when thou art gone out of paradise, if thou shouldst keep thyself from all evil, as one about to die, when again the Resurrection hath come to pass, I will raise thee up and then there shall be given to thee the Tree of Life' (28: 4). In place of the curse of death which he had brought on people there is the promise of his resurrection, 'Again I promise to thee the Resurrection; I will raise thee up in the Resurrection with every man, who is of thy seed' (41: 3 cf. also 13: 3).[53] Such concepts become explicitly linked with the heavenly dimension when the Paradise to which Adam is restored is said to be in heaven. In the Apocalypse of Moses at the end of time Adam is to be raised up to enjoy the benefits of Paradise in the third heaven, 'Lift him up into Paradise unto the third Heaven, and leave him there until that fearful day of my reckoning, which

I will make in the world' (37: 5 cf. also Vita Adae et Evae 25: 3). There
was a belief that the Paradise in which Adam had lived was being kept in
heaven for the last days (cf. 2 Bar. 4: 2-6; 4 Ezra 8: 52), and the concept
of glory associated with Adam was also closely related to heavenly existence. Glory belongs primarily to the transcendent God but men or angels
can absorb and reflect God's splendour as they stand in his presence. In
the Apocalypse of Moses when Eve deceives Adam, he is immediately
aware that he has lost the visible splendour that such glory involves (21:
6), but later God promised that in the resurrection this glory will be
restored ('I will transform thee to thy former glory' - 39: 2). Much of
this appears to be a development of the motif in which the eschatological
glory to be possessed by the righteous in the age to come (cf. 4 Ezra 8: 51;
1 Enoch 39: 9; 50: 1; 58: 2; 103: 2f; 2 Bar. 15: 8; 54: 15, 21) was viewed
as possessed by Adam before the fall (cf. Ecclus 49: 16; 2 Enoch 30: 11
and the Rabbinic tradition of Adam's countenance of glory - Lev. R.
XX, 2; Eccles. R. VIII. 12). A similar pattern of thought can be found in
the Qumran literature, where the glory of Adam is promised to the community (cf. 1QS IV. 23; CD III. 20; 1QH XVII. 15) so that 'the glory in
store for the pious is identical with, or of similar grandeur to, the glory of
Adam in Paradise before the Fall'.[54]

In some places Adam before his fall is seen as essentially a heavenly
creature on earth who led a life of heavenly bliss in Paradise, which included the eating of angels' food (Vita Adae et Evae 4: 2 cf. also 10: 4;
16: 3). In references in the Rabbinic literature Adam's link with heaven is
suggested by his gigantic size which fills the space between earth and
heaven (cf. Gen. R. VIII. 1; XIV. 8; XXI. 3; XXIV. 2; Lev. R. XVIII. 2;
Midr. Ps. 139. 5). Still other passages associate Adam with angelic existence. Just as God created Adam like the angels (cf. 1 Enoch 69: 11; 2
Enoch 30: 11; Gen. R. XXI. 2, 4, 5) so he has something similar in store
for eschatological humanity (cf. 1 Enoch 104; 2 Bar. 51: 10). Adam's
exalted heavenly status is further indicated by the fact that he is considered worthy of the angels' worship and ministration (cf. Vita Adae et
Evae 13: 2; 14: 1f; 33; Apoc. Mos. 7: 2; Jub. 3: 15; 2 Enoch 30: 14;
Gen. R. VIII. 10) and this status also will be restored to eschatological
humanity (cf. 2 Enoch 22: 6; 1 Cor. 6: 3).

Since Paul's reference to the heavenly nature of the second man occurs
in the context of a comparison of the two Adams, it is extremely likely
that this motif of the restoration of heavenly existence to Adam found in
apocalyptic and Rabbinic literature was formative in his thinking. What
was still promise in this tradition Paul sees as accomplished by Christ who
has inaugurated the new heavenly age. After comparing the Apocalypse of

Moses with 1 Corinthians 15 J. L. Sharpe also concludes, 'the characteristics of the exalted eschatological Adam have been used to describe the
resurrected Christ, whom Paul terms "the last Adam".'[55] Unlike the
Gospel of Peter 10: 40 which applies the figure of Adam stretching from
heaven to earth to Christ, Paul's depiction of Christ as heavenly avoids
such overt mythological symbolism.[56]

9. The heavenly nature of believers (15: 48, 49)

By reintroducing his comparison of the two Adams, Paul has not lost sight
of the main point of the discussion, the resurrection body. In verses 48
and 49, by showing that Adam and Christ are representatives of those who
belong with them to an earthly order or a heavenly order, he is able to
build his argument to a powerful climax which speaks directly to the question of the nature of the resurrection body.

The first man's descendants share his characteristics and are designated
οἱ χοϊκοί. Likewise those who belong to the second man can be called οἱ
ἐπουράνιοι by virtue of their relationship to the one who is ὁ ἐπουράνιος
par excellence. They are heavenly not because they came from heaven or
are going to heaven, but because they are 'in Christ' (cf. verse 22) and
share his resurrection life. In the Apocalypse of Moses also Adam's seed is
included in the promise of the restoration of heavenly existence, involving
resurrection and a new paradise (cf. 13: 3f; 41: 3). Despite the Corinthians'
over-realized eschatology Paul is not afraid to grant that those who belong
to Christ are οἱ ἐπουράνιοι. This quality of heavenliness is not something
entirely of the future.[57] But just as Paul could qualify the Corinthians'
claim to be πνευματικοί by showing that they will not be fully spiritual
until they possess a resurrection body completely under the Spirit's
influence, so he qualifies the fact that believers are already heavenly by
maintaining that complete conformity to the image of the heavenly one
awaits possession of that same resurrection body, which can be characterized as a heavenly body. Those who are heavenly must be like the heavenly
one in every respect, including the bodily. The forceful implication of
Paul's argument for the Corinthians is that if they grant that Christ, the
heavenly one, has a resurrection body, and Paul knows they must concede
this, then they as heavenly ones must also have such a body.

Although it is usually rejected because of its difficulty, φορέσωμεν is
the better attested reading in verse 49. While B among the major manuscripts has φορέσομεν, the subjunctive φορέσωμεν is supported by p[46]
ℵ A C D G.[58] In fact this latter reading with its exhortatory climax to the
discussion brings out more satisfactorily both the eschatological tension of
Paul's perspective and the force of his argument. 'We have borne the image

of the earthly one with all that means for bodily existence,' he is saying, 'so now that we are heavenly, let us go on to bear the image of the heavenly one in its full bodily manifestation.' The concept of progressive transformation and renewal in Christ's image is found elsewhere in Paul (cf. 2 Cor. 3: 18; Rom. 12: 2; Col. 3: 10) and the eschatological tension of verses 48, 49 is brought out by paraphrasing the apostle's exhortation as 'Let us become fully what we already are.'[59]

It is clear from the context that Paul's use of εἰκών in the latter part of verse 49 has specific reference to the future resurrection body, yet to the extent that the Corinthians can be described as οἱ ἐπουράνιοι in this life, to that extent it is also true that they already bear the image of the heavenly one.[60] However, full conformity to Christ's image awaits glorification (cf. Rom. 8: 29f; Phil. 3: 21) and thus the answer to any Corinthian queries about the possible nature of a resurrection body is that it will partake of a heavenly mode of existence and that is simply to say that it will share the mode of existence that the body of Christ their heavenly Lord now possesses. In line with the thought of verse 20 where Christ's resurrection is the firstfruits, and where the firstfruits and the full harvest are of the same kind, the heavenly body of the redeemed will be of the same kind as Christ's.

The Corinthians have borne and to some degree still are bearing the image of the earthly one, but there is a second stage in which the image of the heavenly one is to be borne. The metaphorical use of φορέω suggests that the image is seen as a garment, and this sort of language provides a fresh link between εἰκών and the resurrection body, for elsewhere that body is also seen as a garment to be put on (cf. 1 Cor. 15: 53, 54; 2 Cor. 5: 2–4). Such terminology may also be reminiscent in this context of the concept of putting on garments of glory attested in apocalyptic literature, cf. 1 Enoch 62: 15f – 'And they shall have been clothed with garments of glory, And these shall be the garments of life from the Lord of Spirits; And your garments shall not grow old, Nor your glory pass away before the Lord of Spirits', cf. also Apoc. Abr. 13; Asc. Isa. 4: 16f; 8: 14f; 9: 9. In the light of Paul's language earlier in the letter in 11: 7 where in an allusion to Gen. 1: 26 he could refer to the Corinthians' present existence within the earthly body as being 'the image and glory of God', he presumably thought of both stages as compatible with the image of God. His concept of 'image of God', however, clearly had room for progression from bearing that image in the first Adam's earthly existence to bearing it in the last Adam's heavenly existence. The terminology of 'heaven' in connection with that of 'image' provides one way for Paul of expressing the fact that conformity to Christ's image is not simply a restoration of something lost by the first Adam but involves a distinctly new element, a new quality of existence.

The Corinthians' mistake in regard to this appears to have been a two-fold one. They believed that the second stage, that of conformity to a heavenly mode of existence, was already fully operational and that it did not affect bodily existence. Paul corrects the latter error by making bodily existence integral to the concept of 'image' in verse 49, thereby showing that both stages must have corporeal manifestation. If our reading of the subjunctive is correct, then it brings out all the more clearly that Paul corrects the former error by indicating that at present there is an overlap between the two stages. The Corinthians, while they are still in their earthly bodies, will continue to participate in the first stage and to bear the image of the earthly one, yet at the same time, because of their relationship to the decisive event of Christ's resurrection which has already taken place, they bear the image of the heavenly one. They do not however bear this image fully in its bodily form and so the exhortation of verse 49 arises from this 'not yet' of the present overlap.

This balance of realized and future eschatology is maintained in the closing part of Paul's argument. The Corinthians made too much of the 'victorious life' and overestimated their present share in Christ's victory so that in verses 54ff Paul must show that full victory is still future. Yet at the same time he can also use the present participle for the victory that believers have through Christ (verse 57) and in a manner similar to the preceding section (cf. verse 49) can conclude with an exhortation based on the indicative of Christ's conquest of sin and death. The Corinthians are to abound in working for their Lord, since Christ's resurrection has guaranteed the consummation and fulfilment of all such work for his kingdom.

10. Concluding observations

It is because of the Corinthians' confusion about death and the nature of eschatological existence and because of what he knows to have happened to Christ that Paul draws on spatial language about heaven in 1 Corinthians 15. Conceptions of a heavenly angelic form of existence were present elsewhere in Jewish thought and had been taken up by the Corinthians, but Paul's use of this spatial terminology is distinct because it serves his particular view of the history of salvation, and just as that history of salvation has its focus and centre in Christ, so too does the heavenly dimension. Because of Christ's resurrection, heaven has a new significance for Paul; its significance can be said to be no longer merely cosmological but

Christocentric[61] (cf. the difference in the use of ἐπουράνιος in verse 40 and in verses 48, 49).

Since it is so closely linked with Christ and since Christ is set forth as the second man, the last Adam, this concept of the heavenly dimension is also firmly tied in to Paul's view of humanity and its destiny. In his mind therefore the heavenly dimension was not simply a peripheral cosmological trapping, having nothing to do with the real essence of human existence, nor was it an order of existence which completely separated the resurrected Christ from humanity, but rather it was integral to humanity as God intended it to be. Christ became heavenly but remained man. It is the second *man* who is heavenly. Paul no longer has to look at what humanity once was to find God's design for it. Instead he looks to Christ, the true man. Because the resurrected Christ, whom he has encountered, was heavenly, he knows that it is also God's plan for a person's destiny that he or she is to be heavenly. In verse 44*b* Paul could in fact assert that from the outset God in his plan for humanity had an eschatological goal, intending a higher order of existence. Paul describes this first in terms of the spiritual but when the spiritual becomes interchangeable with the heavenly, this seems to be entirely appropriate terminology for the upward direction human existence had originally been intended to take. The eschatological prospect held out to Adam (and to which he failed to attain) is realized and receives its character through the work of the last Adam who has become heavenly. In this way creation and the age to come, protology and eschatology are correlated, the former pointing forward to the latter.[62] From this passage in 1 Corinthians 15 it is not enough to say that the work of Christ restores a person to his or her original humanity, rather it brings that person to the goal for humanity that God intended but humanity before Christ had never reached. This new order of humanity transcends the old and it is the concept of the heavenly dimension which helps the apostle to indicate the eschatological 'plus' factor in the newness of the new creation inaugurated by Christ's resurrection.

The heavenly dimension is so integrally related to the resurrection of Christ that Paul's way of describing the present order of existence entered on by Christ at his resurrection is to speak of it as heavenly.[63] For the apostle heavenly existence is resurrection existence. Because of union with their heavenly Lord believers participate in this existence and can themselves be called heavenly (verse 48). It is the Spirit who constitutes this link with heaven. Through the parallelism of the argument we have seen that the heavenly dimension serves as the functional equivalent of the dimension of the Spirit, for by virtue of the resurrection Christ has become both life-giving Spirit (verse 45) and heavenly (verse 47). As the last Adam shares the life-giving Spirit he has become with those who belong to him, he is also sharing his heavenly existence. To the extent that the Corinthians are truly spiritual, they are also heavenly, for the Spirit provides a foretaste of the fullness of heavenly life. Since, in Paul, resurrection life has both present and future aspects, heavenly existence too is 'already' but also 'not yet'. Despite the emphasis on the future in Paul's polemic against the Corinthians, his realized eschatological perspective in regard to heaven is clearly recognizable. Heavenly existence has begun with the resurrection of Christ. The Corinthians can experience it now through the Spirit, but they are not yet fully heavenly.[64] This will only occur when they bear fully the image of the heavenly man, that is, when their bodies share in heavenly existence. Thus, as Paul sets out the believer's hope in the face of the questions which death poses, he meets the Corinthians' preoccupation with an 'over-realized' heavenly existence and their disparagement of the body by showing that Christ's resurrection from the dead into the heavenly dimension means not only that heavenly life has been opened up for the Corinthians now but also that in the future their bodies will play an essential role in this heavenly order of existence.

3

2 CORINTHIANS, THE HEAVENLY HOUSE AND THE THIRD HEAVEN

1. The polemical setting in the Corinthian correspondence

The two passages in 2 Corinthians in which the concept of heaven figures prominently are 4: 16 – 5: 10 which speaks of the believer's 'heavenly house' and 12: 1-10 which relates Paul's experience of the third heaven or Paradise. Although chapters 10-13 in all probability form a separate and later letter,[1] there is a continuity in life-setting between the two passages. Chapters 10-13 indicate that the innuendoes and criticisms to be found in a number of places in the earlier chapters have now become an outright calling into question of Paul's apostolic claims combined with an attempt by the agitators to supplant his claims by their own. It would seem that at some time after the sending of 1 Corinthians new agitation had been caused by a group coming to Corinth but had been temporarily lulled by Paul's severe letter. Later, after the further letter, 2 Corinthians 1-9, had been received, there was a renewed effort (perhaps a return to Corinth) by these opponents, which undid Paul's conciliatory work and provoked his full-scale counter-attack of 2 Corinthians 10-13. In this way 2 Corinthians 5 and 2 Corinthians 12 have the same opposition in view but at two different stages of development.[2]

The main issue at stake between Paul and his opponents is the nature of apostleship and its accompanying life-style. They emphasize visible manifestations of glory and appear to believe that Paul's suffering and weakness veil the gospel (cf. 4: 3). These opponents have been identified as Gnostics,[3] as Hellenistic-Jewish Christians,[4] or as Palestinian Jewish Christians.[5] We shall simply elaborate on the main features of our own identification which is a variation of the third alternative.[6] The opponents are a particular brand of Judaizers from Palestine, most probably originating from the Jerusalem church. The arguments of Georgi and Friedrich against the Judaizing hypothesis[7] only show that certain traditional issues such as Gentile observance of circumcision are not directly at stake here. We must allow for more than one style of Judaizing. Amongst Jewish Christians with a strict attitude to the Jewish cultus and customs, it is possible to distinguish some who, like James, were prepared to accept Gentile Christians without requiring them to adhere to the law, others who were more rigorous and insisted that all followers of the Messiah must obey the law or at least practise circumcision, and still others who in pressing their Jewishness were willing to adopt syncretistic tactics and accommodate themselves to the thought-patterns of those they were attempting to proselytize.[8] It is this last variety that we find represented by Paul's opponents in 2 Corinthians and in Philippians 3.

Such an identification accounts adequately for their stress on their Jewishness – Hebrew, Israelite, seed of Abraham (11: 22). Indeed, if Ἑβραῖος is a term which could not only denote the national and linguistic characteristics of an Aramaic-speaking Jew from Palestine but also carry religious and cultural connotations of a strict attitude towards the Jewish cultus and customs,[9] then there is no reason why the opponents could not be connected with the diaspora mission of the group within the Jerusalem church described by this term by Luke (cf. Acts 6: 1). At least this hypo-thesis does not share the dilemma of Friedrich's, which identifies those who call themselves Ἑβραῖοι with those who are specifically distinguished from Ἑβραῖοι in Acts 6.

Though the use of letters of recommendation (3: 1) was a common phenomenon, recommendation from the Jerusalem church would most adequately account for the opponents' claims to authority having been so convincing to the Corinthians that they were now almost in the pos-ition of having ousted the very man who had founded the Corinthian church and of being able to set up a rival apostolate in Corinth. Again it is the sort of agreement between Paul and the heads of the Jerusalem church, recounted in Galatians 2: 9, which best explains Paul's charge in 10: 13ff that his opponents are parasites on his mission territory and have over-stepped the agreed limits.[10] It appears also that the criticisms of Paul's practice of financial independence in Corinth are made against the back-ground of a comparison with the custom of the Jerusalem apostles (11: 7–11; 12: 13ff, cf. 1 Cor. 9: 1–18).

The emphasis of the opponents on their Jewishness is certainly meant to impress on the Corinthians their superior position as members of Israel and heirs of the covenant promises. For them Israel had a spiritual primacy in the new order inaugurated by the resurrection. If, as seems probable, διάκονοι δικαιοσύνης (11: 15) is another of their self-designations,[11] then they set themselves up as those who promoted righteousness, and the discussion in 2 Corinthians 3, which again has the opponents in the background, indicates that their zeal for righteousness included a stress on the letter of the law. In the new order the law was still to be seen as the supreme revelation of God's will, even if Gentile Christians were not obliged to submit to it in its fullness. But Paul shows that the glory of the law was transient and pointed forward to the far greater glory of the new covenant in the Spirit. Against those who would have considered the Spirit to be inseparable from the law,[12] he makes clear that the two are not to be linked in their fashion and that only the former deserves the appellation ἡ διακονία τῆς δικαιοσύνης. In fact the law, so far from promoting righteousness, is expressly termed ἡ διακονία τῆς κατακρίσεως (cf. 3: 8, 9). Against those who are bringing another view of the Spirit (cf. 11: 4), Paul insists that the Spirit is directly linked with the Lord (3: 17f). It is quite possible that the other element in their false teaching, that is, 'another Jesus' (11: 4), refers to a view that Jesus as the Christ had established a new era in which the priority of Israel was to be manifest[13] rather than that it indicates a θεῖος ἀνήρ Christology.[14] There is another reference to this false view of Christ in chapter 5. Verse 12 indicates that Paul is engaged in a polemical aside against those who boast about external advantages, a man's outward appearance and status. To Paul such an attitude reveals a this-worldly viewpoint and according to 5: 16, when applied to Christ, it is 'according to the flesh', for Paul distinguished his present view of Christ from views, including his own previous view, which he dubs as 'κατὰ σάρκα'. Before his conversion Paul shared the nationalistic conception of the Messiah which expected him to establish the divinely promised prerogative of Israel to rule the world; his Jewish Christian opponents still retain basically this view.[15] For Paul, however, the coming of the new (cf. verse 17) had brought a break with old outlooks and at no point was this more decisive than in regard to the person of Christ himself.

In comparing the background of Paul's opponents with the so-called 'Jewish mission' Georgi seems to assume that all elements of syncretism in the respective missions must mean a Hellenistic–Jewish identification. The opponents' emphasis on external manifestations of the Spirit such as visions, revelations, miracles (12: 1, 2), their apparent proficiency in the techniques of rhetoric (cf. 10: 5; 11: 6; 13: 3) and the glorification of Moses (cf. 3: 7ff) and Jewish customs (11: 22) are seen as evidence that such men must be Hellenistic–Jewish Christian missionaries.[16] It is now generally recognized however that it is hard to be dogmatic about what is distinctively Palestinian and what is distinctively Hellenistic. The glorification of Moses, the law and Jewish customs was characteristic of the most conservative wing of Jewish Christianity (cf. Acts 15: 5, 21; 21: 20f) and there is no reason why a high regard for visions, which could also be found in Rabbinic Judaism,[17] and an interest in the Spirit's visible manifestations could not have its origin in the pentecostal beginnings of the church's life (cf. for example Acts 2: 17ff; 3: 1ff; 5: 12ff; 6: 8; 10: 10ff). If Paul who claimed to be a Hebrew of the Hebrews (Phil. 3: 5) could make effective use of elements from the tradition of 'apology' in chapters 10–13,[18] then there is also no reason why Jewish Christian opponents could not become proficient in the diatribe and other rhetorical forms. Just as it is being increasingly realized that the Pharisees, who in life-style and customs sharply resisted Hellenization, were in fact very much influenced by hellenistic ideas in parts of their theology, so it may well be that 'syncretistic developments found their earliest and most rapid growth in Christianity not, as has been supposed among the Hellenists but among the Hebrews, not among those who were free in regard to the Law but among those who were most strict in their observance of the Law and prided themselves on their legitimacy'.[19] In order to insinuate their way into the Corinthian church and to gain influence and authority, such Judaizers were willing to adopt the sort of characteristics which most impressed the Corinthians, and when the Corinthians, confronted by rival apostolates, proceeded to evaluate their claims on what some would regard as basically 'hellenistic' grounds, Paul's opponents were willing to accommodate themselves to such criteria.[20]

In taking this view of the opponents we do not share the interpretation, held by some with similar views,[21] that οἱ ὑπερλίαν ἀπόστολοι (11: 5; 12: 11) are to be distinguished from Paul's adversaries in Corinth and seen as a reference to the Jerusalem apostles. Such an interpretation is unnecessary in establishing a Palestinian Jewish Christian background and seems to be forcing a particular hypothesis on Paul's argument. In both references the most natural way to read the text is as a continuation of Paul's interchange with the Corinthians in regard to his immediate opponents. The comparison of himself to the 'super-apostles' in 11: 5 follows directly upon Paul's description of the false apostles' preaching of another Jesus and his mention of a different Spirit and different gospel in verse 4 and is in turn followed in verse 6 by a comparison with these opponents in connection with the charge cited in 10: 10. Just as clearly the comparison to the 'super-apostles' in 12: 11 concludes Paul's piece of folly in indulging in competitive boasting with his opponents which he began in 11: 21*b*. In both instances a reference to the Jerusalem apostles is simply out of place. The argument that it is inexplicable that Paul should have made the modest claim that he was not excelled by those whom he describes later as servants of Satan[22] is weak. It ignores the fact that he proceeds to do something similar in 11: 22 and misses the bitter irony not only in the tone of these comparisons but in the whole of chapters 10–13. οἱ ὑπερλίαν ἀπόστολοι is one way in which Paul most appropriately dubs those whose claims for themselves are always in the superlative because, as he has already suggested, they compare themselves to themselves and boast beyond limit (10: 12–15).

2 CORINTHIANS 4: 16 - 5: 10 AND THE HEAVENLY HOUSE

2. The heavenly perspective (4: 16–18)

Possibly the one point about which there is no dispute with regard to 2 Corinthians 4: 16 - 5: 10 is its difficulty. Numerous attempts in commentaries, theses, monographs and articles[23] have been made to solve its difficulties and within the limited scope of our study we cannot possibly hope to cover all the angles[24] but will highlight the main features of Paul's argument as it focuses on the heavenly dimension and its function. 4: 16 - 5: 10 should not however be seen simply as an eschatological crux but, as part of the apostle's prolonged digression in 2: 14 - 7: 4 which constitutes an apology for his office, it plays its role in the argument by setting out the sufferings and rewards of that office.[25] Though the passage as a whole is not polemical in tone,[26] Paul's apology still has in view the situation in the Corinthian church and the distorted ideas which were being put forward there (cf. 5: 3, 4, 7). At the same time the passage reflects his relief from the depression caused by his anxieties about Titus and Corinth and from his recent affliction in Asia when he had been brought face to face with death. It reflects too his experience of God's comfort which had brought him through the anguish. In the face of attitudes which cast doubt on his apostolicity because of his troubles and his physical weakness and which instead stressed the manifestation of heavenly power and glory, Paul recounts the consolations which he knows to be his in the midst of the afflictions of life in this mortal body.

Chapter 4: 16–18 takes up this theme and with its contrast between τὰ βλεπόμενα and τὰ μὴ βλεπόμενα leads into the comparison between earthly and heavenly existence to be developed further in 5: 1ff. Paul's statements in chapters 3 and 4 can be seen both as a check to those tendencies in the Corinthian church which held that heavenly existence was already being fully enjoyed and that the body was of no significance in this and as set over against the claims of the 'super-apostles' to present glory and to the Spirit's manifestation in their ecstasies, their rhetorical gifts and impressive appearance. For Paul too, even as the 'suffering apostle', there is a progression from glory to glory beginning in this life as believers are transformed into the image of their heavenly Lord through the Spirit (2 Cor. 3: 18 cf. 1 Cor. 15: 47ff), but this is at present a phenomenon only accessible to faith (cf. 4: 18 and 5: 17) and this glory of the heavenly realm is to be lived out in and through mortal bodies (cf. 4: 6, 7). As in 1 Corinthians 15, Paul thinks in terms of earthly and heavenly stages to human existence and holds that for the believer there is at present an overlap in these two stages. Here in 2 Cor. 4: 16 the believer as he or she still bears the image of the earthly is seen as the 'outward man' and in so far as he or she already bears the image of the heavenly is described as the 'inward man'. The heavenly powers of the new age are at work but not in a way that alters that part of a person visible to others, the external bodily form. This is decaying. But in the heart (4: 6; 5: 12), in the centre of a person's being, in the 'inward man' not accessible to sight, the renovating powers of the age to come are in operation. Though the terminology Paul adopts may well come from the framework of a dualistic anthropology, his concept does not, for he is describing the one personality of the Christian believer, who lives in the period of the overlap of the ages, as seen now from the perspective of this age and now from that of the age to come. The latter perspective casts the true light on present suffering – it is producing an eternal weight of glory (4: 17). This makes clear that glory is not an immediately tangible possession; its full possession and its full tangibility await the future.[27] The attitude of faith which prepares for this future heavenly glory is described as one which looks at the earthly in the light of the heavenly. Unlike his opponents, Paul does not simply concentrate on the realm of that which is seen and that which is transient but looks to those things which are as yet invisible and which are eternal (cf. also 5: 7).[28] This is not to describe the heavenly dimension in Platonic fashion. These things are not eternal because they are essentially unable to be seen and are in an ideal realm. On the contrary, both the resurrection body and the heavenly Christ himself are for Paul realities which are to be revealed and seen in all their glory, and they are only at present invisible. Further, αἰώνιος (4: 17, 18; 5: 1) should not be taken in a static sense as referring to that which always has been in existence, but in its contrast with πρόσκαιρος it is meant to highlight the permanence of the realities of the new age. In this context it does not refer to that which is divorced from the realm of time and is without either beginning or end. The realities of the new age may have no end but they do have a beginning.

3. The heavenly house (5: 1)

οἴδαμεν γάρ (5: 1) introduces the reason for concentrating on the as yet unseen heavenly realities; believers can be assured that they will share fully in them. As in 1 Corinthians 15, after showing that heavenly existence must be lived out at present in earthly bodies, Paul goes on to indicate that the consummation of heavenly existence will involve a new bodily form. Again these heavenly realities are contrasted with the earthly, as ἡ ἐπίγειος ἡμῶν οἰκία τοῦ σκήνους is set over against οἰκίαν ἀχειροποίητον αἰώνιον ἐν τοῖς οὐρανοῖς.

The earthly tent-dwelling corresponds to the 'outward man' of the previous verse and also to the earlier 'earthen vessels' (cf. 4: 7), the 'body' (4: 10) and the 'mortal flesh' (4: 11). The tent metaphor for earthly existence is used in LXX Wisd. 9: 15 (the only other place in the LXX or NT where the word σκῆνος occurs in this way) and in the NT in John 1: 14 and 2 Peter 1: 13f. Paul employs it to underline the temporary nature of life in the earthly body and not to speak of the release of the soul from the captivity of corporeal existence as do Plato (e.g. *Phaed.* 81c), Philo (e.g. *Quaest. in Gen.* I, 28) or the *Corpus Hermeticum* (XIII, 15).[29]

If οἰκία in this half of the comparison has reference to the body, then all the indications are that the parallelism is to be maintained and that it will also have reference to the body in the other half. This consideration, together with the parallel to 1 Corinthians 15: 47–9 where it is also earthly and heavenly bodily existence which are being compared, stands decisively against any interpretation which would take the building ἐν τοῖς οὐρανοῖς either in the sense of a mansion in heaven along the lines of John 14: 2f[30] or in the sense of the new temple as the corporate body of Christ.[31] It is the heavenly resurrection body which Paul has in view.

ἐν τοῖς οὐρανοῖς refers primarily to the locality of this resurrection body in the heavenly realm. But depending on the context the local in connection with heaven can shade over into the qualitative. That which belongs primarily in the heavens partakes of the quality of that realm. Elsewhere also ἐν τοῖς οὐρανοῖς can be virtually interchangeable with οὐράνιος and in Matthew 6, for example, πάτερ ἡμῶν ὁ ἐν τοῖς οὐρανοῖς (verse 9 cf. also verse 1) can give way to ὁ πατὴρ ὑμῶν ὁ οὐράνιος (verses 14, 26, 32). Here also the phrase can be viewed as having similar force to ἐπουράνιος in 1 Corinthians 15: 48f. This is further supported by the fact that both here in 2 Corinthians 5: 1 and in 1 Corinthians 15: 48f the contrast is with a form of existence that is described by the adjective ἐπίγειος.

Other phrases used of the resurrection body and which by association shed light on the heavenly dimension are ἐκ θεοῦ, ἀχειροποίητος and αἰώνιος. The connotation of αἰώνιος here is primarily qualitative through association with the life of the age to come, but it carries secondary connotations of permanent duration. As compared with the earthly tent which can be dismantled in death, the heavenly body is indestructible and will last for ever. The building from God and the house not made with hands are virtually synonymous. The resurrection body originates from God as its source and therefore cannot be attributed to human workmanship. ἀχειροποίητος became almost a technical term in Christian usage for the spiritual and heavenly realities of the new order (cf. Col. 2: 11, and for negative formulations using χειροποίητος cf. Acts 7: 48; 17: 24; Heb. 9: 11, 24). The starting point for this usage appears to have been the saying mentioned in Mark 14: 58 and, in view of the parallels with 2 Corinthians 5: 1, Paul may well have had this saying in mind (cf. καταλύσω-καταλυθῇ; οἰκοδομήσω-οἰκοδομήν; ἀχειροποίητον-ἀχειροποίητον).[32] But since in the early church it was taken literally as a reference to the destruction of the temple in Jerusalem in A.D.70, and symbolically as a reference to Christ's resurrection body as the new temple and also to the church as the new temple, Paul's allusion cannot be held to be decisive for determining the reference of οἰκία here. Paul could be referring either to the resurrection body or specifically to Christ's resurrection body or to the new temple and other factors will determine which he has in mind. The significance of the allusion in this passage is to provide a Christological basis for a reference to the believer's resurrection body and thus to develop the point made in 4: 14 – 'knowing that he who raised the Lord Jesus will raise us also with Jesus'. In this way the believer's heavenly existence, as in 1 Corinthians 15: 47ff, is shown to be integrally linked with Christ's.

Paul is talking then of earthly and heavenly bodily existence and of the former he can write ἐὰν ἡ ἐπίγειος ἡμῶν οἰκία τοῦ σκήνους καταλυθῇ . . . The end result of the process of dying (4: 10–12) and decay (4: 16) is the body's destruction in death. To keep Paul's metaphor, at death the earthly tent-dwelling is dismantled (cf. also LXX Isa. 38: 2 where καταλύω is used in this sense). This description is only appropriate to the death of a believer before the parousia and not to what happens to those who survive and are alive at Christ's return. The language Paul employs in the latter case is that of transformation (cf. Phil. 3: 21) which will involve a 'putting on' without the necessity of a prior 'taking off' (cf. verses 2–4; 1 Cor. 15: 51ff). While the earthly body of those still alive must be changed, this will not involve its destruction.[33]

Since the clause has reference to death before the parousia, added weight is given to interpreting ἐάν conditionally as 'if' rather than temporally as 'when' or 'whenever'. This is the normal way ἐάν is used with the aorist subjunctive in the NT. Though Paul may well have taken increasingly seriously the likelihood of his own death before the parousia because of his recent experiences (cf. 1: 8ff), there is still an element of uncertainty and here as in 1 Thessalonians 4: 13ff, 5: 10 and 1 Corinthians 15: 51ff he still reckons with the dual possibility of death or the prior return of Christ, in which case he would not be overtaken by death but rather transformed. As in these other passages the apostle is addressing himself to the dilemma of death before the parousia but here he feels himself more personally and intensely involved in that dilemma. Despite this the assurance he proclaims is no less ringing than that which sounds out in 1 Corinthians 15. In the eventuality of death, he asserts, we know we have a heavenly resurrection body from God.

The present tense ἔχομεν underlines this certainty. Given that the object of the verb is the heavenly body, there are three basic possibilities in regard to the temporal reference. Some see it as a present possession of this body which already exists in heaven.[34] Paul often conceives of objects and events normally associated with the end-time as existing already in heaven (e.g. the Jerusalem above in Galatians 4: 26).[35] This interpretation suggests that he is thinking similarly here of a present possession which would be actualized at some future stage and that when he comes to verse 2 he expresses this in terms of the existence of heavenly garments prior to their being put on. Parallels to such a notion are adduced from 1 Enoch 62: 15; Asc. Isa. 7: 22; 8: 26; 9: 2, 9, 17, 24; 11: 40.[36] Against such an idea being present here however are the considerations that ἐν τοῖς οὐρανοῖς is to be construed primarily with οἰκίαν rather than ἔχομεν, that in this context its local reference shades over into qualitative connotations of the body as heavenly and that the use of αἰώνιος does not signify that this body has always been in existence. Even more central to Paul's thought is the consideration that nowhere else does he conceive of a detached and impersonal body as something desirable and therefore his particular metaphor of the body as a garment to be put on should not be put to a use which would obscure the reality it is meant to signify.[37] In fact Paul himself indicates that his metaphors are not to be pressed too literally by the way in which he merges that of the building and that of the garment into one another. In this way, and most significantly, the resurrection body should probably be seen as an exception to Paul's application of the apocalyptic category of the present anticipation in heaven of the benefits of the end-time.

ἔχομεν is to be taken as designating a future possession of the heavenly body. But here again opinions divide on whether this will be at death or at the parousia. Those who advocate the former hold that ἔχομεν points to an immediate succession between the earthly and the heavenly forms of embodiment and thus if they do not actually treat ἐάν grammatically as temporal they virtually equate it with ὅταν. Though becoming increasingly popular[38] such an interpretation is by no means necessary or convincing in this context. It is exactly the element of immediacy which is missing from the text and which has to be read into it.[39] To be preferred is the view that ἔχομεν is a futuristic present used by Paul because he was so assured of his possession of the resurrection body after the parousia that he could speak of it as present.[40] There are no decisive objections to this interpretation. Harris however puts forward what he considers to be two such objections.[41] He writes, 'Since the receipt of the σῶμα πνευματικόν at the Parousia was (on this view) guaranteed whether or not death had occurred previously, any notion of conditionality in 2 Cor. 5: 1 is virtually obliterated.' But this is only the case if καταλυθῇ is taken to refer to either the parousia or death beforehand. The conditionality remains if the verb refers only to the dismantling in a prior death, for then Paul is saying, 'If we die before the parousia, we still have the resurrection body which only comes after the parousia.' To the further objection that 'the moment when the consolation is needed must be the moment when the consolation is given, and the consolation received at death cannot simply be identical with the assurance of the future acquisition of the resurrection body already possessed during life', we reply that the evidence indicates that Paul would not have agreed. After all, both in 1 Corinthians 15 and in 1 Thessalonians 4 it is just in these terms that he provides consolation for those who are perplexed about those who have died before the parousia. Why should it be any different when his own consolation is more to the fore?[42]

The evidence of 1 Corinthians 15 in regard to the time of the receipt of the resurrection body may also be called in to support this interpretation of ἔχομεν. Paul is writing to the same Christian community and approximately a year later speaking of the same heavenly body about which he had already written at some length. If he made clear then that the time of the receipt of such a body, both for those who had died and those who survived, was at the parousia, then the same must be assumed to be the case here unless it can be proven otherwise.[43] The present tense of ἔχομεν is certainly insufficient evidence that Paul has undergone a radical change of mind. If Paul intended to convey the notion that the resurrection body was to be received immediately upon death, it would be very hard to see why this should be called a 'development' rather than an outright contradiction of what he had previously said. The explicit order of the programme for the defeat of death in 1 Corinthians 15: 23–6 would no longer hold and the mystery proclaimed in 1 Corinthians 15: 51ff that at the last trumpet the dead will be raised imperishable would no longer be true. The change of mind would not only involve a question of chronology but also a quite different idea of the continuity between earthly and heavenly bodies than is suggested in 1 Corinthians 15. Yet there is simply no indication of such a radical break with what he had

previously meant when Paul mentions the resurrection of the dead in 2
Corinthians 1: 9 and 4: 14. It is also strange that when in later letters Paul
dwells on the same theme (cf. Rom. 8: 22-4; Phil. 3: 20f) there is again no
indication of his 'new insights'. We conclude therefore that in 2 Corinthians
5: 1 Paul is anticipating the believer's share in heavenly glory (cf. 4: 17)
and is assured of his future possession of the heavenly body, which, as
everywhere else in his letters, he believes will actually become his at
Christ's coming.

4. Heavenly existence and death before the parousia (5: 2-4)

The γάρ of verse 2 can be seen as introducing further grounds for the
apostle's assurance of receiving a resurrection body. This body, for which
he longs, is designated this time in a variation of terminology as τὸ
οἰκητήριον ἡμῶν τὸ ἐξ οὐρανοῦ. Here heaven is to be seen primarily as the
place of origin, the source of the resurrection body (cf. ἐκ θεοῦ in verse 1).
Again this can take on qualitative connotations; that which comes from
and belongs to the heavenly dimension is heavenly (cf. the force of ἐξ
οὐρανοῦ in 1 Corinthians 15: 47, 48), though there could here also be an
allusion to the resurrection body coming *from* heaven at the parousia.[44]
But this time the heavenly mode of existence is not set over against the
dismantling of the earthly body in death but against the groaning that
takes place in that body during the present life. ἐν τούτῳ in verse 2 refers
to the earthly tent, since ἐν τούτῳ στενάζομεν (verse 2) is parallel to ἐν
τῷ σκήνει στενάζομεν (verse 4). In verse 2 this groaning and the reason for
it are placed in a positive light, but followed in verse 3 by a parenthetical
clause which contains a negative and is aimed at false views in the Corinthian church. Then verse 4 repeats the thought of verse 2 but in the light of
the aside, so that the groaning now includes a negative element alongside
the positive.

On the positive side the reason for the sighing or groaning is Paul's
desire to put on the heavenly habitation over the earthly tent-dwelling.
This is similar to the sentiment expressed in Rom. 8: 23 where the groaning of the believer expresses the tension of living in the overlap of the ages,
eagerly awaiting the redemption of the body. There are two further indications from the terminology of verses 2-4 that Paul's desire will be fulfilled at the parousia rather than at his death. The first is found in the distinctive use of ἐπενδύσασθαι in verses 2 and 4. The force of the prefix ἐπι -
is to give the nuance not simply of putting on a garment but of putting it
on over the top of what one is already wearing. That Paul has such a
notion in view is brought out particularly clearly in verse 4 - 'because we
do not wish to be unclothed but to be further clothed'.[45] His preference is

that he should not have to experience an interval of being unclothed as far as embodiment is concerned but that he should be able simply to put on his future heavenly form of existence over the top of his present earthly form.[46] This imagery is only appropriate to those who survive until the parousia and not to those whose earthly form of clothing has already been taken off through death.[47] 'We may think of a man living in a house or tent; he wishes to put up another, larger house or tent round the one he already inhabits.'[48] It is obvious that this cannot refer to the same event the apostle has in mind when he talks of the earthly tent being dismantled. When Paul has in view the transformation which both the dead in Christ and those alive at his return must undergo he uses the general image conveyed by ἐνδύσασθαι as in 1 Corinthians 15, but when he has the specific experience of those who will be alive in focus, the more particular significance of ἐπενδύσασθαι becomes appropriate. The second indication of the time of the fulfilment of Paul's desire is the notion of verse 4 that when he puts on the heavenly dwelling, then what is mortal will be swallowed up by life. Paul uses very similar terms in 1 Corinthians 15: 54 and there the clear temporal reference of such terminology is to the parousia (cf. verse 52). The presumption is that the same will be the case here unless there are clear indications to the contrary.[49]

Paul's statement of his desire (verse 2) is followed by the parenthetical clause of verse 3 – 'on the assumption, of course, that when we have put it on, we shall not be found naked'.[50] His reason for spelling out this assumption in tautological fashion can only have been to set his goal clearly over against that of some in Corinth so that they could not fail to catch the thrust of what he was saying. This interpretation depends on the meaning given to γυμνός. Some hold that it is to be explained in terms of shame before God at the parousia because of the lack of a robe of righteousness.[51] Such an explanation can call on the imagery of the parable of the wedding garment (Matt. 22: 11–14) and on OT imagery for support but does not fit this context. Where γυμνός is opposed to the concept of being clothed in verse 3 and synonymous with that expressed by ἐκδύσασθαι in verse 4, and where this clothing is expressly seen in terms of embodiment, then γυμνός quite naturally must be seen as referring to a state of disembodiment.[52] That this state of disembodiment is that of unbelievers who will be without a spiritual body[53] is again unlikely for contextual reasons, for Paul is not discussing generally the fate of both believers and unbelievers, but only the future of believers. We hold then that γυμνός refers to the state of disembodiment upon which believers enter at death. To those among his readers who, because of their general disparagement of the body, would consider such a state desirable, Paul is at pains to show that this is not the object of the believer's longing.[54] Those Corinthians who considered themselves to be enjoying heavenly existence to the full already did not envisage a further stage of embodiment. Others may well have gone further and conceived of the lack of a body as a desirable state. Both in verse 3 and in verse 4 Paul shows that this is not the case and that the goal of Christian existence is not the stripping off of the body but a new heavenly form of embodiment.

In order that there should be no mistake on this matter, the apostle repeats his expression of the tension and groaning in present Christian existence in the light of his polemical aside. Not only does disembodiment not constitute the believer's ultimate desire but it in fact introduces a negative aspect into the tension, since the believer actually shrinks from such a state of being unclothed (verse 4). In verse 4 as opposed to verse 2 the groaning is associated with great oppression – βαρούμενοι (cf. ἐβαρήθημεν in 1: 8 which includes both mental and physical oppression in the face of death) – and this is 'because we do not wish to be unclothed but to be clothed upon'.[55] In the light of the distorted viewpoint of some Corinthians, in 2 Corinthians 5: 4 Paul emphasizes that the grounds for this groaning are negatively the fear or dislike of an ἐκδύσασθαι and positively the desire for an ἐπενδύσασθαι. He is oppressed because he does not desire the disembodiment which he knows death before the parousia must involve. Barrett aptly observes,

> Paul is not in the ordinary sense afraid of death; he dreads it precisely for the reason which he proceeds to give – because it would be a much happier thing to survive till the *parousia*, that is, not to die, be buried, pass some time *naked*, and then be raised up, but to be transformed immediately.[56]

Thus, while Paul held a state of nakedness to be undesirable, he nevertheless reckoned with its possibility.

5. The Spirit as the pledge of heavenly existence (5: 5)

The statement of verse 5 that 'he who prepared us for this very thing is God, who gave us the Spirit as a pledge' reinforces the notion that heavenly embodiment is the consummation and goal of Christian existence. αὐτὸ τοῦτο refers to the reception of the heavenly body at the parousia and the giving of the Spirit is seen as part of God's process of preparation for such a fulfilment. The Spirit is the link between the renewal which is taking place now in the inner man (4: 16) and the consummation of this renewal in the heavenly body. He is transforming believers from glory to glory and into the likeness of their heavenly Lord

(3: 18). The term ἀρραβών expresses here in verse 5 (cf. also 1: 22) the nature of the link the Spirit provides. It could be used to mean both 'pledge' and 'first instalment'. There is no reason why both notions cannot be involved in its use here. The Spirit is the pledge God has given that believers will acquire their heavenly inheritance (cf. also Eph. 1: 14), God's guarantee that he will fulfil his promises. At the same time the Spirit functions as the first instalment differing from God's payment in full only in degree, not in kind.[57] Thus the Spirit is the down-payment here and now on that heavenly existence which will find its culmination in embodiment (cf. also Rom. 8: 23).

6. Presence with the heavenly Lord (5: 6–10)

In the light of the guarantee that God will not fail in accomplishing his purpose of providing a heavenly body for the believer, the apostle is of good courage at all times, even when faced with the possibility, introduced in verses 3, 4, of being naked for a period because of death before the parousia. He begins to state further grounds for confidence – 'and knowing that to be at home in the body is to be absent from the Lord'.[58] The presupposition of these grounds, which are stated afresh in verse 8, is the thought that being at home in the body implies absence from the Lord's immediate presence. The apostle has now put aside his 'tent' and 'building' metaphors and in verses 6–10 speaks simply of the body, by which he means the present earthly body. He has left behind too the idea of 'putting on' a new form of embodiment and the verbs he now employs (ἐκδημεῖν and ἐνδημεῖν) introduce new imagery, that of being at home or away from home.[59]

The aside of verse 7 – διὰ πίστεως γὰρ περιπατοῦμεν οὐ διὰ εἴδους – underlines the assertion Paul has introduced and points out why it is true. The believer is absent from Christ in this life because Christ is in heaven and, though the believer on earth can have a faith-relationship with him, for the present his Lord generally remains invisible. We take εἶδος in its more usual passive sense of outward and visible appearance (cf. the other four instances of its use in the NT – Luke 3: 22; 9: 29; John 5: 37; 1 Thess. 5: 22) rather than in its active sense of 'sight'. This would then be similar to the point Paul has made in 4: 18 that he concentrates not on the things that are seen but on those which are unseen. This parenthesis, like that of verse 3, may well have a polemical edge[60] and be aimed at those views of Christian existence in Corinth which tended to neglect the fact that the eschaton had not yet arrived (cf. 1 Cor. 13: 12) and especially the views of the newly arrived opponents who boasted of appearances (cf. 5: 12), emphasizing visible manifestations of power (12: 12) and visions (12:

1ff), not understanding that heavenly glory is not yet visibly demonstrated in the present body.

In verse 8 the apostle begins his thought again, expressing his confidence and his willingness, if faced with the choice of remaining in the present body or departing, to be away from the body because this would be to be at home with the Lord. In this context he can prefer dying because, although it might mean a period of nakedness, it will certainly mean ἐνδημῆσαι πρὸς τὸν κύριον. It is hard to see that this phrase implies the possession of a spiritual corporeality and that Paul is simply continuing the contrast between two stages of embodiment.[61] In itself it only implies enjoyment of fellowship with the Lord in his presence and this could be either in the body or otherwise. But it is precisely the fact that Paul does not say 'to be absent from *this* body' but rather 'to be absent from *the* body' which would indicate that he is not thinking of two successive stages of embodiment.[62] Again it is hard to see that Paul envisages the parousia rather than death as the time when the ἐνδημῆσαι πρὸς τὸν κύριον would occur.[63] On such a view he would simply be expressing his preference for possessing heavenly embodiment as opposed to his present earthly embodiment – a rather obvious and not very profound sentiment. But verses 6, 8, 9 all imply that being at home in the body is coincident with being away from the Lord, so that as soon as one ceases to be at home in the body, one also ceases to be absent from the Lord.[64] 2 Corinthians 5: 8 is therefore similar to Paul's perspective in Philippians 1: 21–3 where, faced with the same choice, he sees dying as 'gain' and as 'far better' because it means being with Christ. Since Christ is in heaven, being at home with him must involve being in heaven in his presence. Death before the parousia will therefore bring a fuller enjoyment of heavenly existence than believers can experience in this life, yet their enjoyment will not be complete until they possess the heavenly body for which God has prepared them.

7. Concluding observations on 2 Corinthians 4: 16 – 5: 10

In the midst of decay and affliction Paul concentrates on the as yet unseen heavenly realities and knows that if he dies before the parousia he will assuredly still receive a heavenly body when Christ returns. He longs to be able to put on that body without first experiencing death. For him the disembodied state, though possible, is undesirable and he knows that ultimately God has prepared him for the reception of the heavenly body and has in fact guaranteed this by giving him the Spirit. In the light of this he is of good courage and knows that even if he dies before the parousia this is something to be preferred because it will mean that he will be present with the Lord.

The usual objection to this interpretation is that it involves Paul in two contradictory attitudes towards dying.[65] At first he shrinks from the nakedness of death and then he can say that, faced with the choice between dying and remaining in this body, he prefers to die because death for him will mean being with the Lord. Yet is this not 'precisely the kind of psychologically sound tension that a man could express when caught in the grasp of strong ambivalent feelings? Death is an enemy; disembodiment is to be abhorred ... But meanwhile, if he must die, ... it will be all right, indeed far better, for it means to be with the Lord even without resurrection.'[66] In addition this interpretation does justice to the way in which Paul has to formulate his own position in the face of the views both of some in the Corinthian congregation and of the opponents who have arrived on the scene. For the Corinthians the life of heaven had nothing to do with the body; for the opponents the life of heaven was to be demonstrated visibly through the present body. Paul steers a course between these two options. In 5: 1f he can stress the future bodily consummation of heavenly life and at the same time in 5: 6f can assert that there is a sense in which he cannot be at home in the present body and being away from it will mean a greater experience of heavenly life. In the face of death the apostle reckons with heavenly realities and it is his very assurance of the reality of the future heavenly body which throws into relief the incompleteness of the state of 'nakedness' and makes death seem so abnormal. Yet even if death destroys the earthly body it cannot alter Paul's indissoluble link with his heavenly Lord which will continue, though the earthly body does not, and which will eventually issue in the reception of the heavenly body.

An excessive fear of finding anything that might smack of a Hellenistic anthropology in this passage has led some commentators to strange alternative interpretations. Yet what is to be seen here in Paul is not an ultimate anthropological dualism but rather a temporary duality brought about by sin and death, which until the consummation of salvation continue to mar the wholeness of human existence.[67] If the possibility of existence in disembodied form is 'Hellenistic', then in any case it had already penetrated the Jewish traditions to which Paul was heir and here, as in Phil. 1: 23, apocalyptic and rabbinic concepts provide the framework in which Paul develops his thoughts about the role which heaven will play for the believer after death.[68] He can combine a concept of an intermediate state in heaven (cf. especially 5: 8) with the expectation of the resurrection of the dead (cf. 4: 14; 5: 1). Thus W. D. Davies is correct in finding behind our passage the twofold conception of the age to come as already existing in heaven and as yet to come.[69] 1 Enoch 39: 4 and 71: 14ff provide examples from apocalyptic writings of the age to come being experienced in heaven at death. For the rabbis also the souls of the righteous entered the age to come as heaven at death, and this preliminary blessedness was to be consummated when through the resurrection of the dead the age to come entered into its second and final phase.[70] Paul in his pre-Christian days would have shared this perspective. It becomes transformed for him however by what has taken place through the resurrection of Christ. Yet this transformation is not of the sort Davies has proposed. The new Christological orientation centres in the reality of the believer's union with the resurrected Lord. The age to come has been opened up already in its initial stages by the resurrection of Christ and can be seen to exist at present in heaven, but not until the consummation will this directly affect the believer's body.[71] It is only at the parousia of Christ from heaven that the believer will receive his or her heavenly body. Union with Christ is determinative for both stages of experience of the age to come. 2 Corinthians 4: 14 assures that 'he who raised the Lord Jesus will raise us also – σὺν 'Ιησοῦ'. Similarly this indissoluble union provides the reason why, even if he or she dies before the parousia, the individual believer will still know that experience of heaven which the apostle thinks of as being at home with the Lord.

2 Corinthians 4: 16 – 5: 10 thus presents no radically new teaching about heavenly resurrection life but a development of that which the apostle had presented earlier in 1 Corinthians 15. He uses new imagery and applies further reflection as he addresses an altered situation both in his own life and in the Corinthian church. All this, it should be remembered, forms part of Paul's demonstration that true apostleship will not over-emphasize present glory but while 'away from the Lord' (5: 6) will involve suffering and yet at the same time know the consolation of certain hope. Union with Christ (cf. 5: 1, 6–8) and the guarantee of the Spirit (5: 5) are the certainties which provide assurance even in the face of the most extreme evidence of apostolic weakness – death before the parousia. For this reason God's power and glory can be revealed through death just as much as through weakness and suffering during life.

2 CORINTHIANS 12: 1-10 AND THE THIRD HEAVEN

8. Paul the visionary

2 Corinthians 12: 1ff gives us a glimpse of heaven in the life of Paul the visionary.[72] The apostle comes to the point where he feels compelled to take up the weapon of his opponents – boasting – and to vindicate himself in regard to visions and revelations – ἐλεύσομαι δὲ εἰς ὀπτασίας καὶ ἀποκαλύψεις κυρίου.[73]

The event Paul proceeds to relate was not a unique occurrence in his life but rather just one outstanding example of his visionary experiences. The dual terminology and the plural forms - ὀπτασίας καὶ ἀποκαλύψεις - may indicate that Paul set out with the intention of relating several visionary experiences[74] and suggest that there is some justification for the description of the apostle as a 'visionary'. Further support from this passage can be found in the phrase in verse 7 - τῇ ὑπερβολῇ τῶν ἀποκαλύψεων - which could refer to either the quality or quantity of the revelations and which has broader reference than merely to the visionary experience mentioned in verses 2–4.[75] We must also assume that the saying of the risen Christ recorded in verse 9 was given to Paul by revelation. There is no indication whether this was given directly to him in a visionary experience or mediated through a prophet. That Paul does not anywhere dwell on this side of Christian existence must not be taken to mean that it was not a valid side or that it only played a very minor part on the periphery of his life.[76] It is simply that he considers such experiences to be a matter between himself and God and in his letters concentrates on what he holds to be of more direct value for building up the churches. His allusion to his ecstatic experiences earlier in 5: 13 is illuminating in this regard. Such ecstasies are not for his own glory - εἴτε γὰρ ἐξέστημεν, θεῷ· εἴτε σωφρονοῦμεν, ὑμῖν. This attitude parallels that expressed in the one mention of his own speaking in tongues in 1 Corinthians 14: 18f where he can make the bold assertion - 'I thank God that I speak in tongues more than you all; nevertheless, in church I would rather speak five words with my mind, in order to instruct others, than ten thousand words in a tongue.' Clearly lack of frequent reference does not necessarily mean lack of frequent experience.

Of the only other references in the apostle's letters to the part which visions and revelations played in his life Galatians 1: 12 (cf. also 1: 16), 1 Corinthians 9: 1; 15: 8f all refer to the most formative vision of all for Paul's life, that of the heavenly Christ, which he received on the road to Damascus, while Galatians 2: 1 has reference to a revelation which initiated a later journey to Jerusalem. In Acts however Luke depicts Paul as experiencing visions on several occasions. There are three accounts of the Damascus road vision - Acts 9: 1–9; 22: 3–16; 26: 9–18 - and the last of these is designated as 'the heavenly vision' (26: 19). Further visions involving the Lord are recorded in Acts 9: 12; 18: 9–11; 22: 17–21; 23: 11.[77] Two other visions which were given to Paul but in which Christ is not directly related to the content are presented by Luke in Acts 16: 9f and 27: 23.

Paul does not say whether he saw the heavenly Christ in the vision recounted in 2 Corinthians 12 or whether it was the Lord who uttered the unspeakable words to him, but since the majority of the visions mentioned in the letters and in Acts involved seeing Christ and receiving a revelation from him we may well assume that the same holds in this case. In the phrase in verse 1 - ὀπτασίας καὶ ἀποκαλύψεις κυρίου - κυρίου is probably to be taken as a subjective genitive denoting the giver of the visions,[78] but too sharp a distinction need not be made and the Lord need not be excluded from also being the content of the visions and revelations (cf. Galatians 1: 12 and 16 where Christ appears to be both giver and content).[79]

9. The context in the 'apology'

To appreciate the force of the passage in its context and the style of Paul's response to his opponents the nature of chapters 10–13 as an 'apology' should be recognized. It is the great merit of H. D. Betz's work, *Der Apostel Paulus und die sokratische Tradition*,[80] to have pointed out parallels with the form of an apology in the Socratic tradition, though it at times succumbs to the temptation to subordinate everything in these four chapters to this single line of interpretation. That Paul uses elements from this particular form does not necessitate attempting to explain all his attitudes in these chapters from the perspective of the Socratic tradition, and indeed Paul is far too passionately involved in the situation and concerned for the cause of Christ to have a basic affinity with Socrates' detached irony.[81] It is unlikely also that Paul is consciously following the Socratic 'apology' as such, as Betz appears to hold, and more likely that he is making effective use of elements from this tradition with which he is acquainted from their employment in popular culture and conventions.

The Corinthian church had been impresssed by the accomplishments of Paul's opponents and the difficult task of the apostle is to free the church from their bewitchment and through his defence to bring its members to self-examination and lead them back to a recognition of the true situation. Betz compares Paul's dilemma to that of Socrates when his disciples were at first astounded by the knowledge of the sophists[82] and provides many examples of the way in which Socrates and subsequent philosophers defended themselves when charged with charlatanism. In conducting his apology the true philosopher rejected the usual means of rhetoric and by the use of irony vindicated himself in the name of philosophy, demonstrating that his poverty and weakness were proof of the genuineness of his claims, exposing his opponents as sophists who had at their disposal wealth, political influence and a whole arsenal of rhetorical tricks, and reducing their claims to absurdity.[83] In such apologies it was not good form for the true philosopher to speak of his own accomplishments, but when necessary this could be done by someone else and in moderation. If absolutely forced to defend himself against false charges then one means he could adopt to avoid boasting about himself directly was to take on the role of 'the fool', because the fool could get away with assertions which would not normally be permissible and could make extravagant claims.[84]

Some general parallels between elements in this tradition and 2 Corinthians 10-13 can be readily seen. Paul too is faced with the charge of charlatanism. He cites this charge against him in 10: 10, having already made an ironic allusion to it in 10: 1. The accusation is that there is a great discrepancy between the image the apostle puts over in his letters and his appearance and speech when present, so that whereas his letters are weighty, his appearance is weak and his ability with words is of no account. The apostle in his concern for the truth (11: 10; 12: 6; 13: 8) and for the Corinthians (11:.2, 11; 12: 15, 19; 13: 9) is forced to defend himself (12: 11) but in so doing rejects the rhetorical form of apology designed for self-recommendation (12: 19).[85] Like the philosopher, but by means of spiritual weapons, Paul sees it as his task to do battle against sophistic rhetoric and to expose it for what it really is (10: 4-6).[86] He does not dispute that he is weak in this area (11: 6), but for him such an admission is only evidence of the genuineness of his claims, as is the list of his weaknesses in 11: 23ff (cf. 12: 9, 10). In his defence, which is at the same time not a defence (cf. 10: 18; 12: 19), Paul resorts to the role of the fool in order to remind the Corinthians of his claims as an apostle (11: 1, 16ff, 21, 23; 12: 6, 11) and the whole is permeated by fierce irony (e.g. 10: 1; 11: 5, 7, 21).[87]

10. Paul's boasting about his vision

Paul brings up this matter of visions, about which he is so reluctant to speak, only because he felt that for the sake of the Corinthians it had to be dealt with as part of the defence of his apostleship. καυχᾶσθαι δεῖ (12: 1) is symptomatic of the whole tone of chapters 10-13, where the concept of boasting occurs nineteen times. The situation has developed since the statements of 3: 1 and 5: 12. Because of the attacks of his opponents and the Corinthians' reaction to them Paul now feels compelled to take up their challenge. What is at stake in all this is the legitimacy of Paul's apostleship.[88] What is more specifically at issue in 2 Corinthians 12 is what is to count as evidence for the legitimacy of claims to apostleship. The Corinthians, with their interest in the more sensational manifestations of the Spirit, were making experience of visions and revelations and the performance of miracles some of their criteria for the recognition of apostolic claims and the intruding 'false apostles' had been all too willing to accommodate themselves to such tests and were making great claims for themselves in these areas. Paul's stress in verse 6 that if he were to continue with his own account of visionary experiences he would be telling the truth may well have in view the fact that his opponents were even laying claim to experiences they had never had.[89]

The apostle's boasting is not to be taken in a straightforward sense. Though he takes up his opponents' weapons and seems to accede formally to the Corinthians' view of what counts as evidence by mentioning visions and revelations, in fact he does not surrender to their requirements but rather succeeds in turning the tables. He not only asserts that there is nothing to be gained by such boasting (12: 1) but demonstrates its futility in the way he carries it out. Quite consciously playing the fool, Paul had begun to match his opponents boast for boast (11: 21*b*) and even to attempt to outdo them (11: 23). But this is such an unnatural role for Paul that he is unable to sustain even this indirect boasting for long and ends with a list of sufferings and weaknesses which gives his boasting an altogether different complexion from that of the opponents. His boasting of the crowning humiliation of being let down in a basket through a window in the Damascus wall (11: 32f) acts as a *reductio ad absurdum*. In 12: 1 the apostle continues in the strain begun in 11: 21*b*, this time matching the opponents' boasts about visions and revelations. But again this is boasting with a difference and would not have been very successful on his opponents' or the Corinthians' view of boasting. He begins with an outstanding vision which had taken place fourteen years previously but comes to a halt and has to start his account again and even then will not allow himself to say anything substantial about the incident. He uses the third person in the narrative and yet is talking about himself as verse 7 makes clear. The best explanation for this is not in terms of 'the objectifying of the I'[90] or of a dualistic anthropology where 'Paul distinguishes two men within himself'[91] or where he distinguishes his present self from his future self.[92] It is also not provided by the convention of the pseudonymity of apocalyptic where an anonymous seer transfers his own experiences to a well-known figure such as Enoch,[93] but rather by Paul's perspective on boasting. One of the elements of the apology in the Socratic tradition was that one must not boast about oneself, but if necessary this may be done by someone else. Paul's use of the third person is his way of observing this sort of convention. He does not praise himself but another described as ἄνθρωπος ἐν Χριστῷ (verse 2), ὁ τοιοῦτος ἄνθρωπος (verse 3) and again ὁ τοιοῦτος (verse 5).[94] Eventually Paul abandons any attempt to boast of further visions, though he could do so if he wanted (cf. verse 6) and returns instead to the theme of his own weaknesses (verse 5). And since boasting of his own weakness is equivalent to boasting of the power of Christ (verse 9*b*), Paul's own perspective on boasting, rather than that of the opponents, is established – 'Let him who boasts, boast of the Lord' (10: 17, cf. also 1 Cor. 1: 31). The very terminology of ἄνθρωπος ἐν Χριστῷ (verse 2) indicates his adherence to the principle of 10: 17. It was not because of anything that he was in himself that Paul had been granted his experience of heaven, not because he possessed special psychic powers or a unique capacity for mystical experience but solely because of his relationship to Christ.

Although Betz in his discussion of this passage[95] goes too far in subordinating content to form and in considering that 12: 2–4 and 7*b*–10 are simply two parodies, there are undoubtedly elements of parody in both sections which enable the apostle to reduce the opponents' type of boasting to absurdity again. Their boasting of visions would climax in the special revelatory word they had been given and they would also give boastful accounts of outstanding miracles. Paul proceeds to tell of a vision but ironically concludes his account with the fact that there is no revelatory word because 'he heard things that cannot be told, which man may not utter' (verse 4), and then gives a miracle story[96] where there is no miracle. Paul's accounts are based on genuine experiences but the ironic twists which give the accounts an element of parody indicate that he is determined not to be judged by what the Corinthians count as evidence.

In this context Paul's ironic boasting of his experience of the third heaven is extremely significant for it is meant to show that outward success and visionary experiences cannot count as proof of the truth of claims. In fact this sort of evidence easily leads to deception and Paul not only hints at this in 12: 6 but says so explicitly in 11: 13–15. It is his opponents who are deceitful, who disguise themselves as servants of righteousness, and who are indeed ψευδαπόστολοι – counterfeit apostles. Paul refrains from reciting further visions and revelations because they can only provide evidence of a sort that cannot be verified and that is removed from the realm of that which others can perceive through seeing or hearing – μή τις εἰς ἐμὲ λογίσηται ὑπὲρ ὃ βλέπει με ἢ ἀκούει (12: 6). Paul will rely only on the evidence that is plainly before the Corinthians' eyes (cf. also 10: 7; 11: 6). All the evidence which is demonstrable in Paul's case is negative and was considered by the opponents as proof of the illegitimacy of his apostleship.[97] He admits the charges of 10: 10 – his presence *is* weak (cf. 11: 21 and the list of sufferings in 11: 23ff) and his speech *is* of no account (cf. 11: 6). But for Paul the two demonstrable proofs – his weaknesses and the existence of the Corinthian church – clinch his case. He asserts this in the concluding – and for him conclusive – arguments of the letter in chapter 13 which again centre around the matter of proof. In this context it becomes clear that Paul introduces his visionary experience of heaven only in order to show that it is not such experiences on which he relies for evidence of his apostleship.

11. The visionary rapture to paradise

Since this is the setting in which Paul introduces his outstanding experience of heaven it is not surprising that he is prepared to reveal only the minimum of information. The two details which are pinned down with any definiteness at all are the chronology and the cosmology. The date is given as fourteen years before the writing of the letter (verse 2) and yet because of our imprecise knowledge of the Pauline chronology as a whole and of the dating of this letter, we are not much closer to ascertaining the exact occasion. If the letter was written sometime between A.D. 55 and 58, then the experience of the third heaven took place sometime between A.D. 41 and 44 which would place it in the obscure early years of Paul's ministry spent in the north-western part of the province Syria-Cilicia. It cannot be identified with any of the visions recorded in Acts and the apostle's purpose in giving a date is presumably simply to make clear that this was a dateable occurrence which actually happened (cf. the insistence that he is speaking the truth in 12: 6). That he could give a date indicates the outstanding nature of this particular vision, but that he could remain silent about it for so long is already an indicator of his assessment of such experiences as credentials for apostleship.

The parallelism of the narrative has given rise to discussion whether Paul might not be describing either two separate events or two separate stages within one experience.[98] But as we shall see there is no decisive evidence that Paul considered Paradise to be one stage further along than the third heaven on his heavenly journey, and since there is only one reference to a date at the beginning of the first part and the content of the experience is only mentioned at the conclusion of the second part, it is most likely that, because of his reluctance to reveal this highly personal and cherished incident, Paul begins and then in a halting manner and with a minimum of variation has to repeat himself before he can bring himself to conclude the account.

The first time Paul gives the heavenly location of his experience as the third heaven (verse 2), while the second time this is varied to Paradise (verse 4). But again even these details are not of great help in being able to identify precisely the apostle's cosmology and it cannot be said with any certainty what system of enumerating the heavens, if any, he adopted.

Some writers hold that Paul's mention of the third heaven has reference to a threefold division of heaven in the OT.[99] Note is made of heaven in terms of a lower atmospheric heaven, then a higher stellar heaven or firmament and finally beyond these two what is described by the phrase 'the heaven of heavens' (cf. Neh. 9: 6, 1 Kgs 8: 27; 2 Chron. 2: 6; 6: 18; Ps. 68: 33; 148: 4). Paul's 'third heaven', it is said, corresponds to the last in this threefold division. It is possible that those passages in Jewish apocalyptic literature which speak of three heavens are based on this OT background but also likely that they, along with references to five, seven or ten heavens, have been influenced by Babylonian ideas about a plurality of heavens.[100] Although the Rabbis had an exegesis of 'the heaven and the heaven of heavens' in 1 Kings 8: 27 which made this a reference to three heavens (cf. Midr. Ps. 114: 2), there is no direct evidence that the 'third heaven' was a common designation for this OT 'heaven of heavens', and it is unlikely that Paul had this in view with his specific reference here.

Others hold with Calvin that the term has no technical cosmological significance but rather a symbolic one, so that 'the number three is used as a perfect number to indicate what is highest and most complete'.[101] There is much to be said for the view that the third heaven must have been the highest for Paul, for had he been thinking of another four heavens above his third heaven, this would have detracted somewhat from the force of his account.[102]

Those who seek the background of the term in the Jewish cosmological views of Paul's time are however on safer ground with regard to method. But even here the assertion that Paul must have believed in seven heavens[103] cannot be established, since contemporary apocalyptic traditions could make the third, fourth, seventh or tenth heaven the final destination of a heavenly journey and could place Paradise sometimes in the third, sometimes near the fourth, sometimes in the highest and sometimes simply in some undetermined region in the beyond. Undoubtedly the number seven was coming to the fore in connection with the heavens. In the Qumran literature, although there is no reference to seven heavens, there is evidence of the number seven becoming increasingly associated with the heavenly realm.[104] At the same time other systems were in circulation. Some writings which contain speculation about cosmology mention only one heaven (e.g. parts of 1 Enoch, 4 Ezra and 2 Baruch). Other parts of 1 Enoch (cf. 1: 4; 71: 1, 5) speak of the 'heaven of heavens'. The idea of two heavens is found in Midr. Ps. 114: 2, B. Chag. 12*b* and Deut. R. 2. The original version of Test. Levi 2, 3 mentions three heavens. 3 Baruch has five, while a later version of Test. Levi refers to seven, as do 2 Enoch, Apoc. Abr., Asc. Isa. and a number of passages in Rabbinic writings (e.g. B. Chag. 11*b*-16*a* where the seven heavens are named; Pesikt. R. 5; Midr. Ps. 92: 2; Aboth R. Nathan 37; Pirke R. Eliezer 154*b*). One version of

2 Enoch has further heavens to bring the number up to ten (cf. 2 Enoch
20: 3*b*; 22ff) and this number is also found in Bemidbar R. 14 on Numbers
7: 78. In 3 Enoch 48: 1 (A) there are nine hundred and fifty five heavens
above the seventh heaven![105] With the possible exception of this mention
of the third heaven by Paul, the NT in contrast is remarkably free from
such speculation about the number of heavens.

Besides 2 Corinthians 12 there are one or two other references where
Paradise is located in the third heaven. 'And the two men placed me
thence and carried me up on to the third heaven, and set me down in the
midst of Paradise' – 2 Enoch 8: 1 (B). In 2 Enoch 31: 1, 2 (A), however,
Paradise is in the East on earth but opened to the third heaven. In the
Apocalypse of Moses 37: 5 the Father of all hands Adam over to the
archangel Michael, saying, 'Lift him up into Paradise unto the third heaven,
and leave him there until that fearful day of my reckoning, which I will
make in the world.' (Cf. also 40: 2; 3 Bar. 4: 8.) Since both Paul and 2
Enoch place Paradise in the third heaven and since 2 Enoch contains
reference to seven heavens, it is held that Paul also must have adhered to
this number. But that this is a by no means necessary deduction is indicated by the fact that the other two parallel references are not dependent
on a system of seven heavens.[106] Undoubtedly Paul shared the cosmological views of his time but there are certain factors which indicate it may
be wrong to try to pin him down to a particular number of heavens. The
great variation in contemporary views, the fact that this is the only place
where he mentions a number and that elsewhere he is quite unconcerned
about numbers or system, and the parallels we have noted in which Paradise as the place of the departed righteous is specifically identified with
the third heaven could well indicate that here in 2 Corinthians 12: 2 Paul
has simply taken over the term 'third heaven' in a formal manner as a
variant designation for Paradise. In this case it would be beside the point
to attempt to ascertain on the basis of this verse how many heavens Paul
actually thought there were.

If Paradise is probably the more significant reference with regard to the
location of Paul's experience, what is its force? Originally it was a Persian
word, denoting an enclosure and thence a nobleman's park, which was
borrowed by both the Hebrew and Greek languages. In the Hebrew OT
פרדס is used, for example in Eccles. 2: 5, to mean a park. In the LXX
παράδεισος is used of the earthly Eden (cf. Gen. 2: 8ff) and translates
גו עדן . But nowhere in the OT does it refer to a future resting place
of the righteous. This was a development which was to take place in apocalyptic literature and one which was natural in the realm of thought which
held that the last days would be like the first (cf. Isa. 51: 3; Ezek. 36: 35

with reference to Eden). In this literature the term came to be used of the abode of the blessed whether after death or after the final judgment. References where paradise appears to be the realm entered upon death include Apoc. Mos. 37: 5; Test. Abr. 20 (A); 10 (B); 1 Enoch 60: 7f, 23; 61: 12; 70: 4; 2 Enoch 9: 1; 42: 3 (A); Apoc. Abr. 21: 6f. That this realm was entered by Enoch and Elijah in bodily form is mentioned in Jub. 4: 23; 1 Enoch 60: 8; 70: 3; 87: 3f; 89: 52; Test. Abr. 11: 3. In the NT Luke 23: 43, containing Jesus' promise to the criminal on the cross, 'Today you will be with me in Paradise', has reference to this present location of the departed righteous. Although there is not always a clear-cut distinction, other passages refer more to the final consummation of blessedness and are often connected with the resurrection. Among these are Test. Levi 18: 10f – 'He himself (the priestly Messiah) will open the gates of Paradise, take away the sword which threatened Adam, and give the saints to eat of the tree of life; then will the spirit of holiness rest upon them'; Test. Dan 5: 12; 1 Enoch 25: 4f; 2 Enoch 65: 9 (A); 4 Ezra 7: 36, 123; 8: 52; Apoc. Mos. 13. In the NT Revelation 2: 7 provides a similar reference to this paradise of the end-time.[107]

In some places, as we have seen, Paradise is located in the third heaven, but this is not always the case and it can be found in other heavens, including the seventh (cf. Asc. Isa. 9: 7; B. Chag. 12*b*). Most frequently it is heavenly in character but it can also be earthly (cf. 4 Ezra 6: 2f where it came into being on the day of creation, or Jub. 2: 4; 2 Enoch 30: 1 where it was created on the third day, or Vita Adae et Evae 48: 6 where it is located on earth) or even combine elements of both (e.g. 2 Enoch 8: 1–8 (A) where Paradise is in the third heaven but the root of the tree of life is in the garden at the earth's end).[108] This combination of the earthly and heavenly could have been suggested by the original story of Paradise in Genesis where God walked in the garden and where even after the fall the cherubim guarded the way to the tree of life, so that while paradise was on earth it also belonged to the invisible world of God. Earthly and heavenly elements were also mixed on account of the pattern of thought which conceived of what originally existed on earth being restored in the future but in the meanwhile existing in heaven.

Paradise seems to be an integral part of Paul's perspective which he does not have to explain. Its significance here in 2 Corinthians 12: 4, since it obviously refers to a presently existing state, is similar to that in Luke 23: 43, and indicates 'the place of the righteous departed'.[109] Paul is granted in this life an experience of this aspect of heaven which thus anticipates both 'the intermediate state' and the glory of the final consummation. In apocalyptic literature similar raptures are often associated with the place of the deceased righteous (e.g. 1 Enoch 39: 3–14; 60: 23; 70: 3; 2 Enoch 8, 9). Bietenhard's conclusion, 'Paulus hat somit eine Offenbarung über das Jenseits, nicht eine solche über die Zukunft, empfangen',[110] while basically correct, drives too sharp a wedge between the beyond and the future, since it is the paradise of the end-time which is conceived of as already existing in heaven now. And while Paul did not receive any revelation about the future which he could communicate to others, it could well be that his anticipatory experience of Paradise is reflected in his perspective on the state of the believer after death.

To Paradise Paul was caught up (ἀρπαγέντα – verse 2; ἡρπάγη – verse 4). This sort of language denotes the rapture of visions and the same verb is found in this sense in apocalyptic accounts (cf. for example, Apoc. Mos. 37: 3). It would seem to indicate that Paul's experience was an involuntary one where God took the initiative rather than one brought about by preparation or special techniques (cf. other uses of ἀρπάζω in the sense of 'to catch up' where God or his Spirit are clearly those who perform the act – Wisd. 4: 11; Acts 8: 39; 1 Thess. 4: 17; Rev. 12: 5). It would not have been impossible for ἀρπάζω to have been used even if mention had been made of preliminary preparations but when taken together with the subjective genitive κυρίου of 12: 1 it provides a fairly strong indication of an involuntary experience.

Paul's repetition of his ignorance and God's knowledge of whether his transcendental experience occurred in or out of the body could be meant simply to stress the fact that the experience was so powerful that it kept him from determining his own state at the time. It could however be a carefully designed statement in the light of the views of his opponents and the views he knew to be popular in the Corinthian church.[111] Since the opponents placed great weight on external and visible claims to the Spirit and charged Paul with bodily weakness as evidence that the Spirit was not working visibly in his body, it would have been consistent if some had felt it necessary to boast that in their visionary experiences their bodies had come into contact with the fullness of divine power to such an extent that in line with other great figures in Jewish tradition they had been lifted bodily into heaven. To some of the Corinthians, however, the body was unimportant so that the significance of such ecstatic visionary experiences was that they provided moments of release from the body.[112] 'The explanation of Paul's intention may thus be that he did not wish to prejudice his account with either side by taking a stand on this issue.'[113] Whereas for others the validity of their claim was affected by whether their experience was in or out of the body, Paul again is content to rest his claim with God alone.

That he comes down on neither side also indicates that for Paul either mode of rapture was a possibility. Precedents could be found for an experience 'in the body' within the OT in the persons of Enoch and Elijah, though they did not return afterwards, and within Jewish tradition in the case of Enoch again, of Ezra (cf. 4 Ezra 14: 49) and of Baruch (cf. 3 Baruch). The exaltation of Christ himself could be considered a precedent and Paul also conceives of those who are alive at the parousia being involved in a type of bodily rapture (cf. 1 Thess. 4: 15–17). That he could conceive also of an experience of Paradise 'out of the body' would underline our conclusions about both 2 Corinthians 5 and Philippians 1: 23 where the apostle envisages an intermediate disembodied state in heaven.[114]

What Paul heard in heaven he describes in the paradoxical phrase ἄρρητα ῥήματα. ἄρρητος can mean both that which cannot be expressed in words and that which for some reason, for example, its sacredness, is not to be mentioned. The clause which follows - ἃ οὐκ ἐξὸν ἀνθρώπῳ λαλῆσαι - indicates that the latter is the case here and that what Paul heard was not to be communicated to others.[115] The idea of a sealed revelation was known from the OT (e.g. Isa. 8: 16; Dan. 12: 4) and that of a secret revelation was even more widespread and could be found not only in apocalyptic literature[116] but also in Rabbinic Judaism where the scribes were viewed as the guardians of secret knowledge such as the esoteric traditions about the Merkabah of Ezekiel or the marvels of creation,[117] and also in the mystery religions. In fact Paul's terminology here parallels that to be found in the mystery religions. Euripides, *Bacch.* 472, speaks of mysteries which are secret except to initiates - ἄρρητ' ἀβακχεύτοισιν εἰδέναι βροτῶν. Aristophanes, *Nub.* 302, refers to the mysteries in terms of ἀρρήτων ἱερῶν and Herodotus VI, 135 mentions the under-priestess who had revealed to Miltiades the rites that no male should know - τὰ ἐς ἔρσενα γόνον ἄρσενα ἱρὰ ἐκφήνασαν Μιλτίαδῃ (cf. also Lucian, *Menipp.* 2; Apuleius, *Metam.* xi. 23).[118] This terminology had been appropriated already by Philo, who, for example, in *De Somn.* I, 191, talks of the sacred word imparting many secret truths which are not allowed to reach the ears of the uninitiated - πολλὰ καὶ τῶν ἀρρήτων ἀναφέρει, ὧν οὐδένα τῶν ἀτελέστων ἐπακοῦσαι θέμις (cf. also *Quod. Det. Pot.* 175; *Leg. Alleg.* II, 57; III, 27). Whereas in the mysteries the secret revelation could usually be passed on to initiates, what Paul heard is to be communicated to no one. Herein lies the ironic twist he gives to his account, for in order to boast about revelations he selects from his many experiences a visionary experience which involved that which could not be revealed to any one else.

We have already mentioned possible backgrounds for the way in which Paul relates aspects of his experience and the same backgrounds provide parallels for the experience itself, though the concept of an ascent into heaven is even more widespread.[119] Accounts of ascents to heaven by living men can be found in Greek literature (cf. especially the story of Er and Proclus' commentary in Plato, *Republic* X, 614ff), and in Hellenistic Jewish writings where Philo talks of the soul or mind being 'borne yet higher to the ether and the circuit of heaven' (*De Op. Mundi* 23) and of himself being 'borne aloft into the heights with a soul possessed by some God-sent inspiration, a fellow-traveller with the sun and moon and the whole heaven and universe' (*De Spec. Leg.* iii. 1). In apocalyptic literature 1 Enoch 71: 1, 5 speaks of an ascent in the spirit,

> And it came to pass after this that my spirit was translated
> And it ascended into the heavens:
> And I saw the holy sons of God.
> And he translated my spirit into the heaven of heavens,
> And I saw there as it were a structure built of crystals,
> And between those crystals tongues of living fire.

An ascent in the body is in view in 1 Enoch 39: 3. 'And in those days a whirlwind carried me off from the earth, and set me down at the end of the heavens' (cf. also 14: 8; 4 Ezra 14: 9; Test. Abr. 7B, 8B; Apoc. Abr. 12; 15; 16; 30; 2 Enoch 3: 1; 36: 1f). One example of an ascent out of the body in Rabbinic Judaism is in Gen. R. 68: 12 on Gen. 28: 12 where Jacob's true appearance is in heaven while his body lies on the earth, and the angels are travelling back and forth between them – 'they ascended on high and saw his features and they descended below and found him sleeping' (cf. also B. Baba Bathra 10b). The account of the four rabbis who entered Paradise in B. Chag. 14b is instructive for an ascent in the body – 'Our Rabbis taught: Four men entered the "Garden", namely Ben 'Azzai and Ben Zoma, Acher and R. Akiba.' Some scholars have suggested that this last account and the tradition of Merkabah mysticism which it represents may indeed provide the closest parallel to Paul's experience.[120] In Johanan b. Zakkai's dream the visionaries and their disciples are allocated to the third category in heaven, 'a Bath Kol was sent to us, saying: Ascend hither, ascend hither! Here are great banqueting chambers, and fine dining couches prepared for you; you and your disciples and your disciples' disciples are designated for the third class.'[121] Also 'the familiar idea that the ecstatic sees in his lifetime what other people see only after death recurs ... in Paul's as well as the rabbis' journey to heaven'.[122] In the account about the four rabbis only R. Akiba returned from Paradise unscathed; of the others, one died, one became demented and one apostatized. Paul too returns unscathed from his actual experience, although it could be argued that since the thorn in the flesh is seen by him as a check against becoming too elated by revelations, he does not in fact escape entirely unscathed.[123] The accounts differ of course in that while the rabbis' journey seems to have been undertaken on their own initiative and was in the body, Paul's was an involuntary experience and one in which he did not know whether he was in the body or not.

It is to be expected that Paul's account will have much in common with claims to similar experiences in the world of the first century.[124] At the same time there are a number of factors which make the apostle's experience distinctively Christian. He stresses that the whole experience is to be attributed to God or Christ (cf. the subjective genitive κυρίου in verse 1; ἡρπάγη in verse 4) and he can repeat that God alone knows how it was done (verses 2, 3) because he believes it was God who did it. In distinction from the mysteries, for Paul this experience of heaven had no soteriological function as a rebirth elevating him to a higher level of existence. There is no hint that he looked at it as the point of arrival in his search for salvation or as that which produced a oneness with the divine and a share in God's immortal being. Rather it came to him as someone who was already a 'man in Christ', and that he was granted such an extraordinary personal assurance of the reality of the heavenly dimension through vision and revelation was purely of grace. In addition the third heaven or Paradise was not for Paul some undefined ethereal sphere or a location that invited detailed cosmological speculation[125] but, as we have seen in the previous chapter, for him heaven had been opened up by Christ and received its character from his work. By his use of the Adam–Christ typology Paul has also indicated that Christ, the heavenly Man, brings back Paradise.[126] The Paradise that will be manifested in the future and can be experienced at death is through the work of Christ already present in the invisible world and can be experienced in vision and revelation now. Paul also knows Christ himself to be in heaven. Thus, since Paradise receives its character from Christ, Paul's anticipation of it should be assumed to be also an anticipation of greater intimacy with his heavenly Lord.[127] In this way also the experience of 2 Corinthians 12: 1ff can be seen as a form of realized eschatology.

12. Heavenly power in earthly weakness

The context well illustrates Paul's view of the role of such experiences of heavenly life in present Christian existence. He places the account of his journey to the third heaven between the accounts of being let down over the wall of Damascus in a basket and of his 'thorn in the flesh'. 'The man who experienced the ineffable "ascent" even to the third heaven was the same man who had experienced the undistinguished "descent" from a window in the Damascus wall.'[128] In this way Paul's remarkable vision of Paradise is set in the midst of humiliations. And it is the link between the apostle's experience of heaven and his experience of humiliation which the account of his thorn in the flesh is designed to emphasize. Verse 7 indicates that the thorn in the flesh, whether it was some physical affliction or the intense opposition of adversaries or whatever it was, was given as a counterbalance to the revelations of heaven – καὶ τῇ ὑπερβολῇ τῶν ἀποκαλύψεων δίο, ἵνα μὴ ὑπεραίρωμαι.[129] The apostle repeats the reason for it being given – 'to keep me from exalting myself'. He admits that it would have been easy to have allowed the experience to go to his head and to have become puffed up. Instead he had to be kept humble, made aware of his weakness and reminded that Christian existence depends on grace. 'My grace is sufficient for you' (verse 9).

Paul's account of his revelation contained no revelation but now in his miracle story without a miracle a revelation is given and the word from the risen Lord is that his power is perfected in weakness. δύναμις ἐν ἀσθενείᾳ (verse 9) sums up Paul's view of Christian existence in 2 Corinthians and he could glory in its paradox – 'Most gladly, therefore, I will rather boast about my weaknesses that the power of Christ may rest upon me' (verse 9 cf. verse 5). Viewed from this perspective weakness was not something of which Paul had to be ashamed in the face of his opponents' claim to glory. It was the surest proof of his being a representative of the crucified Christ who is the Lord. 'He was crucified because of weakness, yet he lives because of the power of God' (13: 4). Because Christ has participated both in this age and the age to come he can be viewed as both weak and strong. As the exalted heavenly Christ he is now strong but while his followers remain part of this age their lives will display the paradox of heavenly life and power being demonstrated in the midst of earthly weakness.[130]

13. The heavenly vision as a manifestation of the Spirit

Paul's experience of the third heaven is classed by him under the category of ὀπτασίαι καὶ ἀποκαλύψεις κυρίου. In 1 Cor. 14: 6, 26 he sees revelations as part of the work of the Spirit in the church. The visions and revelations from the Lord will have been seen no differently. There is therefore no necessity for treating this visionary experience of Paradise as an event which was unique to Paul and happened only this once in the life of the church but it can be seen as part of the charismatic manifestation of the Spirit in the Christian community.[131] This would be a perspective held in common with Acts where Peter's speech in 2: 17–21, as it takes up the prophecy of Joel, treats visions as part of the Spirit's programme for the last days in which the church saw itself living. As a result of the outpouring of the Spirit young men shall see visions and old men shall dream dreams. The apostles may have experienced this manifestation of the Spirit in a more intensive and continuous way than the rest of the church and Paul's experience would have been an outstanding one, but the apostles were certainly not the sole claimants to such experiences as the polemic of this letter indicates. In this revelatory function of the Spirit a variety of means could be employed including visions, raptures – whether in or out of the body, and prophecies, but all were the work of the same Spirit and came from the same Lord. Indeed, his visions, as part of his charismatic experience, would have been one of the factors which helped Paul to the realization not only that such manifestations of the Spirit came from his heavenly Lord but also that the Lord is the Spirit (cf. 1 Corinthians 15: 45). In linking Paul's vision of heaven to the manifestation of the Spirit we see again that the Spirit is active in providing anticipation of the life of heaven.

Yet having said all this, we must still underline the point made earlier that Paul will not use such an experience as evidence for his apostleship, and, since for him the question of apostleship is integrally related to that of the nature of Christian existence, neither will he use it as evidence for his belonging to Christ (cf. 10: 7). This would be to remove Christian existence from the realm of human weakness, from that which others may 'see in him or hear from him' (12: 6). It would be to succumb to the tendencies of his opponents to see heavenly life as completely transforming the structure of human existence whereas for Paul heavenly life was to take shape within those structures and even special anticipations of its fullness were not to be allowed to obscure this perspective. Apostleship is not at one remove from the life of this age on some higher level of existence. Paul freely acknowledges his limitations and weakness (cf. 10: 1; 11: 6, 21, 30; 12: 5, 9, 10, 11) because he knows that in his apostleship participation in the life of the heavenly Man at present also involves bearing his cross.

4

PHILIPPIANS AND THE HEAVENLY COMMONWEALTH

This consideration of Paul's treatment of the heavenly dimension in Philippians centres around Philippians 3: 20, 21 in which the believer's commonwealth or state (τὸ πολίτευμα) is said to be in heaven.

1. The literary setting and genre of 3: 20, 21

A traditional question has been whether chapter 3 can be considered part of the original letter, while more recent discussion has asked whether verses 20, 21 in particular can be considered Pauline, or whether they are not rather a pre-Pauline hymn which has been incorporated, just as 2: 6–11 is commonly held to have been brought into the earlier part of the letter.

A number of scholars have held that two, three or even four fragments of Paul's correspondence with the Philippians were brought together at a later date when his correspondence was collected and were amalgamated into the one letter we now know as Philippians. In most versions of this hypothesis Philippians 3: 2 – 4: 1 forms one fragment or at least a part of one fragment, for some add 4: 8, 9 as part of the same fragment. Yet the great variety in such reconstructions of the fragments and of the places where they are to be joined, the existence of quite satisfactory explanations of the structure of the letter as we now have it and the repetition of certain themes throughout it cast doubt on the necessity for a fragment hypothesis.[1]

The discussion about the literary form of 3: 20, 21 turns on whether Paul is using confessional material in a passage where he expresses himself in a more elevated language and style or whether he has actually taken over a pre-Pauline hymn. E. Lohmeyer spoke of 'die hymnisch beschwingten Worte und Gedanken' and of 'diesem kleinen sechszeiligen Hymnus'.[2] He has been followed in this evaluation by G. Strecker,[3] E. Güttgemanns[4] and J. Becker.[5] Parallelism is adduced. This can be found in verse 21 but it is not at all clear in verse 20. The criterion of relative pronouns, which often stand at the beginning of hymns (cf. Philippians 2: 6 and 1 Timothy 3: 16), would again fit verse 21 but the ἐξ οὗ of verse 20 can scarcely be claimed as belonging to 'dem hymnischen Relativstil'.⁶ Becker's extended discussion of peculiarities in the terminology of these verses is inconclusive. πολίτευμα, for example, is a *hapax legomenon* in Paul but this does not prove it must be from a hymn. It could equally well have been taken over from opponents and in any case seems to have ties with the use of πολιτεύεσθαι in 1: 27. Again, the singular and plural of οὐρανός are used interchangeably in the Pauline corpus (e.g. 2 Corinthians 5: 1, 2), and it seems tenuous to hang much on the use of the plural here.⁷ The title σωτήρ, on the other hand, may well be drawn from traditional material and the full designation κύριος Ἰησοῦς Χριστός, found also in the hymn in 2: 11 and in Paul's opening salutations and farewell greetings, most probably does come originally from the language of worship.⁸

A central consideration is the terminological correspondence between 2: 6-11 and 3: 20, 21:

μορφῇ (2: 6) μορφήν (2: 7)	σύμμορφον (3: 21)
ὑπάρχων (2: 6)	ὑπάρχει (3: 20)
σχήματι (2: 7)	μετασχηματίσει (3: 21)
ἐταπείνωσεν (2: 8)	ταπεινώσεως (3: 21)
ἐπουρανίων (2: 10)	οὐρανοῖς (3: 20)
πᾶν γόνυ καμψῃ ... καὶ πᾶσα	τοῦ δύνασθαι αὐτὸν καὶ
γλῶσσα ἐξομολογήσεται (2: 10, 11)	ὑποτάξαι αὐτῷ τὰ πάντα (3: 21)
κύριος Ἰησοῦς Χριστός (2: 11)	κύριον Ἰησοῦν Χριστόν (3: 20)
δόξαν (2: 11)	δόξης (3: 21)

Some have argued that since the first set of terms and concepts is found in what is commonly assumed to be a hymn, then this provides a strong indication that the second and similar set is also located in a hymn. The striking similarities would thus mean that the two hymns come from the same stratum of tradition⁹ or from the same linguistic and conceptual milieu in Hellenistic Christianity.¹⁰ But an equally powerful argument can be developed in the other direction. Is it not unlikely that the apostle would quote two hymns which happen to have such striking similarities? Is it not more likely that material from the first hymn has been deliberately and skilfully adapted to produce a correspondence which would suit the apostle's purpose at this stage in his argument?¹¹

The first part of verse 20 appears to be too much a part of the apostle's response to his opponents to have formed an integral part of a hymn, even allowing for a different original word-order, such as τὸ πολίτευμα ἡμῶν ἐν οὐρανοῖς ὑπάρχει. The last part of verse 20 may well draw on traditional material of a confessional nature about the parousia (cf. 1 Thessalonians 1: 10). The parallelism of the first part of verse 21 may be seen as reflecting stylistically the apostle's deliberate structure of thought at this stage in his argument. Finally, the last part of verse 21 has a doxological tone which moves beyond what is strictly necessary for Paul's argument and its content is reminiscent of that of parts of Ephesians which have a distinctly liturgical style (cf. Ephesians 1: 19ff; 3: 20f). We conclude that, rather than incorporating a six-line hymn, Philippians 3: 20, 21 climaxes Paul's argument in this chapter in elevated style as the apostle draws on traditional and liturgical material and quite probably has the pattern of 2: 6–11 in mind.[12]

2. The nature of Paul's argument and of his 'earthly-minded' opposition in 3: 1–19

Who are Paul's opponents in Philippians 3? This is perhaps the most vexing issue which must be decided in placing verses 20, 21 in their context. Traditionally the problem has been whether Paul is combating two[13] or three[14] groups in this chapter or whether he is facing a united front throughout.[15] Since Paul's argument seems to be all of one piece with no clear breaks the advocates of the latter solution feel that it is more convincing in dealing with a polemical text to regard it 'as a unified front against only a single heresy',[16] while those who favour an interpretation involving a variety of groups hold that the other viewpoint ignores the distinctiveness of the different sections of the chapter.[17] Our own position will emerge as we outline the three stages of development in Paul's argument in 3: 1–19 in order to see clearly how 3: 20f with its important reference to the heavenly dimension fits into the polemic and why the apostle believes *his* statement about heaven expresses the true eschatological perspective. The first section (verses 2–11) refers to a threat to the Philippian community from Judaizing propagandists and Paul responds to this threat. The apostle then moves his attention to those within the Philippian community liable to succumb to some of this dangerous propaganda (cf. verses 12–16). These are people with a 'perfectionist' viewpoint, who believe they have already attained. But such people are now to take their example from the apostle and his group of co-workers. With this directive in verse 17 Paul moves outside the confines of the Philippian church and this broader reference continues into verse 18 as he speaks of 'the enemies of the cross of Christ'. He elaborates on these enemies in verse 19 in terms which probably take in opponents who have plagued him in a number of places during his ministry and of whom he had often spoken to the Philippians. Although of wider application the description is certainly meant to include those who at that time posed a threat in Philippi and whom the apostle had denounced so vigorously at the beginning of the chapter. This analysis allows for the unified flow of Paul's argument and the overlap of thought as he moves from those threatening the church to those liable to succumb within the church and then out again to the enemies of the cross, and at the same time it does justice to the indications of change of address and the distinctive nuances of the three sections.

(i) Verses 2-11 and knowing Christ

In the light of verse 18 τὰ αὐτά in verse 1b could well refer to warnings Paul has already issued to the congregation about opponents of the faith. The threefold imperative βλέπετε expresses a sharp and urgent warning, which seems to have in view a group of people who have arrived on the scene from outside. The threefold polemical characterization of the opponents which accompanies the warnings provides certain clues about their identity. The term κύνες takes its force from the fact that Jews commonly compared Gentiles to the dog as an unclean animal (cf. 1 Enoch 89: 42; Matt. 7: 6; Mark 7: 27),[18] so that here the apostle is not describing the activity of those who 'dog' his footsteps or who are impertinent intruders[19] but is simply turning his Judaizing opponents' description of uncircumcized Gentiles against themselves. He also calls them τοὺς κακοὺς ἐργάτας. This is not a comment on their insistence on works[20] but rather takes up a term which became almost technical for itinerant missionaries (cf. Matt. 9: 37f; 10: 10; 2 Cor. 11: 13; 1 Tim. 5: 18; Did. 13: 2)[21] and was probably used by the propagandists as a self-designation.[22] For all their missionary activity Paul believes such men to be malicious, ultimately producing harmful and evil effects. The parallel to 2 Cor. 11: 13, where Paul had also called his opponents ἐργάται δόλιοι, is striking. The third epithet in Philippians 3: 2 - κατατομή - provides further evidence of the vigour and skill of the apostle's polemic. In the light of the reference to περιτομή in the next verse, this is undoubtedly a play on words designed to wound the pride of his opponents as they boasted of their circumcision.[23] According to Paul, the circumcision so highly valued by them is in reality a mutilation; κατατέμνω is used in the LXX of forbidden cultic incisions (cf. Lev. 21: 5; 1 Kgs. 18: 28; Hos. 7: 14). In denying true circumcision to the propagandists, the apostle claims this title for himself and the churches he has founded - ἡμεῖς γὰρ ἐσμεν ἡ περιτομή.

The claims Paul makes for the true Christian community in verse 3 are all set over against the assertions of his opponents. With the second claim - οἱ πνεύματι θεοῦ λατρεύοντες - this is implicit. 'We who serve in the Spirit of God' almost certainly indicates that the opponents had made just such a claim to special possession of the Spirit in their activities[24] and there are further indications of this later in the chapter where 'perfection' and revelations are mentioned in connection with those in the church attracted by the propagandists' views (cf. verses 12-16). This would again provide a pointer to similarity with the opponents in 2 Corinthians who saw their mission as a visible demonstration of the Spirit's powers. Paul will not allow his opponents such a claim here in Philippians and insists that it is he and his churches who are serving in the Spirit of God. They boast in Christ Jesus and, unlike the propagandists, put no confidence in the flesh, although the apostle makes clear that if anyone had grounds for such false confidence it is he. Again the argument is reminiscent of 2 Corinthians, for there also Paul indicts those who boast according to the flesh (11: 18) and lays down the principle which he follows here in Philippians 3: 3 - ὁ δὲ καυχώμενος ἐν κυρίῳ καυχάσθω (10:17). As in 2 Corinthians 11: 1-12: 13 where he launches into matters of which he could boast only to dismiss the whole exercise as foolishness, so in Philippians 3: 4-8 on a lesser scale he lists points of which he could boast only to dismiss them as loss or even refuse. But whereas in 2 Corinthians elements in Paul's experience as a Christian were involved, here he deals with matters of which he was proud before his encounter with Christ. By this means he indicates that the points the propagandists emphasize in their missionary activity really have no status at all for believers.[25] However, the change of tense from ἥγημαι (verse 7) to ἡγοῦμαι (verse 8) signifies that there is also a present aspect to the apostle's determination to rely on nothing apart from Christ.

The points Paul lists reflect the qualities his opponents must have valued so highly. They include circumcision, the claim to belong to Israel, to be a Hebrew, and zeal, especially for righteousness based on the law. Paul leaves the Philippians in no doubt that he could outclass anyone on each of these counts and yet that to do so would be to put confidence in the flesh and falsify any claim to serve in the Spirit. As in 2 Corinthians 11: 22 the opponents here appear to have laid claim to the titles Ἰσραήλ and Ἑβραῖος (verse 5) as indications that they were the true people of God and to have thought of themselves as those with a true concern for righteousness which comes through law (verses 5, 6 cf. 2 Cor. 11: 15 - διάκονοι δικαιοσύνης). But for Paul 'knowing Christ' (verse 8) and 'being found in him' (verse 9) bring a whole new perspective on righteousness. It can no longer be based on law, but is righteousness from God that depends on faith in Christ (verse 9). What is clear, despite the brevity of the discussion, is that the opponents who boasted of their Jewish qualities also professed Christ in some way, otherwise this argument would have been by no means convincing.[26]

> The question is not whether 'to be in Christ' or to fulfil the law is the higher value, that is, whether the Christians or Jews are correct. Rather the controversial issue is whether 'to be in Christ' and to fulfil the law are intrinsically bound up with each other, or on the contrary, are mutually exclusive.[27]

Paul's answer is clear – there is now only one way to a right relationship with God; it is no longer through obedience to the law but through knowing Christ.

Although the expression γνῶναι αὐτόν in verse 10 is coloured by LXX usage in connection with the relationship of Jahweh and his people, involving a strong emphasis on the aspect of obedience, the use here goes beyond this to include a transforming power which effects a becoming like the one who is known. This has affinities with the concept of 'knowing' in Hellenistic mystery religions where seeing a deity results in transformation and a participation in the deity[28] and with aspects of the principle in Hellenistic thought about the knowledge of God that 'like is known by like'.[29] That Paul twice uses the terminology of 'knowing' to describe the believer's relationship with Christ (verses 8, 10) and that he is careful to define what he means by this (verse 10) suggest that he may well be responding to a use by opponents which comes originally from such a Hellenistic milieu, and that, as in 2 Corinthians, the Judaizers, as they boast of a knowledge which avoids the real significance of the death and resurrection of Christ, have adapted their views to suit those they are attempting to influence.

As Paul talks about knowing Christ, both present and future aspects of the resurrection hope are featured, for knowing the power of Christ's resurrection is experienced by the apostle during his lifetime and yet he makes clear in verse 11 that there will always remain the final manifestation of this to be experienced. No doubt the opponents would also have claimed to know Christ and his power, and yet they meant by this that they were living right now in full eschatological and pneumatic power and glory. With his two modifiers Paul guards against any such interpretation of his words. Firstly, knowing Christ means knowing the fellowship of his sufferings, becoming like him in his death. Secondly, full conformity to Christ still awaits the final resurrection from the dead. ἡ ἐξανάστασις ἡ ἐκ νεκρῶν (verse 11), as compared with the more straightforward ἡ ἀνάστασις of verse 10, is an expression used only here by Paul, and emphasizes in the strongest way that he has the final bodily resurrection in view. The force of εἴ πως καταντήσω at the beginning of the verse is similar. It has nothing to do with his uncertainty or humility in view of impending death[30] but underlines the very different view of the resurrection that he has in comparison to the opponents, his lack of any presumption to have experienced full salvation already. These verses (verses 10, 11) take us to the heart of the discussion concerning the relation of suffering and glory, of earthly and heavenly modes of existence for the believer, a discussion which surfaces again in verse 21.

(ii) Verses 12-16 and the prize of the heavenly calling

In verses 12-16 it becomes apparent that in his eschatological assertions Paul has in view some in the church at Philippi who are 'otherwise minded' and of whom he can ironically say ὅσοι οὖν τέλειοι (verse 15). Because their own views lean heavily in a 'perfectionist' direction, they are likely to be taken in by any propaganda which announces that the fullness of resurrection existence and heavenly glory can be experienced now. Over against such ideas Paul's viewpoint is characterized by the double 'not already' at the beginning of verse 12 - οὐχ ὅτι ἤδη ἔλαβον ἢ ἤδη τετελείωμαι. This use of the verb τελειόω with the ironic reference to τέλειοι in verse 15 indicates that this was probably a favourite term of the opponents, designating 'the possession of the qualities of salvation in their entirety, the arrival of heaven itself'.[31]

The apostle then sets up a model for Christian existence which excludes the possibility of having already arrived. διώκω, ἐπεκτείνομαι, σκοπός, βραβεῖον all indicate a race which is in progress and in which there can be no dwelling on what has already been achieved (τὰ ὀπίσω) because the prize is yet to be obtained. Significantly for our study the prize is described as ἡ ἄνω κλῆσις τοῦ θεοῦ Χριστῷ Ἰησοῦ and ἄνω is the term Paul uses for the heavenly dimension in Galatians 4: 26 and Col. 3: 1f. Elsewhere in the Pauline corpus (cf. Rom. 11: 29; 1 Cor. 1: 26; 7: 20; 2 Thess. 1: 11; Eph. 1: 18; 4: 1, 4; 2 Tim. 1: 9) ἡ κλῆσις refers to the divine initiative in bringing a person to faith. Here however it cannot mean such a call which has issued from heaven, for the prize lies at the end of the race, not the beginning. There is however a parallel to the language of this verse in Philo, *De Plant.* 23. For Philo men are heavenly and not earthly plants, and in particular those who have been given the desire for special wisdom and knowledge, who have received the divine spirit, are called up to God - πρὸς γὰρ τὸ θεῖον ἄνω καλεῖσθαι. In particular Moses was identified as one called up above (ἀνεκάλεσε Μωυσῆν - *De Plant* 26). It is not unlikely that Paul's Jewish Christian opponents or the group likely to succumb to their teaching in the Philippian church were using this sort of language in their claims to an exalted status. By following in the tradition of Moses and through visionary experience they too claimed to have received the upward call already in this life (cf. the concern of the opponents in 2 Corinthians with Moses and his glory). In this case we would have an eminently plausible explanation for Paul's unusual use of κλῆσις. Such an upward call to heavenly existence is not attained in this life, he is saying, but is the goal for which we aim, the prize which lies ahead at the end of the race. For Paul this could include both the thought of being with Christ (cf. 1: 23) whom he conceived of as in heaven, and the ultimate putting on of heavenly existence in the glorification of the body (cf. 3: 21). It was with the former aspect that an early Christian redactor of 3 Baruch[32] seems to have equated the upward call of Philippians 3: 14, for he describes it as the entry into paradise (cf. 3 Bar. 4: 15 - ἐν αὐτῷ μέλλουσιν τὴν ἄνω κλῆσιν προσλαβεῖν, καὶ τὴν εἰς παράδεισον εἴσοδον).

Paul insists that his view of the 'upward call' be normative, as he ironically places himself alongside those who consider themselves τέλειοι and suggests that they think about the matter in the same way as he. The irony continues throughout verse 15 as the apostle alludes to the revelations about which some are boasting (cf. similar boasts reflected in 2 Cor. 12: 1ff). Those who are not inclined to step into line with his directives because they are too attracted by spectacular claims are in need of another revelation on this matter! καὶ τοῦτο ὁ θεὸς ὑμῖν ἀποκαλύψει - this will be something else which God will have to reveal to them![33] The use of πλήν at the beginning of verse 16 indicates a temporary halt to the irony as the apostle sums up what he means to say. The foundational apostolic mission and tradition are not to be undermined. His readers must hold on to all that had been achieved so far in the building of the Philippian church.

One of the main reasons given by scholars for dividing this chapter into various discrete units is that it is impossible for the two emphases we have noted to have been propagated by the same opposition. Yet, as evidenced by the opposition in 2 Corinthians, a claim to spirituality already attained, to the heavenly call already received and a Judaizing insistence on righteousness through the law are by no means incompatible. The concepts of 'perfection' and 'righteousness' were probably closely associated in the terminology of the opponents and a basic factor in their attitude may have been 'the belief that a complete fulfilment of the law was possible - they had achieved it already and could boast about it! - and brought about the possession of the eschatological promises in full, that is, the Spirit and spiritual experiences of such heavenly gifts as resurrection and freedom from suffering and death'.[34] Such an attitude however does not provide enough evidence for the assertion that the opponents must be seen as typical of early Christian Gnosticism.[35] We hold instead that the opponents in view here are very similar to those with whom the apostle deals in 2

Corinthians, and that this is the explanation for his attack being in strikingly similar terms (cf. 2 Cor. 11: 13-15).[36] These opponents appear to have been Jewish Christian missionaries willing to accommodate themselves to 'Hellenistic' emphases and perfectionist interests. As we have seen from verse 14 and shall see from verse 20, some of their concepts about the heavenly world can be compared with those of Philo. Amongst other things they believed themselves to be servants of righteousness, the true possessors of the Spirit through the law, and held that apostolic existence should especially exhibit the transcendent power of Christ through miracle working, ecstatic visions and a rhetorical capacity for inspired proclamation.[37] Clearly, however, the propagandists in Philippi had not yet made such inroads into the church as those at Corinth, and the apostle still seems to be confident of the faithfulness of the majority of believers there.

(iii) Verses 17–19 and the earthly-minded enemies of the cross

The Philippians are to imitate Paul and also follow the lead of those who live according to the Pauline pattern – 'those who so live as you have an example in us'. ἡμᾶς here refers to Paul and his team of associates who accompanied him. Already by mentioning these fellow-workers the apostle has moved outside the Philippian situation and his attention remains for a while on this broader horizon as he thinks of many who, in their opposition to the Pauline pattern, are living as enemies of the cross of Christ (verse 18). During the apostle's visits to Philippi and perhaps in previous letters he had often spoken of these opponents who trespassed on his mission territory. He now has to speak of them again, since it is some of just such enemies who have arrived on the scene in Philippi and the thought of this situation moves the apostle to tears. What follows can be seen as general enough to take in the Judaizing opponents Paul has encountered elsewhere, especially in Corinth, but with shafts specifically aimed at those who are now troubling the Philippian church.

There are a variety of ways in which those who opposed Paul made themselves 'enemies of Christ's cross' (verse 18), but all of them involve theological viewpoints which somehow derogate from the significance of Christ's death. Here in Philippians the indictment of the propagandists is that they are unwilling to become like Christ in his death (cf. verse 10)[38] and it is significant in this regard that θανάτου δὲ σταυροῦ may well be a Pauline addition to the Christ-hymn of 2: 6–11.[39] Paul had had to stress similar points in 2 Corinthians (cf. 4: 7–11; 13: 4).

The apostle can assert that eschatological destruction awaits such opponents. He had also used τέλος in this way to describe their ultimate destiny in 2 Corinthians 11: 15. It is quite likely that its use here in 3: 19 involves a play on words[40] so that this denunciation particularly strikes home to the Philippian opponents who in their claim to have already achieved their τέλος are only earning themselves ultimate judgment. It is difficult to decide whether ἡ δόξα ἐν τῇ αἰσχύνῃ αὐτῶν is a corresponding statement about judgment or whether it is an allusion to the nakedness required for circumcision.[41] Either alternative is to be preferred to the view which sees a reference to immoral sexual practices.[42] 'Glory' may have had specific force for those claiming to possess heavenly qualities already and perhaps Paul is saying that they glory in these things – their circumcision and their spiritual experience – which will turn out to be their shame and their disgrace at the final judgment. αἰσχύνη is frequently used in the LXX for the experience of God's judgment (e.g. Ps. 34: 26; 70: 13; Mic. 7: 10; Isa. 30: 3, 5; 45: 16) and Paul has already used the cognate verb in a similar sense in this letter in 1: 20.

The other two statements describe the opponents' present attitude rather than their final destiny. ὧν ὁ θεὸς ἡ κοιλία – their god, that which they serve, is the belly. This need by no means refer to libertines who indulge in sensual delights and the pleasures of the table;[43] it could equally well have those who obey Jewish food laws in view. Basically, Paul's use of κοιλία here is the same as that in Romans 16: 18 where he gives a general description of false teachers, who, professing to serve Christ, were in fact serving their own belly. In both cases, whilst probably having food laws specifically in view,[44] the expression also provides an intensified way of saying that such people are serving the flesh, which need have nothing to do with sensual gratification.[45] Similarly οἱ τὰ ἐπίγεια φρονοῦντες indicates that they are bound to the sphere of the flesh (cf. Romans 8: 5). This is the first part of the contrast which the apostle completes in verse 20. ἐπίγειος can simply refer to what is temporal and transient (cf. 1 Cor. 15: 40; 2 Cor. 5: 1f) but here and in Colossians 3: 2, 5 it appears to have a definite negative ethical aspect as descriptive of the sphere of sin and therefore corresponding to Paul's negative use of σάρξ. In this way it can be generally used of Paul's opponents but again it has special force in the context of the polemic in this chapter. F. W. Beare is wrong in thinking that the phrase means that 'they have no thought of heavenly things'.[46] Precisely the opposite is the case with these Philippian opponents who apparently claimed to have already received the heavenly call and to be members of the heavenly realm.[47] They would have prided themselves on being heavenly-minded, but, as he is to do again in Colossians 3: 1ff, the apostle turns the tables on his opponents, shows he by no means approves of all heavenly-mindedness and calls their variety 'earthly'. This constitutes a full-orbed rejection of both their pride in their earthly Jewish privileges and their claims to heavenly experience. As far as Paul is concerned, both are tarred with the same brush, for that which determines their whole pattern of living is ultimately the earthly sphere of sin.[48]

3. The apostle's counter-claim to the heavenly commonwealth: the force of 'Politeuma' (3: 20)

Paul completes the contrast initiated in the last part of verse 19 as he begins verse 20 with the unusual and striking clause – ἡμῶν γὰρ τὸ πολίτευμα ἐν οὐρανοῖς ὑπάρχει. His polemical tactics here remind one immediately of verses 2, 3 where he had proceeded in almost exactly the same way. In the last part of verse 2 Paul had called the opponents the opposite of that which they claimed and had then used the very title of which they boasted for himself and Pauline Christians – ἡμεῖς γὰρ ἐσμεν ἡ περιτομή. The same emphatic word order is followed here in verse 20 – the first person plural pronoun, then γὰρ and then the claim. This parallel with the earlier part of the polemic provides a strong indication that here in verse 20 also the apostle is taking over a catchword of his opponents.[49] As in verse 14 there are parallels to such terminology in the writings of Philo. In *De Conf. Ling.* 78 all whom Moses calls wise are represented as sojourners, and although they may visit earthly nature for a while, the true home of their souls is in heaven, 'To them the heavenly region, where their citizenship lies, is their native land; the earthly region in which they become sojourners is a foreign country' – πατρίδα μὲν τὸν οὐράνιον χῶρον ἐν ᾧ πολιτεύονται. In other places in Philo the actual term πολίτευμα is used of the ideal heavenly world, to which those who possess heavenly wisdom and virtue belong (cf. *De Agr.* 81; *De Conf. Ling.* 109; *De Ios.* 69; *De Spec. Leg.* II, 45; *De Op. Mundi* 143f). This sort of terminology, though not borrowed directly from Philo, seems to have been taken up as part of the propaganda of the Jewish Christian teachers in Philippi. In their view their lives as τέλειοι indicated their heavenly citizenship, their possession of the heavenly call and their enjoyment of the full privileges of heavenly existence. Paul's counter-claim is that he and those who are faithful to the apostolic tradition are those whose commonwealth is in heaven.

πολίτευμα is a *hapax legomenon* in the NT and consequently there has been some discussion over its exact shade of meaning here. The suggested polemical setting makes its general significance clear, but since Paul has chosen to take over the word and to express himself in this particular way we should endeavour to discover as exactly as possible what significance this noun would have had for his readers. The greatest help for such an investigation is the work of W. Ruppel – 'Politeuma. Bedeutungsgeschichte

eines staatsrechtlichen Terminus', which provides a comprehensive study
of the usage of the term in classical literature, inscriptions and papyri.[50]
The two main considerations in surveying the variety of meanings and
nuances which became associated with the term will be to ascertain which
usage predominates and which is most appropriate to the context in
Philippians 3: 20.

As with many nouns ending -μα, πολίτευμα seems to have developed
from the verbal form - πολιτεύειν, πολιτεύεσθαι - signifying the result of
the verb or the force which comes to expression in the verb and thus
political activity or action, usually of individuals, cf. Aeschines, *Tim.* 86;
Demosthenes 18, 108-10; Plutarch, *M. Caton* 26, 1; *Pomp.* 21, 5; 47, 1;
Caes. 8, 4; 13, 2; 14, 9. This meaning remains basic to the term.[51]

πολίτευμα also came to mean the subject of political action and thus
administrative authorities, cf. Plato, *Leges* XII, 945d, and from there
Aristotle could use it for political government in general cf. *Politica* III,
6, 1278b; 7, 1279a, and for any who govern or have a share in it, cf. III,
13, 1283b; IV, 6, 1293a; 13, 1297b. Aristotle, in fact, defines the power
of the state as the constitution, cf. *Politica* III, 6, 1278b - 'A constitution
(πολιτεία) is the arrangement of magistracies in a state (πόλεως), especially
of the highest of all. The government (πολίτευμα) is everywhere sovereign
in the state (πόλεως), and the constitution is in fact the government
(πολίτευμα δ' ἔστιν ἡ πολιτεία)', and also 1279a - 'The words constitution
and government have the same meaning.' In IV, 13, 1297b Aristotle calls
states constitutional governments, and so clearly the constitution is seen
as the political power of the state (cf. also Polybius, III, 118, 9). For this
reason πολίτευμα can take on the meaning of constitution, e.g. Aeschines,
2, 172.

It is only a further short extension from the political power or government of the state to the state or commonwealth itself. Polybius (c. 200-
120 B.C.) provides many instances of the use of πολίτευμα during this
stage, when it is often difficult to decide whether the constitutional
government or the state itself is in view, cf. Polybius, III, 2, 6; 8, 2-3;
VI, 3, 11; 10, 6f; 12, 9; 14, 12; 43, 1; 46, 9; 50, 4; 51, 1, although in II,
47, 3; 70, 1; IV, 25, 7; 81, 14; 84, 5; V, 9, 9; VI, 3, 8; IX, 36, 4; X, 2, 9
the constitution is clearly in view. Similarly in Josephus the state constitution is in view in *c. Ap.* II, 16, 145, 257; *Ant.* II, 157, whereas in *c. Ap.*
II, 184; *Ant.* I, 5, 13 the meaning 'state' or 'commonwealth' is preferable,
and both meanings occur in the passage, *c. Ap.* II, 164f. Also in Plutarch
'state' or 'commonwealth' is meant in *Solon.* 9, 2; *Romulus* 20, 2;
Theseus 35, 4 and 'constitution' in *Them.* 4, 5; *Ages.* 20, 2.[52] In the sole
use of πολίτευμα in the LXX, 2 Macc. 12: 7, the reference is to the
commonwealth of the town of Joppa.

Another use of πολίτευμα which occurs in Aristotle is with reference to citizenship and its privileged political powers, cf. *Politica* V, 3, 1302b. The main instance of this meaning is on inscriptions, one of which reads ἕως ἂν ἑτέρους ἐπινοήσωμεν ἀξίους τοῦ παρ' ὑμῖν πολιτεύματος and the citizenship involves the right of activity for the state.[53]

A further meaning of πολίτευμα is that of a 'colony of foreigners', who took over the laws and religious cult of their homeland for the colony. The Jews in Alexandria, for example, were described as a πολίτευμα, cf. Josephus, Ant. XII, 2, 12, 108 and the Letter of Aristeas, 310.[54]

A number of these attested meanings have been claimed for the use of πολίτευμα in Philippians 3: 20. Some scholars opt for 'citizenship'.[55] This meaning however is one of the least well attested, especially for the NT period.[56] Others prefer the meaning 'colony'.[57] As a translation – 'We are a colony of heaven' will not do, for if Paul had used πολίτευμα in this sense he would have spoken of πολίτευμα οὐρανῶν ἐπὶ τῆς γῆς whereas what he actually says is that the πολίτευμα is in heaven.[58] Other exegetes move via the meaning of 'state' or 'commonwealth' to that of 'homeland' or 'home'.[59] There are good reasons however for ruling out such an interpretation. The meaning 'homeland' is not attested and the two references given by Ruppel for such a meaning[60] – Polybius XXIV, 9, 8 and 10, 4 (ἐν τοῖς ἰδίοις πολιτεύμασιν) – can only be translated 'homeland' because of the accompanying ἰδίοις. In addition, nowhere in the usage of πολίτευμα is the local, territorial sense of 'state' to the fore which is necessarily the case in the meaning 'homeland'.[61] It is here that a contrast with the Philo parallel in *De Conf. Ling.* 78, cited earlier, also becomes apparent, for there 'homeland' is plainly in view, because πατρίς is used, but any such expression is absent in Philippians 3: 20. We conclude that the meaning of πολίτευμα which is best attested in Hellenistic times and which best fits the context in this passage is that of 'state' or 'commonwealth',[62] but that the particular nuance we have found in its usage should also be remembered here, that is, the state as a constitutive force regulating its citizens. In this way something of the interplay between 'constitution' and 'state' is retained.[63] With this active force πολίτευμα can be compared to the significance of the term βασιλεία as reign rather than realm.[64]

These conclusions are reinforced when it is noted that Philo, whose conceptual world may be indirectly influential on the background of our passage, uses πολίτευμα in this figurative sense of state or commonwealth, cf. especially *De Op. Mundi* 143f and *De Agr.* 81 where the ideal world is seen as a realm which determines the quality of the lives of those who belong to it.[65] In Philippians 3 it is this connotation of πολίτευμα as a dynamic constitutive force which best corresponds to the relationship involved in οἱ τὰ ἐπίγεια φρονοῦντες in the first half of the contrast, where that which is the object of φρονέω is seen as determinative of a person's orientation. Similarly the πολίτευμα in heaven is determinative of the Christian's existence – the 'primary binding and governing relationship is in heaven'.[66] Perhaps one way of expressing this connotation of πολίτευμα in translation is the admittedly awkward rendering – 'For our state and constitutive government is in heaven.'

Having assessed the primary thrust of Paul's use of πολίτευμα after he had taken over this terminology from opponents, we should also mention the added colour his use may have taken on in the Philippian setting. The significance of Philippi as a Roman colony for the church situated there is a secondary and derivative factor and is not to be associated with any translation of πολίτευμα as 'colony'. Philippi was very proud of its relation to Rome (cf. the emphasis on this in the Acts 16 narrative). To commemorate his victory in the struggle for control of the empire in 42 B.C. on the plain of Philippi, Octavian had conferred the Roman form of constitutional government on the city. The official language became Latin, Roman coinage was adopted and the two chief magistrates of the city were now appointed in Rome and exempt from any interference by the provincial governor. In fact under the provision of the 'ius Italicum' Philippi was governed as if it was on Italian soil and its administration reflected that of Rome in almost every respect. To the Philippians the πολίτευμα was in Rome, and they would have seen a parallel as the apostle makes the claim about the πολίτευμα of Christians. Their state and constitutive government is in heaven and they are to reflect this rule in every respect.[67]

That such a parallel may well have been intended is further indicated by Paul's use of πολιτεύεσθε in 1: 27, a *hapax legomenon* in the Pauline corpus and occurring elsewhere in the NT only in Acts 23: 1. There has been some debate among commentators whether the verb here is simply being used in its weaker and more general sense of 'to live' or whether it retains its original political connotations of 'to live as a citizen'. In arguing for the latter sense here R. R. Brewer tries to prove too much by insisting that every instance of πολιτεύεσθαι which can be found conforms to the dictum of Thayer, namely, that 'from Thucydides down in Hellenistic writers πολιτεύεσθαι meant to conduct one's self (sic) as pledged to some law of life'.[68] He is right however in believing it to be significant that only in Philippians does Paul use πολιτεύεσθαι as opposed to περιπατεῖν or ζῆν which are each used seventeen times in the letters most generally conceded to him. Although πολιτεύεσθαι could have the weaker sense in Philippians 1: 27, more appears to be involved in this setting where, in allusion to the status of their city, Paul would be saying to the Philippians, 'Live as citizens in a manner worthy of the gospel of Christ', and might well have their dual allegiance in view, for, as he goes on to say, they belong to the heavenly commonwealth and, as its citizens, are to reflect its life.[69]

4. The heavenly dimension: realized and future eschatology (3: 20, 21)

The Christian's commonwealth and government is ἐν οὐρανοῖς and it is there because that is where his or her Lord is, as the following clause clearly implies. If Christ is to come from heaven, then he is envisaged as being there until that time. As elsewhere, Paul views heaven in its place in the history of salvation. Just as τὰ ἐπίγεια take on significance as representative of the sphere in which sin rules, so heaven must be seen as referring to the realm which provides the focus for God's new order centering in Christ. This is why Paul felt it appropriate to take over political terms in this reference to the heavenly dimension. Heaven is the place where Christ rules as Lord from God's right hand (cf. Col. 3: 1f; Eph. 1: 20f) and so naturally the state which governs the believer's life is to be found where his or her Lord is.

The contrast at this point is between the earthly and the heavenly spheres with their particular significance and not, as some recent writers imagine, between the present and the future. Because of his presuppositions about what genuine Pauline eschatology can include, Koester states, 'the emphasis . . . is upon the fact that ours is a πολίτευμα that is not here, but rather in heaven and, therefore, still to come'.[70] But this is to allow temporal categories to swallow up spatial ones and also to ignore the very clear present tense of ὑπάρχει. 'The believer *now is*, in this present world, a citizen of the heavenly commonwealth.'[71] Although not yet fully manifest for what it is, the heavenly commonwealth is a present reality. Though expressed in Hellenistic political terminology, Paul's conception corresponds to the apocalyptic motif we have seen in which the benefits of salvation awaited at the end are already present in heaven (cf. 4 Ezra 7: 14, 83; 13: 18; 2 Bar. 21: 12; 48: 49; 52: 7). Paul is not as afraid of seeming to agree with his enthusiastic opponents at certain points as some scholars suppose.[72] In fact, as we have observed in 1 Corinthians, the apostle often goes as far as possible with a mistaken viewpoint but then modifies it by placing it in his own framework. Here in Philippians 3: 20 Paul affirms a 'realized eschatology' in the sense that the source of the life the believer now enjoys, its determinative power, is in heaven, but he sets off his own perspective by combining such an emphasis with a future eschatological reference. The tension between the present and the future is maintained as spatial (representing the former) and temporal (representing the latter) categories are interwoven.

The future expectation is immediately introduced in the second clause of verse 20 – ἐξ οὗ καὶ σωτῆρα ἀπεκδεχόμεθα κύριον Ἰησοῦν Χριστόν. The relative phrase ἐξ οὗ, strictly grammatically, would refer to the singular πολίτευμα and thus give it a primarily local sense.[73] However, it is preferable to take it as a *constructio ad sensum*, so that it is seen adverbially as an equivalent of ὅθεν which does not occur in Paul. Besides, Paul alternates elsewhere between singular and plural forms of οὐρανός, which though plural in form here is singular in meaning. In 1 Thessalonians 1: 10 he speaks of Christ's coming from heaven and such a reference makes the best sense here also.[74]

A significant factor arising from Paul's treatment of heaven in verse 20 is that his ultimate expectation of salvation is not in terms of heaven itself as a person's final destiny, which is often the impression conveyed by translating πολίτευμα as 'homeland', but rather in terms of Christ coming from heaven to earth. It is not a question of the soul returning to its homeland in the ideal world, as in Philo, but of bodily existence being transformed as Christ returns to earth at the consummation (cf. verse 21). Paul concentrates not on the heavenly 'beyond' but on the believer's body being made like Christ's body of glory. In contrast to those who were claiming likeness to Christ's glory and insisting on its present manifestation in the body, the apostle is quite clear that the transformation of the body awaits the consummation. The resurrection from the dead is not excluded but he appears to have specifically in mind the transformation of those who are still alive, for μετασχηματίσει best corresponds to the concept of being changed by putting on the additional clothing of immortality, which Paul has used in 1 Corinthians 15: 51ff and 2 Corinthians 5: 1ff. That he does not employ the same terminology here but rather a term taken from Hellenistic usage may indicate that he is borrowing this particular formulation, possibly one used by his opponents, and setting it in his own eschatological framework.[75] This suggestion is strengthened when it is noted that μετασχηματίζω, which is found in the NT only in Paul, occurs in 1 Corinthians 4: 6 in an almost technical literary sense and then in 2 Corinthians 11: 13–15. In this latter passage the verb is used in the middle voice three times in describing Paul's opponents, who transform themselves into apostles of Christ and servants of righteousness and thereby show themselves to be servants of Satan who changed his outward appearance to that of an angel of light. It is surely no coincidence that Paul uses the same verb three times in lambasting these opponents. It seems highly probable that he is using one of their favourite terms against them.

In contrast to similar opponents here in Philippians the apostle insists that present bodily existence is characterized by ταπείνωσις. The reference is not to that which is inherently evil, but to the state of humiliation, frailty and weakness which has come about because the body has fallen victim to sin and death.[76] Final salvation will definitely embrace bodily existence and μετασχηματίζω involves not a creation of something entirely new but the transformation of something already there, in this case 'our body of humiliation'. In this way the element of continuity is brought out as both present and future modes of existence involve some kind of σῶμα. The discontinuity is indicated by the contrast between humiliation and that glory which is as yet enjoyed only by Christ – σύμμορφον τῷ σώματι τῆς δόξης αὐτοῦ. His resurrected body is the prototype of the Christian's (cf. also 1 Cor. 15: 49; Rom. 8: 29). The contrast between verse 21 and verse 10 where the verbal form συμμορφιζόμενος is used should be noted. Paul's point is very clear. Knowing Christ now means being conformed to his death; only when he comes from heaven will it mean being conformed to him in all the qualities possessed by his body of glory.

It is the Lord Jesus Christ himself who will bring about this decisive change (verse 21). The sovereign power which it will take to accomplish final salvation he already possesses as he subjects all things to himself. As in 1 Corinthians 15: 27 and Ephesians 1: 22 there is an 'Adamic' reference via the allusion to Psalm 8: 6. It is as the last Adam, to whom has been restored dominion over the cosmos, that Christ has life-giving power to transform believers' bodies. The one who rules the cosmos is well able to achieve full salvation for his people. The present aspect of Christ's rule mentioned here underlines the correctness of seeing the commonwealth in heaven as also a present reality.

5. The heavenly dimension and the apostle's death (1: 23)

Paul's perspective on heavenly life set out in 3: 20, 21 can include both present and future elements, but how does it square with his sentiments expressed earlier in the same letter in 1: 23 where he has his own death in mind and looks forward to this as being with Christ? Does he not in this passage after all see salvation as being with Christ *in heaven*, which is where he envisaged Christ as being?

What is clear is that for Paul in this letter the two perspectives provided no contradiction, for they stand alongside each other without any further discussion or explanation.[77] It should also be underlined that the apostle has no death-wish as such nor in 1: 23 does he treat earthly life as insignificant over against the life of the heavenly realm. The dilemma – life or death – which he sets out in considering the possibility that he will not survive his imprisonment, is a dilemma precisely because he values the significance of his life of service to Christ and the church so highly. He carefully weighs both sides of the matter and still cannot decide. Yet from a purely personal viewpoint death could only be gain (1: 21) because it would mean being with Christ in a far better way than is now possible. Living, which is equated with Christ, and dying, which is gain, are not contrasted but rather the latter is seen as a consequence of the former. Since living right now for Paul involved being taken up with Christ, dying could only mean more of the same but without the difficulties and suffering which would accompany remaining in the flesh.[78] The key terms in the apostle's discussion of this limited individual horizon are ἀναλῦσαι and σὺν Χριστῷ. Some hold that ἀναλῦσαι involves the Hellenistic idea of the immortality of the soul now freed from the body as it sets out on its journey to return to God.[79] But the fact that Paul used this word which had become a euphemism for dying does not mean that he used it in the same technical sense as, say, Plato. Rather he takes a term which was to hand and sets it within his own perspective on death where he neither devalues nor flees from earthly life and where the sole reason why death can be considered better is Christological.[80] Verse 20, where his wish is that whether by life or by death Christ might be magnified in his body, shows that Christ is his central concern and the Christological grounding for his attitude to death is expressed in the phrase σὺν Χριστῷ εἶναι (verse 23). It differs from σὺν Χριστῷ in an eschatological context elsewhere in Paul (cf. 1 Thess. 4: 13, 14, 17; 5: 10; Rom. 6: 8; 2 Cor. 4: 14; 13: 4; Col. 3: 4), in that the others all refer to the parousia but here that which immediately follows Paul's death is in view. The phrase cannot refer to what will follow the resurrection of the dead, otherwise remaining in the flesh with you (verses 24, 25) would not be a genuine alternative to being with Christ (verse 23).[81] Both options in the apostle's dilemma have reference to what is to follow immediately. For Paul the relationship of union with Christ cannot be broken by death but will continue in an even more intimate way where Christ now is, that is, in heaven.[82] Clearly heaven as such is not the attraction for Paul on considering his death but only as it forms the temporary setting for his unbreakable personal relationship with Christ his Lord. Although the apostle knew Jewish apocalyptic traditions about 'paradise' (cf. 2 Cor. 12: 1ff) as the place of the righteous departed, he concentrates not on these but on personal union with Christ.

This concept expressed in 1: 23 need not have been a later development in the apostle's thought as compared to the expectation of the parousia. To those who object that if he had had this concept earlier he would have comforted the Thessalonians with it in 1 Thessalonians 4, the answer must be given that his readers were not asking about the state of those who had 'fallen asleep' but rather about the relationship of such believers to those who would be alive at the parousia. To talk of the present state of such believers would have been wide of the mark. We have seen that in 2 Corinthians 5 the two perspectives stand together and it is likely that this was the case from quite early on in Paul's thinking, and that when faced with the possibility of his own death this intermediate horizon quite naturally becomes more explicit. In Jewish apocalyptic writings also one can find a combination of a concept of an intermediate state in heaven with the expectation of the resurrection of the dead.[83] In similar vein to Paul's 'gain' and 'far better' 1 Enoch 103: 3f indicates that the lot of the righteous dead is abundantly better than the lot of the living, and their resting-place, although not always clearly designated, is said to be with the angels (39: 4) or in heaven (70: 1 - 71: 1). 1 Enoch 103: 3f is surrounded by passages which speak of final eschatological salvation and of the judgment day and the assertions about the state of the dead can be connected with the day of judgment (cf. 102: 5; 104: 5), so that the individual's destiny at death and the corporate eschatological consummation are closely interwoven.[84] The same close relationship can be found also in Rabbinic literature, where categories normally applied to the eschaton, such as the age to come and Paradise, are applied with regard to those who have died. R. Jacobs (A.D. 140–165) said, 'This world is like a vestibule before the world to come; prepare thyself in the vestibule that thou mayest enter into the banquet hall', while in Sifre Deut. 32: 4 (133a) we read, 'Tomorrow my lot will be in the coming world.'[85] In other words the final age to come can be depicted as being proleptically enjoyed in heaven in the intermediate state, so that, for example, in 1 Enoch 45: 2, 5 the community of the elect and the righteous, who are at present in heaven, will appear on a transformed earth in the last days.

That the two expectations stand side by side both in Paul and in apocalyptic and Rabbinic materials suggests very strongly that the latter provided Paul not only with his two age eschatological framework but also with the background for his view of the believer's destiny immediately upon death.[86] In the same way as the two age theory is modified by Paul as he looks back on what God has already done in Christ, so the Jewish view of the intermediate state receives a new Christological orientation. Further preparation for Paul's concept of being with Christ in heaven may be found in the apocalyptic notion of being in the presence of the Messiah, the Elect One, in the intermediate heavenly state – 'And there I saw another vision, the dwelling places of the holy, and the resting-places of the righteous . . . And in that place mine eyes saw the Elect One of righteousness and of faith . . . And the righteous and elect shall be without number before Him for ever and ever.' (1 Enoch 39: 4ff cf. also 70: 1–4). But whereas in apocalyptic this was but one element in eschatological salvation, in Paul the concept of union with Christ is the determinative feature.[87] Thus for Paul even if death precedes the parousia, it is still unable to break his union with the exalted Christ in heaven. In turn this indissoluble union with Christ is the factor which links the intermediate state with the consummation, for it is because believers have been joined to Christ by faith that they will also finally be raised with Christ (cf. 2 Cor. 4: 14).

It is clear from a comparison of Philippians 1: 23 with 3: 20, 21 that the state into which Paul will enter at death is far better, bringing with it a greater closeness of communion with Christ, and yet that it is still a state of expectation, less than the fullness of redemption described in 3: 20f. The limited horizon of heaven as the intermediate place of individual salvation is seen to play a significant but minor part in Paul's thought, for it is mentioned only here and in 2 Corinthians 5 as compared with numerous references to the consummation. That which may well come first for Paul in time sequence does not occupy the pre-eminent place in his eschatological expectation. Here again we can see how spatial and temporal elements are related in Paul's eschatology. The spatial concept of heaven features in the proleptic enjoyment of eschatological salvation in the period between the individual's death and the parousia. At the same time individual death will not be followed by some immediate escape from time, so that in this respect it can be seen that heaven participates in the 'already – not yet' tension of existence during the overlap of the ages.[88]

6. Humiliation as the badge of membership of the heavenly commonwealth

In the context of the polemic of chapter 3, verse 21 is far more than a doxological flight to climax the passage. As we have seen, the term 'glory' figured in the attack on opponents in verse 19 and appears to have been one of the key issues under dispute in 2 Corinthians also (cf. especially 2 Cor. 3 and 4). Both in 2 Corinthians and in Philippians 3 those under attack from the apostle appear to have linked 'glory' with the possession of the Spirit through keeping the law, but Paul will not allow such opponents simply to pass over the reality of bodily existence as $\tau\alpha\pi\epsilon\acute{\iota}\nu\omega\sigma\iota\varsigma$ and to concentrate solely on heavenly glory. He will not allow them to lower the final barrier between earthly and heavenly existence by asserting that they already fully possess the latter (cf. also verses 10, 11). So it is that Paul insists that although Christ has fully achieved the final stage of heavenly power and glory, the believer has not yet done so and must await the coming of his or her Lord from heaven.

At present the believer is still in the process of following Christ who first experienced humiliation and then glory. At this point it becomes evident that our passage has more in common with the Christ-hymn in 2: 6-11 than merely striking verbal similarities. The hymn describes how Christ who was in the form of God – and this is closely linked with possessing the glory of God[89] – achieves God's purpose for humanity in that he refused to exploit his right to heavenly status but took on earthly bodily existence, in which there was nothing extraordinary about his external appearance (καὶ σχήματι εὑρεθεὶς ὡς ἄνθρωπος – 2: 7), and humbled himself (ἐταπείνωσεν ἑαυτόν) to the point of death. Yet precisely because of this God highly exalted him. This Christological pattern of humble suffering as the path to glory in chapter 2 is now applied to believers in chapter 3. There can be no attempts to find short cuts by claiming heavenly status too soon. In other words the programme of the heavenly πολίτευμα as it works itself out on earth is to be the programme followed by the heavenly Christ himself. Because of Christ's exaltation the Philippians too belong to the heavenly commonwealth where Christ in his glory now is but they cannot yet claim all their rights as citizens, for its constitutive power must at present be exercised on earth through their bodies of humiliation. Their Lord is ruling and *his* programme is to be followed. Not until he decrees it by returning from heaven will they be made fully like him. Then this one who was obedient to death and now reigns with power to complete God's purposes for humanity will effect the transformation for his people which God effected for him.[90]

7. Concluding observations

Conclusions from our treatment of Philippians can be summarized under five heads. First, Paul's discussion of the heavenly dimension again arises from a problem in the church situation. It is a response to a particular sort of 'paradise now' mentality held by opponents who threaten to cause trouble in Philippi. In their false evaluation of the heavenly dimension these opponents apparently believed that their reception of the heavenly call, their full membership in the heavenly commonwealth and their possession of heavenly glory had been transmitted to them by Christ through their keeping of the law as true Israelites. But for Paul those who have not grasped the servant character of present eschatological existence are not true followers of the heavenly Christ. Indeed, rather than being controlled by his rule from heaven they can only be designated as 'earthly-minded' (verse 19).

Secondly, the believer's life on earth necessarily transcends the limitations of earthly existence, since the exalted Lord, who is its source, is in heaven. It is because of this close connection with the exalted Christ that the apostle finds a role for the heavenly dimension in his thought. Heaven is not the final goal of salvation. The emphasis is not on heaven in itself as the Christian's homeland, in a Platonic or Philonic sense, a place to which he or she, as a perpetual foreigner on earth, must strive to return.[91] For Paul the heavenly realm is not some static eternal state but rather part of the forward moving history of salvation. As we have seen from 1: 23 it participates in the 'already – not yet' tension of salvation, so that salvation is not simply viewed as a movement from earth below to heaven above. Being with Christ in heaven is a temporary stage prior to the consummation of salvation which will involve a manifestation of Christ in glory *from* heaven (cf. 3: 20f). This final salvation at the parousia is not depicted as Christ taking believers back to heaven with him. Rather Christ's coming from heaven will bring about the redemption of the body as believers are clothed with heavenly glory (3: 21).

Thirdly, heaven functions in this passage not in a negative otherworldly fashion, where the present is viewed simply as the individual's preparation for an after-life in heaven, but has a positive thrust. Because of their relation to the exalted Christ believers are to be governed by the life of the heavenly commonwealth, reflecting the pattern of their Lord as they carry out its programme (cf. also 1: 27). In this way 3: 20, 21 provide further grounds for Paul's command to imitate him (3: 17), for his pattern of life, which involves sharing Christ's sufferings and striving for what has not yet been attained (3: 10ff), is shown to be the pattern of those who belong to the heavenly commonwealth. This in turn, through the similarities with 2: 6–11, is seen to be the pattern of Christ himself, and 3: 7–9 already show that Paul, in renouncing all that of which he could boast, was in fact reflecting something of this Christ-pattern.

Fourthly, the heavenly dimension is depicted in political imagery which is entirely appropriate to the present rule or government of Christ from heaven. As Paul takes up this image he indicates that for him there is a real connection between the heavenly world and this world as the rule of the heavenly Christ projects into and exhibits itself through the lives of believers. Philippians 3: 20 is often compared with Galatians 4: 26. In both places, it is held, this political imagery is used so that believers are seen as citizens of a heavenly city. There are similarities in the treatment of the heavenly commonwealth and the heavenly Jerusalem. Both depend on the presence of Christ in heaven for their force in the argument, both emphasize a realized eschatology and both depict the heavenly dimension as a present reality which activates the lives of believers. At the same time it should be clearly recognized that Jerusalem is not in view in Philippians

3: 20 where πολίτευμα has the force of constitutive government, and Galatians 4: 26 employs not so much political as religious imagery, for Jerusalem figures as the holy city, around which the hopes of the people of God for their salvation centre. Further, the heavenly commonwealth features here as part of a response to a false evaluation of the heavenly realm, while in Galatians 4 the heavenly Jerusalem is employed as part of a response to a false evaluation of the earthly city of Jerusalem in the history of salvation. To merge the two references into one concept of a heavenly city is to do justice to neither passage.[92]

Fifthly, an incipient realization of heaven on earth is clearly involved in Paul's concept, but he is not afraid of being taken for an enthusiast in making his claim, for he is well able to combine both realized eschatology and a future expectation. This is to disagree thoroughly with the pre-suppositions about Pauline eschatology which Koester brings to this passage when he asserts that 'the two so strictly exclude each other that Paul in iii. 20 can introduce his expectation of the heavenly, that is, future realization as the reason for his derogatory judgment of his opponents'. Because he holds such views, for Koester the eschatology of Colossians and Ephesians cannot possibly be Pauline.[93] But if the heavenly dimension appears here in Philippians, which is almost universally regarded as Pauline, in a 'realized' sense, and it clearly does, there can be no *a priori* grounds why similar references in Colossians and Ephesians, which we shall proceed to examine, should be viewed as evidence of non-Pauline eschatology.

5

COLOSSIANS AND HEAVENLY-MINDEDNESS

Our general discussion of Paul's treatment of the heavenly dimension in Colossians leads up to a more detailed examination of the pericope, Colossians 3: 1–4. Unlike the hymn in Colossians 1: 15–20, this passage has the advantage of not being overworked in recent scholarship. The term τὰ ἄνω, which is an equivalent to the heavenly dimension, figures prominently in this passage, and the passage itself is crucial to the structure of the letter as a whole as it provides a bridge from the polemic of chapter 2 into the second half of the letter with its ethical parenesis. Its pivotal place in the letter reflects the centrality of the heavenly realm to the problems in Colossae with which Paul deals.[1]

1. False teaching about the heavenly world in Colossae

There was no lack of interest in the heavenly dimension in Colossae and the form this interest took conditions to a large degree Paul's response and its terminology. It is however not easy to be precise about the form the interest took. Epaphras evidently felt there was cause for some concern at the ailment which was beginning to plague the church and on hearing his report Paul shared this concern and set about prescribing what he knew to be the only cure. Although the prescription for cure comes across reasonably clearly to the present-day reader of Colossians, the ailment defies a really detailed diagnosis on his part. Paul had no reason for clearly defining the teaching involved and merely touches on some of its features, using its catchwords and slogans. In addition, though we now have the Qumran and Nag-Hammadi texts, there remains a paucity of documents from the same period and locality which might shed light on the exact shade of meaning of some of the terms used. Though we must therefore be cautious in the claims made for our reconstruction, it is still important to take up the clues Paul provides and point to similar concepts in the thought of that time in an attempt to obtain as clear a picture as possible of the teaching which caused Paul enough concern to provoke a response.[2]

(i) Visionary experience and asceticism (Colossians 2)

At the heart of the interest of the false teaching in the heavenly dimension appears to be the claim to visions and 'the worship of the angels' connected with such visions. Unfortunately 2: 18 which deals with this visionary penetration into the heavenly realm is one of the most difficult verses in the whole letter. In it Paul urges the Colossians not to submit to any false teacher who would attempt to disqualify others because he himself took pleasure in and was insisting on ταπεινοφροσύνη καὶ θρησκείᾳ τῶν ἀγγέλων ἃ ἑόρακεν ἐμβατεύων. ταπεινοφροσύνη occurs three times in Colossians (2: 18, 23; 3: 12). In the last occurrence the positive virtue of lowliness of mind is enjoined by the apostle. This does not however seem to be in view in the first two instances where the word is used in connection with the false teaching. Because of its close association with 'worship' in both instances it is likely that the term was a technical one in the false teaching and denoted cultic practice rather than a disposition.[3] Lohse holds that the term means 'the eagerness and docility with which a person fulfils the cultic ordinances'.[4] In this context however and with the emphasis of the teaching on external practices associated with food and drink (2: 16, 20f) and on ascetic austerity (2: 23), the term almost certainly has reference to fasting.[5] ταπεινοφροσύνη is a technical term for fasting in Tertullian, De jejun. 12 and Hermas, Vis. III, 10, 6; Sim. V, 3, 7. The related verb ταπεινόω and the noun ταπείνωσις are used in the LXX to denote fasting (cf. Lev. 16: 29, 31; 23: 27, 29, 32; Isa. 58: 3, 5; Ps. 34: 13f; Judith 4: 9).

In apocalyptic writings fasting is often a preparation for visionary experience and for the reception of divine revelations (cf. Dan. 12; 4 Ezra 5: 13, 20; 6: 31, 35; 9: 23-5; 12: 51 - 13: 1; 2 Bar. 5: 7ff; 9: 2ff; 12: 5ff; 21: 1ff; 43: 3; 47: 2ff).[6] Sometimes the preparation is specifically for entrance into the heavenly realm (cf. Apoc. Abr. 9, 12 where, after abstaining from food, Abraham is taken up on a heavenly journey). This combination of fasting and heavenly visions has close parallels with Philo's treatment of Moses' ascent of Sinai which is viewed as an ascent to heaven and preceded by preparatory fasting (cf. *De Vit. Mos.* I, 67-70). In *De Somn.* I, 33-7 that Moses fasted is said to follow necessarily from the fact that he became ἀσώματος and heard the heavenly hymns. The combination of asceticism and heavenly ascent is attested later also, for it plays a prominent part in Jewish merkabah mysticism which had strong halakhic elements[7] and in the *Corpus Hermeticum* where Tat is told it is necessary to hate the body and its senses in order to ascend above through the spheres (cf. IV, 5-8; XIII, 6, 7).

All this is highly relevant to Colossians 2: 18 where the two elements associated with fasting are 'the worship of the angels' and visionary experience. It is unlikely that explicit worship of angels was taking place.[8] If this were the case Paul's response would have been far more forthright. It is more likely that θρησκεία τῶν ἀγγέλων has reference to the angels' worship and is a subjective rather than objective genitive construction. Both usages can be seen in close proximity in Josephus with reference to the Jews' worship of God. In Ant. 12, 253 θρησκεία is in a subjective genitive construction with Ἰουδαίων, while in Ant. 12, 271 it is in an objective genitive construction with θεοῦ. Here in conjunction with fasting the reference is to the participation by the initiate in the heavenly worship of angels.[9] This concept of participation in the angelic liturgy was a familiar one and is mentioned in 2 Enoch 20: 3, 4; 3 Enoch 1: 12; Test. Job. 48–50; Apoc. Abr. 17; Asc. Isa. 7: 37; 8: 17; 9: 28, 31, 33. At Qumran also the community on earth had liturgical fellowship with the inhabitants of heaven (cf. 1QH III, 20-2; XI, 10-12; 1QSb IV, 25, 26)[10] and the concept is by no means foreign to the NT (cf. 1 Cor. 11: 10; Heb. 12: 22f; Rev. 4, 5). It can also be found later in Jewish merkabah mysticism where the Talmudic tradition recorded in B. Chag. 14*b* concerning the four who entered paradise is particularly striking: 'The teacher of R. Jose the priest says he saw them seated on Mt. Sinai; heard heavenly voices saying, "Ascend hither, you and your disciples are destined to be in the third set (of angels) singing continually before the Shekinah." '[11] This Jewish motif lent itself to assimilation into a Hellenistic framework (cf. *Corpus Hermeticum* I, 26) where intermediary powers, thought to exercise a baleful influence over the cosmos and human destinies, had to be appeased. As we shall see, this sort of assimilation appears to have taken place in the syncretism present in Colossae.

The next phrase in Colossians 2: 18 – ἃ ἑόρακεν ἐμβατεύων – again needs comment. Rather than indulging in dubious conjectural emendations,[12] we prefer to deal with the existing text despite its difficulties and translate the phrase literally as 'which he has seen on entering'. In this way ἃ ἑόρακεν is not the object of ἐμβατεύων but a relative clause modifying 'fasting and angelic worship' (cf. the similar neuter plural relative modifying the whole of the preceding phrase in 2: 17 and 3: 6). ἑόρακεν refers then to what has been seen in visions.[13] It is modified temporally by ἐμβατεύων which should be taken in its primary meaning of 'entering'.[14] But into what does the visionary enter? There are two possible solutions. The first sees a reference to entering into the heavenly realm. Where else would a visionary see and participate in angelic worship but in heaven? A. D. Nock first mentions this interpretation – 'it may indicate some claim to special knowledge obtained on a visionary entry into heaven.'[15] In apocalyptic literature such visionary entry into heaven was usually conceived of in terms of the translation of the spirit and its visit to heavenly

places (cf. 1 Enoch 14: 8; 71: 1; 2 Enoch 3: 1; 36: 1, 2; Test. Abr. 7–10;
Apoc. Abr. 12, 15, 16, 30; Test. Levi 2: 5–7, 10; 5: 1, 3; 2 Bar. 6: 4, cf.
also Rev. 4: 1f). The alternative solution connects ἐμβατεύων with a usage
attested by inscriptions from the sanctuary of Apollo at Claros in which
the verb was a technical term employed to indicate a definite stage in the
ritual of the mysteries, entrance into the inner sanctuary which was at the
same time entrance into the presence of the god.[16] On this interpretation
the Colossians reference would involve visionary experience of heaven but
specifically connected with mystery rites. Again this could well be envisaged in a syncretistic teaching. It is true of course that a sanctuary is not
explicitly mentioned in 2: 18,[17] but this is not surprising if Paul is using a
catchword from the so-called 'philosophy' (cf. 2: 8) which would be well
known to the Colossians, and in any case the reference to θρηκεία τῶν
ἀγγέλων could be seen as implying a heavenly sanctuary. Whichever
explanation of ἐμβατεύων is preferred, it is likely that the elements mentioned in Colossians 2: 18 indicate an insistence on fasting as preparation
for visionary experience of and participation in angelic worship in the
heavenly realm.

The rigorous self-discipline in preparation for visionary exaltation
included elements which appear to come from Jewish traditions – an insistence on 'circumcision' (cf. 2: 11), legal ordinances (2: 14), food and drink
regulations, and observances of the festival calendar (2: 16) – and in 2: 20ff
Paul repeats some of the slogans from the asceticism of the local teachers,
who were greatly concerned to check the indulgence of the flesh (cf. 2:
23). To them 'flesh' seems to have meant the lower side of human nature,
including the body (cf. the phrase τὸ σῶμα τῆς σαρκός which Paul takes
up in 1: 22; 2: 11), and by following their detailed regulations they
believed they could strip off the fleshly nature and thereby be in a position to receive visions. This stripping off of the flesh may have involved
actual physical circumcision or 'circumcision' may have been used as a
technical term for the initiatory rites of the 'philosophy'.[18] These ascetic
regulations may well have a further link with the heavenly dimension
through the mention of τὸ καθ᾽ ἡμῶν χειρόγραφον in 2: 14. Rather than
taking the chirograph as a reference to the Mosaic law or simply to a
certificate of indebtedness, we should interpret it in the light of its usage
in Jewish apocalyptic literature.[19] In the first-century B.C. Apocalypse of
Elijah, for example, an accusing angel holds in his hand a book in which
are recorded the sins of the seer who has asked that they may be blotted
out. This book is called a χειρόγραφον and is distinguished from another
chirograph in which the seer's good deeds are recorded. The καθ᾽ ἡμῶν of
Colossians 2: 14 would specifically designate the former. We have noted

other apocalyptic motifs taken up in the Colossian teaching and so it would not be surprising to find the same process in the case of the book of indictment held by an accuser in the heavenly court. The regulations of the 'philosophy', designed to deal with the body of flesh, can be seen as the δόγματα which form the basis of a person's indebtedness to the angelic powers and the angelic indictment would then be the theme, which was to become so characteristic of later Gnosticism, that because of their bodies of flesh people cannot reach God.[20]

(ii) Elemental spirits and dualistic cosmology

Views about the heavenly world characteristic of Jewish apocalyptic appear to have been adapted to the concept of appeasing hostile spirit-powers which played such a significant role in popular hellenistic religion. Decisive in this regard is the interpretation of τὰ στοιχεῖα τοῦ κόσμου (2: 8, 20).[21] With the majority of commentators we favour taking this phrase as a reference to the spirit-powers who were believed to control the affairs of the natural world rather than as 'elementary teaching'. The term στοιχεῖα itself means first of all the component parts of a series and it came to be applied to the physical components of the universe – earth, fire, water and air (cf. Diogenes Laertius 7, 136f; Philo, *Quis Rer. Div. Her.* 134; 2 Pet. 3: 10, 12). Then in Hellenistic syncretism these parts were thought to be under the control of spirit powers. Together with the stars and heavenly bodies they could actually be described as personal beings and were thought to control a person's fate. The Testament of Solomon 8: 2 can call them 'the cosmic rulers of darkness'. Such a reference is the most appropriate for the Colossian context, for elsewhere in the letter Paul emphasizes Christ's supremacy and victory over just such spiritual agencies (cf. 1: 16; 2: 10, 15). It is true that the evidence for this usage of τὰ στοιχεῖα stems from the post-NT period, the earliest being the Testament of Solomon 8: 2 (cf. 15: 5; 17: 4; 18: 1f), while the date of Pseudo-Callisthenes with its reference to King Nectanebos of Egypt who confounds the cosmic elements by his magical arts (I, 12, 1) is uncertain. However there is a great amount of evidence that Jewish apocalyptic literature had already paved the way for this development by associating angels closely with the heavenly bodies. Jubilees 2: 2 shows that each of the elements had its own angel to rule over it and in 1 Enoch 60: 11f the spirits of the various natural elements are mentioned (cf. also 1 Enoch 43: 1f; 80: 6; 86: 1ff; 88: 1ff; 2 Enoch 4: 1f; 4 Ezra 6: 3).[22] For this reason and because of the contextual considerations in Colossians 2 too much weight should not be placed on the lack of explicit usage of τὰ στοιχεῖα as 'elemental spirits' in pre-Pauline writings, for if other factors warrant it, 'it is quite legitimate to make conclusions about earlier traditions on the basis of later witnesses'.[23] It is likely that in the syncretistic teaching being advocated in Colossae these elemental spirits were classed with the angels and seen as controlling the heavenly realm and with it a person's access to the presence of God. One way of placating them was the rigorous subduing of the flesh in order to gain visionary experience of the heavenly dimension and participate in their angelic liturgy. This in turn was a means of gaining fullness of salvation, reaching the divine presence and obtaining the esoteric knowledge that accompanied such visions. All this would be in addition to what the Colossians had heard about Christ, so that in effect he became just another intermediary between humans and God, just one more way of penetrating the heavenly dimension to reach God.

In the light of the way in which the spatial terminology of 'above' and 'below' structures Paul's thought in 3: 1–4 more needs to be said about the relation of upper and lower realms of the cosmos in the conceptual background which probably provides the framework for the syncretistic teaching. In Greek thought from Parmenides onwards there is a continual metaphysical opposition between the realm of eternal being, presenting itself in the ideal spherical form of the heaven, and the phenomenal terrestrial world which is subject to the *anagkē*, the inescapable fate of death. Plato has such a dualism involving an upper invisible and a lower visible realm. A person's soul belongs to the former from where it descends into the realm of bodily existence (cf. *Phaedrus* 246, *Timaeus* 90) and salvation consists in the return of the soul to the higher world (cf. *Phaedo* 81). The figure of the pair of winged horses and the charioteer depicts what is involved. The horse of noble breed, the divine part of the soul, soars upward to the heaven of heavens, whereas the horse of ignoble breed, the lower part of the soul, drags against this, 'weighing down the charioteer to the earth when his steed has not been thoroughly trained' (*Phaedrus* 247). For Plato it is the philosopher who can train the mind and live by reason who is able to wing his way back to the heavenly world (cf. *Theaetetus* 176). That Plato's cosmological dualism persisted in the Hellenistic world is evidenced by the thought of Plutarch towards the end of the first century A.D. For him Osiris was far from the earth and unpolluted by matter, while the souls of people in bodies subject to death can have only a dim vision of the heavenly world. Only souls set free from the confines of bodily existence can have contact with this god and find their home in the heavenly realm (cf. *Isis and Osiris* 373F; *Divine Vengeance* 590). Such salvation is achieved through reason (cf. *Isis and Osiris* 378C) and in conjunction with participation in the mysteries and sacred rites (cf. *Isis and Osiris* 351C). The *Corpus Hermeticum* also places a person between the realm of matter and the higher powers. Through self-knowledge it is possible for the life and light in that person which is related to God to triumph over bodily desires so that he or she takes τὴν πρὸς τὰ ἄνω ὁδόν (*Corp. Herm.* IV, 11), ascends through seven spheres and attains divinization in the heavenly world (cf. *Corp. Herm.* I, 25f; X, 7, 16; XII, 18).

It becomes clear that one of the chief concerns of Hellenistic religious thought was how a person could escape from the lower realm and reach the heavenly world and God, for as the *Corpus Hermeticum* has it, 'None of the heavenly gods will leave heaven and come down to earth' (X, 25).[24] Usually the purified soul was held to ascend after death and to remain 'above'. It was possible however to experience this ascent of the soul during one's lifetime and to enter the heavenly sphere through various ecstatic experiences (cf. especially Plutarch, *De Def. Or.* 39f; *Corp. Herm.* XI, 20). It was of course primarily the mystery cults which fostered this way of ascent. Often such cults demanded strict discipline, but their attraction was that by such means and through initiation into secret rites they promised freedom from the evil body, enlightenment, privileged knowledge, access to the heavenly realm and union with the god or goddess. As people began to conceive that despite the apparent order of the heavenly regions there were powers in them opposed to humanity, not only did mystery religions flourish but also on the popular level magic and superstition became rife. The syncretistic teaching being advocated at Colossae spoke to the same needs and, with its features reminiscent of the mystery religions, was proving attractive for the same reason as these cults.

(iii) The syncretistic teaching and its background

By designating the false interest in the heavenly dimension as 'syncretistic', we take seriously the character of the Colossian church as preponderantly Gentile Christian. Syncretism can be said to have been one of the characteristics of the Hellenistic–Roman period as older and newer forms of religion combined and elements from one people or region merged with those from another, and Phrygia was a soil well-suited for such an amalgam.[25] In such an area Christianity would have been seen as merely another new cult to be accommodated to the concerns of Hellenistic religious philosophy. Both Hellenistic Judaism and the mystery religions called themselves 'philosophy' (cf. 2: 8)[26] and the Colossian 'philosophy' had assimilated Jewish motifs of legalistic asceticism and visionary experience of heaven into a Hellenistic dualistic cosmology with its concern to appease hostile cosmic powers. It offered the Colossian Christians a fuller salvation and attempted to persuade them that in addition to their belief in Christ they should put themselves under the power of other heavenly intermediaries in order to go beyond Christ through the knowledge gained in their visionary experiences.

Because of this syncretism it would be misguided to attempt to tie the philosophy too closely to any one particular system or group. There was certainly a strong Jewish community in the Lycus Valley, for Antiochus the Great had settled two thousand Jewish families in Lydia and Phrygia around the year 200 B.C. and so it would not be surprising for elements in the teaching to have had a Jewish origin. From our earlier chapters it is clear that the concept of upper and lower realms was by no means foreign to Jewish thought. While in the OT and later Judaism there is no ultimate antithesis between higher and lower realms, there was an increasing emphasis in apocalyptic thought on the transcendent realm and the spatial concepts of 'heaven' and 'earth' readily lent themselves to assimilation to a dualistic framework. We have already mentioned that Jewish cultic regulations, apocalyptic interests and techniques of merkabah mysticism find an echo here. We have also seen interests in common with the Qumran community and shall note further terminological parallels. However there is no reference to the Mosaic law as such in Colossians and the use to which strict observance of ascetic and cultic regulations and interest in angelic worship were put is markedly different in the two cases, providing no warrant for too close an identification.[27] Nor should the teaching be identified with Gnosticism, though again certain parallels can be found between its dualism and terminology and what is known of later Gnosticism.[28] What we have is rather a syncretism of nonconformist Jewish elements and speculative Hellenistic ideas and this could perhaps be seen as one stage in a trajectory which leads from the interests of late Judaism via contact with Christianity in a Hellenistic environment to the later Gnosticism we have attested in the Nag Hammadi documents. If this is so, then it is not surprising that Hellenistic Jewish literature provides perhaps the closest conceptual background not only for the syncretism but also for some of the ideas Paul develops in his own way in response. The upper realm is designated the 'above' (cf. Josephus, *Bell.* V, 400; Philo, *Quis Rer. Div. Her.* 70) and in Philo especially the distinction between God and the world is expressed in terms of cosmological speculation about upper and lower realms. Angels are intermediaries between the heavenly and earthly spheres while human beings are caught between them for they are souls which have descended from heaven and entered into mortal bodies. Salvation, a 'soaring upwards back to the place from whence they came', is for the souls of those who have given themselves to philosophy, to studying to die to the life of the body and to a knowledge of the heavenly world and God (*De Gig.* 12f). Sometimes Philo speaks as if this ascent of the soul is possible in this life through ecstatic experiences

> when on soaring wing it [the Mind] has contemplated the atmosphere and all its phases, it is borne yet higher to the ether and the circuit of heaven . . . and on descrying in that world sights of unsurpassing loveliness . . . it is seized by a sober intoxication, like those filled with Corybantic frenzy, and is inspired, possessed by a longing far other than theirs and a nobler desire. Wafted by this to the topmost arch of the things perceptible to mind, it seems to be on it way to the Great King Himself (*De Op. Mundi* 69–71; cf. also *Quis Rer. Div. Her.* 257, 265).

In his exposition of the OT this mystical element is often connected with Moses' ascent of Sinai and his vision of God (cf. *De Vit. Mos.* II, 67ff; *Quaes. in Exod.* II, 27ff). The ascent of the mountain becomes 'an ethereal and heavenly journey' (*Quaes. in Exod.* II, 43) and is preceded by preparatory fasting. Not only so, but the way in which Paul relates Christ to the cosmos and his use of the σῶμα concept may well have as its background the sort of cosmology and teaching about the Logos to be found in Philo.[29]

2. Salvation in Christ as the answer to the threat of hostile heavenly powers

(i) The security of the heavenly hope (1: 5)

In his thanksgiving for the Colossians Paul makes his first reference to the heavenly dimension as he speaks of their faith and love which are grounded in the hope laid up for them in heaven. In Paul 'hope' can refer to both the disposition which awaits the fulfilment of God's promises in confident expectation and the content of that expectation. Romans 8: 24 provides a clear example of these two uses in one verse. Here the emphasis is on the latter. By definition hope has a future temporal reference but now the addition of the spatial referent – ἐν τοῖς οὐρανοῖς – is meant to provide solid grounds for assurance and reflects the apocalyptic concept that what will be manifested in history is already present in heaven, a concept which was also used to indicate the certainty of salvation.[30] The believer's hope is secured in heaven and nothing can alter this. The hope is the gospel's content (1: 23) and it is in heaven because it cannot be separated from the exalted Christ who is above (3: 1) and who is himself the hope of glory (1: 27). Bornkamm is right to note the special meaning of hope in Colossians as the content of the gospel as a present inviolable possession, but wrong in thinking that this is unique to Colossians in contrast with Paul's other correspondence and in ignoring the inevitable future connotation that attaches to it and the situation which calls forth this emphasis.[31] The immediate background for this emphatic hope is not that false teachers were robbing the church of its prospect by asserting the resurrection was past already,[32] but rather that such teachers were placing the prospect in jeopardy by insisting on other means – rigorous observances, esoteric knowledge, visionary experience – in addition to Christ if full salvation was to be attained. In a situation where insecurity was being created among Christians who were being made to feel that what they had been taught was inadequate Paul uses spatial terminology to underline the security of the salvation God has provided for them in Christ.

(ii) A share in the heavenly inheritance (1: 12)

Similarly in 1: 12, as over against those who would disqualify the Colossians by insisting on additional criteria (2: 18), Paul stresses that they have already been qualified to share in the inheritance of the holy ones in light. In Colossians the concept of inheritance has its 'already' and 'not yet' contexts, so that in 3: 24 it is viewed as still to be conferred, while here the reference is to present participation. In the OT the inheritance of God's holy people was in terms of the promised land of Canaan and in fact the nouns used together here in Colossians, μερίς and κλῆρος, are often used together in the LXX with reference to this land (e.g. Deut. 10: 9; 32: 9; Josh. 19: 9). For Paul, as we have already seen in Galatians 4: 26, the inheritance of the true Israel moves beyond the terrestrial and is the transcendent realm of light. 'Light' has ethical connotations of holiness but should also be seen in terms of transcendent splendour. 'Light is the environment of the heavenly world . . . or paradise.'[33] The concept of inheritance had already been developed in this direction in the Qumran literature where 'the lot of God is that of light' (1QM XIII, 5f) and where 'God has given them to His chosen ones as an everlasting possession, and has caused them to inherit the lot of the Holy Ones' (1QS XI, 7, 8) and 'partake of the lot of Thy Holy Ones' (1QH XI, 7f). The 'holy ones' in this literature are the angels in heaven with whom the elect community on earth is joined. Paul's use of ἅγιοι here in Colossians 1: 12 appears to be coloured by this background. In Paul ἅγιοι includes angels in its range of meaning when the context requires (cf. 1 Thess. 3: 13; 2 Thess. 1: 7, 10) and if this is the case here,[34] it is of striking significance in the Colossian setting. No regulations or techniques are needed for participation in angelic worship, for God the Father has already qualified the Colossians to share the lot of the holy ones in light. In providing them with this participation in the heavenly inheritance, God has at the same time delivered them from any hold the cosmic powers might have over them with their dominion of darkness (1: 13).

(iii) The supremacy of Christ and his reconciliation of the heavenly powers (1: 15-20)

The literature on the Colossian hymn, which shows the supremacy of Christ in relation to the heavenly dimension, is voluminous.[35] The limits of our study mean that it will only be possible to make a few comments on these verses in their final form. In verse 16 'visible' and 'invisible' parallel heaven and earth in chiastic fashion, and for Paul there is none of the syncretist's dualism between these two realms, for Christ has united all things in heaven and on earth by virtue of both creation and redemption. Just as Christ has revealed what was hidden (cf. 1: 26), so he has made visible what was invisible, for he is in fact the image of the invisible God (1: 15). Thus in Christ, as had been asserted of the divine word in Ecclesiasticus 24: 5f and Wisdom of Solomon 18: 16, the upper and lower realms meet.

For those so concerned with the invisible heavenly powers Paul spells out some of their names – θρόνοι, κυριότητες, ἀρχαί, ἐξουσίαι. These names are found in apocalyptic literature and in fact all four are listed in 2 Enoch 20–22 where in the seventh heaven ten classes of angels are on ten steps according to their rank.[36] Paul is not attempting any exhaustive classification. His point is simply that all such angelic powers, whatever their name and whatever their place in the hierarchy, are creatures who owe their existence to Christ who is supreme in the universe. If such powers were created in Christ and for him, then they are certainly subject to him and can have no threatening hold over his people. Christ is the head over them (cf. 2: 10) not only by virtue of creation but as the apostle asserts in verse 20 through Christ God has reconciled such powers to himself, for they are included in τὰ πάντα . . . εἴτε τὰ ἐπὶ τῆς γῆς εἴτε τὰ ἐν τοῖς οὐρανοῖς. The implication of the use of ἀποκαταλλάσσειν is of course that at some point the cosmos with its harmonious relationship between heaven and earth had been put out of joint and hostile elements entered so that the whole of created reality became in need of reconciliation through Christ. Harmony has now been restored as God through Christ has reconciled all things to himself. The implicit application is that there is therefore no need for the Colossians to attempt to appease and reconcile the powers. The decisive event has already taken place in Christ's death which had cosmic significance – εἰρηνοποιήσας διὰ τοῦ αἵματος τοῦ σταυροῦ αὐτοῦ. In later Gnostic thought the Redeemer's victory actually takes place in the heavenly regions but here it takes place on earth on the cross and then has consequences for the heavenly realm. Spatial categories are employed to show how Christ's death provides the answer to the urgent questions of Hellenistic religion arising from the separation of earth and heaven and from people viewing themselves as subject to hostile cosmic powers.[37]

(iv) The annulment of the heavenly powers' regulations (Colossians 2)

Over against the angelic indictment of a person's body of flesh Paul stressed that God did not shun the human body but in his fullness dwelt in Christ bodily (cf. σωματικῶς - 2: 9). Christ took this body of flesh to the cross (1: 22; 2: 11) and in this act he was, as it were, putting on the chirograph and taking the full force of the powers' indictment on himself (2: 14).[38] As Christ's body was nailed to the cross God was at the same time nailing the chirograph to the cross and thereby cancelling it. καὶ αὐτὸ ἦρκεν ἐκ τοῦ μέσου - literally, he took it out of the middle, which was the position occupied by the accusing witness at a trial. God has ruled the chirograph out of court, for the crucifixion of Christ was the definitive act that dealt with any hold the powers might claim over humans through the body of flesh.[39]

The Colossians no longer need attempt to strip off their fleshly nature through observance of detailed ascetic regulations. The stripping off (ἀπεκδύσις - 2: 11) of the flesh which counts (for Paul an ethical rather than a physical concept - cf. 3: 9 - ἀπεκδυσάμενοι) has already been accomplished for the Colossians by their union with Christ in his circumcision, that is, his death.[40] Instead of the Colossians having to strip off the flesh to appease the powers, through Christ's death God has in fact stripped the principalities and powers (ἀπεκδυσάμενος is taken as middle with an active sense),[41] leaving them publicly exposed, for they have been robbed of their accusing power (2: 15). Since this is so, the Colossians have died with Christ 'out from under the control of' (ἀπό) the elemental spirits of the universe (2: 20). They have no need to submit to the regulations of the 'philosophy', which, with all its talk about dealing with the flesh, might give an appearance of wisdom and devoted worship but is in reality of no value in checking the indulgence of the flesh (2: 23). For all its talk about the heavenly dimension it still belongs to the world (2: 20) because its religious exercises are a matter of self-willed worship (2: 23 - ἐθελοθρησκία - a self-made religion of human will power and technique). God has triumphed over the heavenly powers in Christ (ἐν αὐτῷ - 2: 15) and for Paul the Colossian believers' freedom from the ascetic and cultic regulations designed to appease such powers is ensured by their union with Christ. He knows only one way to experience liberation from hostile heavenly powers, to enter the heavenly realm and participate in the divine fullness and that is 'in Christ'. In Christ dwells the whole fullness of deity bodily (2: 9); in Christ the Colossians *have been* filled (2: 10); in Christ they were circumcised (2: 11); in Christ they were raised together with him (2: 12). Further work in the form of following rigorous rules or practising cultic rites is not required because everything has already been made available to the Colossians in Christ. All depends then on their appropriation by faith of God's saving actions in history in Christ, and it is this very thing which their baptism proclaimed (cf. 2: 12).

3. True heavenly-mindedness (Colossians 3: 1ff)

(i) Baptism, resurrection and the things above (3: 1)

It is this motif of baptism which Paul develops in his exhortation to heavenly-mindedness because it speaks of incorporation into Christ's resurrection and exaltation. In this way the apostle not only exposes what he considers erroneous in the Colossians' interest in the heavenly dimension but now indicates further his own positive interest. He can do this because, as we have seen in 1 Corinthians 15: 47ff, he considers resurrection existence to be heavenly existence.

The opening clause – εἰ οὖν συνηγέρθητε τῷ Χριστῷ parallels as a positive counterpart the opening clause of 2: 20 – εἰ ἀπεθάνετε σὺν Χριστῷ . . . The Colossians have not realized the significance of their baptism. Not only did it proclaim that they had died with Christ to the elemental spirits of the universe but it also signified that their lives were to be informed by the fact that they had been raised with Christ. The concept of resurrection with Christ is used in close connection with baptism in 2: 12 and it is natural to see this event reflected in the terminology here in 3: 1 and also in that of 'putting off' and 'putting on' in 3: 8–10.

Too much has been read into the fact that here in Colossians Paul can speak of believers as having already been raised with Christ, whereas in Romans 6 he views resurrection with Christ as an event that is still future. Some use this to support the view that Paul could not have written Colossians.[42] At first sight the contrast appears striking. In Romans 6: 5, 8 the future tense is used, whereas in Colossians 3: 1 (also 2: 12, 13) the aorist is involved. However on closer examination it becomes clear that in both passages there are two poles to Paul's thinking about resurrection life. That life has been entered on by the believer in union with Christ yet its consummation still lies in the future. In Romans 6 his main emphasis is on dying with Christ, as, against any accusation of a deficient 'cheap' view of grace, he insists that the believer's present life cannot be one of living in sin because he or she has died to sin (6: 1ff). But dying with Christ is only one side of the coin. It is a precondition which finds its intended completion in the sharing of the new resurrection life of Christ – 'so that as Christ was raised from the dead by the glory of the Father, we too might walk in newness of life' (6: 4). That there is a present aspect of sharing in Christ's resurrection is seen also in 6: 10, 11. Through his resurrection Christ now lives to God and since they are ἐν Χριστῷ Ἰησοῦ and identified with Christ in both his death and his life believers are also to consider themselves alive to God. Unless Paul thought of believers as already having been identified with Christ in his resurrection, this would simply be make-believe. The 'already' pole of his thought is clearly implicit in Romans 6. Similarly the 'not yet' aspect must not be overlooked in Colossians 3, where, although believers have been raised with Christ, the consummation and manifestation of that resurrection life will not be until Christ, who is its embodiment, appears (verse 4). In an important article on these verses Grässer holds that the aorist in 3: 1 indicates the writer's advocacy of perfectionism.[43] His case is weakened however by his equating baptism and the language of this verse with the notion of the heavenly journey of the soul as found in Gnosticism. He holds to a Gnostic background to the Colossian philosophy but seems not to operate with any distinction between an author taking over Gnostic concepts wholesale and an author speaking to Gnostic interests in terms of what has happened in Christ in history. Accordingly Grässer cannot see what is left to take place if the heavenly journey has already occurred in baptism. But for the writer of Colossians the consummation of salvation is not the heavenly journey of the soul but Christ's return in glory and verse 4 demonstrates clearly that this still awaits. That the actual words συνηγέρθητε τῷ Χριστῷ are used here in Colossians but not in Romans remains a significant variation in terminology which is indicative of the apostle's emphasis in this letter. In the light of the content of the two passages this variation should not however be pressed too far and the burden of proof must remain with those who suggest that it represents a concept which Paul could not have entertained.[44]

The imperative that follows from present possession of eschatological resurrection life is phrased in spatial terms – τὰ ἄνω ζητεῖτε. οὐρανός has already been used in 1: 5, 16, 20, 23 and now ἄνω replaces it. Since Colossians 3: 1, 2 is the only place in Paul where the term is used substantively,[45] it could be that this is another of the catchwords of the philosophy and that Paul is using it to his own advantage. Whether this is so or not, we have already noted the prevalence of the concept of an upper world in both apocalyptic and Hellenistic Judaism and have seen Paul's treatment of such a heavenly realm in earlier letters and can therefore appreciate that he would have had no difficulty in assimilating such terminology into his framework. In addition, in Rabbinic Judaism the eschatological schemes of present and future ages could be completely paralleled by the concept of lower and upper worlds[46] and in the Qumran literature the predominantly ethical contrast of light and darkness had clear spatial connotations of upper and lower realms.[47] Here in Colossians 3: 1 we should avoid too quickly reading back a spiritualized or demythologized interpretation into Paul's original meaning. To be sure, seeking the things above has definite ethical significance as the apostle explains later but τὰ ἄνω should not simply be reduced to an ethical way of life. Paul uses it to stand for a transcendent dimension with its own reality and for him there was a valid and legitimate concern with such a dimension in contrast to the misguided concern of the false teaching.

He immediately reveals that he is not recommending seeking this realm for its own sake, nor is he interested in any cosmological geography, nor is his focus 'ein zeitloses Jenseits'.[48] The essential reason for seeking this realm is that it is where Christ is (οὗ ὁ Χριστός ἐστιν). Thus the motivation for the upward direction and heavenly orientation of the believer's life is Christological. The heavenly realm cannot be separated from the Christ who is there (cf. also 4: 1). Paul believed that the resurrected Christ existed in a realm appropriate to and as real as his heavenly body (cf. 1 Cor. 15: 47ff).[49] Here in Colossians 3: 1 also the realm above is very closely related to the sphere of resurrection existence, for those whose whole concern is to be 'the things above', where Christ is, are those and those only who already share his resurrection life. Since resurrection life is heavenly life, by being united with Christ in his resurrection believers participate in the life of the realm above. In this way it becomes clear that Paul's imperative, here as elsewhere, is based on an indicative. In Christ the Colossians have access to the realm above, therefore they are to seek the realm above. The force of the imperative ζητεῖτε in this context is to provide a counterpart to the Colossians' energetic activity in achieving visionary experience. If they really knew what it meant to have been raised with Christ, then instead of such self-willed worship (2: 23) they would expend all their energy in desiring supremely the genuine realm above. This injunction is addressed to *all* the community. It is not just a special group of initiates who by their own techniques have access to the heavenly realm but all those who, through faith and as proclaimed in baptism, have been raised with Christ.

The Colossians not only owe their transference from death to life as a past event to their union with Christ, but because they remain united to him, they must continue to seek their salvation in him (cf. 2: 6). Since he is exalted above at God's right hand, this will mean seeking that which is above. The phrase ἐν δεξιᾷ τοῦ θεοῦ καθήμενος conveys the centrality and supremacy of Christ in the heavenly realm. Here as elsewhere (cf. 1 Cor. 15: 25; Rom. 8: 34; Eph. 1: 20) Paul takes up the Christological interpretation of Psalm 110: 1 common in the early church. As regards syntax it seems preferable to take οὗ ὁ Χριστός ἐστιν and ἐν δεξιᾷ τοῦ θεοῦ καθήμενος as two separate dependent clauses rather than to view ἐστιν and καθήμενος as periphrastic. The allusion to the psalm is thus seen as added by the apostle as an aid to further definition of the realm above in terms of Christ, serving his purpose by emphasizing that Christ has the supreme position over any powers that the Colossians might associate with τὰ ἄνω. Conscious of this, the Colossians need have no fears. The heavenly realm centres around the one with whom they have been raised and since he is in the position of authority at God's right hand, nothing can prevent their access to this realm and to God's presence and there can be no basic insecurity about the salvation they have in him and its final outcome.

(ii) Heavenly-mindedness and earthly-mindedness set in opposition (3: 2)

In the light of Christ's heavenly supremacy Paul issues his imperative again – τὰ ἄνω φρονεῖτε. This time the verb is varied and the exhortation heightened by the contrast with τὰ ἐπὶ τῆς γῆς. The force of φρονεῖν is that of setting one's mind on an object or having a particular mind-set so that the verse amounts to an injunction to be heavenly-minded instead of earthly-minded. This mind-set does not come merely automatically for Paul appeals for an effort to be made. By his use of φρονεῖν with its connotations of sober consideration and firm purpose he indicates that what he has in view is something more than isolated visionary experiences. At the same time cultivating this heavenly mind-set can never be simply a matter for human will power, for its basis and motivating power lie in union with the resurrected heavenly Christ.

Paul gives the contrast between the heavenly and the earthly a strongly ethical content and in this way it closely resembles his more common contrast between flesh and Spirit (cf. especially Rom. 8: 5, 6 where φρονεῖν is employed, as setting the mind on the flesh is opposed to setting the mind on the Spirit). Although 'flesh' occurs several times in the letter and immediately precedes this section in 2: 18, 23, 'Spirit' is only mentioned once (1: 8, cf. the indirect references through the adjective in 1: 9 and 3: 16). The most likely explanation for this is that the Spirit did not figure prominently in the teaching with which Paul was dealing so that the flesh/ Spirit contrast of earlier letters is assimilated into a spatial framework for the Colossian setting.[50]

The spatial contrast functioned very differently for Paul than it did for the dualistic cosmology of the Colossian 'philosophy'. The contrast is not metaphysical in the sense that God belongs to the upper realm which is good because spiritual and has nothing to do with the lower realm which is evil because physical and material. Rather what we see is the OT concept of the two parts of created reality being taken up into Paul's eschatological perspective. Owing to Christ's exaltation heaven highlights the superiority of the life of the new age, so that 'the above' becomes the source for the rule of Christ (3: 1), for life (3: 3), for the new man (3: 10). The earth, on the other hand, has in this verse taken on the connotation of the sphere of sin and of the present evil age. In the light of Genesis 3: 17 (LXX ἐπικατάρατος ἡ γῆ) it is understandable that the earth should be seen as the primary setting of fallen creation. Of course heaven too, as part of created reality, is affected by sin, but when contrasted with the earth it maintains a closer relation to God as a symbol of transcendence. γῆ and ἐπίγειος can be used by Paul without these strong negative overtones (cf. 1 Cor. 15: 47; 2 Cor. 5: 1f; Phil. 2: 10) but here in Colossians 3: 2, 5 and, as we have seen, in Philippians 3: 19 the contrast between heaven and earth is ethically orientated with the earth being viewed as the special theatre of sin.[51] The apostle is not saying that believers' concern with the transcendent realm means that they must not concern themselves with the earthly creation as such. Rather it is the sinfully orientated response to that creation against which he warns. What is at stake is whether earthly created reality is to be given over to the threat of the powers with their dominion of darkness or to the kingdom of Christ (1: 13), to the response of the old man or that of the new man being restored to his original Adamic state (3: 9, 10). τὰ ἐπὶ τῆς γῆς include then the practices of the old man (3: 5–9), the sphere of the flesh (2: 18, 23), life in the 'world' with its bondage to the elemental spirits (2: 20) and in particular the ascetic regulations, the visions and the claims to special knowledge involved in the false teaching.

When one has seen something of the situation in the Colossian church, the apostle's strong twofold exhortation to seek the realm above is all the more striking. Why does Paul follow this dangerous course of telling the Colossians to concentrate on the things above, when their excessive concern with these matters already seems to have led to their particular deviation from his gospel? 'In the light of the Colossian interest in the heavenly hierarchy so violently combatted in the preceding chapter, it is perhaps difficult to imagine any exhortation of which the Colossians would appear to have been less in need. They were positively obsessed by τὰ ἄνω.' This simply highlights the fact that 'what we have here is one more instance of the typically Pauline method of outclassing his opponents on their own ground'.[52] He does not completely disparage their concern with the heavenly realm but rather redirects it. Yet at the same time he exposes its false premises, showing that however spiritual it might appear it was basically encouraging people to seek salvation through what is this-worldly and earthly. For all its emphasis on the upper realm it could only bring people into contact with this realm through legalistic external observances, through regulations about such matters as food and drink. By using its terminology Paul might seem to be simply adding a few of his own modifications to the position of the philosophy, but in fact he succeeds in showing that two antithetical positions are confronting one another. The advocates of the philosophy take the earthly situation as their starting-point from which by their own efforts and techniques they will ascend into the heavenlies. Paul moves in the reverse direction, since he sees the starting-point and source of the believer's life in the resurrected Christ in heaven, from where it works itself out into earthly life (3: 5ff) and from where it will eventually be revealed for what it is (3: 4).

The apostle attempts to guard against his position being swallowed up in the syncretism and its cosmology by making clear to the Colossians that any submission to intermediary heavenly powers in the first place is a manifestation of sin, that his response to the concern for ascension into a higher world depends on the believer's participation in the *history* of salvation, in the events of Christ's death and resurrection, and that the resulting link with the above carries with it clear ethical consequences. Most importantly, Paul turns the tables by taking over spatial terminology in order to point to the exclusiveness and completeness of Christ. Those who held to the syncretism claimed to worship Christ but in addition put themselves under the power of other heavenly intermediaries in order to go beyond Christ through the knowledge gained in their visionary experiences. For Paul there could be no going beyond the one in the supreme position in heaven at God's right hand. For him Christ plus anything else, in this case esoteric heavenly knowledge, is always a perversion of his gospel. Earlier he has spelled out the antithesis clearly. It is not possible to claim allegiance to Christ and to entertain the philosophy, for the latter is 'not according to Christ' (2: 8) and its advocates are 'not holding fast to the Head' (2: 18, 19). In this context Paul's exhortations in verses 1, 2 leave no doubt that the Christian gospel is not to be confused with any form of interest in transcendence and that, so far from all heavenly-mindedness being Christian, much of that to be found in Colossae was distinctly 'earthly'.

(iii) The present hiddenness and future glory of the believer's life (3: 3, 4)

Paul emphasizes again that the dynamic of true heavenly-mindedness lies in the believer's link with Christ. Though ἀποθνήσκω is used absolutely, it is to be implied that this dying is with Christ and involves a dying to the elemental spirits (2: 20) and to what has just been designated τὰ ἐπὶ τῆς γῆς. The Colossians' death to the sphere of sin is inseparably connected with their new life because they are united to Christ in both his death and his resurrection life. ἡ ζωὴ ὑμῶν does not just refer to natural biological existence but to the existence which results from incorporation into Christ. In Paul's writings ζωή is frequently viewed as an eschatological phenomenon, the life of the age to come which will be received at the resurrection (cf., for example, Rom. 6: 8, 23; 8: 11, 13) but which through the resurrection of Christ from the dead has become a present possibility (cf. Rom. 6: 4; 8: 2; 2 Cor. 4: 10, 11). Here in Colossians 3: 3, 4 both present and future aspects are involved. Life is now bound up with Christ, though in a hidden way (verse 3), but will be manifested for what it really is at the parousia (verse 4).[53] It is so closely bound up with Christ that he can be called the believer's life – ἡ ζωὴ ἡμῶν (verse 4). If Christ is 'above' and the believer's life is hidden with him, then the believer's life is already in heaven and the affinity between this passage and Ephesians 2: 6, where believers are said to be seated with Christ in the heavenlies, becomes clear. Further in Colossians 3: 3 the believer's life can be said to be σὺν τῷ θεῷ. In this verse σύν is employed for the present aspect of the believer's relation to Christ, while in verse 4 the same preposition occurs when this relation has a future context. There seems to be no particular significance in the use of σύν in verse 3 and the apostle could equally well have used his more frequent preposition ἐν but seems to have avoided it for the sake of stylistic variation in this particular combination. ἐν τῷ θεῷ modifies both ζωή and the immediately preceding τῷ Χριστῷ; accordingly the Colossians' life is hidden in God because it is incorporated with or in Christ, who is himself in God.[54] As opposed to any ascent of the soul in order to become absorbed into the godhead, the basis of this hidden union is for Paul to be found in the historical events of Christ's death and resurrection. Just as far from his mind is the suggestion that this hidden union means that the believer has a double which is his or her real self in heaven.[55] The force of Paul's statement for the Colossians is that since their life is hidden with Christ in God they need no longer feel any necessity to appease heavenly powers in order to attain the divine presence. Being in God they have completeness and great security.

At present however this relationship remains hidden. The choice of the term κέκρυπται may have been called forth by a predilection on the part of the proponents of the false teaching for this idea of hiddenness, for a secret knowledge belonging only to the initiated. Already in 1: 26f, 2: 2f Paul has taken up this sort of terminology. Central to apocalyptic thought was the view that certain events, especially those connected with the kingdom of God and the Messiah, had been hidden in God's eternal purposes but were now revealed to the seer (cf., for example, 1 Enoch 46: 3), and of course such an idea was susceptible to development along lines in which it became associated with esoteric knowledge available only to an élite. But for Paul, as for Jewish apocalyptic, 'hiddenness' was a historical and not a mystical concept. That which was hidden was not yet revealed. Because he knew that God's plan of salvation had been fulfilled in Christ Paul could see that the mystery hidden for ages had been revealed (Col. 1: 26, 27) but that it also unfolds in two stages so that part remains hidden (3: 3), awaiting revelation at Christ's final coming (3: 4). This concept overlaps with another apocalyptic motif we have frequently encountered, that of future salvation being present in heaven until its revelation.

The believer's heavenly life will only be fully manifest in all its glory when Christ, who embodies that life, appears (verse 4). Though set within the framework of Paul's spatial terminology and starting from the perspective of 'above', this is a very clear reference to the parousia.[56] 'Glory' was a characteristic concept of apocalyptic thought where it pointed to 'a final amalgamation of the earthly and heavenly spheres'[57] and was a familiar theme in Paul's writings where it is also closely associated with heavenly existence. For the believer the future manifestation in glory predicted here will have particular reference to his or her heavenly body (cf. 1 Cor. 15: 43; Phil. 3: 21). τότε makes the apostle's assertion in this verse emphatic. The stress on future consummation not only shows the normal Pauline eschatological reserve emerging forcefully despite his emphasis in this particular situation but could possibly be aimed at the Colossian visionaries and their aspirations to experiences of the divine presence and glory.[58] Paul underlines when and how this glory is to be enjoyed in its fullness. It will not be until the consummation when Christ appears and it will be 'with him'. The present hiddenness of this relationship means that until then Christian existence is predominantly one of faith not sight.[59]

The 'hidden-revealed' motif in connection with the believer's union with Christ demonstrates that the dynamic of this relationship is the dynamic of the history of salvation and that true heavenly-mindedness remains rooted throughout in that history.

(iv) The ethical consequences of true heavenly-mindedness (3: 5ff)

The ascetic regulations insisted on by the advocates of the philosophy were designed to mortify their members on the earth – τὰ μέλη τὰ ἐπὶ τῆς γῆς – that is, their physical bodies dependent on the lower realm of matter. In 3: 5 the apostle gives such an idea his own ethical twist. Νεκρώσατε τὰ μέλη τὰ ἐπὶ τῆς γῆς – then comes the list, not physical members as they might have expected, but immorality, impurity, passion, evil desire and covetousness, all characteristic of man's fallen nature. On this reading there is no necessity for embarrassment at the apparent meaning of Paul's words which would contradict his previous polemic against asceticism and severity to the body.[60] Because it involves union with Christ, genuine interest in the heavenly dimension, unlike that of the philosophy (cf. 2: 23), will have the power to deal effectively with the practices of the flesh. Instead of dividing the church into those with special visionary experiences and knowledge and those without them, true heavenly-mindedness will result in a community where there are no such artificial distinctions but where Christ is all in all (3: 11), where 'perfection' is to be found through mutual love (3: 14), and where the peace of Christ rules in the one body (3: 15). The heavenly life, which flows from its source in the exalted Christ (3: 3), works itself out and takes form within the structures of human existence, not only in the community of the church and its worship (3: 16) but in every aspect of life (3: 17), in the husband–wife, parent–child and master–slave relationships (3: 18 – 4: 1). In fact in 4: 1 the specific motivation for masters to deal justly and fairly with their slaves is with reference to their own Master in heaven (εἰδότες ὅτι καὶ ὑμεῖς ἔχετε κύριον ἐν οὐρανῷ). For Paul having a transcendent point of reference, setting one's mind on the one who is above, was therefore no escape from issues of social concern but was the very thing which should motivate believers to ensure that in their place within the social structure they were embodying the fundamental principles of justice and fairness.

Colossians demonstrates that Paul's view of the heavenliness of Christian existence does not mean that real life is in some other realm and human life on earth is therefore doomed to be a shadowy inauthentic existence. On the contrary he can insist both on the reality of the transcendent dimension where Christian existence has its source in the exalted Christ and on the quality and fullness he expects to see in the personal, domestic, communal and societal aspects of Christian living. It is because the Colossian believers participate in the triumph of the exalted Christ over the cosmic powers that they have been set free to claim the structures of the world for his kingdom and to live out the life of heaven within them.

4. Colossians, heaven and realized eschatology

We have seen that spatial categories and an emphasis on realized eschatology associated with such categories predominate in Colossians because of the setting into which Paul is explaining the implications of his gospel. Instead of arguing from the history of God's dealings with Israel as he does, for example, in Galatians, in Colossians where the major area of concern was the heavenly dimension Paul changes tactics. True, he stresses that the salvation Christ brought occurred in history but he draws out the significance of this in relation to the heavenly realm rather than to the fulfilment of God's promises to Israel. In this way the vertical has a precedence over the horizontal and greater emphasis is placed on the Christian hope being 'above' than on its being ahead. In a Hellenistic syncretistic environment a translation into such categories was needed,[61] but as we have seen they were already to a large extent to hand in the thought world of Jewish apocalyptic and Paul had already used such spatial concepts in earlier letters. Paul can make the extension because from the start he had recognized that Christ's resurrection and exaltation meant a transcendence of temporal categories, not in the sense of a static existence above history, but in terms of inaugurating the new age with its life and rule of the heavenly realm. The syncretistic teaching simply draws out an emphasis on the heavenly realm which is already inherent in Paul's eschatological perspective. In Colossians it is a question of Paul's developing further this understanding of the significance of what God has done in Christ as he sets that event on the cosmic stage of which both earth and heaven are a part. Those troubling the church at Colossae had wrongly related Christ to heaven and therefore had a wrong sort of heavenly-mindedness. Paul puts the Colossians right by showing Christ's true relation to the heavenly realm and their place in this realm through the union with Christ which their baptism so clearly proclaimed.

In his article on Colossians 3: 1–4 Grässer reaches very different conclusions. He believes that Paul's dialectic of eschatological existence has been replaced by a dialectic of transcendent existence.[62] But this is a false antithesis because both eschatological and transcendent perspectives are found together in the undisputed Paulines and right here in Colossians 3: 1–4. In fact for Paul, as we have seen, the eschatological involved the transcendent. Grässer is correct in holding that the thought of Romans 6 is being used to interpret the Colossian situation but not convincing when he adds that in the process the thought of Romans 6 has been considerably altered.[63] He concedes that Paul's pattern of thought in Romans 6 is one where the future of ἐγερθῆναι is understood as already present. But if this is Paul's thought pattern, why does it become unpauline when it is stated explicitly in Colossians 3? Grässer is also not careful enough when he asserts that the author of Colossians is ready to use the noun ἀνάστασις in the same way as the heretics of 2 Timothy 2: 18 - ἀνάστασιν ἤδη γεγονέναι. This is not the case. What the author does is to use the verb ἐγείρω metaphorically in the aorist to speak of the believer's relation to Christ. Yet Grässer cannot see this distinction because he is simply unwilling to allow the 'already - not yet' tension to function here and thinks that if someone is said to have been raised with Christ, this of necessity means that there can be no future resurrection.[64] Grässer objects also that the author, unlike Paul, does not speak in the fashion of apocalyptic about a resurrection of the dead but instead speaks of 'life' as the eschatological gift.[65] Two points should be made here. Firstly, the apocalyptic conception of a resurrection from the dead can be found in this letter in the title ascribed to Christ in 1: 18 with its implications - πρωτότοκος ἐκ τῶν νεκρῶν (cf. 1 Cor. 15: 20), where, even though the author is taking over traditional material in the hymn, he is thereby giving its terminology his approval. Secondly, and more decisively, even in the undisputed Paulines the concepts of the resurrection from the dead and eschatological life are interchangeable (cf. for example Rom. 4: 17; 5: 17, 18, 21; 6: 22, 23; 8: 11; 1 Cor. 15: 45). For Grässer to speak of 'die ganz unapokalyptische Zurückhaltung der Formulierung in v. 3 and 4' is to ignore the fact that the 'hidden-revealed' motif and the concept of glory are both prominent apocalyptic features. His general conclusions that the spatial language and realized eschatology indicate a distinct alteration from a Pauline perspective to one orientated in Hellenistic religious thought[66] are vitiated not only by the above considerations but also by his one-dimensional approach to the letter's setting and to the writer's methods. He does not pay sufficient attention to the Jewish elements in the syncretism at Colossae and does not allow enough for the writer changing the terminology he takes up by setting it in his own framework and thereby giving it his own content.

Lohse offers similar arguments in making a changed eschatology one of the reasons for his decision against Pauline authorship of Colossians. In addition he points to the basis of exhortation in Colossians as baptism, while eschatological themes provide the motivation in Paul.[67] But there is eschatological motivation in Colossians in 3: 4, 6, 24; 4: 5 and there is baptismal motivation elsewhere in Paul. It is simply a matter of emphasis. In Colossians just as Paul has good reason for stressing realized eschatology, so he has good reason for placing the emphasis in his ethical parenesis on the union with Christ proclaimed by baptism. It would be entirely inappropriate to exhort 'work for the end is coming' (cf. Rom. 13: 11ff), for the Colossian philosophy stressed effort and techniques. Rather the apostle points to the powerful motivation found in appropriating what God has already done for them. Thus, Paul's ethical instructions in 3: 5ff are not the means to some goal so much as the outworking of what has been given in Christ (cf. οὖν in verse 5). Believers' seeking of the 'above' and their life in the world are both determined by their life having its source above with Christ and both are the outworking of what God has already given in Christ.

The Pauline 'already – not yet' tension is not broken by the emphasis on the former pole in Colossians.[68] There is future eschatology in 3: 4, 6, 24[69] and it is in precisely the section we have looked at in some detail, 3: 1–4, that the tension is best seen – συνηγέρθητε (verse 1) with τότε . . . φανερωθήσεσθε (verse 4).[70] It would be difficult to hold that a deutero-Paulinist had brought in more traditional apocalyptic material in verses 3, 4 as an erratic reminiscence which is foreign to what precedes and clashes with it, for verses 1, 2 and 3, 4 are integrally linked (cf. γάρ of verse 3). It is significant too that the references to future eschatology are to be found in the latter part of the letter where Paul's pointed response to the particular Colossian situation is receding.

To the observation that Paul comes perilously close to the position he passionately fights in 1 Corinthians 15 we simply reply that in Colossians his opponents are not the Corinthians and the Colossian philosophy is significantly different from the over-realized eschatology of the Corinthians.[71] In Colossians, where the claim is that certain regulations and techniques must be practised before the heavenly dimension can be experienced, the apostle's rejoinder is a stress on the realized aspect of his eschatology.[72] He cannot allow a new sort of legalistic system of works to grow up as the means of entrance to the heavenly realm, for believers already participate in heavenly life in Christ. The principle of grace is at stake. Any special visions given, such as those the apostle himself received[73] will be purely of grace and not achieved through human effort and techniques, about which people can boast (cf. the visions which puff up in 2: 18). Where grace is at stake Paul emphasizes forgiveness. Nothing need be done to appease hostile powers, for believers' sins and failings have already been forgiven (1: 14; 2: 13; 3: 12), the chirograph against them has been cancelled (2: 14). Against those who were removing the basis of Christian living away from grace and towards legalistic observances, knowledge, visionary experiences, Paul insists that God has *already* done everything necessary in Christ. The philosophy was building from the 'not yet' of salvation, treating the gospel that had been received as insufficient for the Colossians' needs. It should not be surprising that out of great pastoral concern for the Colossians believers the apostle skilfully and emphatically underlines the 'already'.[74]

6

EPHESIANS AND HEAVENLY LIFE IN THE CHURCH AT WORSHIP

1. The life-setting and the heavenly dimension

Ephesians is the letter in the Pauline corpus in which the concept of the heavenly dimension is most pervasive. What kind of a letter Ephesians is and in what sense it is Pauline are matters which are still by no means settled in scholarly discussion. Among recent writers some take the traditional view of Paul as the actual author,[1] while others hold that one of Paul's associates was commissioned to do the writing by the apostle and given a free hand,[2] and still others think it more likely that the author was a member of a later Pauline school writing to meet a situation arising in the churches towards the end of the first century.[3] The difficult decision about authorship is closely linked with the perhaps more decisive question of the letter's genre and purpose. Here again hypotheses are produced which can make a good case either for relating the style and intent of Ephesians to a situation in the life of Paul or to a setting after his death. Yet some decision must be made and here a tentative preference is expressed for a setting in the life of Paul which thus allows for either of the first two options regarding authorship. The issue of authorship obviously cannot be pursued here, but it may be helpful to outline briefly one possible reconstruction of the setting and purpose, concentrating on features which help to explain the predominance of the heavenly dimension in this letter.

Ephesians is in the style of a 'liturgical homily'[4] intended to be read at the worship service of churches in Asia Minor not known personally to Paul on an occasion when there would be new converts baptized and with the design that others would be recalled to the meaning of their baptism. While in Colossians Paul had used the terminology of the syncretistic philosophy in order to combat its teaching, here in Ephesians he employs similar language and concepts in developing a more positive understanding of the gospel which would at the same time serve as a safeguard against the infiltration of syncretism into other churches in the Lycus Valley. The homily thus serves as an answer to the needs of those who were looking for further knowledge and insight but might be tempted to look for these in the wrong place – syncretistic mystery cults – and by the wrong means – legalistic observances and visionary experiences. Paul passes on to these predominantly Gentile converts his insights into the great mystery and significance of God's plan of salvation of which they have become a part.

The Christology of the letter involves an extended concentration on Christ's present exalted state in the heavenlies, which in turn colours references to the status of believers and the Church. Consequently realized eschatology, often formulated in spatial language about heaven, is present in Ephesians to an even greater extent than in Colossians.

Positing a worship-setting for Ephesians helps to explain both its particular stylistic features and the presence of so much realized eschatology. This involves taking seriously the worship forms in which the apostle has framed the first three chapters. He begins with an extended 'berakah' or benediction in 1: 3–14, and moves into thanksgiving and intercession (ἐπὶ τῶν προσευχῶν μου, ἵνα ... verses 16f) which then becomes a eulogy of what God has accomplished in exalting Christ to the heavenly realm (verses 20ff). In chapter 3 Paul's great concern for those who were to receive the letter is made clear by the mention of the posture he adopts for the prayer which follows and which he had been about to begin in 3: 1 – κάμπτω τὰ γόνατά μου πρὸς τὸν πατέρα (3: 14). The prayer ends as a doxology in which glory is ascribed to the God who is present in the exalted Christ and in the Church, and this explicitly worship-orientated section of the letter concludes with an ἀμήν.[5] As J. T. Sanders observes, 'the doxology at the end of ch. 3 is a *closing* liturgical element, just as the blessing and thanksgiving in ch. 1 are opening liturgical elements'.[6] This sequence of eulogy, thanksgiving, intercession, doxology was widespread in Jewish and early Christian prayers and is made the framework of the first half of the letter.[7]

As he composes his liturgical homily Paul himself has been contemplating its great themes of the exalted status of Christ and God's purpose in Christ for the Church and the cosmos and has been caught up in worship of the heavenly Christ. But the letter does not only derive from the apostle's own worship, it also incorporates liturgical material which would be common to the worship of many of the apostle's churches. Though it is unlikely that an actual hymn can be found behind 1: 3–14,[8] the passage certainly has hymnic features.[9] Again 1: 20–23 makes use of credal formulations phrased in exalted poetic language,[10] but whether it incorporates a hymn[11] is difficult to determine. Chapter 2: 4–7 employs terminology from a baptismal liturgy,[12] and there are good reasons for believing 2:

14–18 to be the reworking of a hymn.[13] A similar drawing upon traditional material can also be seen in the second half of the letter where 4: 5f contains confessional formulations likely to have had their origin in the church's worship,[14] where 5: 2 also includes a formulation from the liturgical tradition,[15] and where 5: 14 has long been recognized as a citation from a baptismal hymn. Not only these specific features but the general style of the letter with its Semitic sentence-constructions, its relative clauses, prepositional expressions, series of genitives, and wealth of synonyms points clearly to the formal language of worship. The letter in fact contains instructions regarding Spirit-filled worship (5: 18f) and since it was in worship that the churches would experience most powerfully the presence of their heavenly Lord, there would have been no great discrepancy between the atmosphere of devotion which produced the letter and that in which it was received.

A baptismal occasion may be seen as one of the ingredients in this worship-setting. Dahl believes that the benediction of 1: 3–14 should be connected with baptism,[16] and the language of being 'sealed with the promised Holy Spirit' (cf. also 4: 30) and the change from the first person plural which is used until verse 13 when the second person plural is introduced would both be appropriate if a baptismal charge were in view.[17] The whole of chapter 2 can be seen as an exposition of the meaning of baptism: verses 1–10 provide a confessional summary of the change God has accomplished and the new life he has provided, while verses 11–22 in a midrash on Isaiah 57: 19 urge those who have been baptized to remember their change of status and the heritage into which they have now entered. The exhortation to lead a life worthy of this calling (4: 1 – 6: 20) includes the confessional material with its reference to 'one baptism' (4: 5), the language of 'putting off' and 'putting on' (4: 22–4), the citation from the baptismal hymn (5: 14), the language of 5: 26 – 'having cleansed her by the washing of water with the word' and the homily of 6: 10–16 with its exhortation to 'put on' the armour of God. Again such features suggest a possible baptismal setting.[18]

The liturgical and baptismal elements account for the formal style of the letter which carries through to 6: 20. The only personal note is attached as the homily is given the form of a letter (6: 21, 22) and even here the listeners are directed to Tychicus for news of the apostle. Within this formal context, and particularly if we allow some freedom to a loyal associate of Paul's as amanuensis, the references to Paul's ministry and to the other apostles (cf. 3: 1–13), which would seem out of place in Paul's more usual style of letter writing, need no longer appear quite so strange. The baptismal setting also influences strongly the letter's eschatological perspective since 'for Paul, baptism was a sacrament of "realized eschatology"'.[19] As in Colossians where baptismal motivation also figures prominently, the apostle employs baptism to show believers the riches of that which they have already been given by God in Christ.

This possible reconstruction takes seriously the letter's close links with Colossians (cf. Col. 4: 7ff with Eph. 6: 21f) and views the former as having been written not long after the latter. While Colossians had a specific teaching in view, Ephesians is written against the background of the more general concerns of the syncretism of the area and its warnings against false teaching are correspondingly more general (cf. 4: 14, 17ff; 5: 6). The polemical thrust of Colossians has been replaced by the stylized homily and more positive worship-setting of Ephesians. There has been time for the apostle both to polish some of the phraseology of the former letter and to re-apply some of the terminology of the syncretism in order to suit his purposes. Aware of the attractions of syncretism for many of the converts, Paul in Colossians 2: 1–3 had expressed his desire to encourage the churches of the area to have 'all the riches of assured understanding and the knowledge of God's mystery, Christ, in whom are hid all the treasures of wisdom and knowledge'. Ephesians provides such encouragement as the apostle unfolds God's purposes in Christ. Were some in these churches attracted by the prospect of further knowledge and insight into mysteries in order to attain the fullness of salvation? Paul reminds them that he, the apostle to the Gentiles, has been given insight into the mystery of God's plan and been charged not to save this for an initiated élite but to make it known to *all* people (3: 3ff, 9f; cf. 1: 9f). As he expounds more fully the revelation of this mystery in Christ and the Church and its relationship to the cosmos, it is with the intent that those who hear the homily will attain 'to the knowledge of the Son of God, to mature manhood, to the measure of the stature of the fulness of Christ' (4: 13).

Other concerns of the Colossian syncretism, such as freedom from hostile cosmic powers and access to the upper realm and to the fullness of the divine presence, also form a major part of the backdrop for the development of Paul's themes in Ephesians. His insistence throughout that heaven and earth are linked together is aimed at the same sort of cosmological dualism we found reflected in the Colossian philosophy. The world-view of Ephesians 'opposes itself to prevalent notions of a dualistic kind concerning the universe ... there is no room for the idea of two spheres within one universe, mutually excluding each other and separated from one another'.[20] Just as in Colossians Paul had seen that the whole matter of grace was at stake in the quest for visionary experience of the heavenly realm, so here in Ephesians grace is a keynote as he dwells on the believer's salvation and its heavenly dimension (cf. especially 1: 5, 6; 2: 4–10; 3: 2; 4: 7). Syncretism has no prerogative on a cosmic perspective. As Paul shows the cosmic dimensions of the gospel, however, he makes clear that its salvation remains rooted in history, especially in Christ's death (1: 7; 2: 13–16; 5: 2, 25) and that the cosmic unity it proclaims is in one sense an exclusive affair, for it is only 'in Christ' (cf. 1: 10). The Church is to be a pledge of this ultimate unity and more than in Colossians Paul expands on the theme of the Church since he is determined that syncretism should not obscure the Church's significance. Gentile converts are not just members of a new sect whose teachings can be assimilated into syncretism's cosmological interests but they are members of the Church which because of its union with its heavenly Lord has its own most important role in God's plan. They are not simply members of a local congregation but part of a greater whole, chosen in Christ before the foundation of the world (1: 4), with a great historical heritage in and links to the commonwealth of Israel (2: 11ff), and taking its place on both an earthly and a heavenly level. Paul's focus on the Church also contrasts strongly with the individualistic emphasis which syncretism tended to foster as it centered interest on the individual's place in the cosmos and his or her search for salvation and insight through special experiences of the heavenly realm.

Positing a general syncretistic context means that again the Hellenistic-Jewish thought world is likely to provide some of the closest parallels for many concepts in Ephesians,[21] and could also account for the fact that some writers have emphasized an almost exclusively Jewish (with particular reference to Qumran) and non-Gnostic background,[22] while others have looked to Gnosticism for the explanation of the letter's concepts.[23] The background for Ephesians is part of the religious syncretism which had assimilated many Jewish ideas, especially those from esoteric and apocalyptic branches of Judaism, and which contributed so much to the development of later Gnosticism.

2. Blessing for a heavenly and cosmic salvation (1: 3, 9f)

The theme of the extended 'berakah' of 1: 3–14 is God's eternal purpose in history and its realization in Christ and his Church. This can be seen as the theme of the whole letter so that the benediction provides the basis for the development which follows. This applies also in regard to Ephesians' treatment of the concept of heaven. The benediction introduces the recurring formula ἐν τοῖς ἐπουρανίοις (verse 3) and highlights the unity of heaven and earth to be accomplished in Christ (verses 9, 10).

The God and Father of the Lord Jesus Christ is pronounced blessed, because he has first blessed believers with every spiritual blessing 'in the heavenlies' in Christ. What follows can be seen as an elaboration of some of these blessings. ἐν τοῖς ἐπουρανίοις is one of three adverbial phrases which modifies ὁ εὐλογήσας ἡμᾶς though it also tends to qualify the whole clause. In this way not only is the sphere of blessing 'in the heavenlies' but the recipients of the blessing (ἡμᾶς) are also connected with the heavenly realm (cf. also 2: 6).[24]

An examination of ἐν τοῖς ἐπουρανίοις in each of its occurrences (1: 3, 20; 2: 6; 3: 10; 6: 12) indicates that it is used as a formula which retains the same meaning throughout and that the meaning which is most appropriate to all five contexts is a local one.[25] These references give no indication whether the author had a nominative form of the phrase in mind. Whether this was οἱ ἐπουράνιοι (to be completed by τόποι) or whether it was τὰ ἐπουράνια, it appears to be an inclusive summary term, whose gender makes no difference in assigning a local or non-local meaning. The origin of the expression must remain uncertain,[26] though it could well have been a traditional formulation from the Church's worship which Paul takes over for his own use in this letter.[27]

R. M. Pope believes that the references in 3: 10 and 6: 12 are local and Jewish, while the other references are spiritualized and Platonic.[28] For H. Odeberg, who has provided one of the most comprehensive and influential treatments of the formula, the heavenlies are not the equivalent of heaven in its denotation as the celestial regions in distinction from other parts of the universe but represent the whole of spiritual reality in which the Church participates and the realm of the Church in Christ.[29] Most telling against this hypothesis is that it ignores the presence of evil powers in the heavenlies (cf. 3: 10; 6: 12). Käsemann[30] and Conzelmann[31] posit an affinity of the phrase with Gnostic thought, while for Schlier, via Gnostic terminology, it takes on an existentialist significance as a transcendental dimension of human existence which challenges a person to decision.[32] We hold that ἐν τοῖς ἐπουρανίοις is closely related to ἐν τοῖς οὐρανοῖς and over against the above interpretations believe that though Paul is speaking to Hellenistic cosmological interests, he does so from his own framework and that consequently his use of the formula can be most adequately understood in the light of the OT and Jewish conception of heaven.[33] Paul's view of heaven was derived ultimately from the opening statement of the OT. 'In the beginning God created the heavens and the earth' (Gen. 1: 1). Created reality had two major parts. That part known as the heavens could be thought of in terms of the atmospheric heaven (e.g. Ps. 147: 8) or firmament (e.g. Gen. 1: 7, 14). As the upper part of the cosmos it also came to stand for the dwelling-place of God, pointing beyond its own createdness to the divine transcendence (e.g. Ps. 2: 4). Not only so, but the upper limits of the firmament were regarded as concealing a presently invisible created spiritual order (e.g. 2 Kgs. 6: 17; Job. 1: 6; Zech. 3: 1). As we noted in our discussion of 2 Corinthians 12 it is probable that Paul was not so much dependent on specific apocalyptic or Rabbinic speculations on the number of heavens as on this relatively unsophisticated OT perspective. Here heaven had a priority as the upper and controlling element and yet in its created aspect it was involved in God's plan for the ages, for in Jahweh's acts of judgment the heavens as well as the earth are shaken (cf. Isa. 51: 6; Amos 8: 9; Hag. 2: 6) and Isaiah 65: 17 and 66: 22 can speak of the creation of a new heaven and a new earth, pointing to cosmic renewal. In apocalyptic Judaism the evil powers in heaven are judged (cf. 1 Enoch 16: 1–4; 21: 1–6; 89: 59f) before the commencement of this coming new age with its new heaven (cf. 1 Enoch 91: 16). Since Paul also shared this two age eschatological structure which incorporated both heaven and earth in each age and since Jesus Christ as Lord was central in his particular version of this structure, both heaven and earth took on new significance as they were related to the Christ event in his thinking. In Ephesians then it would not be surprising if ἐν τοῖς ἐπουρανίοις were to have reference to heaven as a distinct part of the created universe but one which retains its concealing relation to the spiritual world and to God himself, and thus also its aspect of incomprehensibility. The reference is to this heaven as it takes its place in the cosmic drama of redemption, that is, in that act of the drama which Christ has inaugurated by his resurrection and exaltation.[34] Since Christ is central in God's plan for heaven, the Church 'in Christ' also plays a vital part in this realm. As we shall see, 3: 10 and 6: 12 take their place naturally within this definition of the formula, for heaven is still involved in this present evil age with the consequence that there will remain hostile powers in heaven until the consummation brings in the fullness of the new age with its reconciled and renewed cosmos.

Notwithstanding the new significance heaven takes on for Paul, it does not lose all local connotations.[35] He is speaking to the cosmological concerns of the letter's recipients and showing that the blessing of salvation they have received from God does in fact link them to the heavenly realm. As we have seen, the blessings of salvation are connected with heaven elsewhere in Paul (e.g. 2 Cor. 5: 1, 2; Col. 1: 5). Although these heavenly blessings will only be fully realized in the age to come, through the Christ event the eschatological has become a present heavenly reality for believers. Thus ἐν τοῖς ἐπουρανίοις in 1: 3 has reference not to future blessings viewed as treasure stored up in heaven but to benefits which belong to believers now. Again such an assertion is related to the apocalyptic view-

point which saw aspects of future salvation as present realities in heaven
(cf. 4 Ezra 7: 14, 83; 13: 18; 2 Bar. 21: 12; 48: 49; 52: 7).

As in Colossians, it is made clear that the link with heaven is not one
achieved by human techniques; it is through Christ. God has blessed
believers with every spiritual blessing in the heavenlies ἐν Χριστῷ. Paul's
'berakah' is clearly set off from its Jewish models as this phrase or a
variation of it occurs repeatedly. It is often asserted that the use of the
phrase in Ephesians is distinct from that in the genuine Paulines,[36] and
sometimes such a comparison presupposes that ἐν Χριστῷ has a set meaning in the earlier letters. The work of Büchsel, Neugebauer and Bouttier,[37]
who emphasize that the phrase has a great variety of force which must be
derived from the context in which it is found, provides a necessary cor-
rective. Often it is used instrumentally but a local connotation, in which
'Christ is the "place" in whom believers are and in whom salvation is',[38]
cannot be excluded. This concept of the incorporation of many in one
representative head together with the use of ἐν can be seen in the LXX in
regard to other figures, such as Abraham (Gen. 12: 3) and Isaac (Gen. 21:
12), and in Paul in regard to Adam (1 Cor. 15: 22). In Ephesians the use
of the phrase is accommodated to the letter's liturgical style and it takes
on a formal quality with a predominantly instrumental force.[39] Its significance is not however always *merely* instrumental and in places the more
intensive incorporative force is retained.[40] Thus here in 1: 3 it is not only
that believers experience the blessings of the heavenlies through Christ's
agency but because they are incorporated into the exalted Christ as their
representative who is himself in the heavenlies.[41] In designating the benefits of the heavenly realm as 'spiritual', Paul indicates also that it is
through the Spirit that these benefits are realized (cf. also verses 13, 14
where through participation in the Spirit, who is the guarantee of full
future possession, the believer's inheritance can be appropriated now).
In praising God for the access to heaven the letter's recipients already
have, the apostle shows by his use of ἐν τοῖς ἐπουρανίοις that he sees
heaven in the perspective of the new age brought about in Christ and for
this reason he links its blessings so closely to the Spirit of that age.

The blessings of salvation include the making known of the mystery of
God's will, including his plan for history which embraces the heavenly
realm (1: 9, 10). Again the concerns of the letter's recipients have influenced Paul's formulation of the blessings. Those who believe fullness of
salvation will mean insight into mysteries are shown in this way that the
mystery of God's will has already been made known, that it is not dis-
covered by special techniques but is in accordance with God's grace
demonstrated in Christ (κατὰ τὴν εὐδοκίαν αὐτοῦ ἣν προέθετο ἐν αὐτῷ –

1: 9), and that its content reverses the cosmological framework of the mysteries so highly esteemed by syncretistic groups. Instead of the dualism of the sort we noted in Colossae where heaven and earth are two separated realms, where the lower realm of matter is seen as evil, and where people are under the dominance of heavenly powers, this mystery involves the bringing together and summing up of heaven and earth in Christ.

In responding to syncretism's concern with mysteries Paul draws on the rich Semitic background of the term 'mystery'.[42] As in apocalyptic Paul's use of the term is bound up with aspects of God's plan not yet manifested in history, with God's ordering of history (εἰς οἰκονομίαν τοῦ πληρώματος τῶν καιρῶν - 1: 10), and has both eschatological and cosmic dimensions. In apocalyptic such mysteries are already prepared in heaven so that the apocalyptist can have knowledge of them, but they will only be revealed at the end of history (cf. for example 1 Enoch 9: 6; 103: 2; 4 Ezr. 14: 5).[43] At Qumran however mysteries could also refer to events which were already being realized in the community (cf. for example 1QS XI, 5-8 where the community's participation in the angelic assembly is seen as one of God's marvellous mysteries) and this is true of the concept of mystery which the apostle develops here in Ephesians.[44] The content of the mystery is supplied by the clause ἀνακεφαλαιώσασθαι τὰ πάντα ἐν τῷ Χριστῷ. It is beyond the scope of this study to review the various interpretations this has been given.[45] In elucidating the significance of the aorist middle infinitive however it must be borne in mind that it is derived from κεφάλαιον not κεφαλή. κεφάλαιον refers to the main point, the sum or the summary (cf. Acts 22: 28; Heb. 8: 1) and κεφαλαιόω and ἀνακεφαλαιόω have as their basic meaning 'to sum up' or 'to summarize'. It is noteworthy that Paul uses ἀνακεφαλαιοῦσθαι with this sense in Romans 13: 9 where love is thought of as the comprehensive command which integrates the others, bringing them together under one focal point. In Ephesians 1: 10 by analogy Christ exercises a similar function with respect to the cosmos. Since later in the chapter this relation to the cosmos is seen as one of headship (cf. 1: 22), it is justifiable to link this with 1: 10 and see the summing up of τὰ πάντα as taking place in its subjection to this Head.[46] The concept of 'summing up' involves an element of recapitulation as points already made are drawn together in a conclusion and it is likely that this is something of the force of the prefix ἀνα - indicating a restoration of harmony, with Christ as the point of re-integration. In the Colossians hymn a similar thought had been expressed in terms of reconciliation (1: 20). Both passages presuppose that the cosmos had been plunged into disintegration on account of sin and that it is God's purpose to restore its original harmony in Christ.[47]

The elaboration τὰ ἐπὶ τοῖς οὐρανοῖς καὶ τὰ ἐπὶ τῆς γῆς indicates that
τὰ πάντα is to be taken in its widest sense of all things and all beings,
that is the cosmos as a whole and not just humanity.[48] As we have seen,
such a twofold division of the universe is common to the Jewish world-
view and τὰ ἐπὶ τοῖς οὐρανοῖς are mentioned to emphasize the point made
explicitly at the end of the chapter that no hostile heavenly powers can
thwart God's purpose in Christ.[49] Spatial (cosmic) and temporal (eschatological) categories are combined in Paul's exposition of the mystery. God
has ordered history so as to bring about the fullness of the times and in
this period of fulfilment has exalted Christ to heaven as cosmic Lord,
thereby ensuring an inseparable connection between heaven and earth.
This summing up of the cosmos in Christ has its 'already' and its 'not yet'
aspects. 'Though the dénouement of the redemptive drama has already
been determined, its manifestation awaits the end.'[50]

It is from within the context of the Church that the harmonious cosmic
consummation is viewed, so that the Church which participates in the
benediction is brought to realize that the salvation with which it has been
blessed centres in the same comprehensive Christ in whom God is working
to restore all things. Instead of insecurity and insignificance in the face of
cosmic issues the effect of the blessing is to produce confidence in the God
whose plan of salvation embraces everything in heaven and on earth and to
inspire those who echo it to play their part in God's administration of the
fullness of the times. Believers already have all and more than all that
syncretism can offer. This has become theirs through their having been
blessed with every spiritual blessing (verse 3) and having been sealed with
the promised Holy Spirit (verse 13), terminology appropriate to the
occasion of baptism.[51] Baptism speaks of all that God has given in Christ
and for the apostle the only appropriate response to this overwhelming
grace is the 'berakah' he has formulated in 1: 3–14.

3. The exalted Christ, the Church and the cosmos (1: 20ff)

While 1: 3–14 blesses God for the great salvation he has accomplished, 1:
15–23 is a prayer that the letter's recipients might be enlightened and
might appreciate just how great this salvation is. Paul wants them to know
that their hope includes participation in the glory of the inheritance
among the holy ones (1: 18). As in Colossians 1: 12 salvation is seen to
include this heavenly aspect of fellowship with the angels.[52] The apostle
also wants believers to know the greatness of God's power and the prayer
piles together a number of expressions for power in verse 19 before asserting that the extent of this power has been demonstrated both by the resurrection of Christ and by the exalted position Christ now occupies by virtue
of his enthronement. As he dwells on Christ's heavenly status Paul makes

use of credal formulations about Christ's resurrection and exaltation and develops these with reference to the victory over the powers and to the significance for the Church.

God has made Christ sit at his right hand in the heavenlies (verse 20). The mention of the session at God's right hand makes use of course of Psalm 110: 1, a psalm which may well originally have been employed as an enthronement psalm for the king. In the OT Jahweh's right hand is represented as the position of favour (cf. Ps. 80: 18; Jer. 22: 24), of victory (cf. Ps. 20: 6; 44: 3; 118: 5, 6; Isa. 41: 10) and of power (cf. Exod. 15: 6; Ps. 89: 13; Isa. 48: 13). Prior to the NT the imagery of Psalm 110: 1 had already been given a Messianic interpretation and in the early church came to be applied frequently to Jesus.[53] Paul draws on it here to evoke Christ's position of supreme favour and honour, his place of victory and power associated with his heavenly exaltation. This symbolic significance of 'sitting at the right hand' does not mean that ἐν τοῖς ἐπουρανίοις which accompanies it cannot be thought of as local.[54] The functions of the two phrases are not to be equated, for the former as a symbol of sovereignty is posited only of Christ, not of believers (cf. 2: 6 where despite the other parallels with 1: 20 ἐν δεξιᾷ αὐτοῦ is omitted). Here, as in other places in the NT (cf. Acts 2: 34; Heb. 8: 1), a reference to Psalm 110: 1 is juxtaposed with a local setting of heaven so that while on the one hand Paul speaks of Christ in spatial terms, on the other hand his use of an expression such as ἐν δεξιᾷ αὐτοῦ indicates that he viewed Christ as also breaking through the bounds of such categories (cf. also 4: 10). The fact that Christ has been exalted to heaven, where he now is (cf. 6: 9), is crucial for an understanding of Paul's perspective on heaven in this letter, for it is what has happened to Christ that is determinative for the believer and for the Church in their relationship to the heavenly realm.

Paul shows that Christ cannot be viewed as on the same level as other angelic powers in the cosmic hierarchy, as appears to have been the case in the Colossian syncretism. In exalting Christ God has placed him far above all other heavenly powers (verse 21). The rhetorical flourish - καὶ παντὸς ὀνόματος ὀνομαζομένου οὐ μόνον ἐν τῷ αἰῶνι τούτῳ ἀλλὰ καὶ ἐν τῷ μέλλοντι - underlines the universality of Christ's rule over any imaginable cosmic forces and brings home to believers that they have no possible justification for living any longer under the domination of such hostile powers. The explicit mention of the apocalyptic two age structure provides the only reference in the Pauline corpus to both ages and again shows temporal categories in close connection with spatial ones.[55] Christ's lordship extends over both this evil age and the age to come which has begun with Christ's resurrection but which is still to be revealed fully.[56]

So concerned is Paul to emphasize the supremacy of Christ's heavenly status that he continues to heap up phrases that might be considered redundant. God has put all things under his feet and made him the head over all things (verse 22) and he fills all in all (verse 23). The first of these assertions cites Psalm 8: 6 which itself recalls Genesis 1: 26-8 and honours humanity in particular as created in God's image to exercise dominion over the created order. Paul applies this concept to Christ as the last Adam and in the process of application the cosmic dimension of humanity's dominion becomes explicit, for πάντα has the same scope as τὰ πάντα in 1: 10 so that the whole universe, heaven and earth, angels and people, has now been subordinated to the heavenly man. The absence of the article before πάντα in κεφαλὴν ὑπὲρ πάντα does not mean that this is not a reference to the cosmos,[57] but is to be explained by the fact that Paul is simply taking up the language of the psalm citation in order to elaborate on its significance. By virtue of his position of supremacy in the heavenlies Christ fills the universe - . . . τοῦ τὰ πάντα ἐν πᾶσιν πληρουμένου. These six words have been called 'an unsolved enigma'[58] but our attempt at interpretation takes πληρουμένου as middle with an active sense,[59] τὰ πάντα as its object in the sense of the cosmos (cf. verses 10, 22) and ἐν πᾶσιν as meaning 'in every respect'. There is no indication that the apostle thought of this filling in a physical sense in the way that the primeval man of the Gnostic myth is said to fill the cosmos. Rather the closest parallels are to be found in LXX Jeremiah 23: 24 where God is said to fill heaven and earth and in the cosmological terminology of Philo where on many occasions God can be said to fill τὰ πάντα (e.g. *De Post. Caini* 30; *De Sacrif.* 67f; *Leg. Alleg.* I, 4; *De Gig.* 47; *De Vit. Mos.* II, 238).[60] The heavenly Christ completely fills all things in terms of his sovereign rule as he directs them to their divinely appointed goal, to the restoration of their meaning and harmony (cf. 1: 10; 4: 10). In 1 Corinthians 15: 27f Psalm 8: 6 is cited in the same way as here in Ephesians 1: 22 to underline Christ's cosmic lordship, but whereas there this lordship is to be exercised at the end of history, here the perspective is one of realized eschatology as in the context of worship in the presence of the exalted Lord the end is anticipated.

One of the most significant features of this passage is the status that is given to the Church in its first explicit mention in the letter - καὶ αὐτὸν ἔδωκεν κεφαλὴν ὑπὲρ πάντα τῇ ἐκκλησίᾳ (1: 22b). Christ as cosmic Lord has been given to the Church. Paul's purpose here is not to assert Christ's lordship over the Church as a parallel to his lordship over the cosmos but to subordinate the latter to the former. All the supremacy and power God has given to Christ he has given to be used on behalf of the Church and in this way the Church is seen to have a special role in God's purposes for the cosmos. Instead of seeing themselves as an insignificant new sect, believers are shown that they are part of the universal Church which can only be truly understood when seen in relation to its heavenly Lord who exercises all power on its behalf. Because of Christ's exalted status the Church can confront the powers and the whole universe has been opened up as its sphere of witness (cf. 3: 10).

Christ is the head over the cosmos, but it is only the Church which can be called his body (1: 23). In the earlier letters, when this metaphor is used, it is the crucified body of Christ which is in view (cf. 1 Cor. 10: 16f). Here in Ephesians the focus on the risen and exalted Christ colours the reference to his body and paves the way for the remarkable declaration of the glory of this body – it is his fullness.[61] We take πλήρωμα as in apposition to σῶμα rather than αὐτόν which is twelve words earlier and would make a very awkward grammatical construction. The Church is the fullness of the heavenly Christ in the sense that it is filled by him rather than that it completes him. The passive sense of πλήρωμα is certainly not impossible and attestation can be provided for this meaning from, for example, LXX Psalm 23: 1; *Corpus Hermeticum* 6: 4; 12: 15; 16: 3; Philo, *De Praem. et Poen.* 65. It appears that what in the syncretism of the time was a cosmological term, probably denoting the divine presence stretching from heaven to earth in a series of emanations, has in both Colossians and Ephesians been put to the apostle's own use. In Colossians 1: 19; 2: 9, 10 Paul declares that in Christ is the fullness of God and that the Church comes to fullness of life in him. Here in Ephesians the concept is developed so that the Church can actually be called his fullness. As Christ is filled with God (Col. 1: 19; 2: 9), so his body is filled with Christ (Eph. 1: 23).[62] Although Christ fills all things in terms of his sovereign rule, he fills the Church in a special sense with his gifts and grace (cf. 4: 7ff), so that only the Church *is* his fullness. God has exalted Christ to heaven and the Church enjoys all the benefits of its relationship to its heavenly Lord. Those attracted by syncretism's claims to provide access by various means to the fullness of the divine presence should realize therefore first that that presence dwells in Christ and through his exaltation and rule fills heaven and earth, and then that it is in the fellowship of the Church that this fullness is to be experienced. The significance of the Church's place in the cosmos is that as Christ's fullness it provides the present focus for and demonstration of that presence which now fills the cosmos in a hidden way but which will do so openly and completely.

4. The believer, baptism and the heavenly realm (2: 5, 6)

In his summary of the new life the apostle can say that believers have been made alive together with Christ, raised up with him and made to sit with him in the heavenly places in Christ Jesus (2: 5, 6). The almost exact parallel between the first two of these assertions and those to be found in Colossians 2: 12, 13 where baptism is explicitly mentioned and the link between the third assertion and that in Colossians 3: 1f, for which we have already argued a baptismal context, provide very strong grounds for seeing baptism as the occasion in view here also.[63] The baptismal terminology has however been adapted to the apostle's earlier description of Christ's exaltation so that there are parallels between 1: 19f and 2: 5f. The same divine power is shown to be at work in the exaltation of believers as in that of Christ (2: 4ff cf. 1: 19), both Christ and believers have been raised from the dead and set in heavenly places (the compound verbs συνήγειρεν and συνεκάθισεν of 2: 5f recall the simple verbs ἐγείρας and καθίσας of 1: 20), and ἐν τοῖς αἰῶσιν τοῖς ἐπερχομένοις of 2: 7 balances ἐν τῷ μέλλοντι of 1: 21. In this way the apostle's ecclesiology consciously reflects his Christology. But more than this is involved, for it is only because believers are ἐν Χριστῷ Ἰησοῦ that it can be said that God has done for them what he has already done for Christ. The σύν- compounds together with the phrase ἐν Χριστῷ Ἰησοῦ underline this intimate union between Christ and believers and the statement that believers have been made to sit with Christ in the heavenlies spells out the implications of this relationship of incorporation in Christ in their most developed form in the Pauline corpus.[64] In fact Ephesians 2: 6 only makes explicit what is implicit in Colossians 3: 1ff where the believer is to seek τὰ ἄνω because Christ is above and the believer's life is hid with Christ in God. In both passages Paul is speaking to the concerns of those attracted by the claims of syncretistic teachings to provide access to the heavenly realm, and indicating to believers that their baptism signifies that such an experience of the heavenly realm is already theirs by virtue of their union with Christ. In Ephesians it is union with Christ in his exaltation to heaven which is highlighted. The Colossian philosophy had threatened the principle of grace at the heart of Paul's gospel and here in Ephesians Paul is at pains to emphasize that the believer's session with Christ in the heavenlies and indeed his or her whole salvation is all of grace (cf. 2: 5, 7, 8). Syncretism with its offer of fuller salvation through visions of heaven and knowledge of heavenly secrets has been outdone; God has already accomplished everything necessary for the believer's full salvation – 'you have been saved by grace' (2: 5, 8). The apostle's language in these verses and his use of the perfect tense of σῴζειν[65] is not so much an expression of 'ecclesiastical triumphalism' as an attempt to share his wonder at the immensity of God's grace in providing a total salvation which does not need to be supplemented.

We find such language echoed and ascribed to Paul in the Christian

Gnostic text of the Epistle to Rheginos – 'But then as the Apostle said, we suffered with him, and we arose with him, and we went to heaven with him.'[66] However this later Gnostic use of the combination of Romans 8: 17 and Ephesians 2: 5, 6 cannot help us in any search for background for Paul's concept of believers being seated with Christ in the heavenlies. Although the Gnosticism which developed from the sort of syncretism Paul has an eye on in this letter could speak of the heavenly journey of the soul in liberation from the material world in similar language – ὁ δὲ ἄνθρωπος καὶ εἰς τὸν οὐρανὸν ἀναβαίνει (*Corp. Herm.* X, 25) so that the initiate then perceives – ἐν οὐρανῷ εἰμί (*Corp. Herm.* XIII, 11b),[67] it is unlikely to have been the influence on Paul himself.[68] Perhaps associated ideas from his Jewish background shed greater light on how Paul's thought has developed in his attempt to speak to the converts' cosmological interests. The idea of the righteous entering into eschatological dominion and life and sitting on heavenly thrones was fairly widespread in apocalyptic writings (cf. Dan. 7: 22, 27; Wisd. Sol. 3: 8; 5: 15, 16; 1 Enoch 108: 12; Apoc. Elijah 37: 3, 4; Test. Job 33: 3–5; Rev. 3: 21; Asc. Isa. 9: 18). Closer to the realized eschatology of Ephesians 2: 6 however is the Qumran community's self-understanding that they as the elect on earth already experienced the heavenly realm and formed a liturgical community with the inhabitants of heaven.[69]

> I thank Thee, O Lord, for Thou has redeemed my soul from the Pit, and from the Hell of Abaddon. Thou hast raised me up to everlasting height . . . Thou has cleansed a perverse spirit of great sin that it may stand with the host of the Holy Ones, and that it may enter into community with the congregation of the Sons of Heaven (1QH III, 19–22 cf. also 1QH XI, 10–12).

The present experience of the heavenly world and fellowship with the angels has associations not only with Ephesians 2: 6 but also with 2: 18, 19 with its concepts of access and of fellow citizenship with the holy ones. At Qumran, as here in Ephesians, this realized eschatology was connected with entry into the community and celebrated in liturgy. At Qumran the place of future fellowship with the angels was thought of not only as heaven or the heavenly sanctuary but also as the eschatological temple (cf. 4QFl I, 4; 1QSb IV, 25), and since the community understood itself as the eschatological temple (cf. 1QS VIII, 4ff; IX, 3ff) it could hold that participation with the angels in worship was already taking place.[70] What is of course distinctive about heaven being the place of the Church's life in Paul's thought is that this is totally dependent on his focus on Christ in heaven and the believer's union with him and therefore participation in the life and reign which is his in the heavenlies. Baptism proclaims that this union has taken place and the church at worship is the context in which believers are most aware of this intimate fellowship with their Lord and therefore of their place in the heavenlies. As he speaks to Hellenistic cosmological concerns and stresses that salvation has already been accomplished, Paul underlines the spatial implications of this fact.

Just as this perspective in which believers already share Christ's heavenly rule over the powers should be balanced against that in which they are still involved in battle with the powers (6: 12ff), so the spatial elements of 2: 6 should be balanced against the temporal elements in 2: 7. God has accomplished the believer's resurrection and heavenly session in Christ in order that he might display the immensity of his grace ἐν τοῖς αἰῶσιν τοῖς ἐπερχομένοις. αἰών should be taken in its temporal and spatial connotation of the duration of the world rather than as a personal force and the plural is to be explained as owing to the liturgical influence of the formulae for eternity.[71] In this way although God has accomplished the believer's heavenly session, this remains hidden and will only be truly displayed for the profound act of grace which it is in the age to come. This reinforces the parallel between this passage and Colossians 3: 1–4 where the believer's life is also at present hidden with Christ in heaven to be revealed in its glory only at the parousia.

5. The Church as the heavenly temple (2: 19ff)

Ephesians 2: 19ff concludes the section which begins with 2: 11 and in which the apostle reminds Gentile converts of the heritage into which they have entered since through Christ's death the barrier between Jew and Gentile has been removed and one new entity has been created. As the passage develops however there are hints that behind the historical Jew–Gentile motif there is also a cosmological heaven–earth motif. Perhaps the best explanation for the dual perspective which emerges is that which sees behind verses 14–18 a hymn celebrating Christ as the bringer of cosmic peace, the reconciler of heaven and earth as the two parts of the divided universe. This hymn has been reworked by the apostle to fit his theme of the reconciliation of Jew and Gentile in one new body.[72] Then from verse 17 onwards the heavenly perspective, from which the apostle has already been viewing the Church earlier in the letter, is combined with that which sees the Gentiles being brought near, culminating in the image of the temple.

It is the exalted heavenly Christ who has come and preached peace to those far off and those near (verse 17), and this he has done by his Spirit and through his apostolic messengers. Through him access to the Father in heaven has been provided for both Jews and Gentiles. Such access is no longer confined to a specific locality such as the temple nor is it prevented by hostile powers but rather this access of believers on earth to the Father in heaven is seen to be available through the Spirit - ἐν ἑνὶ πνεύματι (verse 18).

The 'strangers' theme of verse 12 is picked up again in verse 19 but this time the Gentiles are viewed not so much in relation to Israel and her covenants as to the heavenly realm, for they have become fellow citizens with the angels. The interpretation of τῶν ἁγίων as Jewish Christians has much to be said for it (cf. Pauline usage in the context of the collection - Rom. 15: 25, 26, 31; 1 Cor. 16: 1; 2 Cor. 8: 4; 9: 1, 12)[73] but that which sees a reference to the angels, to the inhabitants of the heavenly realm, is still more compelling.[74] We have already encountered ἅγιοι as angels in Colossians 1: 12 and Ephesians 1: 18 and again there are strong parallels in the Qumran writings (cf. 1QS XI, 7f where the concept of fellowship with the angels is closely linked to that of the community as the temple, cf. also 1QH III, 21-3; VI, 10-14; 1QM XII, 1f). Paul has made use of the concept of the believer's attachment to the heavenly city in Galatians 4: 26 and the writer to the Hebrews brings this idea together with that of fellowship with the angels in a way which would correspond to the reference here in Ephesians 2: 19 (cf. Heb. 12: 22 - 'you have come to Mount Zion and to the city of the living God, the heavenly Jerusalem, and to innumerable angels in festal gathering').

In verses 20-22 the temple emerges as the predominant image. The Qumran community had seen itself as the true spiritual temple in contrast to the corrupt cultus in Jerusalem (cf. for example 1QS VIII, 4-10; IX, 5f) and in his earlier letters Paul had applied the temple image both to the body of the individual believer (1 Cor. 6: 19) and to the Christian community (1 Cor. 3: 16f; 2 Cor. 6: 16). In OT prophecy the temple in Jerusalem was to be the universal temple to which in the end time all nations would come to worship and to pray (e.g. Isa. 56: 6, 7). In this context in Ephesians, where Gentiles are being reminded of the heritage into which they have entered, the temple imagery should be seen against this OT background and therefore as having eschatological significance. Through Christ Gentiles have been brought near, given access and in fact have become part of the temple of the Church, the new place in which God supremely manifests his presence (cf. verse 22).

Temple imagery could have not only eschatological but also cosmic connotations. One does not have to turn only to Gnostic literature to find such significance attached to the temple.[75] In the OT and in apocalyptic Jahweh's earthly abode in the temple was seen as the counterpart of his heavenly abode and after the exile the hope of the divine presence in the eschatological temple was increasingly transferred to the transcendental realm with its heavenly temple and heavenly Jerusalem (cf. Wisd. Sol. 9: 8; 1 Enoch 90: 29; 2 Bar. 4: 2–6; Test. Dan 5: 12, 13; Asc. Isa. 7: 10). In Rabbinic thought not only was the earthly temple a counterpart of the heavenly (cf. Gen. R. 55: 7; Ex. R. 33: 4) but via the concept of the sacred rock or stone the temple was also considered as the connection between heaven and earth, the gate to heaven.[76] At Qumran the link between the elect community on earth and the inhabitants of heaven was an intrinsic part of the temple symbolism, for example, 'God . . . has caused them to inherit the lot of the Holy Ones. He has joined their assembly to the Sons of Heaven to be a Council of the Community, a foundation of the Building of Holiness, an eternal Plantation throughout all ages to come.' (1QS XI, 7f). The close parallels in the Qumran writings and the heavenly perspective on the church earlier in this letter make it likely that the temple image here in Ephesians 2 also carries cosmic connotations.[77] That the new temple has a heavenly dimension is given even greater weight by the reference to ἀκρογωνιαῖος in verse 20. In the building in which the apostles and prophets form the foundations, the top stone is seen to be the exalted Christ.

Whether the cornerstone is the foundation stone or the crowning stone of the edifice is of course a disputed point. Jeremias has written several times on this issue and holds that the cornerstone is the final stone of the building which was probably set over the gate. The evidence he adduces for this meaning of the word is to be found in Psalm 118: 22 in Symmachus; LXX 2 Kings 25: 17 where it is used for the head of a pillar; Testament of Solomon 22: 7 and 23: 2–4 which depict the completion of Solomon's temple: Hippolytus, *Elenchos* 5: 7, 35; Tertullian, *Adv. Marc.* 3: 7; Aphraates, *Hom.* 1: 6f and the Peshitta which describes the stone of Isaiah 28: 16 as the 'head of the wall'.[78] In the light of the exalted position ascribed to Christ earlier in the letter (cf. 1: 19ff), the special emphasis on Christ's position as over against the rest of the structure in Ephesians 2: 20 (ὄντος ἀκρογωνιαίου αὐτοῦ Χριστοῦ Ἰησοῦ) favours this interpretation rather than that which makes Christ one stone amongst others in the foundation. 'He is the topstone of the pinnacle of the building . . . As Christ is the κεφαλή of the σῶμα, he is the ἀκρογωνιαῖος of the οἰκοδομή.'[79]

On the other side of the question however is the fact, which Jeremias concedes, that this usage is not found in LXX Isaiah 28: 16 or quotations of it, which identify ἀκρογωνιαῖος with the foundation stone. In the Qumran writings there is a close association between the cornerstone and the foundation as Isaiah 28: 16 is quoted (cf. 1QS V, 6; VIII, 4f). Isaiah 28: 16 is not quoted here in Ephesians 2: 20 but there seems to be an allusion to its terminology. For this reason McKelvey asserts, 'ἀκρογωνιαῖος stands in the same close relation to θεμέλιος in Ephesians 2: 20 as it does in Isaiah 28: 16, and the context ... makes sense only when a Grundstein is in mind'.[80] But his objections based on contextual considerations demand a consistency in use of imagery which is absent from the text and ignore the possibility of the apostle being able to combine this concept of a finished structure with Christ at the head with the dynamic imagery of growth. A comparison with other parts of the letter shows that Paul does exactly that as he views the Church as already Christ's fullness (1: 23) and yet at the same time as having to attain that fullness (4: 13). So here on the one hand the Church is seen as a finished structure with Christ at its head and yet on the other hand joined to that head it must grow into a heavenly temple in him.

The interpretation of the temple as heavenly and especially of Christ as the top stone receives support from the wide range of cosmic ideas associated with the cornerstone which may well have carried over into the Ephesians reference. McKelvey alludes to one strand of this tradition which associated the cornerstone with the underworld and believes that this militates against the top stone interpretation.[81] The concept of the underworld is however foreign to the cosmology of Ephesians and there are other associations which better fit the world-view of this letter. The cornerstone was viewed as the summit of the earth and assigned the role of the link between heaven and earth. In connection with Genesis 28: 17 it was seen as the point of entry into heaven. Still further the stone was believed actually to belong to the heavenly world and thus to be the place of the presence of God and of the inhabitants of heaven (cf. Yoma 54b; Gen. R. 4: 2; 68: 12 on Gen. 28: 12; Yalkut Genesis 120 on Gen. 28: 22; Pirke de R. Eliezer 32: 35; Num. R. 12: 4).[82] Such connotations for the cornerstone are most appropriate to the role of the exalted Christ in Ephesians as the link between heaven and earth, and since no decisive arguments can be brought against the well-attested top stone interpretaion of ἀκρογωνιαῖος we feel justified in finding not only eschatological but also cosmic significance in the temple imagery of Ephesians 2: 19ff.

ἀκρογωνιαῖος is intended to emphasize the primary significance of Jesus Christ in the structure and the whole temple is dominated by him, for it is ἐν κυρίῳ (verse 21). At the same time it is the dwelling place of God ἐν πνεύματι (verse 22). τὸ κατοικητήριον is used in the LXX both for God's abode in the temple in Jerusalem (cf. 1 Kgs. 8: 13) and for his heavenly dwelling place (cf. 1 Kgs. 8: 39, 43, 49). By his formulation here

Paul shows that the presence of the high God of heaven was not separated from humans on earth and therefore to be sought through special techniques but that in fact as Gentile believers were built into their Lord as the Church the God of heaven had chosen to make that very Church his dwelling place. ἐν πνεύματι has reference to the manner of God's dwelling so that, as elsewhere in the letter (cf. 1: 3, 13f), it is the Spirit who provides the link between believers on earth and the heavenly realm, and makes the Church the place where the heavenly and earthly dwelling places of God merge. Again this image of the Church does not derive from a triumphalist attitude of having already arrived, for the building is depicted as still in the process of growth.

6. The Church and the powers in the heavenlies (3: 9, 10)

Paul encourages Gentile converts by depicting the Church's cosmic role from another angle. The mystery of Christ (verse 4) has not only been made known to him (verse 3) and to the apostles and prophets (verse 5) and is to be proclaimed by him to the Gentiles (verses 8, 9) but further it is now to be made known also to the principalities and powers in the heavenlies through the instrumentality of the Church (verse 10). The plan of the mystery, which has been hidden ἀπὸ τῶν αἰώνων - from the beginning of time[83] - and is now made known, is that which is described in verses 3-6, namely, that in Christ Gentiles can become members of the same body as Jews. The God who created all things is well able to carry through this plan and in its realization in the Church his manifold wisdom is demonstrated to the powers.

Paul sees his preaching to the Gentiles as part of the realization of this plan (verses 8, 9), for as Gentiles are being brought into the one body so the mystery is being made known to the powers in the heavenly places. In the Colossian syncretism it was necessary to placate the powers controlling the heavenly realm in order to gain access to mysteries but Paul's thought here reverses such a situation. The mystery is embodied in the Church and through it is being proclaimed to these very powers. In fact the existence of the Church heralds the cosmic implications of Christ's victory and the defeat of the hostile heavenly powers.

That the apostle can conceive of not only Christ and believers but also hostile powers in heavenly places is again to be explained against the background of the cosmic heavens in OT and Jewish apocalyptic thought where angels and spirit powers were often represented as in heaven (e.g. Job 1: 6; Dan. 10: 13; 21; 2 Macc. 5: 2; 1 Enoch 61: 10; 90: 21, 24), a concept which was also developed in Philo (cf. *De Spec. Leg.* I, 66; *De Plant.* 14; *De Gig.* 6f). For Paul God had placed in the heavenly realm creatures in

family groupings just as he had done on earth (cf. 3: 15). Since he shared
the two age eschatological structure of Jewish apocalyptic which incorporated heaven and earth in each age he could think of the present overlap of
the ages brought about by Christ as a period in which heaven was still
involved in the present evil age, so that though the powers had already
been defeated they would not be utterly vanquished until the consummation. In the meantime it is the Church which provides the angelic
powers with a tangible reminder that their authority has been decisively
broken and that all things are to be subject to Christ. The overcoming of
the barriers between Jews and Gentiles as they are united through Christ
in the Church is a pledge of the overcoming of all cosmological dualism
when the universe will be restored to harmony in Christ (cf. 1: 10).

7. Psalm 68, the exalted Christ, the Spirit and the Church (4: 7ff)

Ephesians 4: 7ff which speaks of the ascent of Christ and his status above
all the heavens is a passage which poses a number of difficulties for
interpretation. Some of these are alleviated when the larger context of 4:
1–16 is kept in mind, where Paul's concern is the unity of the Spirit which
is basic to the Church's life (4: 3). 'There is one body and one Spirit' (4: 4
cf. also 2: 16, 18 – ἐν ἑνὶ σώματι . . . ἐν ἑνὶ πνεύματι). The central role of
the Spirit in the train of thought about the Church and its unity which
leads Paul eventually to cite Psalm 68: 18 and to comment on it is of great
significance in understanding these later comments.[84] The passage flows
from the exhortation to maintain the unity of the Spirit (verse 3) through
the mention of the diversity of spiritual gifts (verse 7) and the exalted
Christ as their giver (verses 7ff) to the function of these gifts in building
up the body and ensuring its unity (verses 11ff, especially verse 13). Woven
into this theme is the concern we have already encountered that the
Church should be aware of the status it has through its relation to its
heavenly head and that it should cultivate the completeness and fullness
for which he has made provision by his exaltation and gifts rather than
seeking these things elsewhere and being taken in by the claims of
syncretistic teachings (verses 13ff, cf. Col. 2: 18, 19).

The unity of the Church is that of an organism in which there is a
diversity of functions as is shown by Christ's sovereign distribution of
grace (verse 7). ἡ χάρις here is equivalent to χάρισμα in 1 Corinthians 12:
4, 9 and Romans 12: 6 and is given according to the measure of Christ's
gift. δωρεά could be simply a general reference back to the grace that has
been mentioned (cf. previous references to giving and grace in 3: 2, 7, 8
where however God is in view as the giver) but it is possible that it has a
more specific reference to the Spirit as Christ's gift.[85] In the parallel

passage in 1 Corinthians 12 the charismata are from the Spirit and the terminology of apportioning or measuring is also used (cf. 1 Cor. 12: 4, 11), and elsewhere in the NT the Spirit can be termed δωρεά (cf. Acts 2: 38; 8: 20; 10: 45; 11: 17). This is given plausibility by the prominence of the Spirit in the passage (cf. 4: 3) and by the fact that, as we shall show, Pentecost was associated with the OT citation which follows.[86] According to this interpretation each person shares in Christ's gift of the Spirit (δωρεά) but via the reference to Psalm 68: 18 the various roles mentioned in verses 11ff are seen as particular gifts (δόματα) of Christ in the Spirit. Giving is a key concept in this passage – ἐδόθη, τῆς δωρεᾶς τοῦ Χριστοῦ (verse 7); ἔδωκεν δόματα (verse 8); αὐτὸς ἔδωκεν (verse 11) – and the one which sparks off the citation and enables verse 11 to follow on naturally from verse 7. The primary purpose of the citation is to establish that it is Christ who is the giver of the gifts. Since the psalm mentions only an ascent in connection with giving gifts, to establish his point that the Christ who ascended is the giver of gifts in the Church the apostle must show that a descent is inferred.

As is well-known, in his Scripture citation Paul has modified the LXX text (Ps. 67: 19). The major change is that of the verb so that ἔλαβες has become ἔδωκεν, and along with this there is the change of person from second to third so that ἠχμαλώτευσας has become ἠχμαλώτευσεν, and instead of ἐν ἀνθρώπῳ Paul has τοῖς ἀνθρώποις. It has been held that this modified form of the text closely follows the Syriac Peshitta, but the reading at this point in the Peshitta is probably a corruption and its value as evidence is precarious.[87] More significant however is the fact that in the Targum on the Psalms this verse differs from the MT and the LXX in the same way as Ephesians 4: 8 by changing the concept of receiving to that of giving – 'You have ascended to heaven, that is, Moses the prophet; you have taken captivity captive, you have learnt the words of the Torah; you have given it as gifts to men.'[88] Since the Targum on the Psalms is a late work, it is probable that Paul makes use of an ancient Rabbinic tradition which the Targum has also preserved[89] and that this tradition has interpreted the Hebrew לקח rather than reflected a variant textual tradition which had חלק .[90] The tradition has been taken over by Paul and incorporated into a midrash pesher rendering of the text in which he integrates his exposition of its meaning in the light of fulfilment in Christ into the actual quotation.[91]

The original force of Psalm 68: 18 was in praise of Jahweh's deliverance of his people and he is pictured as triumphantly ascending Mount Zion, driving before him the captives from whom he receives tribute. Jahweh's ascent of Zion is transferred directly to Christ's ascent on high in Ephesians.

It is the triumphant ascent and the gifts which particularly interest Paul as parallels. He does not develop explicitly the concept of leading captivity captive although the idea of triumphing over the evil powers is likely to have been in his mind (cf. 1: 21; Col. 2: 15). In any case this use of Psalm 68: 18 in regard to Christ is in contrast to the use made of it in Rabbinic tradition in ascribing an ascension to heaven to Moses (cf. the Targum; the Midrash Tehillim on Ps. 68: 11; Aboth R. Nathan II, 2a). Psalm 68: 18 was linked with Moses going up Sinai and interpreted as an ascent to heaven to receive not only the Torah but also other heavenly secrets. The 'Moses mysticism' with which this interpretation of Psalm 68: 18 is to be associated was widespread. It can be found elsewhere in the Rabbinic writings (e.g. Midr. Tehillim on Ps. 24: 1 and Ps. 106: 2; B. Shabb. 88b) and in Philo (e.g. *Quaest. Exod.* II, 40, 43; *De Vit. Mos.* I, 158; *De Post. Caini* 14; *De Somn.* I, 186-8).[92] Already Philo had used this tradition to speak to Hellenistic cosmological concerns and it could well be that it was current in the syncretism of the Lycus Valley and quoted in support of its penchant for heavenly visions.[93] In this case Paul would be relating Christ to the similar interests of his readers and showing that Christ has provided a link with the heavenly world that could not be matched by Moses. A 'new Moses' typology does appear to be in operation here.[94] As a greater than Moses, Christ has ascended far above all heavens in order to fill all things by his rule (cf. verse 10). Christ's gift is not the Torah but the Spirit and neither are his gifts heavenly secrets for the enlightenment of a few but rather people whose ministries will build up the whole body.

The reapplication of Psalm 68: 18 to Christ's ascent and his distribution of gifts by the Spirit may well have been aided by the psalm's association with Pentecost.[95] The psalm citation was connected with Moses and the giving of the law, and Pentecost, besides celebrating harvest, was more and more coming to be regarded as the feast which commemorated the law-giving at Sinai. Over against the view that the old form of the feast in which the first fruits and the sacrifices were brought to the temple persisted until the destruction of the temple in A.D. 70 and only then did the giving of the law become associated with Pentecost as an entirely new feature, there is good reason to believe that the latter association existed from the middle of the second century B.C.[96] The Book of Jubilees, which is usually dated between 135 and 105 B.C., makes Pentecost or the Feast of Weeks the most important of the annual festivals in the Jewish liturgical year, associating it with the institution of the various covenants in Israel's history but above all with the covenant at Sinai (cf. 1: 5; 6: 11, 17; 15: 1-24). The Qumran community followed the calendar of the Book of Jubilees which ordered an annual renewal of the covenant (6: 17), and in all probability this was combined with the annual renewal of the members' own oath of entry into the community which took place in the third month of the year, the time of Pentecost's celebration. According to Exodus 19: 1 the giving of the law took place in the third month also, as did the covenant renewal recorded in 2 Chronicles 15: 10–12. The liturgy for the annual renewal at Qumran is given in the Manual of Discipline (cf. 1QS I, 7 – II, 19).[97] Additional evidence is available from the Synagogue liturgy which may have been in existence before the time of Christ. In the triennial cycle of readings both Exodus 19, 20 and Numbers 17, 18 were read at Pentecost, while, according to the Megilla (B. Meg. 31a) representing the tradition which replaced the triennial cycle, the psalms for the day were 29 and 68.[98] Together with these factors the two central themes of Paul's reapplication, the exaltation of Christ and the gift of the Spirit, suggest Pentecost in the background.

The midrash of verses 9, 10, rather than being a parenthesis which digresses from the subject in hand, is meant to function as a support for the apostle's assertion about Christ's gift. Having talked of Christ's exaltation earlier in the letter he can assume that his readers will readily understand the psalm's language of ascension being applied to Christ. Once it is seen that the language of ascent and descent is derived from the OT citation, it will be appreciated that this passage can tell us nothing about Paul's awareness of an ascension tradition in the sense of Luke–Acts, though he clearly held that in the resurrection–exaltation complex of events, on which he focuses, Christ in some sense ascended from earth to heaven.[99] Here Christ is thought of as ascending above all the heavens – ὑπεράνω πάντων τῶν οὐρανῶν (verse 10). Elsewhere the plural of οὐρανός can be explained on the basis of the translation of the Hebrew plural; here however a number of heavens appear to be indicated. Yet as we have noted in relation to 2 Corinthians 12 it is unlikely that the apostle was concerned about a specific number of heavens. Here his terminology has rhetorical force as he asserts that however many heavens his readers may be interested in, Christ is above them all. Thus the local terminology is introduced not to give cosmological teaching but to serve as a backdrop to Christology. The unique status ascribed to Jahweh in the OT and here in verse 6 (ὁ ἐπὶ πάντων) as the high God whom the heavens cannot contain is now ascribed to the exalted Christ. This also indicates the paradoxical nature of the language employed for Christ's exaltation, so that while he can be viewed locally as in heaven (cf. 1: 20; 6: 9), at the same time he is above the heavens, beyond that which can be conceived in terms of created reality.[100] Christ's ascent was in order that he might fill all things. Many commentators who interpret the descent as either a descent into Hades or as the incarnation use the argument that by having Christ descend to the lower parts and then ascend to heaven the requirements for filling the universe are met and they thus interpret this filling in a quasi-physical sense. Strictly speaking, however, the ἵνα clause is connected to the statement about Christ's ascent and not to both the descent and ascent. Noting this enables us not to be misled by the concept of filling and to see the parallel with 1: 22f where it is by virtue of his exaltation that Christ can be said to fill the universe in every respect as he pervades it with his rule.

In facing the problem of the reference of the descent which Paul takes to be an inference from the ascent we should first dismiss a possible variant reading which has been influential in the history of the passage's interpretation but which tends to confuse the issue. The variant has πρῶτον after κατέβη in verse 9 and is read in ℵᶜ B Cᶜ K P and the majority of the Latin manuscripts and via the Textus Receptus is reproduced in the AV. It is omitted however in p⁴⁶ ℵ* A C* D G and the quotations in Irenaeus, Tertullian and Origen, and thus on the weight of the manuscript evidence it is certainly to be omitted. That an early copyist felt it necessary to add this interpretative gloss suggests that in the original the sequence of the ascent and descent could be taken either way and means that the question of the meaning of the descent can be approached without prejudice in this respect. There are three main possibilities – a descent into Hades, the descent of the pre-existent Christ in his incarnation or the descent of the exalted Christ in the Spirit at Pentecost.

The interpretation of a descent into Hades[101] is sometimes associated with the traditional doctrine of a *descensus ad inferos* or sometimes, as in the more appealing case made by Büchsel, seen simply as a reference to Christ's death. It is held by some that if κατώτερα τῆς γῆς is to be in genuine contrast with ὑπεράνω πάντων τῶν οὐρανῶν this requires a reference to an underworld. However the contrast is between an ascent to heaven and a descent from heaven whereas the descent involved in the traditional view of a descent into Hades is not from heaven but from earth to the underworld. If the apostle had had three levels in mind and meant that Christ descended to the deepest level just as he ascended to the greatest height he would have been more likely to have used a superlative than a comparative. Besides, a three-storey cosmology does not fit the world-view we encounter elsewhere in Ephesians where the cosmos is seen as having two main parts – heaven and earth. Others compare this passage to Romans 10: 6f where ascent into heaven is contrasted with descent into the abyss, which is explicitly said to be bringing Christ up from the dead. This is a strong point in favour of the interpretation but καταβαίνειν is not a technical term which means the same in every context, and although

Romans 10: 6f demands a reference to the dead the same is by no means true of Ephesians 4: 9f (cf. also 1 Thess. 4: 16). In fact it is extremely difficult to see how such a descent into Hades could be logically deduced from Christ's ascent which, after all, is Paul's argument or why the identity of the descender and ascender should be stressed. For such reasons other scholars have seen that it is preferable to take τῆς γῆς in τὰ κατώτερα τῆς γῆς as a genitive of apposition which further defines the preceding noun, that is, the lower parts. This particular grammatical feature occurs a number of times in Ephesians (cf. 2: 14, 15, 20; 6: 14, 16, 17). Now τὰ κατώτερα are not the lower parts of the earth, that is, an underworld, but rather the lower parts of the cosmos, that is, the earth, and the apostle is speaking of a descent to the earth. Those who support both the following views hold to this interpretation but differ on whether the descent to earth was before or after the ascent to heaven.

There is much to be said for the view which sees here a prior descent in the incarnation.[102] This has the advantage of following the order in the original meaning of the psalm, for the descent inferred from the ascent of Jahweh to Mt Zion would be the fact that he first came down to deliver his people and triumph over his enemies before going up to his dwelling place. On this view the passage is seen as a typical instance of a κατάβασις - ἀνάβασις Christology to be found elsewhere in the NT, especially in the fourth gospel (cf. Jn 3: 13; 6: 62). However because καταβαίνειν is almost a technical term for the incarnation in John it by no means follows that the same applies for Paul. John 3: 13 is not nearly as strong a parallel as many would like to think, for there Jesus is arguing from the earthly descended Son of Man to the reality of a heavenly ascent, while here in Ephesians the apostle argues in the reverse direction; it is the ascended Lord who is known and the identity of the one who descended is inferred from this.[103] When asserted of Christ 'he ascended' could imply previous descent, yet it is hard to see what this would prove, certainly not the pre-existence of Christ, for that would have to be assumed for a descent to make sense. Further, the only reason for stressing the identity of descender and ascender on this interpretation would be in order to guard against Docetism, and while traces of such a controversy can be found in the Johannine literature it does not figure in the life-setting of this epistle.[104]

To take the descent which the apostle infers as subsequent to the ascent and thus at Pentecost[105] is attractive and may well be preferable because it not only avoids the difficulties pointed out in the other interpretations but is also in keeping with the whole context in which these verses are found. On this interpretation the ascent and the giving of gifts can maintain their central function in the passage. The descent fits easily between the two and is seen to be a necessary and logical deduction in connecting the one who ascended to heaven with the gifts he has given to his Church on earth. The movement of thought from Christ's ascent to his gifts in the Church requires a descent in the Spirit. After speaking of the Spirit's work in the unifying of the body (verse 3f), what more natural than that Paul, in arguing from Christ's gift via his ascent to the gifts he has given to help maintain unity, should include the vital connecting link of the coming of the Spirit. That κατέβη is preceded by καί in verse 9 may indicate this chronological order, which is that followed in the exegetical tradition which applied the psalm to Moses and which is in the background here. After Moses ascended he would have to descend before being able to give the law (cf. the ascents followed by descents throughout the account of the law-giving at Sinai, e.g. Exod. 19: 3, 14; 19: 20, 25; 24: 18 and 32: 15; 34: 4, 29). It is also significant that Philo argued for the necessity of a subsequent descent after the ascent of a mystical experience from Moses' ascent followed by a descent at Sinai –

> The one who is begotten and brought into being is not wont to be God-possessed always, but when he has been divinely inspired for some time he then goes and returns to himself . . . But it is necessary that the most pure and luminous mind should be mixed with the mortal (element) for necessary uses. This is what is indicated by the heavenly ladder, (where) not only an ascent but also a descent of the angels is mentioned. And this is what is said of the prophet [i.e. Moses in Exod. 19: 17ff], (namely) his descent and ascent reveal the swift turning and change of his thoughts (*Quaes. Gen.* IV, 29).

For Paul Psalm 68 is no longer to be viewed as a Jewish Pentecostal psalm concerning Moses but as 'a Christian Pentecostal psalm, celebrating the ascension of Christ and his subsequent descent at Pentecost to bestow spiritual gifts upon the church'.[106] This descent of Christ in the Spirit to give gifts is in line with the similar passage in 1 Corinthians 12 where in regard to the variety of gifts within the one body the Spirit is most prominent in their distribution (cf. verses 3, 4, 7f; 11, 13). On this interpretation it also becomes apparent why the identity is a matter for emphasis – ὁ καταβὰς αὐτός ἐστιν καὶ ὁ ἀναβάς. It brings home to the Church once more its link with its heavenly Lord. The one who by virtue of his ascent became cosmic Lord is the same one who by his Spirit is active in giving gifts to the Church and equipping it for its role. The Christ who by his exaltation unites the cosmos (cf. 1: 10; 4: 10) is the same Christ who by his Spirit unites the Church. We have seen that the Church is to be a pledge of the universe's ultimate unity in Christ and now Paul asserts that it is this

same Christ who by his Spirit's gifts enables them to be so. A close association and indeed virtual interchange between Christ and the Spirit is evidenced elsewhere in Ephesians. In 1: 13 the believer is sealed in Christ with
the Spirit, while in 4: 30 he is sealed in the Spirit. In 3: 16 the Spirit is in
the inner man while in the following verse, 3: 17, Christ dwells in the
heart. In 1: 23 the Church is the fullness of Christ, while in 5: 18 believers
are exhorted to be filled with the Spirit. We have seen also that 2: 17 is
best interpreted as an activity of the exalted Christ in the Spirit through
apostolic messengers. Elsewhere in Paul an identity between Christ and the
Spirit can be found. In 1 Corinthians 15: 45f the last Adam is said to
become life-giving Spirit, in Romans 8: 9-11 the Spirit is called the Spirit
of Christ and the apostle can talk either of the Spirit in the believer or
Christ in the believer, and in 2 Corinthians 3: 17 ('the Lord is the Spirit')
'Lord' may refer not only to Jahweh in the OT text but also to Christ.[107]
Here in Ephesians the stress on this matter is particularly appropriate in
the light of the cosmological dualism on which the apostle has an eye. For
the Church there can be no chasm between heaven and earth, for the
Christ who has been exalted to heaven is integrally linked with his Church
on earth through the Spirit in whom he has descended.[108]

The remainder of the passage elaborates on this link as it shows that the
function of the various ministers in the church is critical for its growth and
that such men are to be seen as part of the royal largesse which Christ dis-
tributes from his position of cosmic lordship after his triumphant ascent.
In Colossians over against the syncretistic philosophy Paul had emphasized
the importance of the apostolic tradition of teaching (1: 5ff, 23; 2: 6, 7)
and its mediation through the ministries of such men as Epaphras (1: 7f;
4: 12f), Tychicus (4: 7f), Onesimus (4: 9) and Archippus (4: 17). Here in
Ephesians also it is the ministries of such men which are to protect the
Church from false teaching (4: 14) and they are to be highly valued as
gifts from the exalted Christ by his Spirit.

In fact Christ has given these men as part of the overall purpose for
which he ascended – that his work of filling all things might be brought to
completion (verse 10). In the apostle's vision the unity of the Spirit in the
Church, as the various ministers of the word build up the whole body into
Christ's fullness, is interwoven with the goal of the ultimate unity of the
cosmos in Christ. By the way in which Paul brings his midrash on Psalm
68 with its focus on Christ's exaltation into his exposition of the Church's
unity and growth we see again that for him the Church was not to be
thought of simply as a new cult or a new social phenomenon but that its
real nature could only be appreciated when seen from the heavenly perspective and in its relationship to its heavenly Lord. The Church's various

ministries, its unity and its growth all derive their significance from him. For the attainment of such unity and completeness the Church is totally dependent on him and fullness of salvation is seen to be a matter of grace, for the heavenly Christ *gives* all that is necessary for reaching this goal (verses 11–13).

8. The heavenly dimension and human relationships (5: 21ff; 6: 5ff)

It is not surprising that Paul's vision of the heavenly Christ, which is so powerfully portrayed in 1: 19ff and which pervades his thought about the Church, also colours his teaching about human relationships. In the 'Haustafel' of 5: 21 – 6: 9 this heavenly Christ is seen as making a difference both in marriage and in the master–slave relationship.

In 5: 21–33 Paul's primary aim is to give instructions about marriage, yet in so doing he bases his exhortations on the relationship of the heavenly bridegroom to his bride, the Church. A detailed exegesis of this passage would take us too far from our main theme; our aim is simply to point out that the heavenly dimension does colour the presentation and that the imagery has certain eschatological implications. Throughout the passage there is the interplay between the earthly and the heavenly, marked out by the use of comparative particles – ὡς (verses 23, 24), καθώς (verses 25, 29) and οὕτως (verses 24, 28). The husband–wife relationship is expounded in verses 22, 23a and supplemented by exposition of the Christ–Church relationship in verses 23b, 24. The latter is then applied to human marriage in verses 24b, 25a and verse 25a again finds its Christological basis in verses 25b–27. This in turn provides the model for the husband's attitude to his wife in verses 28, 29a which is compared once more to Christ and the Church in verses 29b, 30. The two relationships are brought together in verses 31, 32 via the reference to Genesis 2: 24, and the apostle finally underlines his purpose in this parenetical section by summarizing his instructions to husbands and wives in verse 33. From such an outline it can readily be seen that the standard and prototype for such instructions is the marriage between the heavenly bridegroom and the Church, and that Paul 'is arguing from the Heavenly Marriage to human marriage, not vice-versa; he is seeing the human in the light of the heavenly, and therefore will have the human model itself on the heavenly'.[109]

In 5: 27 by means of the language of presentation Paul places the relationship between Christ and the Church in an eschatological context where the consummation of the union awaits the time when the Church will be totally glorious. What Paul had as his goal for the local Corinthian church (cf. 2 Cor. 11: 2), Christ himself will achieve for the universal

Church. The primary source for this imagery is the OT with its analogy of the covenant relationship between Jahweh and Israel as one between husband and wife and this could itself be found in eschatological contexts (cf. Isa. 54: 4ff; 62: 4f), as is its equivalent in Revelation 19: 7ff and 21: 2, 9. It would be a mistake however to conclude that here in Ephesians 5: 21-33 as a whole 'it is only in the End that the Church becomes the Bride . . . We cannot correctly speak of the Church being now the Bride; rather it is what she shall be.'[110] This would be to ignore the fact that the mystery of the marriage union is applied to the presently existing relationship between Christ and the Church in verse 32 and that throughout the passage there are present aspects of this relationship which form the model for husbands and wives to follow. The alternation between present and future so that the Church is at times the betrothed and at times the actual wife could mean that the apostle is not particularly concerned about consistency in his use of imagery or could well arise from the fact that 'according to Jewish law betrothal effects the acquisition of the bride by the bridegroom . . . and so she is a legally married woman from the time of the betrothal'.[111] In any case the emphasis on the present aspects of the relation between Christ and his bride well fits the stress on realized eschatology in Ephesians, while the future element in verse 27 indicates that the 'already–not yet' tension is still in operation.

The exalted Christ gives marriage an exalted status. Paul's focus on the heavenly dimension is not one which makes earthly relationships of no account.[112] In fact the heavenly perspective is used to combat any attempt to devalue the marriage relationship either by those with ascetic tendencies (abstinence from sexual relationships was part of the preparation for visionary experience, cf. Col. 2: 21 where μὴ ἄψῃ may well be a prohibition of sexual relations) or by those with libertine inclinations still remaining from their pagan past (cf. 2: 3; 4: 19f, 22; 5: 3, 5, 18).

In 6: 5ff slaves are exhorted to be obedient to their earthly masters. These masters (τοῖς κατὰ σάρκα κυρίοις) are distinguished from the one Lord or master whom the slaves are to use their situation to serve (verse 7) and in verse 9 the comparison is heightened as this master is shown to be ὁ κύριος . . . ἐν οὐρανοῖς. Not only slaves but also their masters are to work with this perspective and for the latter an element of mutual solidarity should enter the picture with the recognition that, irrespective of social status, both they and their slaves are under the same impartial heavenly Lord (αὐτῶν καὶ ὑμῶν ὁ κύριός ἐστιν ἐν οὐρανοῖς - verse 9).

9. The battle against the powers in the heavenlies (6: 10ff)

The image of Christian existence as a battle is to be found elsewhere in Paul (cf. 1 Thess. 5: 8; Rom. 13: 12; 2 Cor. 6: 7; 10: 4) but in keeping with the themes of this letter the battle is here placed in a cosmic context. The idea of warfare involving heavenly powers occurs in apocalyptic literature (cf. Dan. 10: 13, 20; Test. Abr. 7: 3; Rev. 9: 11; 19: 11–21) and the Qumran community both felt itself threatened by evil powers (cf. 1QH II, 16; VII, 1ff) and expected to be involved in the final cosmic struggle between God and these powers (cf. 'The War Rule' – 1QM; 1QH VI, 29ff). The distinctive feature about Ephesians 6: 10ff is that the apostle views believers as already involved in such a struggle. In addition, whereas the Qumran community expected to fight with actual physical weapons which were consecrated to God's cause, here the weapons are spiritual and supplied by God himself.

Believers find themselves facing a whole array of powers with the devil (verse 11) at their head. The plurality of such powers is depicted not for the sake of some schematic classification but to bring home to the consciousness of the readers the variety and comprehensiveness of the forces their enemy has at his disposal and therefore the absolute necessity of using the only armour which will avail. τὰ πνευματικὰ τῆς πονηρίας ἐν τοῖς ἐπουρανίοις both sums up the spiritual nature of the adversary and indicates again that evil powers can be located in the heavenly realm (cf. 3: 10). In Ephesians 2: 2 the devil is described as 'the prince of the power of the air' (τοῦ ἀέρος) and a question naturally arises concerning the relationship between the heavenlies and the air as the realm of malevolent agencies. In later Judaism the air is thought of as the region under the firmament. 'And I threw him out from the height with his angels, and he was flying in the air continuously above the abyss' (2 Enoch 29: 4, 5 cf. also Test. Benj. 3: 4; Targum of Job 5: 7 and Asc. Isa. 7: 9; 10: 29; 11: 23 where Satan and his angels are represented as living in the firmament). This is a further indication that the apostle takes up terminology from different cosmological schemes and it is not necessary to think that in Ephesians the 'air' is one definite and distinct sphere in a cosmology in which the 'heavenlies' form another. Rather the localities of the evil powers in 2: 2 and 6: 12 are more or less synonymous and 2: 2 represents a variation in terminology for the devil's sphere of dominion (ὁ κόσμος οὗτος and ὁ αἰὼν οὗτος have been used in the previous sentence[113]), which also stresses the proximity of the powers of evil in influencing the lives of people.

Though these forces are formidable, the fact that they are in the heavenlies need no longer pose a threat to believers, for, as we have seen, they are not fighting to break through the hold of such powers and penetrate to the heavenly realm themselves but are rather fighting from a position of victory, having already been seated with Christ in the heavenlies (2: 6). It is a question of making this effective, of appropriating the benefits of this status that has been conferred on them. This is why they are urged to find their strength in their heavenly Lord (6: 10 cf. 6: 9), and 'in the strength of his might'. This heaping up of terms for 'power' recalls that of 1: 19ff where it is God's might which is displayed in Christ's resurrection and victory over evil powers. This same strength is granted by God 'in the Lord' to believers (cf. also 3: 16, 20). The exhortation to take the whole armour of God has similar force for it is an exhortation to appropriate both that which God himself wears (cf. Isa. 59: 17; Wisd. Sol. 5: 17-20) and which he now supplies to his people[114] to enable them to fulfil their role in the cosmic battle. By 'putting on' the armour they will be able to withstand in the evil day. This terminology of the 'evil day' has its background in the apocalyptic concept of the time of climactic tribulation which will immediately precede the end of the world (cf. 1 Enoch 50: 2; 55: 3; 63: 8; 96: 2; 99: 4; Jub. 23: 11ff; Assump. Mos. 1: 18; Test. Levi 5: 5; also 1QM XV, 12; XVIII, 10, 12). Some writers hold that this is the reference here in 6: 13,[115] while others believe any day of special temptation is in view[116] and still others that the reference is to the whole of the present age.[117] It seems best to take the phrase as an apocalyptic concept which has, in common with other such concepts in this letter, been given a present significance (cf. 5: 16 - 'the days are evil' and the way in which the interpretation of the armour is orientated towards a present situation) and which yet retains its apocalyptic overtones. The Church is to recognize that it is already in the last days which will culminate in a climactic 'evil day'.[118]

This homily on the believer's armour serves to put the realized eschatology of the letter in perspective, for it indicates that while this present age lasts the forces of evil are still able to exercise control over a world which will not avail itself of Christ's victory and that believers, while part of this age, are still engaged in an intense battle against such powers in which only the appropriation of Christ's might will enable them to stand. There is no contradiction between the exultation in Christ's victory and the Church's share in it of the earlier chapters and this depiction of the hard realities of battle but rather their juxtaposition clearly shows that the 'already–not yet' tension is still at work in Ephesians and that believers' session in the heavenlies is proleptic and has not removed them from this world. From a position of strength they can fight evil in all its manifestations, while never underestimating the enemy because they recognize its transcendent dimension 'in the heavenlies'.

10. Ephesians, heaven and realized eschatology

The predominance of realized eschatology in Ephesians has been prepared for by the apostle's response to the situation in Colossae. It finds its strongest expression in Ephesians 2: 6 where believers are said to have been seated with Christ in the heavenlies but, as we have seen, this is simply a making explicit of that which was already involved in the concepts of Colossians 3: 1ff. For this reason the same arguments hold for Ephesians as for Colossians whether such eschatology can be Pauline or not.[119] And if Paul has an eye on the same general background of syncretism in this letter which took specific form in the Colossian philosophy, this conclusion would of course be reinforced. We noted the baptismal motivation behind the realized eschatology of Colossians and both the baptismal orientation and the worship-setting would account for the intensification of such eschatology in Ephesians.

In speaking to the cosmological interests of the syncretism Paul appears to draw on concepts evidenced in apocalyptic and Qumran writings. An apocalyptic view of history with its two age structure and its stress on mystery and on insight into the cosmic dimension of the course of history underlies the apostle's formulations but has been modified because he sees the life of the age to come as at work in the Church on account of what God has accomplished in Christ. In common in particular with the Qumran writings is the emphasis on the community's present relationship with the heavenly world, but for Paul the decisive factor in such a relationship was that it had been made effective through union with Christ in his prior exaltation.

The apostle's particular emphasis in this letter by no means necessitates a rejection of futurist eschatology.[120] Reference to the future plays a clear role in 1: 14; 2: 7; 4: 30; 5: 5, 27; 6: 8, 13 and is reflected in the rhetorical flourish of 1: 21. In addition there are concepts such as 'growing' and 'filling' which can be seen as equivalents of future eschatology (cf. 2: 21; 3: 9; 4: 13, 15f).[121] In this way the tension between 'already' and 'not yet' is retained. The relationship between these two poles is similar to that between the Pauline indicative and imperative with its 'Become what you are'. The force of the emphasis on realized eschatology with its spatial terminology in this letter is to highlight what believers are and have in Christ. But this stands side by side with the future references and neither pole should be played down. Schille attempts to play down the realized aspects by stating that these were part of the over-enthusiastic hymnic tradition which the apostle has inherited and wishes to correct.[122] Kirby similarly plays down the future aspects by relegating them to traditional material to which the writer feels he must make concessions.[123] Both aspects of eschatology belong to the Pauline perspective and it is significant that the future aspect becomes stronger in the latter part of the letter, for as Paul moves from the explicitly liturgical form and content of the first three chapters the realized eschatology correspondingly recedes.

The references to heaven are often part of an overall emphasis on the ultimate unity of the cosmos as over against any cosmological dualism, as is the stress that God's plan involves τὰ πάντα (which comprises heavenly and earthly spheres cf. 1: 10). Heaven and earth are shown to be inseparably connected by virtue of God's creation (cf. 3: 9, 15; 4: 6) and by the redemption he has accomplished. Dualism is denied by focusing sometimes on Christ as the integrating point between the two realms (cf. 1: 3, 10, 22f; 2: 6, 20; 4: 10), sometimes on the Spirit as the link (cf. 1: 3; 2: 18, 22; 4: 7ff) and sometimes on the role of the Church on both levels (cf. 1: 3; 2: 6, 20ff; 3: 10; 6: 12).

From this perspective the heavenly dimension cannot be seen as standing in antithesis to earthly life. Indeed it is precisely because of the salvation which climaxed in the exaltation of Christ to heaven that the whole of human life and the cosmos itself has become meaningful, for in him people have been freed from the tyranny of the powers and from the disruptive consequences of sin and are being restored to God's original purpose for them. In the light of the heavenly dimension both marriage (5: 21ff) and the master–slave relationship (6: 9) are given a new perspective and significance. The same Church which participates in the heavenly life of the age to come has the task through its various ministers of growing to maturity and demonstrating unity here on earth, where it is still involved in the present age and the consequent battle against its manifestations of evil and the powers behind them. Neither growth nor security in the battle are automatic but depend on the Church's maintenance of its link with its heavenly head (cf. 4: 15f; 6: 10).

7

HEAVEN AND THE ESCHATOLOGICAL
PERSPECTIVE IN PAULINE THOUGHT

Some of the more significant conclusions about Paul's eschatology arising
from the exegesis have been summarized at the end of each chapter. This
final chapter now aims to relate these and other findings to broader issues
in Paul's thought and its interpretation. The further question of the contemporary relevance of Paul's views expressed in concepts so closely
associated with first century A.D. cosmologies lies beyond the scope of
our study but has been raised in the Introduction.

1. Heaven, realized eschatology and apocalyptic

(i) Apocalyptic parallels to Paul's references to heaven[1]

In the course of this study correspondences in apocalyptic writings to
Paul's references to heaven have often been noted. This is hardly surprising
since Paul was a diaspora Pharisee and apocalyptic ideas had a particularly
strong influence on diaspora Judaism.[2] In several passages we have seen
links between heaven and the general apocalyptic concept of the two ages.
More specifically we found apocalyptic references for the heavenly Jerusalem (Gal. 4: 26), Paradise and the third heaven (2 Cor. 12), the age to
come present in heaven and entered at death (2 Cor. 5; Phil. 1: 23), the
hope laid up in heaven (Col. 1: 5), the 'hidden–revealed' motif and the
theme of glory (Col. 3: 1-4), the mystery of God's cosmic plan (Eph. 1:
10), the session in heaven (Eph. 2: 6), the heavenly temple (Eph. 2: 20ff)
and the cosmic battle (Eph. 6: 10ff). Further, apocalyptic thought about
an exalted eschatological Adam was seen to provide the background for
the heavenly Man of 1 Corinthians 15, Philippians 3: 20 was held to express
in Hellenistic political terminology the apocalyptic motif of the presence
in heaven of the benefits of eschatological salvation, a motif reflected also
in Ephesians 1: 3, and the apocalyptic concept of evil powers in heaven
proved significant for determining the force of the formula ἐν τοῖς
ἐπουρανίοις in Ephesians 3: 10 and 6: 12. In addition, the Qumran literature, as one development of apocalyptic, provided parallels for such

themes as the heavenly Jerusalem (Gal. 4: 26), sharing the lot of the holy ones (Col. 1: 12; Eph. 1: 18; 2: 19), the mystery of God's plan for heaven (Eph. 1: 10), present participation in the heavenly realm (Eph. 2: 6), the community as the heavenly temple (Eph. 2: 20ff) and the cosmic battle (Eph. 6: 10ff). To recall the continuities and discontinuities which have emerged from our study between the use of the above concepts in apocalyptic and Qumran writings and their use by Paul will enable us to evaluate the view of many interpreters of Paul that the 'realized' element of his eschatology which frequently employs spatial language constitutes a decisive break with Jewish apocalypticism.

(ii) Heaven and the two ages

For such an evaluation we should first examine how Paul relates his thought about heaven to the two age doctrine he inherited from apocalypticism.[3] The one verse in which the two ages are explicitly contrasted is Ephesians 1: 21 but the terminology and the structure involved in this contrast play a large part in the apostle's thought. In 1 Corinthians 10: 11 he sees himself and the Corinthian believers as those 'upon whom the end of the ages has come'. Many passages mention 'this age' (cf. Gal. 1: 4; Rom. 12: 2; 1 Cor. 1: 20; 2: 6, 8; 3: 18; 2 Cor. 4: 4; Eph. 2: 2) but apart from Ephesians 1: 21 'the age to come' occurs only in the plural in Ephesians 2: 7.[4] In Romans 8: 38 and 1 Corinthians 3: 22 however 'things present' (ἐνεστῶτα) are contrasted with 'things to come' (μέλλοντα). Elsewhere in contexts where ὁ μέλλων αἰών could conceivably have been employed the apostle prefers ἡ βασιλεία τοῦ θεοῦ (cf. 1 Thess. 2: 12; 2 Thess. 1: 5; Gal. 5: 21; 1 Cor. 6: 9, 10; 15: 50; Eph. 5: 5), or when speaking of a present experience of the life or benefits of the age to come he will often make reference to the heavenly dimension, as our study has shown.

It is at this point that it becomes clear that Paul modified the sharp contrast between the two ages customarily attributed to apocalyptic writings. Cullmann has drawn attention to one aspect of this modification. 'For Judaism the mid-point of the line which signifies salvation lies in the future. The chronologically new thing which Christ brought for the faith of primitive Christianity consists in the fact that for the believing Christian the mid-point, since Easter, no longer lies in the future.'[5] For Paul who believed that the Messiah had already arrived and that in him the age to come had become present reality, the view of history as two successive antithetical ages was inappropriate. The arrival of the coming age did not mark the consummation of history but rather provided a new focus, a 'new division of time'.[6] Paul could continue to refer to the period in which he was living as 'the present age' but holds at the same time that the age to come began at Christ's resurrection, is already a reality in the believer's experience and will come fully at the parousia.

Before Cullmann, Vos had given a similar and fuller interpretation of Paul's modification of the traditional two age structure and is perhaps the only interpreter to have seen the importance of heaven in the apostle's outlook. Vos termed the period in which the ages overlap 'semi-eschatological' and saw that for Paul within this framework a vertical point of view could come to expression as well as a linear or horizontal and that in the midst of this present age the age to come was now realized in principle in heaven.[7] Vos held that while a coexistence of two temporal ages is not possible because the two sequences of time are mutually exclusive, a coexistence of two worlds or states is by no means logically impossible and that in Paul the idea of heaven as the higher world over against earth took the place of the older terminology of the two ages. According to Vos, '"Heaven" offered moreover the advantage of expressing that the provisionally-realized final state lies on a higher plane than the preceding world-development.'[8] By highlighting the concept of heaven in his brief remarks Vos made a valuable initial contribution to the study of Pauline eschatology which has remained unexplored in any depth. His remarks however need not only development but also correction. In the light of our investigation it becomes clear that he was wrong in believing the references to heaven to be evidence of the emergence of an entirely new scheme alongside the continuation of the older one.[9] He did not sufficiently take into account the connection of heaven either with the 'age' concept itself or with other apocalyptic motifs. Both his interpretation and diagram[10] give the impression that heaven figures exclusively in the new situation produced by the inauguration of the age to come, neglecting the fact that in apocalyptic 'this age' also embraced both heaven and earth. Paul's depiction of evil powers in heaven during the present period finds its only adequate explanation in his sharing this conception of an age structure in which heaven as well as earth participated in the evil nature of this present age. While for Vos Paul's references to heaven retain an eschatological force, he did not perceive their apocalyptic links, not recognizing that the basic notion of the anticipation of the age to come in heaven was already present in apocalyptic writings. When he wrote he did not of course have available the further evidence of the Qumran literature for parallels to this motif of the present experience of the heavenly world.

How then does the vertical point of view relate to the age concept in Paul's thought? There should be no surprise at Paul's spatial equivalent for an apparently temporal concept, for the term αἰών which he inherited

already had not only temporal but also spatial connotations. In the LXX
αἰών appears as a translation of the Hebrew עולם . In Hebrew there was
no word for 'world' or 'universe', so that often the circumlocution 'heaven
and earth' was employed or a term such as הכל or eventually עולם .[11]
עולם then had a dual reference either to 'age' or to the 'world' or
'cosmos' and its Greek equivalent αἰών was correspondingly pressed into
double service, so that in its sense of 'time or duration of the world' it
could easily pass over into the sense of 'world' itself and become an equivalent for κόσμος (cf. Paul's use in, for example, 1 Cor. 1: 20; 2: 6; 3: 18,
19 where αἰών and κόσμος are virtually interchangeable).[12] αἰών could
therefore involve a spatio-temporal complex and indicate a period of the
world seen in its cosmic scope of heaven and earth. In apocalyptic both
'this age' and 'the age to come' included heaven and earth.[13] One strand of
apocalypticism however tended to concentrate on the heavenly dimension
of the age to come so that, for example, 1 Enoch 91: 16 in prophesying
about the age to come mentions only the new heaven and not a new earth
and 1 Enoch 104: 2-6 dwells on the heavenly aspects of the salvation of
the righteous (cf. also 2 Bar. 51: 8; Assump. Mos. 10: 9ff).

Paul continued with this basic structure of successive cosmic world-
epochs and the apocalyptic framework was not employed speculatively
but made to serve his exposition of what he knew to have happened to
Christ and the new situation his death, resurrection and exaltation had
effected. Christ's resurrection had inaugurated the age to come with its
heavenly life,[14] but it also raised the question, 'Where is he now?' Paul
held not only that Christ had become heavenly through his resurrection
but also that by virtue of his exaltation he was now in heaven (cf. Phil.
3: 20; Col. 3: 1; 4: 1; Eph. 1: 20f; 2: 6; 6: 9). Christ had not simply dis-
appeared nor had he evaporated into a universal spirit, but he had departed
to a new sphere, that of heaven, which would be appropriate to his transformed incarnate mode of existence. The two age structure, already associated with heaven, does not have to be jettisoned in the apostle's formulation of this state of affairs. Neither does the concept of heaven have to
be introduced for the first time but rather it is given new content and
significance by the dawning of the age to come and by Christ's exaltation
and presence in heaven. In thinking about the believer's present experience
of the age to come Paul's focus can be on heaven, because for him, with
Christ's resurrection and exaltation, the eschatological centre of gravity
had moved to the heavenly realm. Heaven has a new status in the age
structure simply because of Christ's presence there until the parousia. Any
connotations of the superiority of heaven to earth are a secondary factor.
The primary consideration for Paul is what has happened in the history of

salvation. Through union with Christ believers are drawn into this history
and thus also into the heavenly dimension where their Lord now is. It is
this that explains the spatial terminology we have encountered when
experiences of the age to come during the period of the overlap of the
ages are in view. The heavenly Jerusalem is seen as the source of the
Church's life and its liberating power (Gal. 4: 26). Believers who are
united to the heavenly Man are themselves heavenly (1 Cor. 15: 47ff).
Those who die before the parousia are seen as being with Christ in heaven
(2 Cor. 5; Phil. 1: 23). Through the Spirit believers can have visionary
experiences of heaven (2 Cor. 12). That which governs their life, their state
or commonwealth, is in heaven (Phil. 3: 20). They are able to share fellowship with the angels in heaven (Col. 1: 12; Eph. 2: 19) and they are to seek
that which is above where their life is hidden with Christ's (Col. 3: 1ff).
Believers can even be said to be seated with Christ in the heavenlies (Eph.
2: 6) and the Church as a whole is shown to be linked to the heavenly
dimension (Eph. 2: 19ff; 4: 7ff). At the same time during this period of
overlap heaven is also still involved in this present evil age. For this reason
there are still enemy powers in the heavenlies (Eph. 3: 10 cf. also 2: 2)
whom believers must resist in the cosmic warfare in which the Church is
participating on the side of the ultimately victorious forces (Eph. 6: 10ff).
For this reason also the experience of the deceased believer in heaven will
remain incomplete until the parousia and his or her reception of a heavenly
body (cf. on 2 Cor. 5 and Phil. 1: 23).[15] While the present age lasts cosmic
renewal will not be completed, for not until the parousia will everything
in heaven and on earth be summed up in Christ (Eph. 1: 10). An emphasis
on the future is not lost in drawing attention to the overlap of the ages.
The age to come will only arrive in its fullness at Christ's future coming
and it is significant that the only two uses of this term (Eph. 1: 21; 2: 7),
despite the predominantly realized eschatology of the epistle in which
they appear, retain a clearly future reference.

It should be underlined that Paul's primary focus is on Christ. The
structure of the ages simply provided the appropriate vehicle for expressing the significance of what God had accomplished in Christ. It is not as
though Christ is fitted into a system that Paul already firmly holds. His
adherence now is clearly to Christ in a way that requires the reshaping of
old patterns of thought. But just as the linear scheme of the ages could be
taken up, modified and used to interpret Christ's coming as unfolding in
two stages, so also could the vertical elements of that structure illuminate
Christ's present exaltation in heaven. The point to be emphasized here,
however, is that the latter elements were just as much to hand in Jewish
apocalyptic thought as the former. Paul's references to heaven in the

context of realized eschatology are just as much a utilization and adaptation of an original apocalyptic perspective as is his seeing the period between Christ's resurrection and parousia as an anticipation of the age to come. Emphasis on the heavenly dimension as part of Paul's thought is *not* drawn from some new schema alien to the aspects of his eschatology which draw on the apocalyptic view of history in terms of the ages and having to be grafted on to them.

(iii) Paul, heaven and apocalyptic

In a climate of interpretation in which Bultmann's reduction of Paul's eschatology to anthropology was predominant, Käsemann's redirection of attention to the role of apocalyptic with his assertion that 'apocalyptic . . . was the mother of all Christian theology' was bound to prove controversial.[16] For Bultmann the temporal and spatial categories in Paul's eschatology belonged to the mythological framework of Jewish apocalyptic and Gnosticism. The chronological elements were derived largely from apocalypticism while the cosmological came mainly from Gnosticism and both were to be interpreted anthropologically or existentially.[17] Bultmann held that this was not simply imposing a twentieth-century understanding on Paul but was following the lead Paul himself set, because for Paul eschatological existence 'means being a "new creature" (2 Cor. 5: 17). The eschatology of Jewish apocalyptic and of Gnosticism has been emancipated from its accompanying mythology, in so far as the age of salvation has already dawned for the believer and the life of the future has become a present reality.'[18] In this way temporal and cosmic elements retreat in favour of an emphasis on the believing self-understanding. 'In Paul history is swallowed up in eschatology. Thereby eschatology has wholly lost its sense as goal of history and is in fact understood as the goal of the individual human being.'[19] The views of W. Grundmann are similar in this regard. He sees in Paul's eschatology two strands, one represented by temporal apocalyptic categories and the other by categories of personal communication. Only the latter are determinative for Paul's thought.[20] Over against such an interpretation Käsemann's emphasis had the merit of showing the important role which apocalyptic features played in Paul's eschatology and in distinguishing it from that of the Corinthian enthusiasts.[21] He could claim that 'Paul's apostolic self-consciousness is comprehensible only in the light of his apocalyptic and that the same is true of the method and goal of his mission.'[22] He recognized that what he considered to be the present eschatology of Hellenistic enthusiasm still had links with apocalyptic, though it had transformed the latter into a metaphysical dualism.[23]

Käsemann's Paul was not willing to talk, as did the enthusiasts or his own pupils in the Deutero-Paulines, of sharing in Christ's resurrection, experiencing the life of heaven or having victory over the powers, but only of the *nova oboedientia* through which 'the Church proves itself to be the new creation' and to be 'ruled by the power of the resurrection'.[24] But significantly for our study Käsemann did attempt to connect the tension between realized and future elements in Paul's eschatology with apocalyptic.

> Paul cannot and will not speak of an end of history that has already taken place, but . . . he does regard the time of the end as having dawned. This has been the case since the resurrection of Christ, because since then the subjection of the cosmic powers has been taking place. Thus the present eschatology of the enthusiastics is here taken up, but there is a difference from them in that it is anchored in and limited by apocalyptic . . . It is for Paul not an alternative to futurist eschatology but a part of it.[25]

Käsemann's discussion remained general however and he provided no detailed defence of this thesis nor any reference to apocalyptic texts.[26]

For a fuller attempt to root the tension in Paul's eschatology in apocalyptic it is necessary to turn back to the work of Schweitzer. Schweitzer rightly endeavoured to explain what he called Paul's 'mysticism', his experience of the heavenly while still on earth, eschatologically. He saw that for Paul the death and resurrection of Christ constituted a cosmic event which had brought about the dawn of the supernatural age, by which he meant the Messianic kingdom.

> If Jesus has risen, that means, for those who dare to think consistently, that it is now already the supernatural age. And this is Paul's point of view . . . Those who had insight, therefore, did not reckon the duration of the natural world as up to the coming of Jesus in glory, but conceived of the intervening time between his resurrection and the beginning of the Messianic kingdom as a time when the natural and supernatural world are intermingled.[27]

Schweitzer held that this concept of a temporally limited Messianic age played an important role in Paul's view of history which had three future stages – the period from the resurrection to the parousia, the Messianic kingdom, and the final kingdom of God.[28] He noted that one branch of apocalypticism, 2 Baruch and 4 Ezra, also gave this concept a role and believed that it was this apocalyptic source which had also provided the apostle with a model for his perspective on the Christian present as a period in which the natural and supernatural world mingle, for both writings represent the Messianic kingdom as a meeting of the earthly and heavenly and thus overcome a strict separation of the two ages.[29]

Following Schweitzer, H. J. Schoeps also insisted that Paul's thought is rooted in apocalyptic and that 'if we are to understand the eschatology of Paul aright – and it contains the whole Christian conception of saving history – we must make its apocalyptic presuppositions more central in his thought than is usually done'.[30] Unlike Schweitzer, however, he saw no place for a Messianic kingdom at the return of Christ but held rather that for Paul Christ's resurrection had inaugurated the age to come in such a way that the present was the Messianic age. 'In this transitional epoch in which Paul and his churches are living . . . the *olam hazzeh* and the *olam habba* are already mingled, thus indicating that the Messianic age of salvation has dawned.'[31] But Schoeps too believed that Paul as the interpreter of the post-Messianic situation in which the two ages are mingled has links with the speculation about the Messianic age of 4 Ezra 7: 26ff and 2 Baruch 29–30.[32]

Our study indicates that these scholars were right to seek a connection between the concept of the mingling of the ages and apocalyptic but disagrees with them as to the nature of the connection and shows instead that it is precisely in the area of the conception of a present awareness and experience of the heavenly realm that the missing link is to be found. The concept of a temporally limited Messianic kingdom following the parousia does not play the role in Paul's eschatology that Schweitzer imagined.[33] Though Paul does in one place, 1 Corinthians 15: 24ff, make a distinction between the present period extending from Christ's resurrection to his parousia as the kingdom of Christ and the end when this kingdom is to be delivered over to God the Father, the concept of the present as a temporal Messianic age in contrast to a final theocratic age is not a dominant motif in his letters and there is no consistent distinction in terminology between a present kingdom of Christ and a future kingdom of God. Paul sees God exercising his rule through Christ so that the kingdom of God can be referred to as a present reality (cf. Rom. 14: 17; 1 Cor. 4: 20) and the kingdom in its future aspect can also be called the kingdom of Christ (cf. Eph. 5: 5; cf. also 2 Tim. 4: 1, 18). However it is still possible that Schoeps' thesis has some merit and that Paul could have seen the present period in terms of the apocalyptic temporal Messianic age, so that the traditions about this which were incorporated in 2 Baruch and 4 Ezra (cf. also 1 Enoch 91: 12–17; Sib. Or. III, 652ff) would offer some correspondence to the merging of the two ages in the present, and 1 Corinthians 15: 24ff would provide the one possible piece of evidence in Paul's writings that he was familiar with such a tradition, though he had modified it. By comparison it is clear from our study that we are closer to the centre of Paul's eschatology and on more promising ground for the discovery of correspondences with apocalyptic writings in investigating a realized eschatology involving the heavenly dimension.

At the beginning of this chapter we listed some of the more important references to heaven in Paul for which we had noted similarities in apocalyptic and Qumran writings. In some cases one of the differences between Paul and the apocalyptic writings in their employment of similar concepts is that what in apocalyptic was expected in the future, Paul sees as having been inaugurated in the present by Christ. The eschatological heavenly Adam of apocalyptic, for example, is seen to have been manifested already in the resurrected Christ (cf. on 1 Cor. 15: 47ff) and the future dominion and session on heavenly thrones of the righteous has through Christ's exaltation become a present session with him in the heavenlies (cf. on Eph. 2: 6). In the case of the mystery about God's plan for the cosmos and the involvement of heaven in this, apocalyptic writings treated such a mystery as knowable by the seer in the present but still to be revealed in the future, while both at Qumran and in Paul it is already in the process of being realized (cf. on Eph. 1: 10). In the majority of the cases however the references to heaven have a present context in apocalyptic and at Qumran and also in Paul. It is not only the case, as W. D. Davies has already pointed out,[34] that both apocalyptic and Paul show that the age to come can be anticipated in heaven upon the believer's death (cf. on 2 Cor. 5; Phil. 1: 23), but both show also that it can be anticipated by experiences of the heavenly realm before death. A number of these instances come under the broad apocalyptic conception of the benefits of future salvation being present now in heaven (cf. for example, 4 Ezra 7: 14, 26, 83; 8: 52; 13: 18; 2 Bar. 4: 6; 21: 12; 48: 49; 51: 8; 52: 7; 73: 1; 1 Enoch 46: 3; 52: 2; 103: 3).[35] In this light are to be seen the concept of the Colossians' future hope being already present in heaven and of their life being at present hidden in heaven (Col. 1: 5; 3: 3), the idea of the heavenly commonwealth being a present reality (Phil. 3: 20) and the believer's enjoyment of every spiritual blessing in the heavenlies (Eph. 1: 3). The Paradise of the end time is anticipated both by the seer's heavenly journey in apocalyptic and by the apostle's rapture (cf. on 2 Cor. 12). Associated with this perspective also are the eschatological hopes for Jerusalem and for the temple which find anticipation in a present heavenly Jerusalem and a present celestial temple in apocalyptic, at Qumran and in Paul (cf. on Gal. 4: 26 and on Eph. 2: 20ff). Finally in both the Qumran writings and Paul there is a present fellowship with the angels (cf. on Col. 1: 12; Eph. 2: 19) and a present participation in the heavenly realm (cf. on Eph. 2: 6). In all these cases Paul's 'already' does not constitute a radical break from apocalyptic thought-forms but is a development of them. The distinction between Paul and apocalyptic lies not in the 'already' with its spatial terminology but in the Christological content and orientation the apostle has given to it. It might be argued that there are also other distinctions and that in apocalyptic the experience of the benefits of the age to come in heaven is usually no more than a preview for the isolated visionary whereas in Paul it is an actual foretaste by the whole community of believers. This would however be too simple an analysis, for in apocalyptic the heavenly journey of the seer certainly constitutes an experiential anticipation and in the development in the Qumran writings the whole community is already drawn into the present experience of the heavenly dimension.[36] Paul works then with categories to be found in pre- and post-Pauline Jewish apocalyptic and it is solely the Christological factor that produces the decisive differentiation.

Our investigation therefore indicates that the combination of present and future, spatial and temporal elements is not the distinctive feature in Paul's eschatology as over against that found in apocalyptic and at Qumran. M. Hengel has done much to dispel the misconception that spatial terminology must necessarily be Hellenistic and to show the combination of spatial and temporal categories in apocalyptic.[37] He asserts that the motif of the heavenly journey alone should give pause to any attempt to understand apocalyptic onesidedly or exclusively from the temporal aspect of the imminent expectation of the end.[38] There are, of course, a number of apocalypses which reflect great cosmological interest and involve the revelation of heavenly secrets. In regard to Qumran it is recognized that the present experience of the heavenly realm played an important role in the community's thought[39] and that this by no means excluded an expectation of future salvation. In the eschatology of Qumran there was no conflict between present and future elements or between spatial and temporal categories. In each case both are to be found alongside each other, as the work of H.-W. Kuhn in particular has demonstrated.[40] It should not be surprising to find that in Paul also emphasis on heaven in contexts of realized eschatology can exist alongside an expectation of the future parousia of Christ from heaven (cf. Phil. 3: 20f; Col. 3: 1–4).[41]

This tension between present and future is at the centre of Paul's eschatology and since the tension is rooted in apocalyptic thought, there is certainly a sense in which Paul can be seen as an apocalyptist.[42] This is naturally not to deny that there are also important differences between Paul and apocalyptic.[43] In terms of his literary production Paul wrote

letters not apocalypses. We do not find any apocalyptic schema as such in
Paul. Nowhere does he attempt to give a complete eschatological timetable. Rather apocalyptic perspectives function as a major source for his
thought on which he can draw as he addresses the various situations in his
churches. Above all, for Paul, the Messiah awaited in some apocalyptic
writings has now arrived in the person of Jesus and Paul is first and fore-
most a follower of this Jesus Christ, so that what gives his thought its
unique character is not any inherited apocalyptic structure but the resurrected Christ and the new historical situation he has produced. One of the
specific contributions of this study however has been to show that even in
interpreting this proleptic coming of the new age apocalyptic categories
were on hand for Paul to remould and that he did not need to look for an
entirely different framework. Paul's thought is therefore not in conflict
with apocalyptic,[44] but makes use of it, drawing on both sides of its framework, on both its temporally and its spatially orientated structures, and in
this sense the apostle can be called a Christian apocalyptist. But since the
tension between present and future arises for Paul in the first place only
because of Christ's resurrection and exaltation, the decisive qualification
involved in the adjective 'Christian' must be given its full weight in this
description of his eschatology.[45]

Our study of his treatment of the heavenly dimension reveals that
Paul's Christian apocalyptic is defined both by the future and by the
recent past and is about what happens when the life of the age to come has
been made available through Christ's resurrection and how that life does
not remain centered in heaven but works itself out on earth in the present
period of history. In this way Paul avoids one of the negative tendencies of
Jewish apocalyptic, the tendency to minimize the significance of present
history. Within this Christian apocalyptic references to the heavenly
dimension have been given new content by being subordinated by the
apostle to what has happened to his heavenly Lord. After all the most
formative influence on Paul's thought was his encounter with the heavenly
Christ on the Damascus Road when what had previously been just elements
in the conceptual world he had inherited became integral in formulating
the significance of this startlingly dramatic event. According to Luke in
Acts Paul could sum up this event in terms of 'the heavenly vision' (Acts
26: 19 cf. also 9: 3; 22: 6; 26: 13). When he received the traditions about
Christ's resurrection and appearances his own encounter caused him to
think of this resurrection as a resurrection to heavenly existence and his
further visions and revelations of his heavenly Lord reinforced this conception. From now on everything was coloured by the impact of his
experience of the exalted Christ as the bearer of the divine glory. The

significance of the heavenly Jerusalem (Gal. 4: 26) now has to do with
the Church's enjoyment of the life and freedom of the age to come
granted by Christ in heaven, accomplished through his death and made
effective by his Spirit.[46] According to 1 Corinthians 15: 47ff, the 'heavenly'
is the quality of life which flows from Christ in his resurrection existence
and is mediated by him as life-giving Spirit and for the Corinthians to be
heavenly means to be like Christ in every respect which will include their
future possession of a heavenly body. 2 Corinthians 5: 1 integrally links
the believer's heavenly body with that of Christ by its allusion to the
tradition preserved in Mark 14: 58. Existence in heaven after death and
before the parousia is in the presence of the heavenly Lord (2 Cor. 5: 6ff),
so that union with Christ is determinative for this anticipation of the age
to come in heaven (Phil. 1: 23). Christ gives the specific colouring to
Paul's heavenly vision of 2 Corinthians 12 which was given by the Lord
and comes to him as a 'man in Christ'. The paradise he experiences is one
which has been opened up by Christ and receives its character from him.[47]
Believers' government is in heaven because that is the realm from which
their Lord now rules and their present demonstration of that heavenly
rule is to be defined by Christ's character as the one who humbled himself
to the point of death (cf. Phil. 3: 20f). The Colossian believers are only to
seek the things above because that is where Christ is and their life has its
source above because it is hidden with him (Col. 3: 1, 3). The cosmic
reconciliation and unity which involves the heavenly dimension takes place
through Christ's death on the cross and is summed up in him (Col. 1: 20;
Eph. 1: 10). Throughout Ephesians it is what has happened to Christ (cf.
1: 20ff; 4: 7ff; 6: 9) that is determinative for the community's relationship to the heavenly realm, so that the blessings of salvation in the
heavenlies which believers enjoy are 'in Christ' and bound up with the
Spirit (1: 3), they are seated in the heavenlies both in and with Christ (2:
6), the Church can be seen as a heavenly temple because the exalted Christ
is its top stone (2: 20) and it is linked to its heavenly Lord and dependent
on him for unity, ministry and growth as he is present in the Spirit (4: 7ff).
In the interaction in Paul's thought between elements from the apocalyptic framework and Christology the latter is clearly the ultimately
dominant factor. The relationship between the present and the future of
salvation is not determined by the *a prioris* of any apocalyptic schema
but is derived by the apostle from the overwhelming and unexpected way
in which God has acted in Jesus Christ for human salvation and will yet
act.[48]

(iv) Some implications for theories of the development of eschatology within the Pauline corpus

If our findings about the relationship between Paul's use of the concept of heaven and apocalyptic are valid, they give strong grounds for disputing the evolutionary interpretation of Paul's eschatology which sees a movement away from apocalyptic notions in the earlier letters to more Hellenistic ideas in the later letters and considers the emphasis on the heavenly in the later letters as evidence for this. Some scholars, as we have noted earlier in the study, see the development towards realized eschatology using spatial terminology to be so marked in Colossians and Ephesians that for this reason these letters can no longer be considered authentically Pauline.

An older representative of the evolutionary interpretation was F. C. Porter who contrasted the externality of apocalyptic with Paul's inwardness, mysticism and ability to spiritualize so that for him Paul was part of a movement 'away from the apocalyptic toward the spiritual apprehension of the other world and man's relation to it', a movement which had come to recognize that 'it is the religious task of man to have his real home in the heavenly world.'[49] C. H. Dodd also held that Paul began with a strongly Jewish apocalyptic eschatology but developed towards the realized eschatology of a 'Christ-mysticism' which could be summed up in the words of Ephesians 1: 3.[50] The decisive shift in Paul's attitude took place between the writing of 1 Corinthians and 2 Corinthians so that from then on, according to Dodd, 'the thought of the imminence of the Advent retires into the background' and 'the eschatological expectation has come to be subordinated to the thought of the heavenly life (the life of the new age) lived here and now'.[51] On this view Paul's thought is to be understood in the light of its maturity rather than in terms of the earlier stages which the apostle had outgrown.[52] T. Boman believes also that a change took place between the writing of 1 and 2 Corinthians, after which Paul moves more and more to Greek thought-forms. The eternal house in heaven (2 Cor. 5: 1) and the commonwealth in heaven (Phil. 3: 20), according to him, involve concepts which 'belong not to time but to space, not to end-time but to the Beyond, not to the future but to the present, not to becoming but to being ... Greek influence has certainly expressed itself here.' For Boman Colossians 3 and Ephesians are examples of Greek eros-piety which 'expresses itself in the struggle of the religious man to attain that which is above'.[53] The sharp disjuncture between the two thought worlds of apocalypticism and Hellenism involved in most of these theories sounds strange now in the wake of recent insistence on taking seriously the impact of over three centuries of Hellenistic rule of Palestine. Jewish apocalyptic had always had a close relationship with its Hellenistic environment and there is of course much Hellenistic literature about heavenly journeys and revelations which is similar in form to the apocalyptic writings.[54] There are further difficulties for such theories of development; they often depend on a particular chronology of the letters which it is difficult to establish with any certainty and the relatively short span of time in which the letters were written after the early and presumably most formative stage in Paul's thought militates against any major change of direction.[55] But if, as we have shown, Paul does not have to abandon his apocalyptic framework in expanding on the concept of the believer's involvement in the heavenly world, then these theories are made even less likely.

We are on safer hermeneutical ground in taking the course followed in this study of examining the form and function of Paul's eschatological language in its various settings.[56] Particular situations, many of them polemical, evoked particular emphases in the apostle's teachings. It was because deficient views about the heavenly dimension were being aired in such churches as those at Corinth, Philippi and Colossae that Paul was forced to focus his own perspective. We have noted that in doing so he will often make use of 'Hellenistic' terminology (cf. Phil. 1: 23; 3: 20; 2 Cor. 5), but only as new and appropriate ways of expressing to predominantly Gentile congregations his own basic eschatological perspective. We have seen that neither Dodd nor Davies are to be followed in their suggestions about the sort of change in Paul's eschatology which took place between the writing of 1 Corinthians and 2 Corinthians but rather that in addressing an altered situation both in his own life and in the Corinthian church the apostle uses new imagery and applies further reflection but does not go back on anything he has asserted in 1 Corinthians 15. Though Paul increasingly has to come to grips with his own death before the parousia and though earlier letters may reflect his expectation of a more speedy coming of the Lord while later ones suggest an expectation of that coming as simply imminent, his basic eschatological framework, which reckons with the dual possibility of the believer's death or the prior return of Christ, remains constant.[57] Our study has found that realized eschatology using language about heaven is scattered throughout the letters. It occurs not only in Colossians and Ephesians but can be found as early as Galatians with its reference to the heavenly Jerusalem and even in 1 Corinthians 15 where Paul is addressing those with an over-realized eschatology. Both here and in Philippians 3, while correcting opponents on this score, he is not afraid to concede the element of truth in their position and to strike a balance as he acknowledges that believers are heavenly (1 Cor. 15: 47ff) and that their commonwealth and government is now in heaven (Phil. 3: 20). 2 Corinthians 12 shows that heaven can be anticipated in this life through visionary experiences, while 2 Corinthians 5 and Philippians 1: 23 indicate an anticipation of the age to come in heaven at death. As over against scholars such as Käsemann, Lohse, Grässer and Koester,[58] we do not therefore find it surprising that this sort of realized eschatology undergoes expansion in the particular settings of Colossians and Ephesians. If Colossians is directed against a syncretistic 'philosophy' with its dualistic cosmology and if Ephesians in conjunction with its worship-setting also has an eye on this syncretism, then it would be natural for Paul to draw on the spatial concepts already inherent in the framework he has inherited from apocalyptic and to expand on them as he writes to churches under the influence of such Hellenistic syncretism. It was not a question of having to adopt a new framework; the appropriate ideological weapons were already on hand and simply needed to be developed. The worship-setting of Ephesians makes this spatial terminology even more prominent in that letter, but again by analogy with the Qumran writings this is only to be expected, for it is primarily in the hymns of thanksgiving that the community's consciousness of its links with the heavenly realm is reflected. Worship, moreover, is the appropriate setting for realized eschatology, for the goal of creation and of history is doxology and this is anticipated in worship. It is noticeable, in any case, that the more polemical the setting of Paul's letters the fewer references there are to future eschatology – they are lacking in 2 Corinthians 10–13 and scarce in Galatians.[59] In writings aimed at a syncretistic situation which called for a stress on what God had already done for believers in Christ a large number of references to the future would be surprising. Yet, as we have seen, in neither Colossians nor Ephesians are such references entirely eclipsed and it is as the focus of these letters moves from the polemical purpose in the case of Colossians and from the explicitly liturgically orientated part in the case of Ephesians that their references to the future increase. In both letters realized eschatology stands alongside future eschatology without conflict.

An emphasis on heaven does not involve any abrogation of eschatology.[60] Still more significantly, it does not even involve an abandonment of the categories of apocalyptic. The apostle draws on elements from the basic apocalyptic framework for the different situations and needs to which he writes and in doing so maintains a balance between spatial and temporal elements in his eschatology in contrast to the virtually all-pervasive emphasis on the heavenly to be found in some post-apostolic writings.[61] We can agree therefore with those who, like Käsemann, stress Paul's links with apocalyptic and yet, having a fuller knowledge of those links, we need not with him dismiss the emphasis on realized eschatology which utilizes spatial terminology as foreign to the authentic Paul.

2. Heaven and the scope of salvation

In any attempt at a synthesis of the materials with which we have been dealing the fluidity of the term 'heaven' is to be remembered. Our study has centered around passages where οὐρανός and its cognates play a role. In Gal. 4: 26 and Phil. 3: 14 ἄνω was used attributively, while in Col. 3: 1, 2 it was employed substantively in the phrase τὰ ἄνω. The phrase ἐξ οὐρανοῦ occurred in 1 Cor. 15: 47 where it was seen to be equivalent to ἐπουράνιος in verses 48, 49, and it was found again in 2 Cor. 5: 2. In 2 Cor. 5: 1; Col. 1: 5, 20 the phrase ἐν τοῖς οὐρανοῖς appeared and without the article was repeated in the plural in Phil. 3: 20; Eph. 3: 15; 6: 9 and in the singular in Col. 4: 1. There is an unusual variation of the preposition in Eph. 1: 10 with ἐπὶ τοῖς οὐρανοῖς. In Ephesians we found the further distinctive phrases ἐν τοῖς ἐπουρανίοις (1: 3, 20; 2: 6; 3: 10; 6: 12) and ὑπεράνω πάντων τῶν οὐρανῶν (4: 10), while in 2 Cor. 12: 2, 4 ἕως τρίτου οὐρανοῦ and εἰς τὸν παράδεισον are parallel phrases.

As we have seen, from its OT and Jewish usage the term has a variety of references – it can refer to the sky and the cosmic heavens as the upper part of created reality,[62] to a presently invisible created spiritual world which the upper limits of the firmament were thought to conceal, and to the divine abode, as this upper part points beyond its own createdness to the divine transcendence. Since it is a word employed for objects which point beyond themselves, in certain passages its nuances are not clearly distinguished. Thus while it is clear, for example, that the first meaning is in view in 1 Corinthians 15: 40, other references, such as Colossians 1: 20 and Ephesians 1: 10, appear to combine the first and second meanings and to have in view both the cosmic heavens and the spiritual powers behind them, and elsewhere, especially in Ephesians, the second and third meanings appear to be combined for Christ can be said to be both in heaven (1: 20, 6: 9) and also 'at God's right hand' (1: 20) or 'above all the heavens' (4: 10), the latter references pointing to the divine transcendence of spatial categories. In other passages what God has done in Christ has given a special content to the concept of heaven, for it has become involved in a new way in that act of the drama of redemption inaugurated by Christ's resurrection and exaltation. Despite the variation between singular and plural expressions, which, except in Eph. 4: 10, where the addition of πάντων indicates that the plural is significant, is simply a stylistic matter, the passages and their terminology listed above indicate the relative consistency of Paul's references. We have seen again and again that in his use οὐρανός and its cognates have a local, spatial or cosmological connotation which continually shades over into a qualitative force. The realm of heaven also stands for the qualities of life which belong to that realm. It is for this reason that we have frequently chosen the phrase 'heavenly dimension' as the one which perhaps is able to convey best the fluidity and the dual connotations of οὐρανός and its cognates in the majority of uses in the Pauline corpus. The important influences on Paul's use of this concept, as has been indicated earlier, include the apocalyptic framework which he inherited, the situations in the churches which called for references to heaven in the first place and shaped the apostle's response, and above all his own knowledge and experience of the exalted Christ. Since we have endeavoured to be sensitive to these considerations throughout the study, this attempt to draw together some of our findings and to discover how the concept of heaven fits into Paul's overall view of the fulfilment of God's promises of salvation in Christ perhaps avoids some of the pitfalls involved in any systematization of Paul's thought. That Paul spoke to different questions at different times certainly need not mean that he had no coherent overall perspective.[63]

(i) Heaven and the cosmic drama

Too often a consideration of the topic of heaven is reduced to a discussion of what happens to the individual at death, but for Paul this topic was far broader and richer, involving this life and stretching out beyond death to the consummation of history. Perhaps the apocalyptic framework which Paul drew on justifies the attempt to view the function of heaven for him as part of the drama of salvation which was unfolding with Christ as its centre, though again it must be underlined that the apostle himself never presents this as a schema. The drama, that is, the history of salvation, and the setting, that is the cosmos, heaven and earth, are both important. The setting however is not to be thought of simply as a static backdrop because it is caught up and involved in the drama. At the same time while the cosmic setting is important, for Paul the details of cosmology are not. He holds to no fixed doctrine of the number of heavens[64] and while most frequently he operates simply with a two-storey universe of heaven and earth, at other times, such as in the hymn of Philippians 2 or in Romans 10: 6ff, he can take over the three-storey schema with heaven, earth and a realm under the earth.

A synopsis of the drama can be found in 1Thessalonians 1: 10. Here Paul takes up traditional confessional material used in the missionary preaching of the early Jewish Christians[65] and employs it to describe the totally new orientation of the Thessalonian believers on their reception of the apostolic message. They now 'wait for his Son from heaven, whom he raised from the dead, that is Jesus, who delivers us from the wrath to come'. The present is a period in which the Thessalonians are being saved from coming wrath and it is also a time of expectation of the consummation of this salvation which will occur with the coming of God's Son *from* heaven. This of course presupposes that in the interim he is *in* heaven and the beginning of this present period of salvation is marked off by the reference to Christ's resurrection. The use of the name Jesus in this context may be meant to underline the identity of the earthly Jesus with the exalted Lord but the perspective of the statement is clearly that the resurrection of Jesus inaugurated the period of salvation in which he is in heaven and that this period will culminate in his coming from heaven. The rest of what Paul has to say about heaven can be seen as an expansion on the perspective of this traditional formulation.

The opening act involves the resurrection and Paul expands on this event in 1 Corinthians 15, showing how it ushers in the life of the age to come and of the heavenly dimension. It is because of his resurrection that the second Man, Jesus Christ, and those who belong to him can be called heavenly and heavenly existence is seen to be resurrection existence. Not only did the resurrection bring about a transformation of nature for Christ but his ensuing exaltation (cf. Eph. 4: 8ff)[66] also effected a change of place, both of which are seen in terms of heaven. The central figure in the drama of the history of salvation has moved from the setting of earth to that of heaven (cf. Phil. 3: 20f; Col. 3: 1; Eph. 1: 20; 6: 9).

This fact dominates the act which is now in progress and which covers the period between the resurrection and the parousia. Because Christ is in heaven, this realm can be seen as the present sphere of fulfilment of God's promises of salvation to his people in the OT. This is something of the significance of the apostle's reference to the Jerusalem above in Galatians 4: 26 and of his use of Isaiah 54: 1 in that context. Paul regards this prophecy about the new Jerusalem as being fulfilled in the present, as through Christ Jews and Gentiles become one people. For Paul the hope of Israel lies not in the Jerusalem that now is but in Christ who fulfils all that Jerusalem dimly foreshadowed in regard to the presence of God with humanity. Since Christ is now in heaven the fulfilment of the promise to the earthly Jerusalem has been transferred to the heavenly dimension he has opened up and the Gentiles who are children of promise share in this salvation which has its focal point in the Jerusalem above.

The heavenly Christ who fulfils God's promises of salvation also shows the scope of that salvation, for by his death and exaltation he has won the victory over any and all evil cosmic powers and now rules over heaven and earth (cf. Phil. 2: 8–11; Col. 1: 15–20; 2: 10, 15; Eph. 1: 20ff). He fills all things (Eph. 1: 23; 4: 10) in terms of his sovereign rule, as he directs the universe to its divinely appointed end. Yet while there is this decisive 'already' aspect to Christ's victory and rule, 1 Corinthians 15: 24ff, which sets out the stages in Christ's conquest, and Ephesians 6: 10ff, which asserts that the believer's warfare is against spiritual hosts of wickedness in the heavenly places, emphasize that the triumph is not yet final. Heaven is still involved in the present age with the consequence that war in heaven will continue until the consummatory victory brings in the fullness of the new age with its reconciled cosmos.

Christ as Lord in heaven is not remote from his people on earth. Because of their link with him both individual believers and the Church as a whole have been drawn into the cosmic drama. The believer's faith-union with Christ is not only a union in his death and resurrection but extends to his heavenly exaltation (Eph. 2: 6). His or her life is hid with Christ above (Col. 3: 1ff) and indeed he or she can be called 'heavenly' (1 Cor. 15: 48). For Paul the Church also could only be truly understood when seen in relation to its Lord in heaven who was exercising all power on its behalf (Eph. 1: 22f). In fact the Church is to provide the angelic powers with tangible evidence that all things are to be subject to Christ (Eph. 3: 10). Its life is governed by the heavenly dimension and the Jerusalem above is the mother who nourishes it (Gal. 4: 26). There can be no suspicion that Christ is remote, for Ephesians 5 pictures the relationship between Christ and the Church in terms of the marriage of the heavenly bridegroom to his bride, a union where the two become one in the strongest sense (5: 31, 32). The Church itself takes on a heavenly character in Ephesians 2: 20–22 where it is seen as the new temple linked to the heavenly realm with the exalted Christ as the top stone in its structure. It is the Spirit who constitutes the vital bond between the people of God on earth and the heavenly dimension, for as the heavenly temple the Church is the dwelling place of God in the Spirit (Eph. 2: 22). In 1 Corinthians 15: 44ff the order of the Spirit and the dimension of heaven serve as functional equivalents, while in Galatians 4: 29 the children of the Jerusalem above are described as those born according to the Spirit. The benefits which belong to believers by virtue of Christ's exaltation are mediated by the Spirit (Eph. 1: 3) who is the pledge and guarantee of full possession of the heavenly inheritance (Eph. 1: 13; 2 Cor. 5: 5). The same Christ who ascended to become cosmic Lord is intimately involved in building up the Church's life because he has also descended in the Spirit (Eph. 4: 7ff).

During the present act of the drama the life of heaven is to be worked out on earth by believers (cf. Phil. 3: 20; Col. 3: 1ff). The paradox of this situation however is that this heavenly life and power are to be displayed in the midst of a state of humiliation (cf. Phil. 3: 20f with 2: 5–11) and through decaying earthly bodies that are still part of the present evil age (cf. 2 Cor. 5, 12). Yet Paul indicates that in this period between the resurrection and the parousia there can be four high points in believers' anticipation of the fullness of heavenly life. The first is at baptism, seen as a complex of 'conversion-initiation',[67] when believers enter on the new heavenly life that is theirs by virtue of their union with Christ (cf. on Col. 3: 1ff; Eph. 1: 3; 2: 6). Another high point is in worship, for here the final union of the earthly and heavenly worlds is anticipated as believers focus their attention on the exalted Christ and experience fellowship with the angels (cf. 1 Cor. 11: 10; Eph. 2: 19; cf. also Col. 1: 12). Ephesians with its liturgical elements and accompanying realized eschatology of heaven is witness to the fact that the Church is at its most heavenly in worship. Special visionary experiences such as that granted to Paul and mentioned in 2 Corinthians 12 also bring an anticipation of the fullness of heavenly existence. The other point at which this occurs is at the death of the believer. In Philippians 1: 23 and 2 Corinthians 5: 6ff believers can be said to be 'with the Lord' or 'present with the Lord' in the state into which they enter at death, and because the Lord is at present in heaven the setting for this state is the heavenly dimension. Yet heaven as such and entrance to it upon death are not seen as the final goal of salvation. Even in this context heaven participates in the 'already–not yet' tension of existence in the period when the ages overlap.

The real dénouement of the history of salvation takes place at the coming of Christ from heaven to earth to open the final act of the drama. In the imagery of 1 Thessalonians 4: 16 – 'The Lord himself will descend from heaven with a shout, with the voice of the archangel, and with the trumpet of God.' In speaking of the encounter this awesome event will involve for those who are still alive, Paul uses the phrase εἰς ἀπάντησιν. This was a phrase associated with the official visits of a ruling dignitary to a Hellenistic city when in a public ceremony the populace would go outside the city walls to meet the ruler and form a triumphal procession escorting him back into the city.[68] If, as seems most likely, this is the nuance the apostle has in mind here, then those who 'will be caught up in the clouds . . . to meet the Lord in the air' (1 Thess. 4: 17) will escort him in his triumphant descent to earth.[69] Christ will bring the glory of heaven to earth. 'Believers will be revealed with him in glory' (Col. 3: 4), 'glory' signifying 'a final amalgamation of the earthly and heavenly spheres'.[70] Philippians 3: 20, 21 also connect Christ's coming from heaven with the transformation of believers' bodies 'into conformity with the body of his glory'. As the life of heaven is brought to earth both earthly bodies and the earth itself are transformed and glorified. The bodies of believers become heavenly bodies, because for Paul heavenly life could not be complete without taking on bodily form (1 Cor. 15: 49; 2 Cor. 5: 1). The coming of the Lord will also effect a transformation of the cosmos, for, as Philippians 3: 21 emphasizes, the power with which Christ will change the bodies of believers is the same power which enables him also to subject all things (τὰ πάντα) to himself. The whole creation will be redeemed (cf. Rom. 8: 18–23), as the new creation, already begun in the lives of men and women (2 Cor. 5: 17; Gal. 6: 15), is brought to completion.[71] In other words the coming from heaven inaugurates not withdrawal from this world into some other but the fullness of the age to come with its transformed heaven and earth.[72] In this magnificent finale attention will remain riveted on the figure through whom all this has been brought about. Jesus Christ is the one who unites heaven and earth. In Ephesians 1: 9, 10 the apostle indicates that God's plan is that the goal of history should be embodied in Christ as he sums up and restores to harmony everything in heaven and on earth and this redounds to the glory of the one who created it all.[73] In this way the drama ends on a doxological note, for as Christ's cosmic lordship is openly confessed God the Father is glorified (Phil. 2: 9–11; 1 Cor. 15: 28; cf. also Rom. 11: 36).

(ii) Heaven and the destiny of humanity

Why does Paul see the realization and fulfilment of human personality as taking the form of some sort of celestial existence? 1 Corinthians 15 provides the clearest evidence of his perspective on this question. Since his discussion there is so dependent on the concept of Christ as the second man, the last Adam, what he has to say about the heavenly dimension is rooted in his view of humanity and its destiny.

Sometimes in Paul the comparison between Christ and Adam is used in contexts of an analogy between the first things and the last and also of a restitution of creation through redemption[74] and we have noted the idea of a restoration of humanity's original links with heaven in Paul. In Ephesians 1: 22 in connection with Christ's lordship over heaven and earth and the angelic powers the apostle cites Psalm 8: 6, which honours humanity as created in God's image to exercise dominion, and shows that what the first man forfeited God has restored to Christ as the last Adam. Through Christ this restoration comes to the believer, as Ephesians 2: 6 indicates with its assertion that the believer shares Christ's dominion in the heavenlies. We have noted that in the Jewish traditions to which Paul was heir Adam was often linked to the heavenly dimension and sometimes in highly speculative and exaggerated forms; he was said, for example, to be physically large enough to span heaven and earth.[75] But for Paul it was enough to think of humanity as being originally made in God's image (cf. Col. 3: 10) and possessing God's glory (cf. Rom. 3: 23). The very concept of being made in God's image involved spiritual transcendence, the potential for being linked with the transcendent Creator in heaven. 'Glory' in particular carried with it associations with the heavenly realm and Paul thought of humanity as at present having lost its share in this glory (Rom. 3: 23). The concepts of glory and image were for Paul closely related. Both δόξα and εἰκών were used to translate תמונה in the LXX and Paul himself uses the two terms together in 1 Corinthians 11: 7 and 2 Corinthians 3: 18; 4: 4. In 1 Corinthians 15 too both glory (verse 43) and image (verse 49) are used in connection with the new heavenly order of existence. Whereas, after the fall, humanity retained something of the image of God but the glory of God became only an eschatological hope, Paul sees Christ, who is God's image, as having been raised in the glory of God, so that he is the heavenly man in whom both the glory and the image are fully present (cf. also 2 Cor. 3: 18; 4: 4). There are degrees of glory (cf. 1 Cor. 15: 40) and the implication of the main thrust of Paul's argument in 1 Corinthians 15 is that all speculation about the original glory of the first man is relatively insignificant now that the second man has been revealed, because his resurrection not only involves a restoration to humanity's original glory but accomplishes a confirmation in glory, that higher state of heavenly glory the first man failed to achieve.

In Paul's perspective the criterion of judgment of what is appropriate to human destiny is neither humanity as it now is nor even humanity as it was before the fall, but rather humanity as God intended it to be. Verses 44*b*–46 of 1 Corinthians 15 indicate that from creation a different kind of body and a different order of existence have been in view for humanity. This higher order of existence is described both as spiritual and as heavenly. The eschatological prospect to which the first man failed to attain is realized and receives its character through the resurrection of the second man who has become heavenly. For Paul it was not enough simply to say that Christ restores humanity to its original condition, rather he brings humanity to that destiny which God had intended but which humanity before Christ had never reached. The concept of a heavenly dimension enabled the apostle to express something of the superiority of the new creation which had begun with Christ's resurrection and to show that as the one who bears the heavenly image, the resurrected Christ provides the only adequate definition of humanity, the fulfilment of a person's inherent potential for transcendence. In his mind this heavenly dimension was not a sphere remote from all that it means to be authentically human but was integral to a person's fulfilment. Christ became heavenly but remained human. It is the second *man* who is heavenly (1 Cor. 15: 47). Having encountered this heavenly Christ and having recognized that the eschatological future of glory had arrived in him, Paul knew that it was God's plan for men and women to become like Christ, that is, heavenly. Paul's use of 'image' in 1 Corinthians 15: 49 has specific reference to the future resurrection body, indicating that the fulfilment of humanity involves the whole personality. Christ's resurrection to heavenly existence had demonstrated once and for all that a person's true identity included the body. For Paul now one of the acid tests of the genuineness of a claim to heavenliness was whether it took the body seriously, for he knew that the fullness of heavenly life did not have to do with souls detached from bodies in a vaporous state but with heavenly bodies.

(iii) Heaven and the tension of Christian existence

What is the nature of the tension between this-worldliness and otherworldliness produced by Paul's emphasis on a heavenly dimension? Does it involve for him an inevitable dualism in the believer's and the Church's existence?

Because of the destiny that lay ahead of the believer and because Christ was in heaven Paul certainly expected there to be a genuine heavenly-mindedness on the part of Christians. 'Seek the things that are above, where Christ is', he urges the Colossians (Col. 3: 1f) and in 2 Corinthians 4 and 5, in expressing his assurance in the face of death, he holds the heavenly realities before him and indicates that the attitude of faith is one which looks at the earthly in the light of the heavenly. We have seen that the contrast of 2 Corinthians 4: 17f between 'the things that are seen' and 'the things that are unseen' is not of the same variety as that in Platonic dualism, for the heavenly realities are only at present unseen. As 'an eternal weight of glory' they will be openly revealed when the heavenly dimension transforms humanity and its world. Nor did the importance Paul placed on heavenly-mindedness involve him in a dualism between this world and the other world such as that to be found in the cosmological dualisms of the syncretistic teachings he has in view in Colossians and Ephesians or that to be found in later Christian thought in regard to nature and grace. To talk of such dualisms with regard to Paul is to pose false problems and it is important therefore to establish that there is a profound distinction between the duality of heaven and earth which figures in Paul's thought and any metaphysical or cosmological dualism involving these two realms. For Paul heaven and earth, though distinct aspects of reality, formed part of one structure, one created cosmos (cf. Col. 1: 16; Eph. 3: 9, 15; 4: 6). Not only were both created by the same God, but both were affected by humanity's fall. The assertions of Colossians 1: 20 and Ephesians 1: 10, as we have seen, presuppose that the whole cosmos was plunged into disintegration because of sin and that hostile elements now exist in the heavenly realm which need to be reconciled. Ephesians 3: 10 and 6: 12 also reflect the view that both heaven and earth are involved in the present evil age. Above all heaven and earth are shown to be inseparably connected by the redemption which God has accomplished in Christ (cf. Col. 1: 20; Eph. 1: 10, 22f; 4: 10). For Paul Christ's cosmic lordship established that there was not the least segment of created reality over which he could not claim the exclusive right.

In the apostle's perspective, therefore, there were not two realms set over against each other, earth over against heaven, this world over against the other world, but rather one structure of created reality (the cosmos of heaven and earth) and human response to that structure involving two ethical directions. The sinful response brought about disunity in the cosmos and this direction of disobedience can be called 'earthly'. In Philippians 3: 19 and Colossians 3: 2, 5 'earthly' is contrasted to 'heavenly' and takes on the connotation of sinful, with the earth being viewed as the primary setting of fallen creation (cf. LXX Gen. 3: 17). In Colossians τὰ ἐπὶ τῆς γῆς in this sense are shown to include the practices of the 'old man' (3: 5-9), the sphere of the flesh (2: 18, 23) and life in the 'world' with its bondage to the elemental spirits (2: 20). On the other hand the direction of obedience, exemplified by the obedience of the second man (Rom. 5: 19), is associated with the heavenly (1 Cor. 15: 47). The resurrection and exaltation of Christ accomplish a new unity between heaven and earth, for Christ now has a heavenly body (1 Cor. 15: 42ff), a body of glory (Phil. 3: 21) and his humanity is now in heaven (Phil. 3: 20f; Col. 3: 1; Eph. 1: 20ff; 6: 9), and both serve as a pledge of the ultimate unity of the cosmos in Christ (Eph. 1: 10).

Believers, as they continue in obedient response to God's salvation in Christ, become part of this heavenly direction, so that they can be called 'heavenly' (1 Cor. 15: 48) and be exhorted to be heavenly-minded (Col. 3: 1f). They can now experience the substantial restoration of links with the heavenly world. We have already noted that the Spirit enables the life of heaven to be experienced on earth, that the Church itself through its exalted Lord is linked to the heavenly dimension and that experiences such as baptism, worship and visions play an important role in the anticipation of this life of the age to come. This stress on believers' association with heaven through union with Christ does not close the earth or this world to believers but opens them. Because they belong to Christ all things belong to believers, including the world (cf. 1 Cor. 3: 22 – εἴτε κόσμος . . . εἴτε ἐνεστῶτα εἴτε μέλλοντα, πάντα ὑμῶν). Colossians demonstrates that it is because believers participate in the triumph of the exalted Christ over the powers that they have been set free to use this world and its structures.[76] Indeed believers are to bring the life of heaven to earth as they reflect and live out that life. The force of Philippians 3: 20 is not, as has often been thought, that heaven as such is the homeland of Christians to which they, as perpetual foreigners on earth, must strive to return, but rather that since their Lord is in heaven their life is to be governed by the heavenly commonwealth and that this realm is to be determinative for all aspects of their life. Colossians 3 again shows that Paul does not believe that real life is in this other world and that as a consequence life on earth has relatively little significance but that heavenly life is to take form within the structures of human existence, in the husband–wife, parent–child, master–slave relationships (cf. also Eph. 5 and 6 and in particular the view that earthly marriages are to reflect the heavenly marriage between the exalted Christ and his bride, the Church). The apostle can insist both on the necessity of heavenly-mindedness and on the fullness he expects to see in the personal, domestic, communal and societal aspects of Christian living. The quality of the concentration on the things above where Christ is will ensure that the present sphere of his rule will not remain simply in heaven but will be demonstrated in the lives of his people on earth.

Despite this substantial restoration of the ties between heaven and earth, for the believer there remain elements of duality in Paul's perspective owing to the present overlap of the ages. In 1 Corinthians 15: 47 'earthly' characterizes the present order, while 'heavenly' characterizes the order of the age to come. Simply to be in the present body is to be part of the earthly order, even without reference to sin, according to both 1 Corinthians 15: 47 and 2 Corinthians 5: 1, so that while the body remains as it is fullness of heavenly life cannot be experienced. Because Christ has been exalted to heaven, heaven rather than earth temporarily provides the chief focus for salvation and for the believer's orientation until Christ's coming from heaven when salvation will then embrace heaven and earth. Correspondingly, during this present period, although, as we have seen, heaven is still affected by evil and Christ's victory over the powers is not yet complete, it is the earth which is seen as the special theatre of sin. Because believers are on earth the influence of this sphere acts as a drag on them so that they have to be exhorted to 'put to death those parts of you which belong to the earth' (Col. 3: 5 NEB). These elements of duality inevitably produce a certain tension for the believer. The aspect of hiddenness also plays its part in this. Believers are already linked to the realm above where Christ is but they know that the real nature of this relationship to the heavenly dimension will remain hidden until the parousia and the accompanying revelation in glory (Col. 3: 3f). Though they know themselves to have been seated with Christ in the heavenlies (Eph. 2: 6), they must for the present remain on earth in the midst of battle (Eph. 6: 10ff). The tension is highlighted by the approach of death. Paul ultimately looks for the consummation of salvation with the reception of a heavenly body at the coming of his Lord from heaven, yet because of his union with Christ his longings for fuller salvation can also focus on the heavenly dimension where Christ now is and on furtherance of that union by being in his presence. In this way, although he entertains no death-wish, when brought face to face with death the apostle can count it as gain to depart from this earth, since being with Christ is far better (cf. Phil. 1: 23; 2 Cor. 5: 6ff). Factors such as increasing age, extreme sickness or imprisonment (the latter two especially appear to have been operative in the settings of 2 Cor. 5 and Phil. 1), which confront the believer with impending death, therefore cause heaven to loom larger than earth on his or her horizon. Above all, the tension which the heaven–earth duality produces for Christian existence is characterized by the paradox that heavenly life is to be demonstrated through a state of humiliation and weakness. In comparing Philippians 3: 20f with 2: 6–11 we observed that for Paul the programme of the heavenly commonwealth as it works itself out on earth is to be the programme followed by Christ. There can be no attempts to find any short cuts to glory, for although believers already belong to the heavenly commonwealth they cannot yet claim all their rights as citizens. Unlike those whom Paul designates 'enemies of the cross' (3: 19), believers are to be pilgrims of the cross on their way to a new heaven and earth. The point of Paul's reference to his experience of heaven in 2 Corinthians 12 is not to glory in this but to point out that it occurred in a context of humiliations. Heavenly existence at present is not at one remove from earthly life but is demonstrated in the midst of it. Paul had learned the lesson that heavenly power is perfected in earthly weakness (cf. 12: 9) and therefore considered his weakness rather than his visionary experience of the third heaven the proof that he was a representative of the crucified Christ who is Lord. The sufferings inherent in life in this present evil age provide the presupposition for this paradox in the believer's life-style. In the midst of such sufferings belief in heavenly realities is to provide consolation (2 Cor. 4: 16ff) and, because of union with Christ and possession of the Spirit, even death, as the extreme of the process of suffering and decay, is to become a setting for the revelation of heavenly power, so that the life of Jesus may be manifested not only in the believer's mortal flesh (2 Cor. 4: 11) but also through death itself (cf. 2 Cor. 5: 1ff), embodying the paradox of the apostle's words 'as dying, and behold we live' (2 Cor. 6: 9).

The apostle's emphasis on heaven involves the believer in an anticipation of the fullness of the age to come. It is an active anticipation because the Lord in heaven is to be obeyed as the life of the heavenly dimension is demonstrated on earth, and yet it is an active anticipation which bears the sign of the cross since the exalted Lord in heaven is at the same time the crucified Servant. It must be underlined that this tension between heavenly and earthly life is temporary, for the completion of salvation will involve heaven being brought to earth at Christ's return.[77] It is this eschatological perspective which provides the ultimate unifying factor for the duality of this-worldly and other-worldly elements in Paul's thought. Where such a perspective has been lost, 'the other-worldliness has deviated into a dualistic asceticism or a pietistic 'blosse Innerlichkeit', and the positive attitude to the world has resulted in tendencies towards an ecclesiastical world-domination, or in a cultural optimism and evolutionism on a religious basis'.[78]

It is this perspective which also nurtures the visionary realism in Paul's thought which allowed the believer to live fully in this world without demanding from it or any of its institutions the ultimate fulfilment since he or she knew that this was only to be found in the new heaven and earth to be brought in at Christ's coming from heaven. The believer could throw himself or herself with abandon into God's programme for the cosmos because he or she knew that the future was secured in hope and that even fragmentary activity undertaken in obedience to the heavenly Lord would not be in vain (1 Cor. 15: 58). In fact the Corinthians could be exhorted to abound in working for their Lord, since through Christ's resurrection God had guaranteed the consummation and fulfilment of all such work for his kingdom. In this way Paul's vision of a renewed cosmos is shown to have its roots in history. Yet his thought seeks the ultimate meaning of life and the ultimate achievement of God's purposes beyond the history of this world. For him both the present heavenly dimension where Christ now is and the future consummation of heavenly life when Christ ultimately unites heaven and earth are as real as the fact that God raised Christ from the dead. Any perspective that ceased to reckon with the reality of a heavenly dimension in its endeavour to transform the present world would for the apostle no longer be recognizable as Christian, for to combine his arguments of 1 Corinthians 15: 14ff and 15: 47ff – 'If there is no heavenly dimension, then Christ is not risen and your faith is in vain.'

NOTES

Introduction

1 (New York, 1961) p. 293.
2 (New York, 1965).
3 *The Making of a Counter Culture* (New York, 1968).
4 (Harvard, 1969).
5 (New York, 1969). Cf. also Martin E. Marty and Dean G. Peerman (eds.) *The Recovery of Transcendence*, New Theology, no. 7 (New York, 1970) esp. pp. 9–22.
6 Cf. especially Carl Braaten's development and popularization of aspects of Moltmann's and Pannenberg's thought in *Christ and Counter-Christ* (Philadelphia, 1972) and *Eschatology and Ethics* (Minneapolis, 1974).
7 (Philadelphia, 1969).
8 *Ibid.*, pp. 11, 37f.
9 (Harmondsworth, 1971).
10 The 'Hartford Declaration' emerged out of a conference held at the Hartford Seminary Foundation on 24–6 January 1975. The text of the declaration can be found in *Theology Today* 32 (1975), 94–6. Cf. also P. Berger and R. J. Neuhaus (eds.) *Against the World for the World: The Hartford Appeal and the Future of American Religion* (New York, 1976).
11 E.g., R. S. Anderson, *Historical Transcendence and the Reality of God* (Grand Rapids, Michigan, 1975); J. H. Gill, 'Transcendence: An Incarnational Model', *Encounter* 39 (1978), 39–44.
12 (Philadelphia, 1972).
13 Cf. H. Blamires' protest in *The Christian Mind* (London, 1963), p. 67, where he insists that 'a prime mark of the Christian mind is that it cultivates the eternal perspective. That is to say, it looks beyond this life to another one. It is supernaturally orientated, and brings to bear upon earthly considerations the fact of Heaven and the fact of Hell.'
14 In H. W. Bartsch (ed.), *Kerygma and Myth* (New York, 1961), p. 4.
15 Cf. the discussion of some of the questions raised by the Bible's symbolic language in the studies by Thomas Fawcett, *The Symbolic Language of Religion* (London, 1970) and *Hebrew Myth and Christian Gospel* (London, 1973).
16 H. G. Gadamer, *Truth and Method* (New York, 1975), pp. 270–4.
17 A. N. Wilder, *Theopoetic* (Philadelphia, 1976), p. 93.
18 Cf. P. Minear, 'The Cosmology of the Apocalypse', *Current Issues in New Testament Interpretation*, ed. W. Klassen and G. Snyder (New York,

1962), especially p. 34.

19 R. J. Sider, 'The Pauline Conception of the Resurrection Body in 1 Corinthians XV. 35–54' *NTS* 21 (1975), 438, who provides a good discussion of the issue of continuity and discontinuity.

20 Cf. *Christ and Time* (3rd edn, London, 1967).

21 (Chicago, 1968).

22 Cf. also S. Smalley, 'The Theatre of Parousia', *SJT* 17 (1964), 406–13; K. Hanhart, *The Intermediate State* (Groningen, 1966), pp. 43ff. For further theological reflection on this, see T. F. Torrance, *Space, Time and Resurrection* (Grand Rapids, 1976).

23 (Tübingen, 1951).

24 (London, 1958).

25 (Grand Rapids, Michigan, 1966).

26 F.-J. Steinmetz, *Protologische Heilszuversicht: Die Strukturen des soteriologischen und christologischen Denkens im Kolosser- und Epheserbrief* (Frankfurt, 1969), discusses spatial categories in general in relation to Colossians and Ephesians, while R. G. Hamerton-Kelly, *Pre-existence, Wisdom and the Son of Man* (Cambridge, 1973), touches on this area as it affects his theme of pre-existence in the NT rather than as it bears on eschatology; J. Baumgarten, *Paulus und die Apokalyptik* (Neukirchen-Vluyn, 1975), p. 147 n. 2, comments, 'Abgesehen von der Qumran-Forschung ist die "himmlische Welt" auch sonst nur selten ein Thema neuerer Forschung.'

27 The term 'realized' should, strictly speaking, be limited to views such as C. H. Dodd's that 'all that prophecy and apocalyptic had asserted of the supernatural messianic community was fulfilled in the Church' (*The Apostolic Preaching and Its Developments* (London, 1936), p. 145). Dodd later conceded that the term he had coined was 'not altogether felicitous' (*The Interpretation of the Fourth Gospel* (Cambridge, 1953), p. 447 n. 1). Yet because of the wide currency it enjoys in NT scholarship, even among those who preserve the element of a still future fulfilment, the term 'realized' will be retained to designate what might more accurately be called 'inaugurated' or 'proleptic' eschatology.

28 On this, see Baumgarten, *Paulus*, who concentrates primarily on Paul's relation to early Christian apocalyptic and on future elements in eschatology.

29 Since the completion of the revision of this dissertation I would in fact be inclined to opt for a different view about Paul as the actual author from that outlined tentatively at the beginning of chapter 6. But whether the author is Paul or a disciple of his, the findings of chapter 6 in regard to heaven and eschatology remain important in assessing the relationship of Ephesians to the rest of the Pauline corpus.

Galatians and the heavenly Jerusalem

1 Cf. J. Eckert, *Die urchristliche Verkündigung im Streit zwischen Paulus und seinen Gegnern nach dem Galaterbrief* (Regensburg, 1971); R. Jewett, 'The Agitators and the Galatian Congregation', *NTS* 17 (1971), 198–212; F. F. Bruce, 'Galatian Problems. 3. The "Other" Gospel', *BJRL* 53 (1971), 253–71.

2 F. C. Baur, *Paul His Life and Works* (London, 1875), vol. I, pp. 113, 119–30, 251–3 held that the apostles themselves were among the Judaizers in Galatia. J. Munck, *Paul and the Salvation of Mankind* (London, 1959), pp. 87ff went to the other extreme in insisting that there were no Judaizers in the Jerusalem church and that those causing trouble for Paul in Galatia were Galatian Gentiles. W. Lütgert, *Gesetz und Geist, eine Untersuchung zur Vorgeschichte des Galaterbriefes*, (Gütersloh, 1919) and J. H. Ropes, *The Singular Problem of the Epistle to the Galatians* (Harvard, 1929), believed that the apostle had to fight on two fronts against both legalists and libertines. For Lütgert the legalists were Jewish Christians loosely associated with the Jerusalem church, while for Ropes they were Gentiles. W. Schmithals, 'Die Häretiker in Galatien', *ZNW* 47 (1956), 26–67 sees the adversaries as part of a unified opposition faced by Paul and designates them as Jewish-Christian Gnostic, while Jewett, 'Agitators', p. 205, finds a political background to the agitation – 'My hypothesis . . .is that Jewish Christians in Judea were stimulated by Zealotic pressures into a nomistic campaign among their fellow Christians in the late forties and early fifties. Their goal was to avert the suspicion that they were in communion with lawless Gentiles.'

3 Cf. also J. W. Drane, *Paul, Libertine or Legalist?* (London, 1975), pp. 78–94; F. Mussner, *Der Galaterbrief* (Freiburg, 1974), pp. 14–29, who is, however, more hesitant about their Jerusalem connection.

4 Cf. H. Schlier, *Der Brief an die Galater* (3rd edn, Göttingen, 1962), p. 19; Eckert, *Die urchristliche Verkündigung*, pp. 22–9, 129.

5 Cf. R. Longenecker, *Paul, Apostle of Liberty* (New York, 1964), p. 214.

6 Cf. also J. B. Lightfoot, *The Epistle of St. Paul to the Galatians* (London, 1890), p. 371.;

7 Cf. A. Oepke, *Der Brief des Paulus an die Galater* (2nd edn, Berlin, 1964), pp. 122, 170; D. Guthrie, *Galatians* (London, 1969), p. 140; Eckert, *Die urchristliche Verkündigung*, p. 45.

8 Cf. Jewett, 'Agitators', p. 201, who credits H. J. Holtzmann, *Lehrbuch der historisch-kritischen Einleitung in das Neue Testament* (2nd edn, Freiburg, 1886), p. 243, with this suggestion.

9 Cf. C. K. Barrett, 'The Allegory of Abraham, Sarah, and Hagar in the Argument of Galatians' in J. Friedrich, W. Pöhlmann and P. Stuhlmacher (eds.), *Rechtfertigung* (Tübingen, 1976), p. 8.

10 Cf. section 8 below.

11 Cf. Barrett, 'Abraham, Sarah and Hagar', pp. 9ff; Drane, *Paul, Libertine or Legalist?*, pp. 43f; K. P. Donfried, *The Setting of Second Clement in Early Christianity* (Leiden, 1974), p. 199 n. 1.

12 Cf. Barrett, 'Abraham, Sarah and Hagar', p. 15.

13 Cf. F. F. Bruce, '"Abraham Had Two Sons" – A Study in Pauline Hermeneutics' in H. L. Drumwright and C. Vaughan (eds.), *New Testament Studies* (Waco, Texas, 1975), pp. 75f.

14 Cf. F. Büchsel, 'ἀλληγορέω', *TDNT* I, p. 260.

15 *Ibid.*; Oepke, *Der Brief des Paulus*, p. 116; K. Woollcombe in G. W. H. Lampe and K. Woollcombe, *Essays on Typology* (London, 1957), p. 50 n. 1; L. Goppelt, *Typos* (2nd edn, Darmstadt, 1969), p. 5 n. 4; A. T. Hanson, *Studies in Paul's Technique and Theology* (London, 1974), pp. 92ff.

16   H. J. Schoeps, *Paul* (London, 1961), pp. 234, 238 n. 3.

17   Cf. J. Bligh, *Galatians* (London, 1969), p. 395; A. T. Hanson, *Paul's Technique*, p. 101; Bruce, 'Abraham Had Two Sons', pp. 83f.

18   Cf. R. T. France, *Jesus and the Old Testament* (London, 1971), p. 41.

19   Cf. Bruce, 'Abraham Had Two Sons', p. 84.

20   For Philo on Abraham, Sarah and Hagar cf. especially *Leg. Alleg.* III, 244; *De Cherub.* 3-8; *De Post. Caini* 130; *De Congress. quaer. Erud. grat.* 1f, 71-3, 121f; *De Mutat. Nom.* 255; *Quaes. in Gen.* III, 21.

21   J. Barr, *Old and New in Interpretation* (London, 1966), pp. 103-11, disputes the clear distinction that is often made in modern scholarship between allegory and typology. In so far as the proponents of this distinction hold that allegory is always non-historical or anti-historical, Barr's dissent is to be supported. It should not however prevent the present-day reader from making relative distinctions in terms of the sort of correspondence the NT writers may have employed. We work with such a distinction as proposed by R. P. C. Hanson, *Allegory and Event* (London, 1959), p. 7,

> Typology is the interpreting of an event belonging to the present or recent past as the fulfilment of a similar situation recorded or prophesied in Scripture. Allegory is the interpretation of an object or person or a number of objects or persons as in reality meaning some object or person of a later time, with no attempt made to trace a relationship of 'similar situation' between them.

22   Cf. also Lampe in Lampe and Woollcombe, *Essays*, p. 35; Woollcombe in Lampe and Woollcombe, *Essays*, p. 56 n. 4; E. E. Ellis, *Paul's Use of the Old Testament* (Edinburgh, 1957), pp. 52f, 130; Goppelt, *Typos*, pp. 167f; R. P. C. Hanson, *Allegory and Event*, p. 83. 'Allegory' should not be considered a 'dirty word' in hermeneutical discussion. As Barr, *Old and New in Interpretation*, p. 108, suggests, a great deal depends on the system into which the interpretation runs out rather than on the method of allegory as such.

23   Cf. D. Patte, *Early Jewish Hermeneutic in Palestine* (Missoula, Montana, 1975), pp. 117ff; also Mussner, *Galaterbrief*, p. 337.

24   The inclusion of Ἁγάρ in the text follows on most naturally from the previous statement and is attested by A B D[gr] K P Ψ it[d.e] syr[h mg. pal] cop[bo]. The preferred reading also best accounts for the other variants. Cf. also B. Metzger, *A Textual Commentary on the Greek New Testament* (London, 1971), p. 596; E. de Witt Burton, *A Critical and Exegetical Commentary on the Epistle to the Galatians* (Edinburgh, 1921), p. 260. For a presentation of the case in favour of omitting δὲ Ἁγάρ cf. Lightfoot, *St. Paul to the Galatians*, pp. 192f; F. Mussner, 'Hagar, Sinai, Jerusalem - zum Text von Gal. 4, 25a', *TQ* 135 (1955), 56-60.

25   A. Deissmann, *Light from the Ancient East* (London, 1910), pp. 275ff.

26   This is advocated by e.g. Burton, *Commentary on Galatians*, p. 259; Oepke, *Der Brief des Paulus*, p. 113; R. Bring, *Commentary on Galatians* (Philadelphia, 1961), p. 230; Goppelt, *Typos*, p. 167; R. P. C. Hanson, *Allegory and Event*, p. 81; Bietenhard, *Die himmlische Welt*, p. 197.

27   For this viewpoint cf. especially Lightfoot, *St Paul to the Galatians*, p. 181.

28   This has been proposed by Mussner, 'Hagar, Sinai, Jerusalem', p. 59, 'Freilich (=δέ) liegt das Sinaigebirge in der Arabia; aber (=das zweite δέ) es

entspricht (in meiner allegorischen Schau) dem heutigen Jerusalem.' This proposal which omits Ἀγάρ from the text could be modified for the reading we have preferred. Cf. also H. Ridderbos, *The Epistle to the Galatians* (London, 1954), p. 177 n. 9; J. Bligh, *Galatians in Greek* (Detroit, 1966), p. 182.

29   The subject of συστοιχεῖ can be either Hagar or Mt Sinai depending on how one construes the rest of the verse. In our construction Sinai is clearly the appropriate subject. On the possibility of συστοιχεῖν referring to a columnar arrangement of the elements in the allegory, cf. Ellis, *Paul's Use of the OT*, p. 52 n. 4; Bligh, *Galatians in Greek*, pp. 182f.

30   So Schlier, *Der Brief an die Galater*, p. 221; Guthrie, *Galatians*, p. 131; Bligh, *Galatians in Greek*, p. 181, who thinks Paul intended to say that the Abrahamic covenant came from the heavenly Jerusalem, and in this may have been dependent on a tradition preserved in Gen. R. LIII, 4.

31   So Lightfoot, *St Paul to the Galatians*, p. 181; Bietenhard, *Die himmlische Welt*, p. 197; Ellis, *Paul's Use of the OT*, p. 52 n. 4; A. T. Hanson, *Paul's Technique*, p. 94.

32   So also J. C. de Young, *Jerusalem in the New Testament* (Kampen, 1960), p. 104; Bligh, *Galatians*, p. 35; Jewett, 'Agitators', p. 204; Mussner, *Galaterbrief*, p. 325.

33   Cf. Holtzmann, *Lehrbuch*, p. 219; Eckert, *Die urchristliche Verkündigung*, p. 217 n. 2; Jewett, 'Agitators', p. 201; Mussner, *Galaterbrief*, pp. 13, 325.

34   Jewett, 'Agitators', p. 204.

35   Cf. E. Lohse, 'Σιών, Ἰερουσαλήμ', *TDNT* VII, pp. 333f.

36   Paul's ἡ ἄνω Ἰερουσαλήμ is equivalent to Hebrews' Ἰερουσαλήμ ἐπουρανία (12: 22) and can be compared with ἡ καινή Ἰερουσαλήμ, ἡ καταβαίνουσα ἐκ τοῦ οὐρανοῦ in the Apocalypse (Rev. 3: 12, cf. 21: 2, 10). His spelling of 'Jerusalem' here and in verse 25 is in accordance with the Hebrew form which he uses predominantly (cf. also Rom. 15: 19, 25, 26, 31; 1 Cor. 16: 3). The only exceptions where he employs the Greek form Ἰεροσόλυμα occur earlier in this letter in 1: 17, 18; 2: 2. There appears to be no particular schema behind this alternation. De Young's thesis that Hierosolyma never has extended connotations and Jerusalem is never used for a geographical reference so that 'Hierosolyma is used of the earthly, while Jerusalem is used of the heavenly, eschatological city' will not hold (cf. *Jerusalem in the NT*, pp. 14, 27). J. Jeremias, 'ΙΕΡΟΥΣΑΛΗΜ/ΙΕΡΟΣΟΛΥΜΑ' *ZNW* 65 (1974), p. 275, proposes a similar thesis. It does not alleviate their difficulties to claim that the exceptions are not simply geographical references, for while this is true of Gal. 4: 25, it is stretching the point to allege that the references in Rom. 15 and 1 Cor. 16 have an ecclesiastical context where Jerusalem is practically synonymous with the church at Jerusalem.

37   Pace R. H. Charles (ed.), *Apocrypha and Pseudepigrapha of the Old Testament* (Oxford, 1913), vol. II, p. 259; Bietenhard, *Die himmlische Welt*, p. 195.

38   M. Baillet, 'Fragments araméens de Qumran 2, description de la Jérusalem nouvelle', *RB* 62 (1955), pp. 222–45.

39   For evidence of this in the Rabbinic material, cf. H. L. Strack and P. Billerbeck, *Kommentar zum Neuen Testament aus Talmud und Midrasch* (Munich, 1926), vol. III, pp. 849f; IV, pp. 919ff.

40 Cf. Targum on Ps. 122: 3; cf. also *B. Taan.* 5a, 'Thus said R. Johanan: The Holy One, blessed be He, said, I will not enter the heavenly Jerusalem until I can enter the earthly Jerusalem.' Cf. Strack–Billerbeck, *Kommentar*, III, p. 573.

41 Cf. Strack–Billerbeck, *Kommentar*, IV, p. 883; Bietenhard, *Die himmlische Welt*, p. 196; Lohse, 'Σιών, Ἰερουσαλήμ', p. 326 n. 202; W. D. Davies, *The Gospel and the Land* (Berkeley, 1974), p. 148.

42 Cf. Charles (ed.), *Apocrypha*, II, p. 482.

43 Cf. Y. Yadin's reconstruction of this passage in 'Some Notes on the Newly Published Pesharim of Isaiah', *IEJ* 9 (1959), pp. 40f.

44 G. Jeremias, *Der Lehrer der Gerechtigkeit* (Göttingen, 1963), pp. 245–9; cf. also H.-W. Kuhn, *Enderwartung und gegenwärtiges Heil* (Göttingen, 1966), p. 188; G. Klinzing, *Die Umdeutung des Kultus in der Qumrangemeinde und im Neuen Testament* (Göttingen, 1971), pp. 59f, 90.

45 There is a somewhat similar application of the apocalyptic concept in Philo who can use it to polemicize against identifying the heavenly city with the earthly Jerusalem, cf. *De Somn.* II, 250.

46 Cf. also Strack–Billerbeck, *Kommentar*, III, p. 573; Lightfoot, *St Paul to the Galatians*, p. 182; Bietenhard, *Die himmlische Welt*, p. 198; de Young, *Jerusalem in the NT*, p. 120; *pace* Hamerton-Kelly, *Pre-existence*, p. 111.

47 *Pace* Oepke, *Der Brief des Paulus*, p. 113.

48 See further section 6 below.

49 de Young, *Jerusalem in the NT*, p. 118; cf. also Bietenhard, *Die himmlische Welt*, p. 198.

50 Cf. also Mussner, *Galaterbrief*, pp. 326f.

51 Cf. also Schlier, *Der Brief an die Epheser*, p. 233; Bring, *Commentary on Galatians*, p. 231; Eckert, *Die urchristliche Verkündigung*, p. 97; A. T. Hanson, *Paul's Technique*, p. 97. K. L. Schmidt, *Die Polis in Kirche und Welt* (Basel, 1939), p. 37, and W. Bieder, *Ekklesia und Polis im Neuen Testament und in der alten Kirche* (Zürich, 1941), p. 12, express the significance of the heavenly Jerusalem in terms of the kingdom of God.

52 Here in Gal. 4: 26 the uninterpolated text without πάντων is strongly to be preferred on grounds of external evidence, cf. also Metzger, *Greek NT*, p. 596.

53 M. C. Callaway, 'The Mistress and the Maid: Midrashic Traditions Behind Galatians 4: 21–31', *Radical Religion* 2 (1975), 94–101, critiques the 'class reading' of Genesis which she sees perpetuated in Paul's discussion of the women in the narrative.

54 Cf. Strack–Billerbeck, *Kommentar*, III, pp. 574f, for rabbinic application of Isa. 54: 1 to Jerusalem.

55 Jerusalem or Zion is mentioned in 40: 2, 9; 41: 27; 44: 26–8; 46: 13; 49: 14; 51: 3, 11, 16, 17; 52: 1, 2, 7, 8, 9; 59: 20; 60: 14; 61: 3; 62: 1, 6, 7, 11; 64: 10; 65: 18, 19; 66: 8, 10, 13, 20.

56 P. Richardson's attempt to show that the phrase refers to part of the Israelite nation who are as yet unenlightened but for whose conversion Paul is concerned fails to convince in the context of this letter and also as syntax, cf. *Israel in the Apostolic Church* (Cambridge, 1969), pp. 74–84.

57 Marcion reworked the text of Gal. 4: 25–6, substituting τὴν συναγωγὴν τῶν Ἰουδαίων for the present Jerusalem and ἁγίαν ἐκκλησίαν for the

Jerusalem above. Cf. later Augustine, *De Civ.* 20, 17, and for further evidence cf. K. L. Schmidt, *Die Polis in Kirche und Welt*, pp. 68ff. *Pace* Schlier, *Der Brief an die Galater*, p. 223 n. 5; R. J. McKelvey, *The New Temple* (Oxford, 1969), p. 143; E. Schweizer, 'Christus und Geist im Kolosserbrief', in B. Lindars and S. Smalley (eds.), *Christ and Spirit in the New Testament* (Cambridge, 1973), p. 306; A. T. Hanson, *Paul's Technique*, p. 97, who appear to make the identification of the heavenly Jerusalem with the church.

58 Cyril of Jerusalem in his 18th Baptismal Catechesis (18, 26), alluding to Gal. 4: 26, calls the earthly church 'the mother of us all', 'the copy of the heavenly Jerusalem which is the free mother of us all'.

59 *Pace* de Young, *Jerusalem in the NT*, p. 134.

60 Cf. also Mussner, *Galaterbrief*, p. 327.

61 Cf. also Eckert, *Die urchristliche Verkündigung*, p. 99 n. 1.

62 We follow the United Bible Societies text as the best attested reading and that which best accounts for the origin of the variants, cf. Metzger, *Greek NT*, p. 597.

63 Cf. 3: 14; 4: 6 and the parallel between 5: 16 and 5: 24 for the close association of the Spirit with Christ in this letter.

64 Within the OT there is also the tradition that Ishmael was quarrelsome and fought with his brothers (cf. Gen. 16: 12; 25: 18).

65 That the children of the Jerusalem above are those born according to the Spirit provides one of the closest correspondences in Paul to the categories of John 3 where the evangelist has Jesus speak of those born from above – (3: 3) – and of the Spirit (3: 5ff).

66 So also O. Merk, 'Der Beginn der Paränese im Galaterbrief', *ZNW* 60 (1969), p. 96; Mussner, *Galaterbrief*, p. 331; *pace* Oepke, *Der Brief des Paulus*, pp. 114f; Schlier, *Der Brief an die Galater*, pp. 226f; Donfried, *Second Clement*, p. 196, n. 1.

67 Paul differs from both the MT and the LXX in order to tie in the quotation with his preceding interpretation and make his application clear, and thus substitutes μετὰ τοῦ υἱοῦ τῆς ἐλευθέρας for μετὰ τοῦ υἱοῦ τοῦ Ἰσαάκ in the LXX.

68 So also O. Merk, 'Paränese im Galaterbrief', pp. 96f; Mussner, *Galaterbrief*, p. 332; *pace* Schlier, *Der Brief an die Galater*, p. 227; Eckert, *Die urchristliche Verkündigung*, p. 98; Barrett, 'Abraham, Sarah and Hagar', p. 13, who curiously takes it as 'the command of God to his (angelic) agents'.

69 While we should not read back into this term all the patristic connotations of ecclesiastical excommunication, it certainly carried implications for church discipline.

70 Cf. Bligh, *Galatians*, pp. 35, 390f.

71 As Donfried, *Second Clement*, p. 194, observes with reference to the Jerusalem above, 'the tension which Paul was able to maintain was lost by many after him; either they overstressed the present reality of the heavenly existence, or they overemphasized the futurity of that new existence, as did 2 Clement'.

72 Cf. the similar conclusion of Davies, *The Gospel*, pp. 217–20, that theologically the centre of gravity of Paul's ministry had moved away from an apocalyptic geography centering in Jerusalem.

73 Cf. Eckert, *Die urchristliche Verkündigung*, pp. 104, 106.

74 Because of the differing situations to which they are addressed the rather different emphases of Rom. 9–11 with its hope for Israel (cf. 11: 25f) and of Galatians 4 should be allowed their full force before an attempt is made to fit them together in some larger scheme of interpretation. Richardson, *Apostolic Church*, pp. 74–84, in his treatment of Gal. 6: 16 fails to observe this and is guilty of reading Rom. 11: 25f into the Galatian situation. It must, of course, be kept in view that Paul's discussion in Galatians is not, as in Romans 11 where it is directed against Gentile arrogance, about Israel as such; his formulation is determined by the conflict between the alleged claims of the *law* and freedom from that law.

75 Cf. K. Holl, 'Der Kirchenbegriff des Paulus in seinem Verhältnis zu dem der Urgemeinde', in *Das Paulusbild in der neueren deutschen Forschung*, ed. K. H. Rengstorf (2nd edn, Darmstadt, 1969), p. 174, 'Indem Paulus den Kirchenbegriff vergeistigte, hat er *die Bindung an den Ort gebrochen* und die Beziehung zu bestimmten Personen zwar nicht aufgehoben, aber gelockert.' Cf. also Bligh, *Galatians*, p. 408.

76 Cf. Eckert, *Die urchristliche Verkündigung*, p. 192 'Damit ist eine gewisse Vorrangstellung Jerusalems, um die auch Paulus nicht herumkommt (vgl. seine Jerusalemreisen) anerkannt, jedoch keine kirchenrechtlichen Charakters.'

2. 1 Corinthians and heavenly existence

1 The situation of the church in 1 Corinthians is significantly different from that evidenced by 2 Corinthians and is therefore being treated independently.

2 With R. McL. Wilson, 'How Gnostic Were the Corinthians?' *NTS* 19 (1972), 74, we hold that these and other characteristics of the Corinthians are 'at most only the first tentative beginnings of what was later to develop into full-scale Gnosticism'.

3 Cf. J. C. Hurd, *The Origin of 1 Corinthians* (London, 1965), pp. 276f.

4 Cf. J. B. Hurley, 'Did Paul Require Veils or the Silence of Women?' *WTJ* 35 (1973), 201.

5 *Ibid.* p. 209; cf. also the references to angels in 6: 3 and 11: 10.

6 *Pace* K. G. Kuhn, 'πανοπλία', *TDNT* V, 299 n. 21, this is not a self-designation of the community but rather a reference to the angels.

7 E. Käsemann, *Jesus Means Freedom* (London, 1969), p. 63; 'On The Topic of Primitive Christian Apocalyptic', *JThCh* VI (1969), 119.

8 For a survey of the main options cf. B. Spörlein, *Die Leugnung der Auferstehung* (Regensburg, 1971), esp. pp. 1–30.

9 Cf. also A. Schlatter, *Die korinthische Theologie* (Gütersloh, 1914), especially pp. 62–6; A. Schweitzer, *The Mysticism of Paul the Apostle* (London, 1931), p. 93; W. L. Knox, *St. Paul and the Church of the Gentiles* (Cambridge, 1939), pp. 126f; Hurd, *Origin*, p. 231; R. Scroggs, 'The Exaltation of the Spirit by Some Early Christians', *JBL* 84 (1965), 372; Spörlein, *Die Leugnung*, pp. 190ff; D. J. Doughty, 'The Presence and Future of Salvation in Corinth' *ZNW* 66 (1975), 78 n. 66.

10 Scroggs, 'Exaltation', p. 372. Doughty, 'Presence and Future', p. 77 n. 65.

11 This view is held by e.g. F. Godet, *Commentary on St. Paul's First Epistle*

to the Corinthians, II (Edinburgh, 1898), pp. 323f; H. von Soden, 'Sakrament und Ethik bei Paulus' in *Urchristentum und Geschichte*, I (Tübingen, 1951), pp. 239–75; J. Schniewind, 'Die Leugner der Auferstehung in Korinth', in *Nachgelassene Reden und Aufsätze* (Berlin, 1952), p. 114; H. Lietzmann and W. Kümmel, *An die Korinther I/II* (Tübingen, 1949), p. 192f; E. Brandenburger, *Adam und Christus* (Neukirchen, 1962), pp. 70ff; Käsemann, 'Apocalyptic', pp. 119f; E. Güttgemanns, *Der leidende Apostel und sein Herr* (Göttingen, 1966), pp. 67ff; J. H. Wilson, 'The Corinthians Who Say There Is No Resurrection of the Dead', *ZNW* 59 (1968), 90–107; K.-A. Bauer, *Leiblichkeit, das Ende aller Werke Gottes* (Gütersloh, 1971), pp. 90f; Baumgarten, *Paulus*, p. 99.

12 To assume with R. Bultmann, *Theology of the New Testament*, I (New York, 1951), p. 169; H. Conzelmann, *I Corinthians* (Philadelphia, 1975), p. 262; W. Schmithals, *Gnosticism in Corinth* (Nashville, 1971), pp. 155–9; P. Hoffmann, *Die Toten in Christus* (Münster, 1966), pp. 245f; R. Jewett, *Paul's Anthropological Terms* (Leiden, 1971), p. 265, that Paul mistakes what the Corinthians believe, is simply to move further away from any objective evidence for reconstructing the situation.

13 Cf. Spörlein, *Die Leugnung*, p. 190 – 'Paulus kennt in seinen Ausführungen nur die Alternative: Heil durch Auferstehung oder Unheil.' Doughty, 'Presence and Future', pp. 75f.

14 Cf. A. J. M. Wedderburn, 'Adam and Christ' (unpublished Ph.D. thesis, Cambridge, 1970), p. 51; also 'The Body of Christ and Related Concepts in 1 Corinthians', *SJT* 24 (1971), 90ff; A. C. Thiselton 'Realized Eschatology at Corinth', *NTS* 24 (1978), 523ff. Cf. also the critique of the present resurrection view in Spörlein, *Die Leugnung*, pp. 176–81.

15 Cf. J. Jeremias, '"Flesh and Blood Cannot Inherit the Kingdom of God" (1 Cor. XV. 50)', *NTS* 2 (1955–6), 151–9.

16 Cf. also 1 Cor. 6: 13, 14, where Paul's response to the problem about the the body and sexual morality is bound up with his belief in the resurrection of the body.

17 *Pace* H. Traub, 'οὐρανός', *TDNT* V, 541; J. Héring, *The First Epistle of St. Paul to the Corinthians* (London, 1962), p. 174; Bauer, *Leiblichkeit . . .*, pp. 95f.

18 So also R. Scroggs, *The Last Adam* (Oxford, 1966), p. 85; H. Ridderbos, *Paul* (Grand Rapids, Michigan, 1975), p. 541.

19 A. Robertson and A. Plummer, *A Critical and Exegetical Commentary on the First Epistle of St. Paul to the Corinthians* (Edinburgh, 1929), p. 371.

20 We shall employ the somewhat awkward translation of ψυχικός as 'psychical' to avoid the misunderstandings produced by such renderings as 'physical', 'natural', or 'psychic'.

21 *Die hellenistischen Mysterienreligionen* (Stuttgart, 1910), now translated as *Hellenistic Mystery-Religions* (Pittsburgh, 1978), cf. especially pp. 68ff, 364–500; followed by J. Weiss, *Der erste Korintherbrief* (Göttingen, 1925), pp. 70, 371ff; H. Jonas, *Gnosis und spätantiker Geist*, I (Göttingen, 1954); U. Wilckens, *Weisheit und Torheit. Eine exegetische-religionsgeschichtliche Untersuchung zu 1 Kor. 1 und 2* (Tübingen, 1959); Schmithals, *Gnosticism*, pp. 169, 170; Brandenburger, *Adam und Christus*, pp. 73ff; Jewett, *Terms*, pp. 334–46, 352–6; J. Jervell, *Imago Dei*

(Göttingen, 1960), pp. 260ff; M. Winter, *Pneumatiker und Psychiker in Korinth* (Marburg, 1975).

22 Cf. for example R. McL. Wilson, 'Corinthians', pp. 65–74; E. Yamauchi, *Pre-Christian Gnosticism: A Survey of the Proposed Evidences* (London, 1973), esp. pp. 39ff.

23 Jewett, *Terms*, p. 344.

24 Cf. B. A. Pearson, *The Pneumatikos-Psychikos Terminology in 1 Corinthians* (Missoula, Montana, 1973); Wedderburn, *Adam*; Spörlein, *Die Leugnung*, esp. pp. 103ff, 171ff.

25 Cf. J. Dupont, *Gnosis: La connaissance religieuse dans les épîtres de Saint Paul* (Paris, 1949), pp. 172–180.

26 Cf. the critique of this part of Pearson's thesis by R. A. Horsley, 'Pneumatikos vs. Psychikos: Distinctions of Spiritual Status among the Corinthians', *HTR* 69 (1976), 270–3.

27 *Pneumatikos*, p. 38f.

28 Cf. Horsley, 'Pneumatikos', pp. 276ff; 284ff.

29 Cf. Wedderburn, *Adam*, p. 196.

30 Cf. W. D. Davies, *Paul and Rabbinic Judaism* (3rd edn, New York, 1967), p. 308.

31 Cf. E. Schweizer, 'πνεῦμα', *TDNT* VI, 421; C. F. D. Moule, 'St. Paul and Dualism', *NTS* 12 (1965–6), 108, who comments that this 'is a word denoting a quality not of substance but of relationship'.

32 Ellis, *Paul's use of the OT*, pp. 36 n. 4, 143 n. 3; W. D. Davies, *Rabbinic Judaism*, pp. 43ff; J. D. G. Dunn, '1 Corinthians 15: 45 – Last Adam, Life-Giving Spirit', in *Christ and Spirit in the New Testament* (Cambridge, 1973), p. 130; Conzelmann, *I Corinthians*, p. 284, believes Paul treats an earlier exegetical tradition as part of Scripture at this point.

33 For this line of interpretation cf. G. Vos, *The Pauline Eschatology* (2nd edn, Grand Rapids, Michigan, 1961), pp. 169 f n. 19, 183; Ridderbos, *Paul*, p. 542 n. 152. R. B. Gaffin, 'Resurrection and Redemption in Pauline Soteriology' (unpublished Th.D. dissertation, Philadelphia, 1969), pp. 109–12; Sider, 'Pauline Conception', p. 434 n. 1, *contra* H. Clavier, 'Brèves Remarques sur la notion de σῶμα πνευματικόν', in W. D. Davies and D. Daube (eds.), *The Background of the New Testament and Its Eschatology* (Cambridge, 1956), p. 351; Scroggs, *Adam*, p. 85 n. 27; Bauer, *Leiblichkeit*, p. 101; Jewett, *Terms*, p. 354.

34 *Eschatology*, p. 169 n. 19; cf. also Godet, *Commentary*, p. 425.

35 Cf. W. D. Davies, *Rabbinic Judaism*, pp. 51ff; E.-B. Allo, *St Paul: Première Épître aux Corinthiens* (2nd edn, Paris, 1956), p. 427f; Héring, *1 Cor.*, p. 178; Jervell, *Imago Dei*, pp. 260ff; C. K. Barrett, *The First Epistle to the Corinthians* (London, 1971), pp. 374ff; Pearson, *Pneumatikos*, pp. 17ff; Horsley, 'Pneumatikos', pp. 276ff.

36 The Philonic background is rejected by Lietzmann–Kümmel, *An die Korinther*, p. 195; Scroggs, *Adam*, pp. 87 n. 30, 115–22; Spörlein, *Die Leugnung*, p. 105 n. 3; B. A. Stegmann, *Christ, the 'Man from Heaven'. A Study of 1 Corinthians 15: 45–47 in the Light of the Anthropology of Philo Judaeus* (Washington, 1927), *passim.*; Wedderburn, *Adam*, pp. 197ff; and 'Philo's "Heavenly Man"', *NT* 15 (1973), pp. 301–26.

37 Cf. Schmithals, *Gnosticism*, pp. 169f; Winter, *Pneumatiker und Psychiker*,

pp. 226ff, and the literature cited above in connection with a suggested Gnostic background for the ψυχικός/πνευματικός distinction in general.

38 Cf. Wedderburn, 'Body', pp. 93f.

39 *I Corinthians*, p. 287.

40 Wedderburn, 'Philo', p. 302; cf. also *Adam*, p. 203; Spörlein, *Die Leugnung*, p. 107.

41 The earthly character of the first man mentioned here is primarily with reference to the creation, though, as we have seen with the connotations of ψυχή in this passage, it may also take in the effects of the fall, cf. Gen. 3: 19 – 'you are dust and to dust you shall return' and also 2 Bar. 48: 42ff where Adam's origin from the dust and his disobedience are connected. So also Sider, 'Pauline Conception', p. 434.

42 Cf. Ridderbos, *Paul*, p. 544 n. 157; so also Scroggs, *Adam*, p. 88.

43 *Contra* Traub, 'οὐρανός', p. 529.

44 Cf. Vos, *Eschatology*, p. 167; F. C. Porter, *The Mind of Christ in Paul* (London, 1930), p. 247; *pace* Barrett, *1 Cor.*, p. 375.

45 This is not an equivalent to a Johannine descent from heaven (cf. Jn. 3: 13), *pace* O. Cullmann, *The Christology of the New Testament* (London, 1963), p. 169; F. Grosheide, *Commentary on the First Epistle to the Corinthians* (Grand Rapids, Michigan, 1953), p. 425; Héring, *1 Cor.*, p. 179; Traub, 'οὐρανός', p. 529, who sees this as a secondary reference.

46 This is not an equivalent to the descent ἐκ τῶν οὐρανῶν of 1 Thess. 1: 10 or ἀπ' οὐρανοῦ of 1 Thess. 4: 16, *pace* Robertson–Plummer, *Critical and Exegetical Commentary*, p. 374; Barrett, *1 Cor.*, p. 376.

47 Cf. G. Vos, 'The Eschatological Aspect of the Pauline Conception of the Spirit' in *Biblical and Theological Studies* (New York, 1912), p. 245 – 'the distinction between the earthly and the heavenly is not cosmologically but eschatologically conceived . . . this whole opposition between a heavenly and an earthly order of things and the anchoring of the Christian life in the former is a direct offshoot of the eschatological distinction between two ages'.

48 Cf. the comments above on the background of the ψυχικός/πνευματικός distinction.

49 Cf. 'The Pauline Doctrine of the Second Adam', *SJT* 7 (1954), 171; cf. also M. Hengel, *The Son of God* (Philadelphia, 1976), pp. 33–5; C. H. Talbert, 'The Myth of a Descending-Ascending Redeemer in Mediterranean Antiquity', *NTS* 22 (1976), 418–40. For critiques of Reitzenstein's original reconstruction of the heavenly Man redemption myth, cf. J. M. Creed, 'The Heavenly Man', *JTS* 26 (1925), 113–36; W. Manson, *Jesus the Messiah* (London, 1943), pp. 174–90; C. Colpe, *Die religionsgeschichtliche Schule* (Göttingen, 1961). For more recent advocacy of the myth as the background to 1 Cor. 15 cf. Brandenburger, *Adam und Christus*, pp. 76–110, and for critical evaluations of his work cf. Scroggs, *Adam*, pp. xviii–xxiv; Wedderburn, *Adam*, *passim*.

50 *Adam*, p. 87 n. 30.

51 *Ibid.*, p. 122, cf. also Stegmann, *Christ, the 'Man from Heaven'*, p. 48.

52 Cf. also Wedderburn, 'Philo', pp. 301–26.

53 Cf. J. L. Sharpe, 'The Second Adam in the Apocalypse of Moses', *CBQ* 35 (1973), pp. 35–46.

54   P. C. H. Wernberg-Møller, *The Manual of Discipline* (Leiden, 1957), p. 87 n. 80.

55   Sharpe, 'Second Adam', p. 35. He dates the Apocalypse of Moses in the first century B.C., cf. p. 35 n. 1.

56   There is another eschatological figure in Jewish thought sometimes connected by scholars with 1 Cor. 15. This is the 'one like a son of man' (cf. Dan. 7: 13; 4 Ezra 13: 3), who is also associated with heaven. In Daniel he is said to come with the clouds of heaven, while in 1 Enoch 46: 1f the Son of Man is described as one 'whose countenance had the appearance of a man, and his face was full of graciousness, like one of the holy angels'. The figure who is like a son of man is perhaps best regarded as the heavenly representative of Israel, 'the transposition into the angelic realm of God's appointed man' (Wedderburn, *Adam*, p. 100). Heaven is not simply connected with the Son of Man as the place of his appearing, but its quality of life becomes his, for those who dwell in heaven or visit there are held to become heavenly. We have seen that in 1 Cor. 15: 47 Paul's emphasis is not on heaven as Christ's place of origin but on the quality of life that comes from being associated with this sphere. If the concept of the Son of Man has any minor part in the background of Paul's thought here, then it would be in this connection rather than as a reference to an appearance in heaven or a coming from heaven. For the more general background of descent and ascent to heaven, see C. H. Talbert, 'Myth', pp. 418–40, who sets out the evidence for the notion of a descending-ascending figure in soteriological contexts in Hellenistic Jewish speculation, where it could be expressed in terms of either Wisdom, Word, Angel or Son or a combination of these traditions.

57   So also E. Schweizer, '$\pi\nu\epsilon\hat{\upsilon}\mu\alpha$', p. 420; *pace* Pearson, *Pneumatikos*, pp. 24f.

58   Metzger, *Greek NT*, p. 569, in explaining the choice of the indicative in the United Bible Societies' text, concedes that it was a decision about the nature of the context being didactic and not hortatory that 'led the Committee to prefer the future indicative, despite its rather slender external support'.

59   Others who opt for $\phi o\rho\acute{\epsilon}\sigma\omega\mu\epsilon\nu$ include F. C. Porter, *Mind of Christ*, p. 254; Grosheide, *Commentary*, p. 389; Allo, *St. Paul*, p. 429; Clavier, 'Brèves Remarques', p. 348 n. 9; Héring, *1 Cor.*, p. 179; Scroggs, *Adam*, with hesitation p. 89 n. 35 ('perhaps'); Sider, 'Pauline Conception', p. 434. Robertson–Plummer, *Critical and Exegetical Commentary*, p. 375, reject the subjunctive because it would imply that the attaining to the glorified body depends on a person's own effort. But this exhortation is in fact only pushing to its final stage the familiar Pauline imperative of 'Become what you are' and a person's response remains dependent on God's gift of resurrection existence in Christ.

60   So also J. Weiss, *Der erste Korintherbrief*, p. 376, who sees this as 'eine ungeheurere Prolepse'; Héring, *1 Cor.*, p. 179; Porter, *Mind of Christ*, p. 254 – 'the heavenly Christ . . . is already making new men of heavenly and spiritual nature'.

61   Cf. also Bietenhard, *Die himmlische Welt*, p. 253.

62   Cf. also N. A. Dahl, 'Christ, Creation and the Church', in *The Background of the New Testament and Its Eschatology* (Cambridge, 1956), pp. 426f.

63 Cf. W. D. Davies, *Rabbinic Judaism*, p. 317, 'he now believed that the Age to come eternally existent in the Heavens had already appeared in its initial stages in the Resurrection of Jesus'.

64 C. K. Barrett, *From First Adam to Last* (London, 1962), p. 104, comments 'It must never be forgotten that in the present age this heavenly life is truly anticipated, but only anticipated.'

3. 2 Corinthians, the heavenly house and the third heaven

1 So also, for example, H. Windisch, *Der Zweite Korintherbrief* (Göttingen, 1970, reprint of 1924 edition), pp. 16–18, 431–3; Munck, *Salvation*, pp. 168–71; F. F. Bruce, *1 and 2 Corinthians* (London, 1971), pp. 169f; C. K. Barrett, *The Second Epistle to the Corinthians* (London, 1973), pp. 10, 21, 243–5.

2 Cf. also D. Georgi, *Die Gegner des Paulus im 2. Korintherbrief* (Neukirchen-Vluyn, 1964), pp. 23f, 219ff; C. K. Barrett, 'Paul's Opponents in II Corinthians', *NTS* 17 (1971), 236.

3 Cf. W. Lütgert, *Freiheitspredigt und Schwarmgeister in Korinth* (Gütersloh, 1908); R. Bultmann, 'Exegetische Probleme des Zweiten Korintherbriefes' in *Exegetica*, ed. E. Dinkler (Tübingen, 1967), pp. 298–322; Schmithals, *Gnosticism*.

4 Cf. G. Bornkamm, *Die Vorgeschichte des sogenannten Zweiten Korintherbriefes* (Sitzungsberichte der Heidelberger Akademie der Wissenschaften, Philosophisch-historische Klasse 2, 1961); Georgi, *Die Gegner . . .*; G. Friedrich, 'Die Gegner des Paulus im 2. Korintherbrief' in *Abraham unser Vater*, ed. O. Betz, M. Hengel, P. Schmidt (Leiden, 1963), pp. 181–215, who connects the opponents specifically with the Stephen circle in Acts.

5 Cf. F. C. Baur, 'Die Christuspartei der korinthischen Gemeinde' (1831) in *Ausgewählte Werke*, I (Stuttgart-Bad Cannstatt, 1963), pp. 1–146; Windisch, *2 Korintherbrief*, esp. pp. 23–6; E. Käsemann, 'Die Legitimität des Apostels', *ZNW* 41 (1942), 33–71, also in *Das Paulusbild in der neueren deutschen Forschung*, ed. K. H. Rengstorf (Darmstadt, 1969), pp. 475–521; D. W. Oostendorp, *Another Jesus: A Gospel of Jewish-Christian Superiority in II Corinthians* (Kampen, 1967); Barrett, 'Opponents'.

6 C. J. A. Hickling, 'Is the Second Epistle to the Corinthians a Source for Early Church History?' *ZNW* 66 (1975), 284–7, correctly warns against too much dogmatism in this area of discussion.

7 Cf. Georgi, *Die Gegner . . .*, pp. 248f; Friedrich, 'Die Gegner', p. 192.

8 Cf. E. E. Ellis, '"Those of the Circumcision" and the Early Christian Mission' in F. L. Cross (ed.), *Studia Evangelica* IV (Berlin, 1968), p. 395; 'Paul and His Opponents' in *Christianity, Judaism and Other Greco-Roman Cults*, ed. J. Neusner (Leiden, 1975), vol. I, pp. 287f; Barrett, 'Opponents', p. 254; *2 Cor.*, p. 287.

9 Cf. O. Cullmann, 'The Significance of the Qumran Texts for Research into the Beginnings of Christianity' in *The Scrolls and the New Testament*, ed. K. Stendahl (London, 1958), pp. 25–8; M. Black, *The Scrolls and Christian Origins* (London, 1961), p. 79; W. Gutbrod, 'Ἰσραήλ κτλ.', *TDNT* III, 372–5, 389–91; Ellis, 'Mission', p. 391ff.

10 Cf. Barrett, 'Christianity at Corinth', *BJRL* 46 (1964), 291–4; 'Opponents',

pp. 237f.

11 Käsemann, 'Legitimität', p. 479; Friedrich, 'Die Gegner', pp. 185–8; Oostendorp, *Another Jesus*, p. 11.
12 Cf. Oostendorp, *Another Jesus*, pp. 35f, 45f.
13 Cf. Oostendorp, *Another Jesus*, pp. 52–8; F. F. Bruce, *New Testament History* (London, 1969), p. 314.
14 Cf. Georgi, *Die Gegner . . .*, p. 286.
15 Cf. F. C. Baur, *Paulus, Der Apostel Jesu Christi*, I (Leipzig, 1866), p. 304; T. W. Manson, *Studies in the Gospels and Epistles* (Manchester, 1962), p. 224; Oostendorp, *Another Jesus*, pp. 54f; Barrett, *2 Cor.*, pp. 41f, 171, considers this sort of interpretation a possibility.
16 Georgi, *Die Gegner*, pp. 187–205.
17 Cf. W. D. Davies, *Rabbinic Judaism*, pp. 198, 210ff.
18 See section 9 below.
19 Ellis, 'Mission', p. 398.
20 Cf. Barrett, 'Opponents', pp. 251, 254; *2 Cor.*, pp. 30, 40.
21 Cf. Käsemann, 'Legitimität', pp. 485ff; A. Schlatter, *Paulus, der Bote Jesu* (4th edn, Stuttgart, 1969), pp. 636f; Bruce, *1 and 2 Cor.*, pp. 236f, 249; Barrett, 'Opponents', pp. 242–4; *2 Cor.*, pp. 30f, 277f, 320.
22 Cf. Käsemann, 'Legitimität', p. 486; Schlatter, *Paulus*, p. 637; Barrett, 'Opponents', pp. 242f; *2 Cor.*, pp. 31, 278. Bultmann, 'Probleme', pp. 318f, has the better of the exegetical argument against Käsemann about the relation of 11: 5 to 11: 1. Barrett's more recent discussion ('Opponents', pp. 242–4) does nothing to alter this and once the nature of Paul's apology is realized, his comment, that 'the admission made in the opening words of v. 6 would completely ruin Paul's case' in a comparison with his opponents, falls away, for in Paul's view his lack of rhetorical tricks only serves to validate his apostleship, cf. also H. D. Betz, *Der Apostel Paulus und die sokratische Tradition* (Tübingen, 1972), pp. 59–69; Ellis, 'Opponents', p. 286 n. 71.
23 For a survey of the history of exegesis, cf. esp. F. G. Lang, *2 Korinther 5, 1–10 in der neueren Forschung* (Tübingen, 1973), pp. 9–161; also Hoffmann, *Die Toten*, pp. 254–67; M. J. Harris, *The Interpretation of 2 Corinthians 5: 1–10 and Its Place in Pauline Eschatology* (unpublished Ph.D. thesis, Manchester, 1970).
24 In particular, the new line of interpretation suggested by N. Baumert, *Täglich Sterben und Auferstehen: Der Literalsinn von 2 Kor 4, 12–5, 10* (München, 1973), and set out in detail in that work, deserves extensive interaction. Lack of space means that we can only mention that Baumert makes an attractive argument for the passage not dealing with events of the end such as death before the parousia or an intermediate state or the reception of a resurrection body but with a present event, namely, as the title indicates, daily participation in the death and resurrection of Christ, and the accompanying experiences of suffering and glory. He argues that the language about heaven in 5: 1, 2 refers to present participation in the life of the new age, which would, if correct, support one of the main points of our own thesis about such a concept not being confined to the later Colossians or Ephesians. However, despite his intricate analysis, it is unlikely that Baumert's overall interpretation can stand. Some basic presuppositions

of the whole work (cf. especially pp. 120–5; 142–50), that any notion of anthropological duality is totally foreign to Paul's thought and that σῶμα is not to be interpreted physically, are at least called into question by R. H. Gundry's *Sōma in Biblical Theology with Emphasis on Pauline Anthropology* (Cambridge, 1976). Though he promises further work in such areas, at present Baumert's proposal does not sufficiently take into account the similarities between 2 Cor. 5 and 1 Cor. 15 or the way in which a polemical background with disputes about the place of the body affects Paul's argument here. He allows one exception to his argument; 5: 1a does refer to physical death. But this makes it hard to see why 5: 1b does not also specifically involve the physical consummation of the new life and not just its general enjoyment and difficult to understand that 5: 2 with its language of putting on the further clothing of the dwelling from heaven is reverting to a description of the overlapping of earthly and heavenly forms of existence in this life. The exegesis also appears strained in a number of places for the sake of this particular interpretation, for example in 4: 14 with ἐγερεῖ, in 5: 8 where the contrast has to be qualified and in 5: 9 where too much has to be read in to enable it to be correlated with the interpretation of 'at home in the body' and 'away from the Lord' which Baumert advances.

25 Since this is part of the apostolic apology, Baumert, *Täglich Sterben*, pp. 25–36, is right to stress that the 'we' of this passage has primary reference to the apostle himself. Yet many aspects of what Paul describes are experiences which he would have in common with the Corinthians and with believers in general.

26 *Pace* Lang, *2 Korinther*, pp. 173ff, 194, whose own solution depends on seeing the whole passage as polemically oriented.

27 Cf. also J.-F. Collange, *Énigmes de la deuxième épître de Paul aux Corinthiens* (Cambridge, 1972), p. 178.

28 Cf. Lang, *2 Korinther*, pp. 175f.

29 Spörlein, *Die Leugnung*, pp. 136f argues that σκῆνος was such a common term for the body in Greek that it was probably no longer a metaphor by the time of Paul's use and therefore should simply be translated as 'body', cf. also Collange, *Énigmes*, p. 194; Baumert, *Täglich Sterben*, pp. 142f. Lang, *2 Korinther*, pp. 178–285, makes a plausible case for the building imagery being derived from the polemical context but not for its reference being to 'die umfassende Lebenswirklichkeit' (p. 194) rather than specifically to the body.

30 Cf. R. V. G. Tasker, *The Second Epistle of Paul to the Corinthians* (London, 1958), pp. 78, 80; K. Hanhart, 'Paul's Hope in the Face of Death', *JBL* 88 (1969), 453f, who sees it as a local metaphor signifying a person's dwelling in the presence of God.

31 Cf. E. Ellis, 'The Structure of Pauline Eschatology (II Corinthians V. 1–10)' in *Paul and His Recent Interpreters* (Grand Rapids, Michigan, 1961), pp. 41ff; J. A. T. Robinson, *The Body* (London, 1952), pp. 75–80. While it is true that in 1 Corinthians θεοῦ οἰκοδομή ἐστε (3: 9) and ὑμεῖς δὲ ἐστε σῶμα Χριστοῦ (12: 27) are related in that both refer to the church, it cannot be deduced from this that they are therefore interchangeable. A. Feuillet, 'La Demeure Céleste et la Destinée des Chrétiens', *Recherches de*

Science Réligieuse 44 (1956), 361–78, believes the reference is to the
heavenly Man of 1 Cor. 15: 47f and thus to his glorified body which then
includes the glorified bodies of Christians. His basic position is preferred by
Collange, *Énigmes*, pp. 190f.

32 Cf. Feuillet, 'La Demeure', pp. 361–70; Collange, *Énigmes*, pp. 183ff, who
believes that δἴδαμεν indicates Paul is referring to a traditional formulation
such as this.

33 Cf. also Windisch, *2 Korintherbrief*, p. 159; Lietzmann–Kümmel, *Korinther
I/II*, p. 117; A. Plummer, *A Critical and Exegetical Commentary on the
Second Epistle of St. Paul to the Corinthians* (Edinburgh, 1915), p. 141;
P. E. Hughes, *Commentary on the Second Epistle to the Corinthians*
(Grand Rapids, Michigan, 1962), p. 160; Ridderbos, *Paul*, p. 500 n. 31;
Hoffmann, *Die Toten*, p. 263; Hanhart, *Intermediate State*, p. 447. *Pace*
Harris, *Interpretation*, p. 33; Barrett, *2 Cor.*, p. 151, who however appears
to contradict himself, for on p. 153 he writes, 'he hopes not to have the
old tent taken down in death, but by surviving till the *parousia*, to receive
the new dwelling in addition'.

34 Cf. Windisch, *2 Korintherbrief*, pp. 160f, 164; Lietzmann–Kümmel,
Korinther I/II, pp. 117, 118; Knox, *St. Paul*, pp. 136–9; Bietenhard, *Die
himmlische Welt*, p. 219; J. Héring, *The Second Epistle of St. Paul to the
Corinthians* (London, 1967), p. 36; R. Berry, 'Death and Life in Christ:
The Meaning of 2 Cor. 5: 1–10', *SJT* 14 (1961), 62; Hamerton-Kelly, *Pre-
existence*, p. 149; Ridderbos, *Paul*, pp. 500f, wants to combine this
interpretation with that of the futuristic present.

35 *Pace* M. Rissi, *Studien zum zweiten Korintherbrief* (Zürich, 1969), p. 80
n. 200, who most surprisingly asserts, 'Die apokalyptische Vorstellung von
der Präexistenz des Eschatologischen im Himmel ist unpaulinisch.'

36 But cf. Feuillet, 'La Demeure', pp. 177–9, on these alleged parallels.

37 M. J. Harris, 'Paul's View of Death in 2 Corinthians 5: 1–10' in R. N.
Longenecker and M. C. Tenney (eds.), *New Dimensions in New Testament
Study* (Grand Rapids, 1974), p. 322, correctly rules out the notion of
some type of heavenly 'body-bank', noting that just as the dwelling is not
ἐξ οὐρανοῦ (verse 2) until the time for putting on, so the house is not ἐν
τοῖς οὐρανοῖς (verse 1) at least until the dismantling of the earthly tent.

38 Cf. Windisch, *2 Korintherbrief*, pp. 157–61, 163, 168; Schlatter, *Paulus*,
p. 544; Knox, *St. Paul*, pp. 137, 139, 141; W. D. Davies, *Rabbinic Judaism*,
pp. 314ff; R. Hettlinger, '2 Corinthians 5: 1–10', *SJT* 10 (1957), pp. 185ff;
Simon, *Heaven*, pp. 214f; Ellis, *Interpreters*, p. 43, speaks of a 'psycho-
somatic organism which envelops and pervades the whole personality' at
death; Bruce, *1 and 2 Cor.*, pp. 200f, 205; Harris, *Interpretation*, pp. 79–82.

39 So also Bultmann, 'Probleme', p. 301; Vos, *Eschatology*, pp. 187f; Rissi,
Studien..., p. 84.

40 Cf. Plummer, *Commentary*, pp. 144, 161ff; Lietzmann–Kümmel, *Korinther
I/II*, pp. 118f; Vos, *Eschatology*, p. 188; Hughes, *Commentary*, p. 163 n.
19; Hoffmann, *Die Toten*, p. 270; Ridderbos, *Paul*, p. 501; Rissi,
Studien..., p. 86; Barrett, *2 Cor.*, p. 151; Gundry, *Sōma*, p. 150.

41 *Interpretation*, p. 78.

42 So also Berry, 'Death and Life', p. 61.

43 Though this is by no means a decisive consideration, the introductory

οἴδαμεν γὰρ ὅτι is an unlikely way of introducing a new teaching which had been made clear to Paul only recently, cf. also Hoffmann, *Die Toten*, p. 268 n. 79.

44 Cf. Windisch, *2 Korintherbrief*, p. 161, who mentions the concept of the angelic retinue of the Messiah bearing heavenly garments; Feuillet, 'La Demeure', p. 375 and n. 21; Ridderbos, *Paul*, p. 501; Barrett, *2 Cor.*, p. 152; Collange, *Énigmes*, p. 204, takes the whole verse as alluding to the return of Christ from heaven.

45 RSV uses the adverb 'further' to convey this force, while NEB translates as 'put on over'. Hughes, *Commentary*, p. 168 n. 31, points out a number of references where ἐπενδύσασθαι has this specific sense, cf. e.g. Herodotus, *Hist.* I, 195; Josephus, *Ant. Jud.* V, i, 12; Plutarch, *Pelop.* II, and mentions the cognate nouns ἐπένδυμα and ἐπενδύτης as denoting an outer garment.

46 So also Plummer, *Commentary*, pp. 145f; Hughes, *Commentary*, pp. 168–71; Bruce, *1 and 2 Cor.*, pp. 202ff; Hoffmann, *Die Toten*, pp. 273f; Barrett, *2 Cor.*, pp. 152f, 156; Gundry, *Sōma*, p. 152; *pace* Bultmann, 'Probleme', pp. 304f; Hanhart, *Intermediate State*, p. 451; Ridderbos, *Paul*, p. 501; C. F. D. Moule, 'St. Paul and Dualism', *NTS* 12 (1965–6), p. 120, agrees with this interpretation of ἐπενδύεσθαι, but then argues that Paul says here in contrast to 1 Cor. 15 that this notion of addition is wrong and has to be replaced by that of exchange, a viewpoint which we cannot find in this passage.

47 So also Vos, *Eschatology*, pp. 189f; Berry, *Death and Life*, p. 63 n. 1.

48 Barrett, *2 Cor.*, pp. 152f.

49 *Pace* Bruce, *1 and 2 Cor.*, p. 204; Harris, *Interpretation*, p. 115 and n. 3.

50 The reading εἴ γε (ℵ C K L P) is probably to be preferred to εἴπερ (p⁴⁶ BDFG) and 'introduces a statement which makes explicit an assumption which lay behind some preceding assertion, and by doing so may also guard against a possible misinterpretation (e.g. Gal. 3: 4; Col. 1: 23)'. (Harris, *Interpretation*, p. 126). It depends on the context whether such a strengthened 'if' implies doubt or confident assumption, cf. C. D. F. Moule, *An Idiom-Book of New Testament Greek* (Cambridge, 1968), p. 164. The καί strengthens the force even further but again is not determinative of doubt or confidence. Moule, 'St. Paul and Dualism', p. 121, holds that the force is one of casting doubt to the extent that this verse 'expresses not a Christian expectation at all, but simply a spasm of unbelief which passes like a cloud across the sun but is also as parenthetic as the cloud'. But this interpretation is not a necessary deduction from the use of εἴ γε καί, and M. E. Thrall, *Greek Particles in the New Testament* (Leiden, 1962), pp. 86–91, concludes from an examination of εἴ γε both in Paul and in secular literature that it expresses assurance rather than doubt in 2 Corinthians 5: 3; cf. also Baumert, *Täglich Sterben*, pp. 380–6.

51 Cf. Ellis, *Interpreters*, pp. 44ff; Hanhart, *Intermediate State*, pp. 447, 454–6, who believes the reference is to shame as a result of a fruitless ministry.

52 Cf. also Plummer, *Commentary*, pp. 147ff; Lietzmann-Kümmel, *Korinther I/II*, p. 120; Hughes, *Commentary*, p. 170; Barrett, *2 Cor.*, p. 155; Gundry, *Sōma*, pp. 151f. For parallels to this use of γυμνός, cf. Plato, *Gorgias* 523, 524; *Cratylus* 403B; Philo, *Leg. Alleg.* ii, 59; *De Virt.* 76; Gospel of Philip 23, 24; Gospel of Thomas log. 20, 37. Cf. also J. Sevenster, 'Some Remarks

on the ΓΥΜΝΟΣ in II Cor. V. 3' in *Studia Paulina in honorem J. de Zwaan* (Haarlem, 1953), pp. 203, 207–9, 211.

53 Cf. A. Oepke, 'γυμνός κτλ.', *TDNT* I, pp. 774f; Bietenhard, *Die himmlische Welt*, p. 226.

54 Cf. also, though with varying interpretations of the opposing views, Bultmann, 'Probleme', p. 299; Schmithals, *Gnosticism*, pp. 259ff; Hoffmann, *Die Toten*, pp. 272, 276–8, 285; Bauer, *Leiblichkeit*, p. 120; Spörlein, *Die Leugnung*, p. 159; Rissi, *Studien*, p. 89; Harris, *Interpretation*, pp. 135–45, who makes the telling point that the οὐ ... ἀλλά antithesis in verse 4 is employed frequently by Paul, and especially in the Corinthian correspondence, to refer either implicitly or explicitly to people or ideas of which he disapproves, e.g. 1 Cor. 4: 19f; 6: 13; 2 Cor. 1: 12, 24; 2: 17; 3: 5; 4: 5; 5: 12; 7: 12; 10: 4, 13, 18; 12: 14.

55 While ἐφ' ᾧ can mean 'on condition that' in classical and Hellenistic Greek, here it is to be taken causally, cf. Moule, *Idiom-Book*, p. 132, 'Dualism', p. 118 n. 1; Harris, *Interpretation*, pp. 105–8; Barrett, *2 Cor.*, pp. 155f; *pace* Thrall, *Greek Particles*, pp. 93f; Bruce, *1 and 2 Cor.*, p. 203. It is imperative that the apostle's word order be observed. He writes ἐφ' ᾧ οὐ θέλομεν and not οὐκ ἐφ' ᾧ θέλομεν as many interpreters assume.

56 Barrett, *2 Cor.*, p. 156; cf. also Plummer, *Commentary*, p. 148; Hughes, *Commentary*, pp. 169–71; Rissi, *Studien*, p. 90.

57 Cf. Vos, *Eschatology*, p. 165; Hughes, *Commentary*, pp. 41f; Barrett, *2 Cor.*, p. 80.

58 εἰδότες in verse 6 is a causal participle and, together with θαρροῦντες, is in anacolouthon, for after the parenthesis of verse 7 Paul begins his thought again in verse 8.

59 This is preferable to the view which treats the verbs in terms of 'taking up residence' and then links them with the 'building' metaphors of verse 1f, *pace* Feuillet, 'La Demeure', pp. 386ff; Hanhart, *Intermediate State*, p. 446; Harris, *Interpretation*, p. 168; Collange, *Énigmes*, p. 229.

60 Cf. Bultmann, 'Probleme', p. 305; Schmithals, *Gnosticism*, pp. 269f; Hoffmann, *Die Toten*, pp. 280 and n. 126, 285; Rissi, *Studien*, p. 95; Lang, *2 Korinther*, pp. 189–93, though his interpretation of the contrast as that between a wrong attitude of finding one's home or security in the body and a right attitude of finding this with the Lord comes to grief with verse 9, for which his own explanation is too forced.

61 *Pace* Hoffmann, *Die Toten*, p. 284; Harris, *Interpretation*, pp. 166–71.

62 Cf. also Vos, *Eschatology*, p. 194 – 'the state in ... a new body would hardly be describable as the state of one absent from the body'; Berry, *Death and Life*, p. 65.

63 *Pace* Lietzmann-Kümmel, *Korinther I/II*, pp. 117ff, 121; Ellis, *Interpreters*, p. 46; Hoffmann, *Die Toten*, pp. 279–85.

64 So also Harris, 'Paul's View of Death in 2 Cor. 5: 1–10', p. 324.

65 Hettlinger, '2 Cor. 5: 1–10', pp. 176ff, makes much of this.

66 G. E. Ladd, *The Pattern of New Testament Truth* (Grand Rapids, Michigan, 1968), pp. 106f; cf. also Plummer, *Commentary*, p. 163; Berry, *Death and Life*, p. 67 – 'Paul was in two minds about death'; Gundry, *Sōma*, p. 152.

67 For a further discussion of anthropological duality in Paul, see Gundry, *Sōma*, esp. pp. 135–6.

68 For further discussion of this background and of the notion of an intermediate state, see chapter 4 section 5 below.

69 W. D. Davies, *Rabbinic Judaism*, pp. 315ff.

70 Cf. Strack–Billerbeck, *Kommentar*, IV, pp. 819ff.

71 *Pace* Davies, *Rabbinic Judaism*, pp. 317f.

72 The resurgence of interest in transcendental experiences has brought new interest in Paul's experience but sheds no greater light as J. L. Cheek's inconclusive article 'Paul's Mysticism in the Light of Psychedelic Experience', *JAmAR* 38 (1970), 381–9, illustrates. Relating the episode to 'charismatic' experiences has however proved more fruitful, cf. J. D. G. Dunn, *Jesus and the Spirit* (London, 1975), esp. pp. 212ff. For a fuller treatment of this passage, cf. my article '"Paul the Visionary": The Setting and Significance of the Rapture to Paradise in II Corinthians XII. 1–10', *NTS* 25 (1979), 204–20.

73 There are many variant readings of the text for the first part of verse 1 but the best attested appears to be καυχᾶσθαι δεῖ· οὐ συμφέρον μέν, ἐλεύσομαι δέ ... For more detailed discussion and evidence, cf. Windisch, *Der Zweite*, p. 367; Metzger, *Greek NT*, p. 584; Barrett, *2 Cor.*, p. 305 n. 1.

74 Cf. Bietenhard, *Die himmlische Welt*, p. 165; E. Benz, *Paulus als Visionär* (Wiesbaden, 1952), p. 110.

75 *Pace* Dunn, *Jesus*, p. 215, in view of Paul's general stance of weakness in relation to his opponents and his specific claim to be speaking the truth in verse 6 it is unlikely that ὑπερβολή is an exaggerated claim.

76 Cf. also Benz, *Paulus*, pp. 77–121. H. Saake, 'Paulus als Ekstatiker', *NT* 15 (1973), pp. 154, 156, 160. *Pace* Barrett, *2 Cor.*, p. 308.

77 Any distinction drawn between Paul's Damascus road experience and his later visions needs to be expressed carefully. Barrett, however, argues that Paul did not regard the Damascus road experience as a vision because 'he then saw Jesus our Lord objectively' (*2 Cor.*, p. 308). It is doubtful whether the apostle would have operated with anything like our objective/subjective distinction in order to differentiate the Damascus road experience from later ones. To be sure, Paul thought of the seeing Jesus involved in his conversion as distinctive, but the distinctiveness was not a matter of the mode of appearance, which was revelatory and visionary in the case of the conversion as in the experience of the third heaven and which was also just as real for Paul in each instance. Cf. Windisch, *2 Korintherbrief*, p. 380; and for a discussion which takes account of the complexities of the issue, see Dunn, *Jesus*, pp. 97–109.

78 *Pace* Schlatter, *Paulus*, p. 658.

79 Cf. also Windisch, *2 Korintherbrief*, p. 377; Hughes, *Commentary*, p. 428 n. 97; Barrett, *2 Cor.*, p. 307; Dunn, *Jesus*, p. 414 n. 88.

80 (Tübingen, 1972).

81 Cf. also E. A. Judge, 'St. Paul and Classical Society', *Jahrbuch für Antike und Christentum* 15 (1972), p. 35.

82 Betz, *Der Apostel Paulus*, p. 89.

83 *Ibid.* pp. 15–18, 20–38.

84 *Ibid.* pp. 75–82.

85 Cf. Windisch, *2 Korintherbrief*, pp. 406f; Betz, *Der Apostel Paulus*, pp. 14f, 39; Barrett, *2 Cor.*, p. 328.

86 Cf. also Windisch, *2 Korintherbrief*, pp. 297ff, Betz, *Der Apostel Paulus*, pp. 68f.

87 Cf. also Betz, *Der Apostel Paulus*, pp. 86-9.

88 As Käsemann, 'Legitimität', pp. 475-521, so clearly demonstrated.

89 Cf. also Barrett, *2 Cor.*, p. 312.

90 *Pace* Dunn, *Jesus*, pp. 214f, who follows J. Lindblom, *Gesichte und Offenbarungen* (Lund, 1968), p. 45.

91 *Pace* Barrett, *2 Cor.*, p. 307.

92 *Pace* E. Güttgemanns, *Der leidende Apostel*, pp. 160f.

93 Or by other aspects of apocalyptic style, *pace* Baumgarten, *Paulus*, pp. 143f, who cites references which are not nearly similar enough to be considered parallels to the phenomenon here.

94 Cf. Windisch, *2 Korintherbrief*, pp. 370, 380, on this 'Bescheidenheitsstil', R. Spittler, 'The Limits of Ecstasy: An Exegesis of 2 Corinthians 12: 1-10' in *Current Issues in Biblical and Patristic Interpretation*, ed. G. F. Hawthorne (Grand Rapids, Michigan, 1975), p. 264, who speaks of 'a device Paul uses to mark himself off from the demonstrational, propagandistic uses of ecstasy (and esotericism) utilized by his opponents' and Betz, *Der Apostel Paulus*, pp. 70, 91, 95.

95 Cf. Betz, *Der Apostel Paulus*, pp. 89-100.

96 Verses 7b-10 contain features of an aretalogy, cf. Betz, *Der Apostel Paulus*, pp. 92ff, 'Eine Christus-Aretalogie bei Paulus', *ZThK* 66 (1969), 288-305.

97 Cf. Betz, *Der Apostel Paulus*, p. 96; Spittler, 'The Limits', p. 265.

98 Cf. Plummer, *Commentary*, p. 344; Schlatter, *Paulus*, p. 663; Betz, *Der Apostel Paulus*, p. 91; Saake, 'Paulus', p. 154.

99 Cf. Hughes, *Commentary*, p. 433; Schoonhoven, *The Wrath*, p. 64.

100 Cf. Bietenhard, *Die himmlische Welt*, pp. 11f; Traub, 'οὐρανός', pp. 511f.

101 J. Calvin, *The Second Epistle of Paul the Apostle to the Corinthians and the Epistles to Timothy, Titus and Philemon*, trans. T. A. Smail (Edinburgh, 1964), p. 156; cf. also Barrett, *2 Cor.*, p. 310.

102 Cf. Plummer, *Commentary*, p. 343, though this argument cannot be connected in any way with Paul's use of ἕως; Hanhart, *Intermediate State*, p. 40 n. 3.

103 Cf. R. H. Charles, *The Book of the Secrets of Enoch* (Oxford, 1896), p. xl; Bietenhard, *Die himmlische Welt*, p. 166; J. Strugnell, 'The Angelic Liturgy at Qumran' in *Congress Volume* (Oxford, 1959), Supplement to *Vetus Testamentum* VII (Leiden, 1961), p. 329; Simon, *Heaven*, p. 42.

104 Cf. Strugnell, 'Angelic Liturgy', pp. 318-45.

105 Cf. also Strack-Billerbeck, *Kommentar*, III, pp. 531ff; Bietenhard, *Die himmlische Welt*, pp. 3ff; Traub, 'οὐρανός', pp. 511f.

106 Bietenhard, an advocate of this view, himself concedes, 'wir können Paulus nicht einfach auf den 2 Hen. reduzieren und daraus erklären. Wir können das im Text des Paulus Fehlende nicht einfach aus dem 2 Hen. ergänzen.' (*Die himmlische Welt*, p. 168).

107 Cf. J. Jeremias, 'παράδεισος', *TDNT* V, pp. 765-73; Strack-Billerbeck, *Kommentar*, IV, pp. 1130-65; P. Volz, *Die Eschatologie der jüdischen Gemeinde* (2nd edn, Hildesheim, 1966), pp. 413f, for further references to Paradise.

108 Cf. also D. S. Russell, *The Method and Message of Jewish Apocalyptic*

(London, 1964), p. 283.

109 Cf. J. Jeremias, 'παράδεισος', p. 770; Baumgarten, *Paulus*, p. 140.
110 *Die himmlische Welt*, p. 167.
111 Cf. Oostendorp, *Another Jesus*, p. 14; Jewett, *Terms*, p. 278.
112 Schmithals, *Gnosticism*, pp. 214ff, emphasizes this aspect and is followed by Baumgarten, *Paulus*, pp. 142f.
113 Jewett, *Terms*, p. 278.
114 Cf. also Gundry, *Sōma*, pp. 146f; *pace* Baumgarten, *Paulus*, p. 142.
115 Cf. also Spittler, 'The Limits', pp. 263f; *pace* Dunn, *Jesus*, p. 215, who stresses the ineffability of such mystical and ecstatic experiences.
116 Cf. Russell, *Method*, pp. 107–18; also Rev. 10: 4.
117 Cf. J. Jeremias, *Jerusalem in the Time of Jesus* (London, 1969), pp. 237–41.
118 Cf. also Windisch, *2 Korintherbrief*, pp. 377f.
119 Cf. W. Bousset, *Die Himmelsreise der Seele* (2nd edn, Darmstadt, 1971) (reprint of articles in *ARW* 4, 1901); M. Eliade, *Shamanism* (New York, 1964), pp. 115–44; 181–288; 392ff; 477ff; C. Colpe, 'Die "Himmelsreise der Seele" als philosophie- und religionsgeschichtliches Problem', in *Festschrift für Joseph Klein* (Göttingen, 1967), pp. 85–104; G. Widengren, *The Ascension of the Apostle and the Heavenly Books* (UUA) (Uppsala, 1950); Talbert, 'Descending-Ascending Redeemer', pp. 418–40.
120 Cf. Windisch, *2 Korintherbrief*, p. 376; G. Scholem, *Jewish Gnosticism, Merkabah Mysticism and Talmudic Tradition* (New York, 1960), pp. 14–19; J. W. Bowker, '"Merkabah" Visions and the Visions of Paul', *JSS* 16 (1971), 157–73.
121 Cf. Bowker, 'Merkabah', pp. 163, 167, on this.
122 Scholem, *Jewish Gnosticism*, pp. 17f.
123 For the notion of danger being attached to heavenly journeys cf. 1 Enoch 40: 7; Apoc. Abr. 17; Asc. Isa. 9: 1, 2; also J. Maier, 'Das Gefährdungsmotiv bei der Himmelsreise in der jüdischen Apokalyptik und "Gnosis"', *Kairos* 5 (1963), pp. 18–40; Bowker, 'Merkabah', p. 157, who explains it in terms of the physical danger of approaching the holy in a state of uncleanness.
124 As Windisch, *2 Korintherbrief*, p. 377, says, 'Ein echtes Erlebnis beschreibt er uns; nur ist Form und Inhalt, soweit er darüber Andeutungen macht, durch die überlieferten Vorstellungen der Zeit bestimmt.'
125 How free the account is of this element can be seen by comparison not only with accounts of ascents in apocalyptic literature but also with both the descriptions based on this passage, the gnostic Apocalypse of Paul (in J. M. Robinson (ed.), *The Nag Hammadi Library* (New York, 1977), pp. 239–41) and the later Apocalypse of Paul (in E. Hennecke and W. Schneemelcher (eds.), *New Testament Apocrypha*, II (London, 1965), pp. 755–98).
126 Cf. chapter 2 and the discussion of 1 Cor. 15: 47ff; also J. Jeremias, 'παράδεισος', p. 772.
127 Cf. also Windisch, *2 Korintherbrief*, p. 375.
128 Hughes, *Commentary*, p. 422.
129 Though it is omitted by p⁴⁶ D K it vg syr Irenaeus Origen, we retain the διό as the more difficult reading and relate the first phrase to verse 7 rather

than to parts of verse 6. The διό is redundant but not impossible and anticipates the ἵνα for emphasis, cf. Heb. 13: 12.

130 Cf. also Käsemann, 'Legitimität', p. 502.

131 Cf. also Benz, *Paulus*, pp. 93f, 111; Dunn, *Jesus*, pp. 212ff, *pace* Käsemann, 'Legitimität', pp. 513, 515.

4. Philippians and the heavenly commonwealth

1 Cf. especially B. S. Mackay, 'Further Thoughts on Philippians', *NTS* 7 (1960–1), 161–70; T. E. Pollard, 'The Integrity of Philippians', *NTS* 13 (1966–7), 57–66; R. Jewett, 'The Epistolary Thanksgiving and the Integrity of Philippians', *NT* 12 (1970), 40–53; R. P. Martin, *Philippians* (London, 1976), pp. 10–22.

2 E. Lohmeyer, *Der Brief an die Philipper* (Göttingen, 1964), p. 156.

3 'Redaktion und Tradition im Christushymnus Phil 2', *ZNW* 55 (1964), 75ff.

4 *Der leidende Apostel*, pp. 240ff. One is inclined to be suspicious of Güttgemanns' work at this point because his whole thesis regarding Paul's use of σῶμα depends on his being able to show that in this passage Paul could not have meant that the resurrected Christ had a body. It is obviously easier for him to make a case for this position if 3: 20f can be shown to be a pre-Pauline hymn and thus not really a part of Paul's theological framework. His views on this passage are effectively critiqued in Gundry, *Sōma*, pp. 177–83.

5 'Erwägungen zu Phil. 3, 20–21', *TZ* 27 (1971), 16–29.

6 *Pace* Güttgemanns, *Der leidende Apostel*, p. 243.

7 *Pace* Becker, 'Erwägungen', p. 19.

8 Cf. Becker, 'Erwägungen', p. 21.

9 So Strecker, 'Redaktion', p. 76.

10 So Güttgemanns, *Der leidende Apostel*, p. 241.

11 Cf. also M. D. Hooker, 'Interchange in Christ', *JTS* 22 (1971), 356, 7; Gundry, *Sōma*, p. 180.

12 Cf. similar verdicts in J. Gnilka, *Der Philipperbrief* (Freiburg, 1968), p. 209; P. Siber, *Mit Christus leben* (Zürich, 1971), pp. 122ff; Baumgarten, *Paulus*, pp. 76f.

13 Cf. F. W. Beare, *A Commentary on the Epistle to the Philippians* (London, 1959), pp. 101f – Jews in verses 2–16; libertines in 3: 17–4: 1; R. P. Martin, *The Epistle of Paul to the Philippians* (London, 1959), pp. 136f, 160 – Judaizers in verses 2ff and 17ff; perfectionists in verses 12f; G. B. Caird, *Paul's Letters from Prison* (Oxford, 1976), pp. 130–69 – Jews in verses 2ff and Christians with a wrong attitude to the cross in verses 17ff; Martin, *Philippians* (1976), pp. 33f – Judaizing missionaries in verses 2ff; hellenistic libertinism in verses 18ff, though linked by an attitude of triumphalism.

14 Cf. R. Jewett, 'Conflicting Movements in the Early Church as Reflected in Philippians', *NT* 12 (1970), 362–90 – Judaizing missionaries in verses 2ff, Hellenistic enthusiastic piety in verses 12ff and libertinists expelled from the Philippian church in verses 17ff, though he finds a common denominator in the notion of perfection.

15 Cf. W. Schmithals, 'Die Irrlehrer des Philipperbriefes', *ZThK* 54 (1957), 297–341 – Gnostic libertines of Jewish origin; H. Koester, 'The Purpose of

the Polemic of a Pauline Fragment', *NTS* 8 (1962), 317–32 – Jewish Christians who combined a perfectionist doctrine of law with a 'radicalized spiritualistic eschatology in a manner typical of early Christian Gnosticism'; A. F. J. Klijn, 'Paul's Opponents in Philippians 3', *NT* 7 (1965), 278ff – non-Christian Jews; Gnilka, *Der Philipperbrief*, pp. 211ff – Hellenistic Jewish 'divine man' missionaries; J. L. Houlden, *Paul's Letters From Prison* (Harmondsworth, 1970), pp. 103ff – non-Christian Hellenistic Jews; P. Siber, *Mit Christus leben*, p. 102 – Jewish Christian 'enthusiasts'; J. B. Tyson, 'Paul's opponents at Philippi', *Perspectives in Religious Studies* 3 (1976), 82–95 – Christians who claimed both a Jewish heritage and Gnostic prerogatives.

16 Cf. Koester, 'The Purpose', p. 318; also Siber, *Mit Christus leben*, p. 102.

17 Cf. Beare, *A Commentary*, p. 133; Jewett, 'Conflicting Movements', p. 373 n. 1.

18 Cf. also Strack–Billerbeck, *Kommentar*, I, pp. 724f; III, pp. 621f.

19 *Pace* Martin, *Philippians* (1959), p. 137; Jewett, 'Conflicting Movements', p. 385.

20 *Pace* K. Barth, *Philippians* (London, 1962), p. 93; Martin, *Philippians* (1959), p. 137.

21 Cf. also Jewett, 'Conflicting Movements', p. 382; Georgi, *Die Gegner*, pp. 49f; Siber, *Mit Christus leben*, p. 102.

22 Cf. also Koester, 'The Purpose', p. 320.

23 Cf. also Schmithals, 'Irrlehrer', p. 313; Gnilka, *Der Philipperbrief*, pp. 186f.

24 Cf. Koester, 'The Purpose', p. 321; Gnilka, *Der Philipperbrief*, p. 188.

25 Cf. Koester, 'The Purpose', p. 322.

26 *Pace* Klijn, 'Paul's Opponents', pp. 278ff; Houlden, *Paul's Letters*, pp. 103ff.

27 Koester, 'The Purpose', p. 322.

28 Cf. M. Dibelius, *An die Thessalonicher I, II. An die Philipper* (3rd edn, Tübingen, 1937), p. 69; Beare, *A Commentary*, p. 114.

29 Cf. B. Gärtner's discussion of this principle in Hermetic literature, Stoicism, Philo and Gnosticism and Paul's adaptation of it from his own perspective in 1 Cor. 2: 6–16 in 'The Pauline and Johannine Idea of "to know God" against the Hellenistic Background', *NTS* 14 (1968), 209–31.

30 *Pace* M. R. Vincent, *A Critical and Exegetical Commentary on the Epistles to the Philippians and to Philemon* (Edinburgh, 1897), p. 106; Martin, *Philippians* (1959), p. 150.

31 Koester, 'The Purpose', p. 322.

32 Cf. Charles, *Apocrypha and Pseudepigrapha*, II, pp. 529f.

33 καὶ τοῦτο implies previous revelations. Cf. Schmithals, 'Irrlehrer', p. 327; Gnilka, *Der Philipperbrief*, p. 201; Martin, *Philippians* (1976), pp. 140f. Of course, the irony of the first part of the verse includes the nuance that real perfection involves a realization that one is not yet perfect.

34 Koester, 'The Purpose', p. 331.

35 *Pace* Koester, 'The Purpose'; Schmithals, 'Irrlehrer', pp. 319–21. We do not think that verses 17ff indicate a libertinist view, and an over-realized eschatology cannot in itself be a conclusive criterion for identifying Gnosticism, cf. M. L. Peel, *The Epistle to Rheginos* (London, 1969), p. 153; 'Gnostic Eschatology and the New Testament', *NT* 12 (1970), 141–65.

36 So also G. Bornkamm, 'Der Philipperbrief als paulinische Briefsammlung' in *Neotestamentica et Patristica* (Leiden, 1962), p. 199; Gnilka, *Der Philipperbrief*, pp. 211ff; Siber, *Mit Christus leben*, pp. 104f; Martin, *Philippians* (1976), pp. 29f; Ellis, 'Paul and His Opponents', pp. 291f.

37 Cf. also Jewett, 'Conflicting Movements', p. 368.

38 Cf. Dibelius, *Thessalonicher*, p. 93.

39 So also Jewett, 'Conflicting Movements', p. 378.

40 So also Koester, 'The Purpose', p. 326; Gnilka, *Der Philipperbrief*, p. 206; Jewett, 'Conflicting Movements', p. 378; Martin, *Philippians* (1976), p. 145.

41 Cf. K. Barth, *Philippians*, p. 113.

42 *Pace* Schmithals, 'Irrlehrer', pp. 334ff; Jewett, 'Conflicting Movements', p. 381.

43 *Pace* M. R. Vincent, *A Critical and Exegetical Commentary on the Epistles to the Philippians and to Philemon* (Edinburgh, 1897), p. 117; Beare, *A Commentary*, p. 136; Jewett, 'Conflicting Movements', p. 380; P. C. Böttger, 'Die eschatologische Existenz der Christen: Erwägungen zu Philipper 3: 20', *ZNW* 60 (1969), 254 n. 75; Martin, *Philippians* (1976), p. 145.

44 Cf. Koester, 'The Purpose', p. 326; C. K. Barrett, *Romans* (London, 1957), p. 285; J. Behm, 'κοιλία', *TDNT* III, 788.

45 Cf. also Gnilka, *Der Philipperbrief*, pp. 205f; Koester, 'The Purpose', p. 327; Houlden, *Paul's Letters*, p. 103; Behm, 'κοιλία', p. 788; Klijn, 'Paul's Opponents', p. 283.

46 *A Commentary*, p. 136.

47 See below on verse 20.

48 Cf. also Böttger, 'Die eschatologische', p. 255; Siber, *Mit Christus leben*, pp. 132f.

49 So also Gnilka, *Der Philipperbrief*, p. 206; Böttger, 'Die eschatologische', p. 260; Martin, *Philippians* (1976), p. 147.

50 In *Philologus* 82 (1927), pp. 268-312, 433-54. Both H. Strathmann's treatment, 'πόλις κτλ', *TDNT* VI, pp. 516-35, and P. C. Böttger's investigation, 'Die eschatologische', pp. 244-63, rely heavily on Ruppel's work, as do we in our summary of the discussion.

51 Cf. Ruppel, 'Politeuma. Bedeutungsgeschichte eines staatsrechtlichen Terminus', *Philologus*, 82 (1927), 453; Schmidt, *Die Polis*, p. 8; Böttger, 'Die eschatologische', p. 246. For further references cf. Ruppel, 'Politeuma', pp. 289f.

52 Cf. Ruppel, 'Politeuma', pp. 275-9, 291; Böttger, 'Die eschatologische', pp. 248f, for further examples of the way in which the meanings of πόλις, πολιτεία and πολίτευμα tend to merge.

53 Cf. W. Dittenberger, *Sylloge inscriptionum Graecarum* (Leipzig, 1915-24), esp. 543, lines 6 and 32; also Ruppel, 'Politeuma', pp. 290, 297f. In other references adduced by Böttger, 'Die eschatologische', p. 247, for this meaning, it is better seen as the governing body elected by and representing the citizens.

54 Cf. Ruppel, 'Politeuma', pp. 299-306, 310, for other instances.

55 Cf. RV; Bietenhard, *Die himmlische Welt*, p. 199. Vincent, *Commentary*, p. 118 (allows it); de Young, *Jerusalem*, p. 125; K. L. Schmidt, *Die Polis*, p. 22 (allows it); K. Barth, *Philippians*, p. 114 (although he gives the term

his own meaning, which is closer to our conclusions).

56 Cf. also Böttger, 'Die eschatologische', p. 252. De Young's argument about relationship is insufficient to establish the nature of that relationship as citizenship and Bietenhard incorrectly believes citizenship to be involved because he holds that the first part of Paul's contrast in verse 19 refers to Jews who stressed their allegiance to an earthly city.

57 Cf. Moffatt's translation (Moffatt possibly did not think that πολίτευμα means colony and was simply giving a loose translation, but others have taken this sense of πολίτευμα as the actual meaning); W. F. Arndt and F.W. Gingrich, trs, of W. Bauer, *A Greek-English Lexicon of the New Testament* (Chicago, 1957), p. 692 (allow it); Dibelius, *Thessalonicher*, pp. 71f; Schmidt, *Die Polis*, p. 24 (allows it); T. W. Manson, *The Teaching of Jesus* (2nd edn, Cambridge, 1967), pp. 138 n. 2, 190; Klijn, 'Paul's Opponents', p. 283; A. Sherwin-White, *Roman Society and Roman Law in the New Testament* (Oxford, 1963), pp. 184f [followed by Martin, *Philippians* (1976), p. 147]; Güttgemanns, *Der leidende Apostel*, p. 243 n. 19; Houlden, *Paul's Letters*, p. 104 (allows it).

58 For similar objections cf. Koester, 'The Purpose', p. 330 n. 1; de Young, *Jerusalem*, p. 125 n. 26; Strathmann, 'πόλις κτλ', p. 535. Güttgemanns is more consistent on this interpretation and believes that a colony in heaven could be in view and that since πολίτευμα was used to designate Jewish diaspora communities, it is now being used to speak of the Philippian church as a transcendent entity. Klijn and Sherwin-White also hold that in contrast to Jewish colonies on earth, the Christian's colony is in heaven, while Dibelius, followed by Manson, started from the meaning of colony but moved from this to that of the home state which corresponds to such a colony.

59 Cf. Beare, *A Commentary*, p. 136; Lohmeyer, *Der Brief*, pp. 157f; Strathmann, 'πόλις κτλ.', p. 535, includes this nuance.

60 'Politeuma', p. 277.

61 Cf. Böttger, 'Die eschatologische', pp. 242, 252.

62 Cf. RSV; Vincent, *Commentary*, p. 118; Strathmann, 'πόλις κτλ.', p. 535; Koester, 'The Purpose', p. 330; E. Stauffer, *New Testament Theology* (London, 1955), p. 296 n. 518, who localizes this to 'capital city'; R. R. Brewer, 'The Meaning of Politeuesthe in Philippians 1: 27', *JBL* 73 (1954), p. 82; Baumgarten, *Paulus*, p. 78; Caird, *Paul's Letters*, p. 147.

63 Cf. also Böttger, 'Die eschatologische', p. 253 – 'Dabei wäre der Staat in erster Linie als dynamische Grösse, als Subjekt politischer Machtausübung zu verstehen, die durch die Staatsverfassung reguliert wird', and Barth caught something of this nuance when he wrote 'It is the constitution or judicial order which is authoritative for us . . .' (*Philippians*, p. 114).

64 Strathmann, 'πόλις κτλ.', goes as far as to say, 'The βασιλεία τῶν οὐρανῶν is the πολίτευμα of Christians.'

65 Cf. also the references from Philo noted above at the beginning of this section.

66 De Young, *Jerusalem*, p. 126.

67 Cf. Stauffer, *NT Theology*, p. 296 n. 518; Martin, *Philippians* (1959), p. 161; Houlden, *Paul's Letters*, p. 105; Brewer, 'Politeuesthe', p. 82. Although Manson is incorrect in starting from the view that πολίτευμα

means 'colony', his conclusion catches something of this force when he writes 'the sense of the passage is that the Christian community on earth is a colony whose constitution reproduces in miniature the constitution of the Kingdom in heaven' (*Teaching*, p. 190).

68 'Politeuesthe', p. 77.

69 Cf. Houlden, *Paul's Letters*, p. 66; Martin, *Philippians* (1959), pp. 83f; Beare, *A Commentary*, p. 66; Vincent, *Commentary*, p. 32; Barth, *Philippians*, pp. 45f; Schmidt, *Die Polis*, p. 18; Gnilka, *Der Philipperbrief*, p. 98 n. 16; Brewer, 'Politeuesthe', p. 83. Other indications of Paul's consciousness of the 'Romanness' of Philippi can be seen in his mention of the praetorian guard in 1: 13 and his sending greetings from those of 'Caesar's household' in 4: 22. In addition φιλιππήσιοι instead of φίλιπποι in 4: 15 is from the Latin form and probably reflects the self-designation of the inhabitants of the city.

70 'The Purpose', p. 330, followed by Gnilka, *Der Philipperbrief*, p. 206; Jewett, 'Conflicting Movements., p. 378.

71 Vincent, *Commentary*, pp. 118f; Lohmeyer, *Der Brief*, p. 158; de Young, *Jerusalem*, p. 126 n. 28; Böttger, 'Die eschatologische', p. 259.

72 *Pace* Gnilka, *Der Philipperbrief*, p. 206.

73 Cf. Stauffer, *NT Theology*, p. 296 n. 518; Güttgemanns, *Der leidende Apostel*, p. 243; Lohmeyer, *Der Brief*, p. 158; Martin, *Philippians* (1959), p. 161; Schmidt, *Die Polis*, p. 23.

74 So also Gnilka, *Der Philipperbrief*, p. 207 n. 123; Vincent, *Commentary*, p. 119; de Young, *Jerusalem*, p. 127 n. 31; Siber, *Mit Christus leben*, p. 133 n. 113; Martin, *Philippians* (1976), p. 148.

75 Cf. Güttgemanns, *Der leidende Apostel*, p. 245; Gnilka, *Der Philipperbrief*, p. 210; Spörlein, *Die Leugnung*, p. 170; cf. also the comments on the concept of 'knowing' which appears to have similar associations.

76 *Pace* Gnilka, *Der Philipperbrief*, p. 207.

77 *Pace* Bultmann, *Theology*, p. 346; G. B. Caird, *Paul's Letters*, pp. 113f. Even if one considers that 3: 20, 21 stand in a different letter, the parousia expectations expressed in 1: 6, 10; 2: 16; 4: 5 would be in the same letter as 1: 23, and it is difficult to believe Paul would have contradicted himself in the same letter on an issue to which he was obviously giving great thought.

78 D. W. Palmer '"To Die is Gain" (Philippians 1 21)' *NT* 17 (1975), 203–18, emphasizes this latter point and compares Paul's sentiments to those of Greek writers who also expressed the thought that death is gain. C. J. de Vogel 'Reflections on Philipp. i 23–24', *NT* 19 (1977), 262–74, queries this approach, but her own belabouring of the view that the passage involves a body–soul relation and that the soul enjoys fullness of life after death does not further the discussion because it fails to relate this to Paul's view of the fullness of salvation involving the resurrection of the body.

79 Cf. for example, J. Dupont, ΣΥΝ ΧΡΙΣΤΩΙ, *L'Union avec le Christ suivant Saint Paul*, I (Louvain, 1952), pp. 177ff.

80 So also Hoffmann, *Die Toten*, pp. 296ff; Gnilka, *Der Philipperbrief*, p. 74; Martin, *Philippians* (1976), pp. 78f; Baumgarten, *Paulus*, pp. 119f.

81 Cf. also Gundry, *Sōma*, p. 148, 'Paul writes of absence *from the Philippian Christians*, which could characterize only the intermediate state, not the

final state when the saved are united in heavenly bliss'; Palmer, 'To die is gain', p. 207.

82 *Pace* Baumgarten, *Paulus*, p. 120.

83 Cf. H. C. C. Cavallin, *Life After Death*, I (Lund, 1974), esp. pp. 78, 82–5, 117, 121, 123, 127; Gundry, *Sōma*, pp. 88f.

84 Cf. Hoffmann, *Die Toten*, p. 126; Gnilka, *Der Philipperbrief*, p. 90; Cavallin, *Life After Death*, pp. 43–8.

85 Cf. also Hoffmann, *Die Toten*, pp. 156–74; Strack–Billerbeck, *Kommentar*, IV, pp. 1118–65, on Gan Eden; W. D. Davies, *Rabbinic Judaism*, pp. 315f; Hanhart, *Intermediate State*, pp. 64f; Cavallin, *Life After Death*, pp. 171–86, who attempts to limit his discussion to material before 100 A.D.

86 Gundry, *Sōma*, p. 108, can summarize this background, in discussing the anthropological duality of the Judaism of NT times, as follows, 'The soul/spirit inhabits the body during life and leaves it at death. Despite incompleteness, the soul/spirit of the righteous consciously enjoys bliss; that of the wicked consciously suffers torment. At the resurrection (if that is held) body and soul reunite.' Cf. also G. W. E. Nickelsburg, *Resurrection, Immortality and Eternal Life in Intertestamental Judaism* (Cambridge, 1972), pp. 179f; Cavallin, *Life After Death*, p. 201, who makes the necessary reminder that frequently, however, the perspectives of immediate salvation for the righteous after death and a final resurrection exist side by side without the explicit logical harmonization of an intermediate state.

87 Cf. Hoffmann, *Die Toten*, p. 318.

88 *Pace* Hanhart, *The Intermediate State*, p. 184; Caird, *Paul's Letters*, p. 114, who holds that the image of sleep in Paul, which is not however mentioned in this passage, involves the collapse of all temporal categories.

89 Cf. R. P. Martin, *Carmen Christi* (Cambridge, 1967), pp. 102–19.

90 Others who have noted a parallel between 2: 6ff and 3: 20f are Dibelius, *Thessalonicher*, p. 72; Porter, *The Mind of Christ*, p. 217; N. Flanagan, 'A Note on Philippians 3, 20–21', *CBQ* 18 (1956), 8, 9; M. Bouttier, *Christianity According To Paul* (London, 1966), p. 18; Hooker, 'Interchange', p. 357; Martin, *Philippians* (1976), p. 150.

91 Lohmeyer, *Der Brief*, p. 157, interprets the passage in this way with salvation being orientated towards a timeless beyond, when he says of the commonwealth in heaven 'dass der Inhalt des Wortes von Zeit und Raum völlig fern und in ein Jenseits gerückt ist . . . "Der Himmel" wird hier also zur Heimat der Seelen, vor der die Erde als Bezirk des Gottlosen versinkt; und damit die Gläubigen zu "Pilgrimen" auf Erden, die nach ihrer himmlischen Heimat wallen.'

92 *Pace* de Young, *Jerusalem*, pp. 125ff; K. L. Schmidt, 'Jerusalem als Urbild und Abbild', *Eranos Jahrbuch* 18 (1950), 209.

93 Cf. Koester, 'The Purpose', pp. 330, 329 n. 2.

5. Colossians and heavenly-mindedness

1 Cf. also J. Lähnemann, *Der Kolosserbrief* (Gütersloh, 1971), p. 30.

2 For a helpful collection of significant attempts to do this, see F. O. Francis and W. A. Meeks (eds.), *Conflict at Colossae: A Problem in the Interpretation of Early Christianity Illustrated by Selected Modern Studies* (Missoula, Montana, 1973). M. D. Hooker's essay, 'Were There False Teachers in

Colossae?' in B. Lindars and S. Smalley (eds.), *Christ and Spirit in the New Testament* (Cambridge, 1973), pp. 315–31, perhaps cautions against seeing the teaching as having made great inroads into the Colossian church, but her own solution fails to take account of too many factors for it to provide a satisfactory alternative to the view that Paul had a specific teaching in mind.

3 Cf. W. Grundmann, 'ταπεινός κτλ.', *TDNT* VIII, p. 22; E. Lohse, *Colossians and Philemon* (Philadelphia, 1971), p. 118; *pace* N. Kehl, 'Erniedrigung und Erhöhung in Qumran und Kolossä', *ZKTh* 91 (1969), pp. 374ff, who sees a reference to the same lowliness of mind which is found in the piety of the Qumran community.

4 Lohse, *Colossians*, p. 118.

5 Cf. E. Percy, *Die Probleme der Kolosser- und Epheserbriefe*, (sic) (Lund, 1946), pp. 148f; Grundmann, 'ταπεινός κτλ', p. 22; C. F. D. Moule, *The Epistles of Paul the Apostle to the Colossians and to Philemon* (Cambridge, 1957), p. 104; F. O. Francis, 'Humility and Angelic Worship in Col. 2: 18', *ST* 16 (1962), 115ff; Caird, *Paul's Letters*, p. 198.

6 Cf. also Francis, 'Humility'; Russell, *The Method*, pp. 169f.

7 Cf. Scholem, *Jewish Gnosticism*, pp. 9ff.

8 Though there is more evidence of this in the Judaism of the time than A. Lukyn Williams, 'The Cult of the Angels at Colossae', *JTS* 10 (1909), 413–38, was able to find.

9 Francis, 'Humility', has convincingly championed this interpretation, though his overall view of the false teaching, treating it almost solely from a Jewish background, is probably too one-sided. Lohse, *Colossians*, p. 119 n. 36, believes that 'Francis' interpretation falls because of v. 23 where "self-chosen worship" (ἐθελοθρησκία) specifically characterizes the concept "worship" (θρησκεία) as performed by men.' He is followed by R. P. Martin, *Colossians: The Church's Lord and the Christian's Liberty* (Exeter, 1972), p. 92; *Colossians and Philemon* (London, 1974), pp. 93f; E. Schweizer, *Der Brief an die Kolosser* (Zürich, 1976), pp. 122f. But this objection is by no means decisive because the worship of verse 23 *is* performed by humans as they join in the angels' worship. It is precisely the worship which involves participation in angelic worship by means of ascetic techniques that Paul can designate as 'self-willed'.

10 Cf. also J. Strugnell, 'Angelic Liturgy', pp. 318–45.

11 Cf. Scholem, *Jewish Gnosticism*, pp. 20–30.

12 E.g. that of J. B. Lightfoot, *St Paul's Epistles to the Colossians and to Philemon* (London, 1892), p. 197.

13 There is nothing strange in 'fasting' being part of what was seen in visions. As Francis, 'Humility', p. 130, points out, 'This is a common pattern: instruction in humility for the purpose of obtaining visions is itself the subject of visions.'

14 Cf. Euripides, *Electra* 595; 1 Macc. 12: 25; 13: 20; cf. also Bauer, (Arndt-Gingrich, trs.) *Lexicon*, p. 253; H. Preisker, 'ἐμβατεύω', *TDNT* II, 535.

15 Though he himself prefers to link the verb with the antecedent of ἃ ἑόρακεν, cf. A. D. Nock, 'The Vocabulary of the New Testament', *JBL* 52 (1933), 132f. The interpretation of entry into heaven is, however, held by Francis, 'Humility', pp. 122f, and Schweizer, *Brief*, p. 124. In a later

essay 'The Background of Embateuein (Col. 2: 18) in Legal Papyri and Oracle Inscriptions' in Francis and Meeks (eds.), *Conflict at Colossae*, pp. 197–207, Francis opts more specifically for the most common connotation of the verb as entering into the possession of property and associates this in the Colossian context with entering heaven to possess salvation or a portion in the Lord.

16 This solution was first proposed by Sir William Ramsay, *The Teaching of Paul in Terms of the Present Day* (London, 1913), pp. 283–305, and then by M. Dibelius, 'Die Isisweihe bei Apuleius und verwandte Initiations-Riten', (1917) in *Botschaft und Geschichte*, II (Tübingen, 1956), pp. 30–79. Martin, *Colossians* (1974), pp. 94f. favours an interpretation akin to this.

17 So Preisker, 'ἐμβατεύω', pp. 535f; Percy, *Die Probleme*, pp. 172f.

18 Cf. Lohse, *Colossians*, p. 102.

19 Cf. O. Blanchette, 'Does the Cheirographon of Col. 2, 14 Represent Christ Himself?', *CBQ* 23 (1961), 206–12; A. Bandstra, *The Law and the Elements of the World* (Kampen, 1964), pp. 158ff; J. Daniélou, *The Theology of Jewish Christianity* (London, 1964), pp. 201ff; Martin, *Colossians* (1972), pp. 79, 80; Martin, *Colossians* (1974), pp. 84f; H. Weiss, 'The Law in the Epistle to the Colossians', *CBQ* 34 (1972), 294–314.

20 Cf. also Lähnemann, *Der Kolosserbrief*, p. 128 n. 68.

21 In addition to the commentaries and major studies on Colossians, cf. Burton, *Galatians*, pp. 510–18; G. Delling, 'στοιχεῖον', *TDNT* VII, pp. 670–87; J. Blinzler, 'Lexikalisches zu dem Terminus τὰ στοιχεῖα τοῦ κόσμου bei Paulus', in *Analecta Biblica* 18 (Rome, 1963), pp. 429–43; A. Bandstra, *The Law*; E. Schweizer, 'Die "Elemente der Welt" Gal. 4: 3, 9; Kol. 2: 8, 20', in O. Bocher and K. Haacker (eds.), *Verborum Veritas* (Wuppertal, 1970), pp. 245–59.

22 Cf. Russell, *The Method*, p. 244.

23 Lohse, *Colossians*, p. 99 n. 41.

24 Cf. also E. Schweizer, *Lordship and Discipleship* (London, 1960), p. 105; *Erniedrigung und Erhöhung bei Jesus und seinen Nachfolgern* (Zürich, 1962), pp. 148–50.

25 For a discussion of Phrygian syncretism cf. Lähnemann, *Der Kolosserbrief*, pp. 82–100. The cult of the god Sabazios is illustrative of its character. This local god was given the attributes of such gods as Zeus, Dionysos, Mithra and fertility and underworld deities, and some Jews of Phrygia combined allegiance to this cult with worship of Jahweh.

26 Cf. Lohse, *Colossians*, pp. 94–6.

27 Cf. E. Yamauchi, 'Sectarian Parallels: Qumran and Colossae', *BS* 121 (1964), 141–52; Lohse, *Colossians*, pp. 115 n. 11, 129 n. 118; E. W. Saunders, 'The Colossian Heresy and Qumran Theology' in B. L. Daniels and M. J. Suggs (eds.), *Studies in the History and Text of the New Testament* (Salt Lake City, 1967), pp. 133–45; *pace* P. Benoit, 'Qumran and the New Testament', in J. Murphy-O'Connor (ed.), *Paul and Qumran* (London, 1968), pp. 16f; N. Kehl, 'Erniedrigung', pp. 364–94.

28 Cf. H. Hegermann, *Die Vorstellung vom Schöpfungsmittler im hellen-istischen Judentum und Urchristentum* (Berlin, 1961), p. 163; *pace* G. Bornkamm, 'Die Häresie des Kolosserbriefes' in *Das Ende des Gesetzes*

(München, 1966), pp. 139–56.

29   Cf. Hegermann, *Die Vorstellung*, pp. 189ff, for a summary of the place of the heavenly world in Philo. He is followed by Lohse, *Colossians*, especially pp. 46–55.

30   Cf. Volz, *Die Eschatologie*, pp. 114–16.

31   Cf. G. Bornkamm, 'Die Hoffnung im Kolosserbrief', in *Studien zum Neuen Testament und zur Patristik* (E. Klostermann zum 90. Geburtstag, Berlin, 1961), pp. 56–64.

32   *Pace* Martin, *Colossians* (1972), pp. 27, 105; Martin, *Colossians* (1974), pp. 34f, 48.

33   E. Käsemann, 'A Primitive Christian Baptismal Liturgy', in *Essays on New Testament Themes* (London, 1964), p. 160.

34   *Ibid.*; Lohse, *Colossians*, pp. 35f; Martin, *Colossians* (1974), p. 54; *pace* E. Schweizer, *Brief*, pp. 47f.

35   Among the more important writings other than commentaries are:- E. Bammel, 'Versuch zu Col. 1: 15–20', *ZNW* 52 (1961), 88–95; P. Benoit, 'L'hymne christologique de Col. 1, 15–20' in J. Neusner (ed.), *Christianity, Judaism and Other Greco-Roman Cults*, I (Leiden, 1975), pp. 226–63; C. Burger, *Schöpfung und Versöhnung*, (Neukirchen-Vluyn, 1975). R. Deichgräber, *Gotteshymnus und Christushymnus in der frühen Christenheit* (Göttingen, 1967), esp. pp. 143–55; H.-J. Gabathuler, *Jesus Christus, Haupt der Kirche - Haupt der Welt* (Zürich, 1965); J. G. Gibbs, *Creation and Redemption. A Study in Pauline Theology* (Leiden, 1971), pp. 94–114; Hegermann, *Die Vorstellung*, esp. pp. 88–157; Käsemann, 'Baptismal Liturgy', pp. 149–68; N. Kehl, *Der Christushymnus Kol. 1, 12–20* (Stuttgart, 1967); R. P. Martin, 'An Early Christian Hymn (Col. 1: 15–20)', *EQ* 36 (1964), 195–205; J. M. Robinson, 'A Formal Analysis of Colossians 1: 15–20', *JBL* 76 (1957), 270–87; J. T. Sanders, *The New Testament Christological Hymns* (Cambridge, 1971), pp. 75–87; G. Schille, *Frühchristliche Hymnen* (Berlin, 1965), pp. 81ff; E. Schweizer, 'The Church as the Missionary Body of Christ', *NTS* 8 (1961–2), 1–11; F. Zeilinger, *Der Erstgeborene der Schöpfung* (Vienna, 1974), pp. 179–205.

36   Cf. further W. Foerster, 'ἐξουσία', *TDNT* II, pp. 571f.

37   Cf. E. Schweizer, *Erniedrigung*, pp. 145ff, also *Brief*, pp. 103, 104.

38   In the light of the Odes of Solomon 23, Gospel of Truth 19: 17ff and also Rev. 5 Daniélou, *Theology*, pp. 201ff, has indicated an early Jewish Christian interpretation of Col. 2: 14 in which Christ came to be identified with the chirograph. Gospel of Truth 20: 23ff in particular shows how such an identification could be made.

39   Cf. Blanchette, 'Cheirographon', pp. 306–12; Bandstra, *The Law*, pp. 158ff, who develops this line of interpretation in a slightly different direction.

40   The 'circumcision of Christ' is taken here as an objective genitive construction, cf. C. A. A. Scott, *Christianity According to St. Paul* (Cambridge, 1932), pp. 36f; Moule, *Colossians*, pp. 95f; Martin, *Colossians* (1972), pp. 77f; Martin, *Colossians* (1974), pp. 82f.

41   Cf. F. Blass and A. Debrunner, *A Greek Grammar of the New Testament and other Early Christian Literature* (Translation and Revision by R. W. Funk) (Chicago, 1961), § 316 (1).

42   E.g. E. Käsemann, *Leib und Leib Christi* (Tübingen, 1933), p. 143;

Käsemann, 'Apocalyptic', p.128; Koester, 'The Purpose', p.329; E. Grässer, 'Kol. 3, 1–4 als Beispiel einer Interpretation secundum homines recipientes', *ZThK* 64 (1967), 139–68; Lohse, *Colossians*, pp. 104, 134 n. 13, 180.

43 Grässer, 'Kol. 3, 1–4', pp. 161f.

44 Cf. also Percy, *Die Probleme*, p. 110; G. R. Beasley-Murray, *Baptism in the New Testament* (London, 1962), pp. 138f; Houlden, *Paul's Letters*, pp. 202f.

45 See above on Gal. 4: 26 and Phil. 3: 14 where ἄνω is attributive.

46 Cf. B. Chag. 2: 1 – 'My fathers gathered treasures for below, I gathered treasures for above . . . my fathers gathered treasures in this world, and I gathered treasures for the future world', cf. also Strack–Billerbeck, *Kommentar*, I, pp. 395, 977; II, pp. 116, 133, 430.

47 Cf. H. W. Huppenbauer, *Der Mensch zwischen zwei Welten* (Zürich, 1959), pp. 103ff.

48 *Pace* Bornkamm, 'Hoffnung', p. 62 n. 1.

49 Zeilinger, *Der Erstgeborene*, p. 149, misses the significance of the distinction between heaven and earth for Paul's thinking about the period between the resurrection and the parousia when he states, 'τὰ ἄνω stellt also eine Chiffre dar, um die Himmel und Erde umfassende Wirklichkeit des neuen Äons zu umschreiben.'

50 *Pace* E. Schweizer, 'Christus und Geist', pp. 311f, who holds that rash talking about the Spirit in the enthusiastic false faith of the Colossians has made it difficult for the writer to refer to the Spirit.

51 Cf. also H. Sasse, 'γῆ'; *TDNT* I, p. 680.

52 H. Chadwick, 'All Things to All Men', *NTS* I (1955), p. 272.

53 *Pace* Grässer, 'Kol. 3, 1–4', pp. 161f, who holds that a future reference is exclusively in view. However, the use of ζωοποιεῖν in 2: 13 has already provided an indication that there is a present aspect to 'life' in this letter.

54 *Pace* Dodd, *Apostolic Preaching*, p. 193, who asserts that 'Paul never speaks of Christ as being "in God" as we are in Him.' For parallels to the believer being in God, cf. 1 Thess. 1: 1; 2 Thess. 1: 1.

55 *Pace* E. Lohmeyer, *Die Briefe an die Philipper, an die Kolosser und an Philemon* (Göttingen, 1930), p. 134, followed by Grässer, 'Kol. 3, 1–4', p. 158.

56 *Pace* Steinmetz, *Protologische*, pp. 29ff, who can find here at the most only traces of future eschatology and who overemphasizes the uniqueness of the concept of believers being revealed with Christ, cf. a similar concept in 1 Thess. 4: 14.

57 Cf. K. Koch, *The Rediscovery of Apocalyptic* (London, 1972), pp. 32f.

58 Such aspirations would correspond to certain of the characteristics of Jewish merkabah mysticism, where the visionary would join in hymns sung by the angels and celebrate his participation in the Shekinah presence. Scholem, *Jewish Gnosticism*, pp. 17, 21, 22, holds that this tradition goes back to the apocalypticists and shows that the final vision is always of the divine glory itself.

59 Cf. also E. Schweizer, *Brief*, pp. 133ff, who underlines the significance of this. 'Die Gemeinde besitzt also die Zukunft nicht so, dass sie darüber verfügen könnte, sondern nur so, dass sie sich von ihr stets neu bewegen lassen darf.'

60 *Pace* C. Masson, *L'Epître de Saint Paul aux Colossiens* (Neuchatel, 1950), p. 142, who resorts to taking τὰ μέλη as a vocative, referring to Christians as members of Christ's body.

61 Cf. E. Schweizer, *Erniedrigung*, p. 178.

62 Cf. Grässer, 'Kol. 3, 1–4', p. 165.

63 *Ibid.*, p. 150 n. 32; cf. also section 3 (i) above.

64 'Kol. 3, 1–4', p. 161 – 'Wer bereits mit Christus auferweckt wurde, wird nicht noch einmal auferstehen.'

65 *Ibid.*; cf. also Lohse, *Colossians*, pp. 104, 134 n. 16.

66 'Kol. 3, 1–4', pp. 166f.

67 Cf. Lohse, *Colossians*, esp. p. 180.

68 Cf. Houlden, *Paul's Letters*, pp. 136, 203; *pace* Grässer, Lohse, Käsemann and Koester (cf. n. 42 above).

69 Steinmetz, *Protologische*, pp. 31f, finds traces of future eschatology in 4: 11 also.

70 Cf. also Percy, *Die Probleme*, p. 116.

71 Cf. also Lähnemann, *Der Kolosserbrief*, p. 156 n. 7.

72 Cf. Kehl, 'Erniedrigung', pp. 384 n. 77, 392, who also asserts that the letter's realized eschatology, which is a response to the Colossian situation, should not be used as an argument against authenticity.

73 See chapter 3 above.

74 Cf. also Lähnemann, *Der Kolosserbrief*, p. 161. Zeilinger, *Der Erstgeborene*, pp. 27, 207ff, on the pastoral and theological significance of this realized aspect of eschatology.

6. Ephesians and heavenly life in the Church at worship

1 Cf. for example, Percy, *Die Probleme*, pp. 179–474; G. Schille, 'Der Autor des Epheserbriefes', *TLZ* 82 (1957), 325–334; H. Schlier, *Der Brief an die Epheser* (5th edn, Düsseldorf, 1965), pp. 22–8; A. van Roon, *The Authenticity of Ephesians* (Leiden, 1974); M. Barth, *Ephesians* (New York, 1974), pp. 36–50; Caird, *Paul's Letters*, pp. 11–29.

2 Cf. for example, R. P. Martin, 'An Epistle in Search of a Life-Setting', *ET* 79 (1968), 296–302, and also *New Testament Foundations*, Vol. 2 (Grand Rapids, Michigan, 1978), pp. 223–38, who opts for Luke; G. H. P. Thompson, *The Letters of Paul to the Ephesians, to the Colossians and to Philemon* (Cambridge, 1967), pp. 17ff, who opts for Tychicus; J. J. Gunther, *St. Paul's Opponents and Their Background* (Leiden, 1973), p. 16, who opts for Timothy.

3 Cf. for example, C. L. Mitton, *The Epistle to the Ephesians* (Oxford, 1951), esp. pp. 243–69, and *Ephesians* (London, 1976), pp. 2–32; J. Gnilka, *Der Epheserbrief* (Freiburg, 1971), esp. pp. 13ff; K. M. Fischer, *Tendenz und Absicht des Epheserbriefes* (Göttingen, 1973).

4 Cf. also Gnilka, *Epheserbrief*, p. 33.

5 Cf. O. Cullmann, *Early Christian Worship* (London, 1953), pp. 23f – 'The liturgical Amen, likewise taken over from Judaism, is said by the congregation, as we see from 1 Cor. 14: 16'; cf. also J. C. Kirby, *Ephesians, Baptism and Pentecost* (London, 1968), p. 88.

6 J. T. Sanders, 'Hymnic Elements in Ephesians 1–3', *ZNW* 56 (1965), 214.

7 Cf. Gnilka, *Epheserbrief*, p. 27; Kirby, *Ephesians*, pp. 84–9; 126–38.

8 *Pace* J. Coutts, 'Ephesians 1, 3-14 and 1 Peter 1, 3-12', *NTS* 3 (1956-7), pp. 115ff; Schille, *Hymnen*, pp. 67ff; Deichgräber, *Gotteshymnus*, pp. 65ff; Fischer, *Tendenz*, pp. 111-18.

9 Cf. also Schlier, *Epheser*, p. 41; Sanders, 'Elements', pp. 223-32; Gnilka, *Epheserbrief*, pp. 57ff; M. Barth, *Ephesians*, pp. 97ff; van Roon, *Authenticity*, pp. 185f; C. C. Caragounis, *The Ephesian Mysterion* (Lund, 1977), pp. 41-5.

10 Cf. Schlier, *Epheser*, p. 86; M. Dibelius, *An die Kolosser, Epheser, an Philemon* (Tübingen, 1953), p. 64; Kirby, *Ephesians*, p. 139; Deichgräber, *Gotteshymnus*, pp. 163f; H. Conzelmann, *Der Brief an die Epheser* (Göttingen, 1968), p. 63; Gnilka, *Epheserbrief*, pp. 93f; M. Barth, *Ephesians*, p. 153.

11 Cf. Schille, *Hymnen*, p. 103 n. 4; Sanders, 'Elements', pp. 220-3 (possibly); Fischer, *Tendenz*, pp. 118-20.

12 Cf. for example, Schille, *Hymnen*, pp. 53ff; Gnilka, *Epheserbrief*, p. 119; Fischer, *Tendenz*, pp. 121ff; Sanders, 'Elements', pp. 218-23.

13 Cf. Schille, *Hymnen*, pp. 24ff; Sanders, 'Elements', p. 217; Gnilka, *Epheserbrief*, pp. 147-51; Fischer, *Tendenz*, pp. 131-7; M. Barth, *Ephesians*, pp. 261f; Burger, *Schöpfung*, pp. 117-57.

14 Cf. for example, Dibelius, *Kolosser*, p. 79; Gnilka, *Epheserbrief*, p. 203; Fischer, *Tendenz*, pp. 137f; M. Barth, *Ephesians*, pp. 462ff.

15 Cf. Schlier, *Epheser*, p. 232; Gnilka, *Epheserbrief*, p. 245; Fischer, *Tendenz*, p. 140; M. Barth, *Ephesians*, p. 557.

16 N. A. Dahl, 'Adresse und Proömium des Epheserbriefes', *TZ* 7 (1951), 263f.

17 Cf. *ibid.*, pp. 259f, 264; R. A. Wilson, '"We" and "You" in the Epistle to the Ephesians' in F. L. Cross (ed.), *Studia Evangelica*, II (Berlin, 1964), pp. 676-80.

18 Those who acknowledge a close link with a baptismal setting include Coutts, 'Ephesians', p. 124; Dahl, 'Adresse', pp. 263f; Percy, *Die Probleme*, p. 447; Schlier, *Epheser*, p. 21; Kirby, *Ephesians*, pp. 150-61.

19 A. M. Hunter, *Paul and his Predecessors* (London, 1961), p. 135.

20 H. Odeberg, *The View of the Universe in the Epistle to the Ephesians* (Lund, 1934), p. 4.

21 Cf. Hegermann, *Die Vorstellung*, esp. pp. 47-87; Gnilka, *Epheserbrief*, pp. 39-45.

22 Cf. F. Mussner, *Christus, das All und die Kirche* (Trier, 1955); also 'Contributions made by Qumran to the Understanding of the Epistle to the Ephesians' in J. Murphy-O'Connor (ed.), *Paul and Qumran* (London, 1968), pp. 159-78; K. G. Kuhn, 'The Epistle to the Ephesians in the Light of the Qumran Texts' in *Paul and Qumran*, pp. 116-20.

23 Cf. Käsemann, *Leib*, pp. 50-94, 138-59; H. Schlier, *Christus und die Kirche im Epheserbrief* (Tübingen, 1930), *passim*; *Epheser, passim*; Conzelmann, *Epheser, passim*.

24 Cf. also Percy, *Die Probleme*, p. 181 n. 5; Schille, *Hymnen*, pp. 69f; Schlier, *Epheser*, p. 44; Gnilka, *Epheserbrief*, pp. 62f.

25 So also T. K. Abbott, *The Epistles to the Ephesians and to the Colossians* (Edinburgh, 1897), p. 5; Percy, *Die Probleme*, p. 181; Dibelius, *Kolosser*, p. 58; Schlier, *Epheser*, p. 45; Gnilka, *Epheserbrief*, pp. 62f.

26 *Pace* Dibelius, *Kolosser*, p. 58, who suggested that the much later Mandaean text Qolasta 17 provided a parallel.
27 Cf. Schille, *Hymnen*, p. 68.
28 Cf. R. M. Pope, 'Studies in Pauline Vocabulary: of the Heavenly Places', *ET* 23 (1912), 365ff.
29 Odeberg, *The View*, pp. 12, 13.
30 Käsemann, 'Epheserbrief' in *RGG* II (1958), 518.
31 Conzelmann, *Epheser*, p. 57.
32 Schlier, *Epheser*, pp. 45–58.
33 For a more detailed critique of the opposing interpretations and a fuller defence of the viewpoint put forward here, cf. the present writer's earlier article, 'A Re-Examination of "The Heavenlies" in Ephesians', *NTS* 19 (1973), 468–83, especially pp. 476–80.
34 Cf. the similar suggestion now made by Caragounis, *Mysterion*, pp. 146–52.
35 Just as W. D. Davies, *Rabbinic Judaism*, p. 308, in commenting on σῶμα πνευματικόν, warns us not to think of the spiritual as immaterial, so we should not think of the heavenly as necessarily a-spatial, *pace* Gibbs, *Creation*, p. 131, who speaks of heaven for Paul as a reality which is a-spatial and limits the meaning of ἐν τοῖς ἐπουρανίοις to simply a symbol of sovereignty. Van Roon, *Authenticity*, pp. 213f, correctly emphasizes both local and qualitative connotations.
36 Cf. especially J. A. Allan, 'The "In Christ" Formula in Ephesians', *NTS* 5 (1958–9), 54ff.
37 Cf. F. Büchsel, '"In Christus" bei Paulus', *ZNW* 42 (1949), 141–58; F. Neugebauer, 'Das Paulinische "in Christo"', *NTS* 4 (1957–8), 124ff; M. Bouttier, *En Christ, étude d'exégèse et de théologie pauliniennes* (Paris, 1962).
38 Cf. E. Best, *One Body in Christ* (London, 1955), p. 8.
39 Cf. Allan, 'In Christ', p. 59; Gnilka, *Epheserbrief*, pp. 66–9.
40 Cf. also Caragounis, *Mysterion*, pp. 152–7, and his criticisms of Allan's viewpoint.
41 See section 4 below on 2: 6.
42 Cf. R. E. Brown, *The Semitic Background of the Term 'Mystery' in the New Testament* (Philadelphia, 1968); Caragounis, *Mysterion*, pp. 121–35.
43 Cf. Brown, *Semitic Background*, pp. 12–22; G. Bornkamm, 'μυστήριον', *TDNT* IV, pp. 815f.
44 Cf. also Brown, *Semitic Background*, pp. 22–9; H.-W. Kuhn, *Enderwartung*, pp. 166–75; Gnilka, *Epheserbrief*, p. 78.
45 Cf. S. Hanson, *The Unity of the Church in the New Testament* (Uppsala, 1946), pp. 124ff; Schlier, *Epheser*, p. 64 n. 3.
46 So also Schlier, *Epheser*, p. 65; Gnilka, *Epheserbrief*, p. 80; M. Barth, *Ephesians*, pp. 89ff. While κεφαλή in extra-Biblical Greek could also be used metaphorically for completion or total, since sums were added from the bottom upwards to the head of the list, cf. S. Hanson, *Unity*, p. 123; H. G. Liddell and R. Scott, *A Greek-English Lexicon* (Oxford, 1948), p. 945, the reverse is not the case, so that the connotation of headship cannot be read into the actual verb ἀνακεφαλαιόω.
47 *Pace* Caird, *Paul's Letters*, p. 38.
48 *Pace* W. D. Davies, *Rabbinic Judaism*, p. 57, and Mitton, *Ephesians* (1976),

pp. 56f, who prefers to emphasize humanity.

49 ἐπί with the dative rather than ἐν is unusual in this particular phrase, cf. Col. 1: 16, 20. Moule, *Idiom-Book*, p. 49, thinks that this 'looks like a merely stylistic variation', while Percy, *Die Probleme*, p. 181 n. 7, holds that the phrase has been influenced by the formula ἐν τοῖς ἐπουρανίοις.

50 E. Roels, *God's Mission: the Epistle to the Ephesians in Mission Perspective* (Franeker, 1962), p. 71. *Pace* Roels and Gnilka, *Epheserbrief*, p. 81, the aspect of accomplishment cannot be demonstrated from the aorist form, cf. F. Stagg, 'The Abused Aorist', *JBL* 91 (1972), 222–31.

51 Cf. also Gnilka, *Epheserbrief*, pp. 30, 61, 85f; Dahl, 'Adresse', p. 260; Deichgräber, *Gotteshymnus*, p. 76; though, *pace* Dahl and Deichgräber, the aorist form cannot be adduced as evidence for this conclusion.

52 See chapter 5 section 2 (ii) on Col. 1: 12; cf. also Schlier, *Epheser*, p. 84; Gnilka, *Epheserbrief*, p. 91.

53 Cf. W. Grundmann, 'δεξιός', *TDNT* II, pp. 37ff; D. M. Hay, *Glory At The Right Hand* (Nashville, 1973), pp. 59–153.

54 *Pace* Abbott, *Epistles*, pp. 31f.

55 *Pace* Schille, *Hymnen*, p. 103 n. 4 this is not Paul correcting too great an emphasis on realized eschatology in the traditional material he is using.

56 Cf. Schlier, *Epheser*, p. 88 – 'Der künftig offenbare Äon ist schon verborgen gegenwärtige Realität'.

57 *Pace* Bauer (Arndt–Gingrich, trs.), *Lexicon*, p. 847; S. Hanson, *Unity*, p. 127; Best, *One Body*, pp. 146f; Mussner, *Christus*, pp. 30f, who takes verse 22b to indicate supreme headship over the church.

58 Mitton, *Ephesians* (1976), p. 96.

59 Cf. Blass–Debrunner, *Greek Grammar*, section 316 (1); Moule, *Idiom-Book*, p. 25; J. H. Moulton, *A Grammar of New Testament Greek*, III (N. Turner) (Edinburgh, 1963), p. 55. Examples of the middle being used with an active sense are found in Xenophon, *Hellenica* VI, 2, 14 and Plutarch, *Alcibiades* 35, 6.

60 Cf. also Mussner, *Christus*, pp. 46–64.

61 On the problems of this part of verse 23 cf. especially G. Delling, 'πλήρης κτλ.', *TDNT* VI, pp. 283–311; C. F. D. Moule, '"Fulness" and "Fill" in the New Testament', *SJT* 4 (1951), 79–86; J. Ernst, *Pleroma und Pleroma Christi* (Regensburg, 1970), a comprehensive study which insists however on reading sacramental significance into these terms; R. Yates, 'A Re-examination of Ephesians 1: 23', *ET* 83 (1972), 146–51; M. Barth, *Ephesians*, pp. 200–10.

62 Cf. also Best, *One Body*, pp. 141f.

63 Cf. also Mussner, *Christus*, p. 91; Schille, *Hymnen*, pp. 53ff; Schlier, *Epheser*, pp. 110f; R. Schnackenburg, *Baptism in the Thought of St. Paul* (Oxford, 1964), pp. 73ff; Kirby, *Ephesians*, pp. 154ff; Gnilka, *Epheserbrief*, pp. 119, 126.

64 Cf. also Schlier, *Epheser*, p. 111, *pace* Allan, 'In Christ', p. 58; Gnilka, *Epheserbrief*, p. 120, who do not allow the idea of incorporation into Christ in Ephesians.

65 Cf. also Rom. 8: 24 where the aorist passive is employed, though in connection with τῇ ἐλπίδι In discussions of the perfect tenses of 2: 5, 8 it often appears to be forgotten that they point of course to the continuing

effects of the accomplishment of salvation for the present and are also balanced by the future orientation of 2: 7.

66 Cf. M. Malinine, H.-C. Puech, G. Quispel, W. Till, *De Resurrectione* (Zürich, 1963), pp. 45, lines 24ff, 62.
67 Cf. Traub, 'οὐρανός', p. 501.
68 *Pace* Conzelmann, *Epheser*, p. 66.
69 Cf. H.-W. Kuhn, *Enderwartung*, pp. 44ff; Mussner, 'Contributions', pp. 164–7; Gnilka, *Epheserbrief*, pp. 123f.
70 Cf. Klinzing, *Die Umdeutung*, p. 129.
71 Cf. H. Sasse, 'αἰών', *TDNT* I, pp. 206f; Gnilka, *Epheserbrief*, p. 121.
72 Cf. especially Gnilka, *Epheserbrief*, pp. 147–52, though his reconstruction of the original hymn is not as convincing as that of Sanders, 'Elements', p. 217; cf. also Schille, *Hymnen*, pp. 24ff; Fischer, *Tendenz*, pp. 131–7; Burger, *Schöpfung und Versöhnung*, pp. 115–57; M. Barth, *Ephesians*, p. 261. In the reworking the dividing wall (verse 14) which was originally the cosmic wall between heaven and earth (cf. 1 Enoch 14: 9; 3 Bar. 2: 1ff; Test. Levi 2: 7 and for later Gnostic usage cf. Schlier, *Epheser*, pp. 129f) has become the law which isolates Jews from Gentiles and causes hostility between them (cf. Letter of Aristeas 139, 142).
73 Cf. O. Procksch, 'ἅγιος', *TDNT* I, p. 106; Roels, *God's Mission*, p. 145; P. Vielhauer, *Oikodome* (Karlsruhe-Durlach, 1940), p. 123; Caird, *Paul's Letters*, p. 60.
74 Cf. also B. Gärtner, *The Temple and the Community in Qumran and the New Testament* (Cambridge, 1965), p. 63; Schlier, *Epheser*, pp. 140f; Mussner, 'Contributions', p. 166, who considers his previous interpretation in *Christus*, pp. 105f, no longer tenable; Steinmetz, *Protologische*, p. 48 n. 63; Klinzing, *Die Umdeutung*, p. 185; Gnilka, *Epheserbrief*, p. 154.
75 For Gnostic references cf. Schlier, *Christus*, pp. 49–60; *Epheser*, p. 144; Vielhauer, *Oikodome*, p. 125.
76 Cf. the discussion of the connotations of the 'cornerstone' concept below.
77 Cf. also S. Hanson, *Unity*, p. 130; L. Cerfaux, *The Church in the Theology of St. Paul* (New York, 1959), pp. 345f; Schlier, *Epheser*, p. 140; Gärtner, *The Temple*, p. 64; Gnilka, *Epheserbrief*, p. 155. Mussner, 'Contributions', p. 173, has changed his view in favour of this interpretation in contrast to his earlier *Christus*, p. 117. McKelvey, *New Temple*, is ambivalent at this point, cf. p. 119 and p. 120.
78 Cf. J. Jeremias, 'Κεφαλὴ γωνίας – Ἀκρογωνιαῖος', *ZNW* 29 (1930), pp. 264–80; 'γωνία κτλ.', *TDNT* I, p. 792; 'λίθος', *TDNT* IV, p. 275.
79 S. Hanson, *Unity*, p. 131. Others who support this interpretation include Cerfaux, *The Church*, pp. 345f; Best, *One Body*, pp. 165f; Vielhauer, *Oikodome*, pp. 125ff; Schlier, *Epheser*, p. 142; Gnilka, *Epheserbrief*, p. 158; Caird, *Paul's Letters*, p. 61; M. Barth, *Ephesians*, pp. 317–19.
80 *New Temple*, p. 201. Others who see a reference to the stone at the bottom corner of the structure which joins together the walls and the foundation are Abbott, *Epistles*, p. 71; Mussner, *Christus*, pp. 108f; 'Contributions', p. 172 n. 59; Gärtner, *Temple*, p. 64 n. 4; Mitton, *Ephesians* (1976), pp. 113, 114.
81 *New Temple*, pp. 203f.
82 Cf. also J. Jeremias, *Golgotha* (Leipzig, 1926), pp. 51ff.

83 Cf. Mussner, *Christus*, p. 26; Gnilka, *Epheserbrief*, p. 172; *pace* Schlier, *Epheser*, p. 153 n. 1, who opts for the personal connotation of αἰών, finding another instance of Gnostic influence, and M. Barth, *Ephesians*, pp. 343f, who wishes to combine both temporal and personal meanings. It is very interesting, as R. McL. Wilson points out in 'The Trimorphic Protennoia' in M. Krause (ed.), *Gnosis and Gnosticism* (Leiden, 1977), p. 54 n. 13, that this gnostic text appears to have taken the phrase 'hidden from the ages' in a temporal sense, cf. the German translation 'das von Ewigkeit her verborgene Myst[e]rium' in 'Die dreigestaltige Protennoia', *TLZ* 99 (1974), 741, and the clearly temporal context shown by the English translation in J. M. Robinson (ed.), *The Nag Hammadi Library*, p. 467 – 'for you have become worthy of the mystery hidden from the Aeons, so that [you might be perfect]. And the consummation of this Aeon [that is and] of the life of injustice [has approached, and there dawns the] beginning of the [Aeon to come] which [has no change forever].'

84 Cf. also R. Schnackenburg, 'Christus, Geist und Gemeinde (Eph. 4: 1–16)', in B. Lindars and S. Smalley (eds.), *Christ and Spirit in the New Testament* (Cambridge, 1973), p. 283.

85 Cf. Bietenhard, *Die himmlische Welt*, p. 238; R. P. Martin, 'Ephesians' in *Broadman Bible Commentary*, vol. 11 (London, 1971), p. 155.

86 Cf. B. Lindars's discussion of the probable role of Ps. 68: 19 in the formation of the theologumenon 'the gift of the Spirit' in *New Testament Apologetic* (London, 1961), p. 51.

87 Cf. Lindars, *Apologetic*, p. 52 n. 2.

88 Cf. Strack–Billerbeck, *Kommentar*, III, pp. 596f.

89 *Pace* Lindars, *Apologetic*, p. 53, who argues for simple coincidence.

90 Cf. Lindars, *Apologetic*, p. 52 n. 2; Ellis, *Paul's Use*, p. 144; M. Barth, *Ephesians*, p. 475 n. 246.

91 Cf. also Lindars, *Apologetic*, p. 53; Ellis, *Paul's Use*, p. 144; *pace* Mitton, *Ephesians* (1976), pp. 145f, who surprisingly thinks the quotation involves an unintentional mistake because he finds it hard to believe that a Christian writer would deliberately change a text of Scripture to support his own contention. Such a procedure is of course not at all unusual in the contemporary Jewish exegetical techniques or elsewhere in the use of the OT in the NT.

92 Cf. further W. Meeks, *The Prophet-King* (Leiden, 1967), pp. 122–5, 205–9. For hints of this motif in Josephus cf. p. 141 and for elaboration in Samaritan writings cf. pp. 232ff, 241ff.

93 See chapter 5 section 1 above.

94 Cf. Knox, *St. Paul*, pp. 194f; J. Jeremias, 'Μωυσῆς', *TDNT* IV, pp. 848f; J. Cambier, 'La Signification Christologique d'Eph. 4: 7–10', *NTS* 9 (1962–3), 265; *pace* Lindars, *Apologetic*, p. 59 n. 1.

95 Cf. G. B. Caird, 'The Descent of Christ in Ephesians 4: 7–11', in *Studia Evangelica* II (Berlin, 1964), p. 544; Kirby, *Ephesians*, pp. 138f, 146.

96 *Pace* E. Lohse, 'πεντηκοστή', *TDNT* VI, p. 48.

97 Cf. also J. van Goudoever, *Biblical Calendars* (Leiden, 1959), pp. 139ff; Kirby, *Ephesians*, pp. 61–9.

98 Cf. Goudoever, *Biblical Calendars*, p. 201; Caird, 'Descent', p. 54 n. 1;

R. de Vaux, *Ancient Israel*, II (New York, 1965), p. 494; Kirby, *Ephesians*, pp. 92ff.

99   Cf. G. Lohfink, *Die Himmelfahrt Jesu* (München, 1971), p. 87. The present writer's earlier article, 'The Heavenlies', pp. 471, 482, needs to be more carefully worded at this point, as does the work of J. G. Davies, *He Ascended into Heaven* (London, 1958), pp. 28ff, 60ff.

100 This explanation differs from that of Traub, 'οὐρανός', pp. 525f, who views verse 10 as Gnostically influenced and the heavens as cosmic spheres which were not the goal of Christ's ascent; he only passed through them. However, Paul's intention is not to declare that in going beyond the heavens, Christ went somewhere which cannot be designated as heaven.

101 Cf. P. Benoit, 'L'Horizon Paulinien de l'Épître aux Éphésiens', *RB* 46 (1937), p. 348; Blass–Debrunner, *Greek Grammar*, p. 92; F. Büchsel, 'κάτω κτλ.', *TDNT* III, pp. 641f; Odeberg, *The View*, pp. 17f; J. A. Robinson, *St. Paul's Epistle to the Ephesians* (2nd edn, London, 1928), p. 180; J. Schneider, 'μέρος', *TDNT* IV, pp. 597f, who was convinced by Büchsel's article and changed the view he had expressed in 'ἀναβαίνω κτλ.', *TDNT* I, pp. 521f.

102 Cf. Bietenhard, *Die himmlische Welt*, p. 237; Bultmann, *Theology*, p. 175; Cambier, 'Signification', pp. 262–75; Dibelius, *Kolosser*, pp. 80f; Ernst, *Pleroma*, p. 136; F. Foulkes, *The Epistle of Paul to the Ephesians* (London, 1963), p. 116; Knox, *St. Paul*, pp. 194f; Mussner, *Christus*, pp. 28, 41ff; Percy, *Die Probleme*, pp. 273f; Schlier, *Epheser*, pp. 192f; Longenecker, *Christology*, p. 60; Traub, 'οὐρανός', p. 525; Schnackenburg, 'Christus', pp. 288f; Gnilka, *Epheserbrief*, p. 209; M. Barth, *Ephesians*, pp. 433f, who also includes the crucifixion; Mitton, *Ephesians* (1976), pp. 147f.

103 Cf. Caird, 'Descent', p. 536.

104 Cf. also Abbott, *Epistles*, p. 115; Caird, 'Descent', p. 536.

105 Cf. H. von Soden, *Der Brief an die Epheser* (Freiburg, 1891), p. 132; Abbott, *Epistles*, p. 116; Simon, *Heaven*, p. 158 n. 3 (probably); Roels, *God's Mission*, pp. 162f; Caird, 'Descent', pp. 537ff; *Paul's Letters*, pp. 73–5; C. H. Porter, 'The Descent of Christ: An Exegetical Study of Eph. 4: 7–11', in R. L. Simpson (ed.), *One Faith* (Oklahoma, 1966), p. 47; Kirby, *Ephesians*, p. 187 n. 51; Houlden, *Paul's Letters*, pp. 310f; Martin, 'Ephesians', p. 156.

106 Caird, 'Descent', p. 541.

107 The main difficulty of the view we are suggesting, however, is that it remains unusual for Pentecost to be spoken of as a descent of *Christ*, cf. Mitton, *Ephesians* (1976), p. 148. Nevertheless N. Q. Hamilton's comment on 2 Cor. 3: 17 in *The Holy Spirit and Eschatology in Paul* (Edinburgh, 1957), p. 6, whatever its accuracy in regard to that particular text, does capture Paul's thought about the relation between Christ and the Spirit and is pertinent to the re nce to the descent here in Ephesians – 'The Spirit so effectively performs His office of communicating to men the benefits of the risen Christ that for all intents and purposes of faith the Lord Himself is present bestowing grace on His own. The Spirit brings the ascended Lord to earth again.'

108 To object with Foulkes, *Epistle*, p. 116, that 'Strongly against this is the association of the giving of gifts to men with his ascension rather than his

descent (verse 8)' is to miss the point of Paul's argument which is that precisely because no descent is mentioned in the citation in verse 8 this is something that has to be deduced from the ascent. No more decisive is the objection of Schnackenburg, 'Christus', p. 287, to a subsequent descent – 'Wenn diese Exegese für v. 9 noch möglich ist, so wird sie durch v. 10 zunichte gemacht. Denn die Aussage dieses Verses tendiert auf den Aufstieg Christi, "um das All zu erfüllen".' The author clearly did not find the assertion of verse 10 any obstacle to speaking of a *subsequent* giving of gifts, so it need not be seen as an insuperable obstacle to a subsequent descent.

109 C. Chavasse, *The Bride of Christ* (London, 1940), p. 77; cf. also I. A. Muirhead, 'The Bride of Christ', *SJT* 5 (1952), 186.

110 Muirhead, 'Bride', p. 184.

111 J. Jeremias, 'νύμφη, νυμφίος', *TDNT* IV, p. 1099.

112 *Pace* Chavasse, *Bride*, p. 75, who sees earthly marriages as only shadows or E. Goodspeed, *The Meaning of Ephesians* (Chicago, 1933), pp. 60ff, who holds that the writer is more interested in marriage as a symbol than in the actual relationship.

113 Cf. Percy, *Die Probleme*, pp. 255f.

114 For this interpretation of τοῦ θεοῦ cf. Schlier, *Epheser*, pp. 289f.

115 Cf. Dibelius, *Kolosser*, p. 98; Schlier, *Epheser*, p. 292; Kirby, *Ephesians*, p. 144; Caird, *Paul's Letters*, p. 92.

116 Cf. Abbott, *Epistles*, p. 184; Percy, *Die Probleme*, p. 259; Mitton, *Ephesians* (1976), p. 223.

117 Cf. Martin, 'Ephesians', p. 175.

118 Cf. also Gnilka, *Epheserbrief*, p. 308; M. Barth, *Ephesians*, pp. 804f.

119 Again this is, of course, not to say that there are not difficulties about Pauline authorship with regard to other aspects of Ephesians, such as the view which it reflects of Paul's apostleship or of the relation between Jews and Gentiles within the Church, but the limitations of this study prevent an evaluation of these here, cf. also Kehl, 'Erniedrigung', p. 384, n. 77; M. Barth, *Ephesians*, pp. 116f.

120 By comparison the particular emphasis of the earlier Galatians had left virtually no room for references to future eschatology.

121 Cf. also Steinmetz, *Protologische*, pp. 114–21.

122 Cf. Schille, *Hymnen*, pp. 104f.

123 Cf. Kirby, *Ephesians*, p. 161.

7. Heaven and the eschatological perspective in Pauline thought

1 In using the term 'apocalyptic' we follow in the main Koch's attempt at a preliminary definition, *Rediscovery*, pp. 18–35. He suggests it should be defined in terms of a body of writings which are apocalypses and in terms of the characteristics which can be found in those writings. He lists some of the main characteristics, including concern with cosmic history, the future disappearance of the barriers between earthly and supernatural history, the return of the beginnings in the last day, the theme of the two ages and glory. Koch also correctly notes that 'it is all too easily overlooked that the kingdom of God, or the future aeon, is undoubtedly thought of as being already present, though in concealed form' (p. 31).

2 Cf. M. Hengel, *Judaism and Hellenism*, I (London, 1974), pp. 175ff, 200, 202-10, 253f. Of course the influence on Paul should not be thought of as always direct but as frequently involving pre-Pauline early Christian apocalyptic, cf. Baumgarten, *Paulus*, pp. 43-53.

3 Cf. Sasse, 'αἰών', pp. 206f; Strack–Billerbeck, *Kommentar*, IV, pp. 799ff, for the two ages in apocalyptic and Rabbinic literature. This terminology emerged comparatively late in apocalyptic and apparently became popular only in the first century A.D. Our discussion of the two ages is not meant to suggest that this doctrine is the exclusive basis for Paul's perspective on history.

4 See chapter 6 section 4.

5 *Christ and Time*, p. 81.

6 Cf. Cullmann, *Christ and Time*, p. 92.

7 Cf. Vos, *Eschatology* (originally published in 1930), p. 38.

8 Cf. *ibid.*, pp. 37-9.

9 Cf. *ibid.*, p. 37, though curiously enough the wording 'the two ages still labor to bring forth their respective worlds' in an earlier essay by Vos, 'Conception of the Spirit', p. 245, suggests a somewhat closer link.

10 *Eschatology*, p. 38.

11 Cf. Sasse, 'αἰών', p. 204.

12 *Ibid.*, pp. 202f.

13 See chapter 6 section 2 on 'the heavenlies' in Ephesians. Cf. also Schoonhoven, *Wrath*, pp. 109-11.

14 See chapter 2 above on 1 Cor. 15: 47ff.

15 Cf. also Schoonhoven, *Wrath*, pp. 77-80.

16 Cf. 'The Beginnings of Christian Theology', *JThCh*, VI (1969), p. 40.

17 Cf. 'New Testament and Mythology', pp. 3-11, 15f.

18 Bultmann, 'Mythology', p. 20; cf. also *Theology*, I, pp. 23, 289f, 306f, 329f.

19 Bultmann, 'History and Eschatology in the New Testament', *NTS* 1 (1954-5), p. 13; cf. also Bultmann's exposition of Paul's transformation of the apocalyptic view of history on the basis of his anthropology in *History and Eschatology* (Edinburgh, 1957), pp. 40-7.

20 Cf. 'Überlieferung und Eigenaussage im eschatologischen Denken des Apostels Paulus', *NTS* 8 (1961-2), pp. 12-26, esp. p. 17; cf. also J. Becker, 'Erwägungen zur apokalyptischen Tradition in der paulinischen Theologie', *EvT*, 30 (1970), pp. 593-609.

21 Cf. 'Apocalyptic', pp. 119f, 128f.

22 *Ibid.*, p. 126.

23 *Ibid.*, pp. 124, 126.

24 *Ibid.*, pp. 128, 130.

25 *Ibid.*, p. 129.

26 The more recent work of J. Baumgarten, *Paulus und die Apokalyptik* does not further this aspect of the discussion, though it does provide a more detailed study of the relation of Paul to apocalyptic, concentrating on the apostle's interpretation of traditional categories which he inherited from early Christian apocalyptic. His conclusions are similar to those of Becker (see above). The cosmic and apocalyptic elements in Paul are seen as traditional, while Paul's interpretation is judged always to tend towards a

reduction and demythologization of such elements as he takes them up in Christological, anthropological, paraenetic or polemical contexts. While this approach has value, the judgments about tradition and interpretation are frequently debatable, and despite Baumgarten's disavowals (pp. 239ff), in the interaction between tradition and interpretation, the traditional apocalyptic features often lose their force as an integral part of the apostle's thought. More importantly in relation to our own study, Baumgarten's conclusions about the lack of a cosmic emphasis in Paul's thought are heavily influenced by his exclusion of Colossians and Ephesians from consideration. Further, he believes the realized aspect of Paul's eschatology constitutes a radical break with apocalyptic (p. 234) and that generally the emphasis on the present is Paul's interpretation, while future notes come from the tradition (p. 235). His negative conclusions about treating the apostle as a Christian apocalyptist (pp. 227ff, 238f) have therefore taken no account of the way in which the realized aspects of Paul's eschatology, expressed in language about heaven, have links with Jewish apocalyptic.

27 A. Schweitzer, *Mysticism*, pp. 97f, 99.
28 Cf. *ibid.*, pp. 65ff, 90ff.
29 Cf. *ibid.*, pp. 84ff.
30 Schoeps, *Paul*, p. 99.
31 *Ibid.*
32 Cf. *ibid.*, pp. 97-100.
33 Cf. also Vos, *Eschatology*, pp. 226ff; W. D. Davies, *Rabbinic Judaism*, pp. 287ff; H. A. Wilcke, *Das Problem eines messianischen Zwischenreichs bei Paulus* (Zürich, 1967), esp. pp. 100ff.
34 Cf. *Rabbinic Judaism*, pp. 315ff.
35 Cf. also P. Volz, *Die Eschatologie*, pp. 113ff, who emphasizes, 'Dass in den angeführten Belegen eine reale Präexistenz der Heilsgüter gemeint sein will, darf nicht geleugnet werden; sie sind nicht bloss geplant, sondern wirklich da . . . die Theorie von den im Himmel präexistenten Gütern hat wohl mit dazu beigetragen, dass sich der Fromme schon in der Gegenwart im Jenseits einlebte, und dass an die Stelle des zeitlichen Jenseits immer mehr das örtliche Jenseits getreten ist'; and J. J. Collins, 'Apocalyptic Eschatology as the Transcendence of Death', *CBQ* 36 (1974), pp. 21-43, who argues that the focus on heavenly realities with its accompanying hope for the transcendence of death is the distinctive characteristic of apocalyptic as over against prophetic eschatology and that this belief inevitably opened the way for some form of mystic participation in the higher heavenly life. In this regard for the apocalypticists present experience and future hope were intrinsically connected, for if the future hope involved elevation to a heavenly life, then any revelation of heavenly secrets, of information about the heavenly regions during this life, was relevant to that hope (cf. esp. pp. 30, 37, 43).
36 Further Hengel, *Judaism and Hellenism*, p. 208, has argued that in apocalyptic the revelation of eschatological heavenly secrets to the righteous is in fact to be seen as both a preparation for and foretaste of their participation in the perfect wisdom of the salvation of the end time, cf. also the previous note.
37 In connection with the influence of apocalyptic on Palestinian Judaism

Hengel writes, 'Thus in it salvation in the present and the expectation of
salvation in the future do not form exclusive opposites, nor do a temporal
conception of the future and spatial concepts of heaven. This is a point
which should be observed in the interpretation of Paul or Hebrews.'
(*Judaism and Hellenism*, p. 253); cf. also E. Schweizer, *Erniedrigung*, pp.
179-81.

38 Cf. *Judaism and Hellenism*, p. 373.
39 S. Holm-Nielsen, *Hodayot. Psalms from Qumran* (Aarhus, 1960), p. 66,
writes about the term עולם וֹם , 'So far as it can be shown that the
expression here also represents the heavenly heights, it must be taken as a
characteristic of the community that man's expectation of heavenly glory
is realized in the existence of the community.' H.-W. Kuhn, *Enderwartung*,
pp. 54ff, explains the same expression in terms of heaven as an extension
of the OT concept of life being in the presence of God, and Kehl,
'Erniedrigung', p. 384, takes this up in his explanation of the community's
experience – 'durch die Gegenwart Gottes in der Gemeinde sind der
Himmel und die "Himmlischen" die "Welt", in der die Gemeinde lebt.'
40 Cf. *Enderwartung, passim*, esp. p. 186, on the balance of spatial and
temporal terms.
41 Cf. also P. Stuhlmacher, 'Erwägungen zum Problem von Gegenwart und
Zukunft in der paulinischen Eschatologie', *ZThK* 64 (1967), p. 444 – 'Das
In- und Miteinander von Heilsansage und Heilserwartung ist ja nur die
plastische "Innenschau" der apokalyptisch–kosmologischen Vorstellung,
dass sich in der letzten Zeit vor dem Ende neuer und alter Äon sowohl
zeitlich wie räumlich in- und übereinanderschieben.' He also points to
apocalyptic and Qumran as possible background for such a combination,
cf. pp. 428 n. 8, 444.
42 It must be acknowledged that there are dangers in arguing from the study
of one motif, in this case, heaven, to conclusions about a whole pattern of
thought, here, the apocalypticism of Paul's thought. In this instance, however, it can be claimed that there is some justification, since this motif is
associated with the overlap between the present and the future which is
central to Paul's eschatology. In turn, it can be further claimed, following
Schweitzer, *Mysticism*, and Vos, *Eschatology*, that Paul's eschatology
rather than, for example, justification by faith, is central to his whole
pattern of thought, cf. also, amongst others, Ridderbos, *Paul*, pp. 44-53,
who speaks in terms of a Christological eschatology providing the fundamental structure or Sanders, *Paul and Palestinian Judaism*, esp. p. 552, who
expresses this in terms of 'participationist eschatology'.
43 Cf. W. G. Rollins, 'The New Testament and Apocalyptic', *NTS* 17 (1971),
pp. 454-76, for some suggested differences between the NT in general and
apocalyptic.
44 *Pace* Rollins, 'NT and Apocalyptic', p. 454, whose thesis is that the NT
'represented a theological orientation in fundamental conflict with Jewish
apocalypticism'.
45 This is to agree with B. Vawter, '"And He Shall Come Again With Glory":
Paul and Christian Apocalyptic' in *Studiorum Paulinorum Congressus*
(1961) (Rome, 1963), p. 147, that 'Christian apocalyptic therefore differs
from the Jewish but it has not ceased to be apocalyptic.'

46 See chapter 1 section 7.

47 See chapter 3 section 11.

48 Cf. Ridderbos, *Paul*, p. 53; Stuhlmacher, 'Erwägungen', pp. 433, 443, who holds the primary factor in Paul's combination of present and future to be 'die vorzeitige christologische Selbstauslegung Gottes'.

49 F. C. Porter, 'The Place of Apocalyptical Conceptions in the Thought of Paul', *JBL* 41 (1922), pp. 191, 192, cf. also pp. 184, 195ff, 204.

50 Cf. *Apostolic Preaching*, pp. 148f.

51 Cf. 'The Mind of Paul: II', in *New Testament Studies* (Manchester, 1953), pp. 111, 112.

52 Cf. *ibid.*, p. 128.

53 'Hebraic and Greek Thought-Forms in the New Testament', in W. Klassen and G. F. Snyder (eds.), *Current Issues in New Testament Interpretation* (London, 1962), pp. 6, 10.

54 Cf. Hengel, *Judaism and Hellenism*, pp. 210–18; H. D. Betz, 'On the Problem of the Religio-Historical Understanding of Apocalypticism' in R. W. Funk (ed.), *Apocalypticism, JThCh* VI (New York, 1969), 134–56, esp. p. 138; 'We have to free ourselves from the idea of treating apocalypticism as an isolated and purely inner-Jewish phenomenon. Rather, we must learn to understand apocalypticism as a peculiar manifestation within the entire course of Hellenistic-oriental syncreticism.' J. J. Collins in 'Cosmos and Salvation: Jewish Wisdom and Apocalyptic in the Hellenistic Age', *History of Religions* 17 (1977), 142, concludes, 'The explanation of the common emphasis on the cosmos which Jewish apocalyptic shares with the Wisdom of Solomon and which distinguishes both from the earlier biblical tradition must be sought in their common environment in the Hellenistic age.' Cf. also J. J. Collins, 'Jewish Apocalyptic against its Hellenistic Near Eastern Environment', *BASOR* 220 (1975), 27–36.

55 Cf. Hurd, *The Origin of 1 Corinthians*, pp. 6–42; Hoffmann, *Die Toten*, pp. 323–9; Baumgarten, *Paulus*, pp. 236–8, for discussion of some of these issues. Our comments do not reflect an opposition to all views of development in Paul's theology. It is simply that they must take careful account of matters of chronology and circumstances and that in the area of realized eschatology those theories proposed are unconvincing.

56 This is to follow the lead of C. F. D. Moule, 'The Influence of Circumstances on the Use of Eschatological Terms', *JTS* 15 (1964), 1–15; cf. also W. Baird, 'Pauline Eschatology in Hermeneutical Perspective', *NTS* 17 (1971), 314–27; E. P. Sanders, *Paul and Palestinian Judaism* (Philadelphia, 1977), p. 432 n. 9, who rightly prefers to talk of 'developments in *presentation* and *argument*' rather than of changes in thought. The work of Steinmetz, *Protologische*, though it provides a useful catalogue of eschatological terms in Colossians and Ephesians, is particularly unsatisfactory at this point for it never asks why the writer has chosen these terms or how they function in the settings of these letters.

57 Cf. chapter 3 section 3; also Baird, 'Pauline Eschatology', p. 316, 'a wide reading of the epistles indicates that belief in the imminence of the end is maintained throughout the Pauline corpus (1 Thess. iv. 17; 1 Cor. vii. 29; Rom. xiii. 11; Phil. iv. 5). On the other hand, the possibility that Paul

might die before the end seems to have been recognized as early as 1 Thess.
v. 10.'
58 See chapter 5 above.
59 Cf. also Baird, 'Pauline Eschatology', p. 321.
60 Cf. Vos, *Eschatology*, pp. 39f - 'Precisely because it is to a large degree
incipient realization, it bears the signature of eschatology written clear on
its face.'
61 Cf. F. H. Kettler, 'Enderwartung und himmlischer Stufenbau im Kirchenbegriff des nachapostolischen Zeitalters', *TLZ* 79 (1954), 385ff; Böttger,
'Die eschatologische', pp. 261, 263.
62 For further discussion of this aspect, see L. Stadelmann, *The Hebrew
Conception of the World* (Rome, 1970), pp. 37-126.
63 Cf. also Sanders, *Palestinian Judaism*, p. 448. In what follows we are aware
of the question of how closely the Ephesians material is to be associated
with Paul himself. If it is attributed to a follower, then our contention is
that in regard to eschatology the author remains so much in continuity
with the apostle that in this area the material can still be used to provide a
'Pauline' perspective.
64 See chapter 3 section 11.
65 Cf. E. Best, *The First and Second Epistles to the Thessalonians* (London,
1972), pp. 85-7.
66 See chapter 6 section 7.
67 Cf. J. D. G. Dunn, *Baptism in the Holy Spirit* (London, 1970), esp. pp. 5ff.
68 Cf. E. Peterson, 'Die Einholung des Kyrios', *ZST* 7 (1929-30), pp. 682-
702.
69 *Pace* Vos, *Eschatology*, p. 136, who holds that they remain in the air. It is
unlikely that they are envisaged as in a state of suspension between heaven
and earth, and in any case 'the air' is associated with evil cosmic powers
(cf. Eph. 2: 2). It is also unlikely that Paul meant that believers were to be
taken back up to heaven, for as Best, *Thessalonians*, p. 200, well says, 'then
why should the Lord come down half-way from heaven? The saints might
as well have been snatched up the full way'.
70 Koch, *Rediscovery*, p. 32.
71 Cf. P. Stuhlmacher, 'Erwägungen zum ontologischen Charakter der καινὴ
κτίσις bei Paulus', *EvT* 27 (1967), 1-35; cf. also W. Schrage, 'Die Stellung
zur Welt bei Paulus, Epiktet und in der Apokalyptik: Ein Beitrag zu 1 Kor
7, 29-31', *ZThK* 61 (1964), 127f; *pace* Baumgarten, *Paulus*, pp. 163-79.
72 Cf. Ladd, *Pattern*, p. 90. 'Although Paul does not use the idiom of the new
heaven and new earth, it is the same theology of a redeemed and transformed creation.'
73 Cf. the doxological context of these verses - 1: 3, 14; also 3: 21.
74 Cf. Dahl, 'Christ', p. 426.
75 See chapter 2 section 8.
76 See chapter 5 section 3 (iv).
77 Cf. also Ladd, *Pattern*, p. 110.
78 Dahl, 'Christ', p. 440.

BIBLIOGRAPHY

Only works cited in the course of this study are listed here.

Abbott, T. K., *The Epistles to the Ephesians and to the Colossians* (Edinburgh, 1897).

Allan, J. A., 'The "In Christ" Formula in Ephesians', *NTS* 5 (1958-9), 54-62.

Allo, E.-B., *St. Paul: Première Épître aux Corinthiens* (2nd edn, Paris, 1956).

Anderson, R. S., *Historical Transcendence and the Reality of God* (Grand Rapids, Michigan, 1975).

Baillet, M., 'Fragments araméens de Qumran 2, description de la Jérusalem nouvelle', *RB* 62 (1955), 222-45.

Baird, W., 'Pauline Eschatology in Hermeneutical Perspective', *NTS* 17 (1971), 314-27.

Bammel, E., 'Versuch zu Col. 1: 15-20', *ZNW* 52 (1961), 88-95.

Bandstra, A. *The Law and the Elements of the World* (Kampen, 1964).

Barr, J., *Old and New in Interpretation* (London, 1966).

Barrett, C. K., 'The Allegory of Abraham, Sarah and Hagar in the Argument of Galatians', in *Rechtfertigung*, ed. J. Friedrich, W. Pöhlmann and P. Stuhlmacher (Tübingen, 1976), pp. 1-16.

'Christianity at Corinth', *BJRL* 46 (1964), 269-97.

From First Adam to Last (London, 1962).

'Paul's Opponents in II Corinthians', *NTS* 17 (1971), 233-54.

Romans (London, 1957).

The First Epistle to the Corinthians (London, 1971).

The Second Epistle to the Corinthians (London, 1973).

'ΨΕΥΔΑΠΟΣΤΟΛΟΙ (II Cor. xi. 13)', in *Mélanges Bibliques en hommage au R. P. Béda Rigaux*, ed. A. Descamps and A. de Halleux (Gembloux, 1970), pp. 377-96.

Barth, K., *Philippians* (London, 1962).

Barth, M., *Ephesians* (New York, 1974).

Bauer, K.-A., *Leiblichkeit, das Ende aller Werke Gottes* (Gütersloh, 1971).

Bauer, W., *A Greek-English Lexicon of the New Testament and other Early Christian Literature*, trans. W. F. Arndt and F. W. Gingrich (Chicago, 1957).

Baumert, N., *Täglich Sterben und Auferstehen* (München, 1973).

Baumgarten, J., *Paulus und die Apokalyptik* (Neukirchen-Vluyn, 1975).

Baur, F. C., 'Die Christuspartei der korinthischen Gemeinde' (1831), in *Ausgewählte Werke*, 1 (Stuttgart-Bad Cannstatt, 1963), pp. 1–146.
Paulus, Der Apostel Jesu Christi, I (Leipzig, 1866).
Paul, His Life and Works (vol. 1) (London, 1875).
Beare, F. W., *A Commentary on the Epistle to the Philippians* (London, 1959).
Beasley-Murray, G. R., *Baptism in the New Testament* (London, 1962).
Becker, J., 'Erwägungen zur apokalyptischen Tradition in der paulinischen Theologie', *EvT* 30 (1970), 593–609.
'Erwägungen zu Phil. 3, 20–21', *TZ* 27 (1971), 16–29.
Behm, J., 'κοιλία', *TDNT*, III, 786–9.
Benoit, P., 'L'Horizon Paulinien de l'Épître aux Éphésiens', *RB* 46 (1937), 342–61, 506–25.
'L'hymne christologique de Col. 1, 15–20' in *Christianity, Judaism and Other Greco-Roman Cults*, I, ed. J. Neusner (Leiden, 1975), 226–63.
'Qumran and the New Testament', in *Paul and Qumran*, ed. J. Murphy-O'Connor (London, 1968), 1–30.
Benz, E., *Paulus als Visionär* (Wiesbaden, 1952).
Berger, P., *A Rumour of Angels* (New York, 1969).
eds. Berger, P. and Neuhaus, R. J., *Against the World for the World: The Hartford Appeal and the Future of American Religion* (New York, 1976).
Berry, R., 'Death and Life in Christ: The Meaning of 2 Cor. 5: 1–10', *SJT* 14 (1961), 60–76.
Best, E., *One Body in Christ* (London, 1955).
The First and Second Epistles to the Thessalonians (London, 1972).
Betz, H. D., *Der Apostel Paulus und die sokratische Tradition* (Tübingen, 1972).
'Eine Christus-Aretalogie bei Paulus', *ZThK* 66 (1969), 288–305.
'On the Problem of the Religio-Historical Understanding of Apocalypticism', in *Apocalypticism*, ed. R. W. Funk, *JThCh* VI (New York, 1969), 134–56.
Bieder, W., *Ekklesia und Polis im Neuen Testament und in der alten Kirche* (Zürich, 1941).
Bietenhard, H., *Die himmlische Welt im Urchristentum und Spätjudentum* (Tübingen, 1951).
Black, M., 'The Pauline Doctrine of the Second Adam', *SJT* 7 (1954), 170–9.
The Scrolls and Christian Origins (London, 1961).
Blamires, H., *The Christian Mind* (London, 1963).
Blanchette, O., 'Does the Cheirographon of Col. 2, 14 Represent Christ Himself?', *CBQ* 23 (1961), 206–12.
Blass, F. and Debrunner, A., *A Greek Grammar of the New Testament and other Early Christian Literature*, translation and revision by R. W. Funk (Chicago, 1961).
Bligh, J., *Galatians* (London, 1969).
Galatians in Greek (Detroit, 1966).
Blinzler, J., 'Lexikalisches zu dem Terminus τὰ στοιχεῖα τοῦ κόσμου bei Paulus', in *Studiorum Paulinorum Congressus Internationalis*

Catholicus, 1961, *Analecta Biblica*, 18 (Rome, 1963), 429–43.

Boman, T., 'Hebraic and Greek Thought-Forms in the New Testament', in *Current Issues in New Testament Interpretation*, ed. W. Klassen and G. F. Snyder (London, 1962), 1–22.

Bornkamm, G., 'Der Philipperbrief als paulinische Briefsammlung', in *Neotestamentica et Patristica* (supplements to *NT*, vol. VI) (Leiden, 1962), 192–202.

'Die Häresie des Kolosserbriefes', in *Das Ende des Gesetzes* (München, 1966), pp. 139–56.

'Die Hoffnung im Kolosserbrief', in *Studien zum Neuen Testament und zur Patristik* (E. Klostermann zum 90. Geburtstag, Berlin, 1961), pp. 56–64.

Die Vorgeschichte des sogenannten Zweiten Korintherbriefes (Sitzungsberichte der Heidelberger Akademie der Wissenschaften, Philosophisch-historische Klasse 2, 1961).

'μυστήριον', *TDNT* IV, 802–28.

Böttger, P. C., 'Die eschatologische Existenz der Christen: Erwägungen zu Philipper 3: 20', *ZNW* 60 (1969), pp. 244–63.

Bousset, W., *Die Himmelsreise der Seele* (2nd edn, Darmstadt, 1971).

Bouttier, M., *Christianity According to Paul* (London, 1966).

En Christ, étude d'exégèse et de théologie pauliniennes (Paris, 1962).

Bowker, J. W., '"Merkabah" Visions and the Visions of Paul', *JSS* 16 (1971), 157–73.

Braaten, C., *Christ and Counter-Christ* (Philadelphia, 1972).

Eschatology and Ethics (Minneapolis, 1974).

Brandenburger, E., *Adam und Christus* (Neukirchen, 1962).

Brewer, R. R., 'The Meaning of Politeuesthe in Philippians 1: 27', *JBL* 73 (1954), 76–83.

Bring, R., *Commentary on Galatians* (Philadelphia, 1961).

Brown, R. E., *The Semitic Background of the Term 'Mystery' in the New Testament* (Philadelphia, 1968).

Bruce, F. F., '"Abraham Had Two Sons" – A Study in Pauline Hermeneutics', in *New Testament Studies*, ed. H. L. Drumwright and C. Vaughan (Waco, Texas, 1975), pp. 71–84.

1 and 2 Corinthians (London, 1971).

'Galatian Problems. 3. The "Other" Gospel', *BJRL* 53 (1971), 253–71.

New Testament History (London, 1969).

Büchsel, F., 'ἀλληγορέω', *TDNT* I, 260–3.

'"In Christus" bei Paulus', *ZNW* 42 (1949), 141–58.

'κάτω κτλ.', *TDNT* III, 640–2.

Bultmann, R., 'Exegetische Probleme des Zweiten Korintherbriefes', in *Exegetica*, ed. E. Dinkler (Tübingen, 1967), pp. 298–322.

History and Eschatology (Edinburgh, 1957).

'History and Eschatology in the New Testament', *NTS* 1 (1954–5), 5–16.

'The New Testament and Mythology', in *Kerygma and Myth*, ed. H. W. Bartsch (New York, 1961), pp. 1–44.

Theology of the New Testament (2 vols.) (New York, 1951 and 1955).

Burger, C., *Schöpfung und Versöhnung* (Neukirchen-Vluyn, 1975).

Burton, E. de Witt, *A Critical and Exegetical Commentary on the Epistle to the Galatians* (Edinburgh, 1921).

Caird, G. B., 'The Descent of Christ in Ephesians 4: 7–11', in *Studia Evangelica*, II, ed. F. L. Cross (Berlin, 1964), pp. 535–45.

Paul's Letters From Prison (Oxford, 1976).

Callaway, M. C., 'The Mistress and the Maid: Midrashic Traditions Behind Galatians 4: 21–31', *Radical Religion* 2 (1975), 94–101.

Calvin, J., *The Second Epistle of Paul the Apostle to the Corinthians and the Epistles to Timothy, Titus and Philemon*, trans. T. A. Smail (Edinburgh, 1964).

Cambier, J., 'La Signification Christologique d'Eph. 4: 7–10', *NTS* 9 (1962–3), 262–75.

Capps, W. H., *Time Invades the Cathedral: Tensions in the School of Hope* (Philadelphia, 1972).

Caragounis, C. C., *The Ephesian Mysterion* (Lund, 1977).

Cavallin, H. C. C., *Life After Death*, I (Lund, 1974).

Cerfaux, L., *The Church in the Theology of St. Paul* (New York, 1959).

Chadwick, H., 'All Things to All Men', *NTS* 1 (1955), 261–75.

Charles, R. H. (ed.), *Apocrypha and Pseudepigrapha of the Old Testament* (2 vols.) (Oxford, 1913).

The Book of the Secrets of Enoch (Oxford, 1896).

Chavasse, C., *The Bride of Christ* (London, 1940).

Cheek, J. L., 'Paul's Mysticism in the Light of Psychedelic Experience', *JAmAR* 38 (1970), 381–9.

Clavier, H., 'Brèves Remarques sur la notion de σῶμα πνευματικόν', in *The Background of the New Testament and Its Eschatology*, ed. W. D. Davies and D. Daube (Cambridge, 1956), pp. 342–67.

Collange, J.-F., *Énigmes de la deuxième épître de Paul aux Corinthiens* (Cambridge, 1972).

Collins, J. J., 'Apocalyptic Eschatology as the Transcendence of Death', *CBQ* 36 (1974), 21–43.

'Cosmos and Salvation: Jewish Wisdom and Apocalyptic in the Hellenistic Age', *History of Religions* 17 (1977), pp. 121–42.

'Jewish Apocalyptic against its Hellenistic Near Eastern Environment' *BASOR* 220 (1975), 27–36.

Colpe, C., 'Die "Himmelsreise der Seele" als philosophie- und religions-geschichtliches Problem', in *Festschrift für Joseph Klein* (Göttingen, 1967), pp. 85–104.

Die religionsgeschichtliche Schule (Göttingen, 1961).

Conzelmann, H., *Der Brief an die Epheser* (Göttingen, 1968).

I Corinthians (Philadelphia, 1975).

Coutts, J., 'Ephesians 1, 3–14 and 1 Peter 1, 3–12', *NTS* 3 (1956–7), 115–27.

Cox, H., *The Feast of Fools* (Harvard, 1969).

The Secular City (New York, 1965).

Creed, J. M., 'The Heavenly Man', *JTS* 26 (1925), 113–36.

Cullmann, O., *Christ and Time* (London, 3rd edn, 1967).

Early Christian Worship (London, 1953).

The Christology of the New Testament (London, 1963).

'The Significance of the Qumran Texts for Research into the Beginnings of Christianity' in *The Scrolls and the New Testament*, ed. K. Stendahl (London, 1958), 18–32.

Dahl, N. A., 'Adresse und Proömium des Epheserbriefes', *TZ* 7 (1951), 241–64.

'Christ, Creation and the Church', in *The Background to the New Testament and Its Eschatology*, ed. W. D. Davies and D. Daube (Cambridge, 1956), pp. 422–43.

Daniélou, J., *The Theology of Jewish Christianity* (London, 1964).

Davies, J. G., *He Ascended into Heaven* (London, 1958).

Davies, W. D., *The Gospel and the Land* (Berkeley, 1974).

Paul and Rabbinic Judaism (3rd edn, New York, 1967).

Deichgräber, R., *Gotteshymnus und Christushymnus in der frühen Christenheit* (Göttingen, 1967).

Deissmann, A., *Light from the Ancient East* (London, 1910).

Delling, G., 'πλήρης κτλ.', *TDNT* VI, 283–311.

'στοιχεῖον', *TDNT* VII, 670–87.

Dibelius, M., *An die Kolosser, Epheser, an Philemon* (Tübingen, 1953).

An die Thessalonicher I, II. An die Philipper (Tübingen, 1937).

'Die Isisweihe bei Apuleius und verwandte Initiations-Riten' (1917), in *Botschaft und Geschichte*, II, ed. G. Bornkamm (Tübingen, 1956), pp. 30–79.

Dittenberger, W., *Sylloge inscriptionum Graecarum* (4 vols.) (Leipzig, 1915–24).

Dodd, C. H., *The Apostolic Preaching and Its Developments* (London, 1936).

The Interpretation of the Fourth Gospel (Cambridge, 1953).

'The Mind of Paul: II', in *New Testament Studies* (Manchester, 1953), pp. 83–128.

Donfried, K. P., *The Setting of Second Clement in Early Christianity* (Leiden, 1974).

Doughty, D. J., 'The Presence and Future of Salvation in Corinth', *ZNW* 66 (1975), 61–90.

Drane, J. W., *Paul, Libertine or Legalist?* (London, 1975).

Dunn, J. D. G., *Baptism in the Holy Spirit* (London, 1970).

'1 Corinthians 15: 45 – Last Adam, Life-Giving Spirit', in *Christ and Spirit in the New Testament*, ed. B. Lindars and S. Smalley (Cambridge, 1973), pp. 127–41.

Jesus and the Spirit (London, 1975).

Dupont, J., *Gnosis: La connaissance religieuse dans les épîtres de Saint Paul* (Paris, 1949).

ΣΥΝ ΧΡΙΣΤΩΙ, *L'Union avec le Christ suivant Saint Paul*, 1 (Louvain, 1952).

Eckert, J., *Die urchristliche Verkündigung im Streit zwischen Paulus und seinen Gegnern nach dem Galaterbrief* (Regensburg, 1971).

Eliade, M., *Shamanism* (New York, 1964).

Ellis, E. E., 'Paul and His Opponents' in *Christianity, Judaism and Other Greco-Roman Cults*, I, ed. J. Neusner (Leiden, 1975), 264–98.

Paul and His Recent Interpreters (Grand Rapids, Michigan, 1961).

Paul's Use of the Old Testament (Edinburgh, 1957).

'"Those of the Circumcision" and the Early Christian Mission', *Studia Evangelica*, IV, ed. F. L. Cross (Berlin, 1968), pp. 390–400.

Ernst, J., *Pleroma und Pleroma Christi* (Regensburg, 1970).

Fawcett, T., *Hebrew Myth and Christian Gospel* (London, 1973).

The Symbolic Language of Religion (London, 1970).

Feuillet, A., 'La Demeure Céleste et la Destinée des Chrétiens', *Recherches de Science Religieuse*, 44 (1956), 161–92, 360–402.

Fischer, K. M., *Tendenz und Absicht des Epheserbriefes* (Göttingen, 1973).

Flanagan, N., 'A Note on Philippians 3, 20–21', *CBQ* 18 (1956), 8, 9.

Foerster, W., 'ἐξουσία', *TDNT* II, 560–75.

Fohrer, G. and Lohse, E., 'Σιών, Ἰερουσαλήμ', *TDNT* VII, 292–338.

Foulkes, F., *The Epistle of Paul to the Ephesians* (London, 1963).

France, R. T., *Jesus and the Old Testament* (London, 1971).

Francis, F. O., 'The Background of Embateuein (Col. 2: 18) in Legal Papyri and Oracle Inscriptions' in *Conflict at Colossae*, ed. F. O. Francis and W. A. Meeks (Missoula, Montana, 1973), pp. 197–207.

'Humility and Angelic Worship in Col. 2: 18', *ST* 16 (1962), 109–34.

eds. Francis, F. O. and Meeks W. A., *Conflict at Colossae: A Problem in the Interpretation of Early Christianity Illustrated by Selected Modern Studies* (Missoula, Montana, 1973).

Friedrich, G., 'Die Gegner des Paulus im 2. Korintherbrief', in *Abraham unser Vater*, ed. O. Betz, M. Hengel and P. Schmidt (Leiden, 1963), pp. 181–215.

Gabathuler, H.-J., *Jesus Christus, Haupt der Kirche - Haupt der Welt* (Zürich, 1965).

Gadamer, H. G., *Truth and Method* (New York, 1975).

Gaffin, R. B., 'Resurrection and Redemption in Pauline Soteriology', unpublished Th.D. dissertation (Philadelphia, 1969).

Gärtner, B., 'The Pauline and Johannine Idea of "to know God" against the Hellenistic Background', *NTS* 14 (1968), 209–31.

The Temple and the Community in Qumran and the New Testament (Cambridge, 1965).

Georgi, D., *Die Gegner des Paulus im 2. Korintherbrief* (Neukirchen-Vluyn, 1964).

Gibbs, J. G., *Creation and Redemption. A Study in Pauline Theology* (Leiden, 1971).

Gill, J. H., 'Transcendence: An Incarnational Model', *Encounter*, 39 (1978), 39–44.

Gnilka, J., *Der Epheserbrief* (Freiburg, 1971).

Der Philipperbrief (Freiburg, 1968).

Godet, F., *Commentary on St. Paul's First Epistle to the Corinthians*, vol. II (Edinburgh, 1898).

Goodspeed, E., *The Meaning of Ephesians* (Chicago, 1933).

Goppelt, L., *Typos* (Darmstadt, 2nd edn, 1969).

Goudoever, J. van, *Biblical Calendars* (Leiden, 1959).

Grässer, E., 'Kol. 3, 1–4 als Beispiel einer Interpretation secundum homines recipientes', *ZThK* 64 (1967), 139–68.

Grosheide, F., *Commentary on the First Epistle to the Corinthians*

(Grand Rapids, Michigan, 1953).

Grundmann, W., 'δεξιός', *TDNT* II, 37–40.

'ταπεινός κτλ.', *TDNT* VIII, 1–26.

'Überlieferung und Eigenaussage im eschatologischen Denken des Apostels Paulus', *NTS* 8 (1961–2), 12–26.

Gundry, R. H., *Sōma in Biblical Theology* (Cambridge, 1976).

Gunther, J. J., *St. Paul's Opponents and Their Background* (Leiden, 1973).

Gutbrod, W., ''Ισραήλ κτλ.', *TDNT* III, 369–91.

Guthrie, D., *Galatians* (London, 1969).

Güttgemanns, E., *Der leidende Apostel und sein Herr* (Göttingen, 1966).

Hamerton-Kelly, R. G., *Pre-existence, Wisdom and the Son of Man* (Cambridge, 1973).

Hamilton, N. Q., *The Holy Spirit and Eschatology in Paul* (Edinburgh, 1957).

Jesus for a No-God World (Philadelphia, 1969).

Hanhart, K., *The Intermediate State* (Groningen, 1966).

'Paul's Hope in the Face of Death', *JBL* 88 (1969), 445–57.

Hanson, A. T., *Studies in Paul's Technique and Theology* (London, 1974).

Hanson, R. P. C., *Allegory and Event* (London, 1959).

Hanson, S., *The Unity of the Church in the New Testament* (Uppsala, 1946).

Harris, M. J., *The Interpretation of 2 Corinthians 5: 1–10 and Its Place in Pauline Eschatology*, unpublished Ph.D. thesis (Manchester, 1970).

'Paul's View of Death in 2 Corinthians 5: 1–10' in *New Dimensions in New Testament Study*, ed. R. N. Longenecker and M. C. Tenney (Grand Rapids, 1974), pp. 317–28.

Hay, D. M., *Glory At The Right Hand* (Nashville, 1973).

Hegermann, H., *Die Vorstellung vom Schöpfungsmittler im hellenistischen Judentum und Urchristentum* (Berlin, 1961).

Heller, J., *Catch-22* (New York, 1961).

Hengel, M., *Judaism and Hellenism* (London, 1974).

The Son of God (Philadelphia, 1976).

eds. Hennecke E. and Schneemelcher, W., *New Testament Apocrypha*, vol. II (London, 1965).

Héring, J., *The First Epistle of St. Paul to the Corinthians* (London, 1962). *The Second Epistle of St. Paul to the Corinthians* (London, 1967).

Hettlinger, R., '2 Corinthians 5: 1–10', *SJT* 10 (1957), 174–94.

Hickling, C. J. A., 'Is the Second Epistle to the Corinthians a Source for Early Church History?' *ZNW* 66 (1975), 284–7.

Hoffmann, P., *Die Toten in Christus* (Münster, 1966).

Holl, K., 'Der Kirchenbegriff des Paulus in seinem Verhältnis zu dem der Urgemeinde', in *Das Paulusbild in der neueren deutschen Forschung*, ed. K. H. Rengstorf (2nd edn, Darmstadt, 1969), pp. 144–78.

Holm-Nielsen, S., *Hodayot. Psalms from Qumran* (Aarhus, 1960).

Holtzmann, H. J., *Lehrbuch der historisch-kritischen Einleitung in das Neue Testament* (2nd edn, Freiburg, 1886).

Hooker, M. D., 'Interchange in Christ', *JTS* 22 (1971), 349–61.

'Were There False Teachers in Colossae?', in *Christ and Spirit in the New Testament*, ed. B. Lindars and S. Smalley (Cambridge, 1973), pp. 315–31.

Horsley, R. A., 'Pneumatikos vs. Psychikos: Distinctions of Spiritual Status among the Corinthians', *HTR* 69 (1976), 269–88.

Houlden, J. L., *Paul's Letters From Prison* (Harmondsworth, 1970).

Hughes, P. E., *Commentary on the Second Epistle to the Corinthians* (Grand Rapids, Michigan, 1962).

Hunter, A. M., *Paul and his Predecessors* (London, 1961).

Huppenbauer, H. W., *Der Mensch zwischen zwei Welten* (Zürich, 1959).

Hurd, J. C., *The Origin of 1 Corinthians* (London, 1965).

Hurley, J. B., 'Did Paul Require Veils or the Silence of Women?', *WTJ* 35 (1973), 190–220.

Jeremias, G., *Der Lehrer der Gerechtigkeit* (Göttingen, 1963).

Jeremias, J., 'γωνία κτλ.', *TDNT* I, 791–3.

'"Flesh and Blood Cannot Inherit the Kingdom of God" (1 Cor. XV. 50)', *NTS* 2 (1955–6), pp. 151–9.

Golgotha (Leipzig, 1926).

Jerusalem in the Time of Jesus (London, 1969).

'ΙΕΡΟΥΣΑΛΗΜ/ΙΕΡΟΣΟΛΥΜΑ', *ZNW* 65 (1974), 273–6.

'Κεφαλὴ γωνίας – Ἀκρογωνιαῖος', *ZNW* 29 (1930), 264–80.

'λίθος', *TDNT* IV, 268–80.

'Μωυσῆς', *TDNT* IV, 848–73.

'νύμφη, νυμφίος', *TDNT* IV, 1099–106.

'παράδεισος', *TDNT* V, 765–73.

Jervell, J., *Imago Dei* (Göttingen, 1960).

Jewett, R., 'Conflicting Movements in the Early Church as Reflected in Philippians', *NT* 12 (1970), 362–90.

Paul's Anthropological Terms (Leiden, 1971).

'The Agitators and the Galatian Congregation', *NTS* 17 (1971), 198–212.

'The Epistolary Thanksgiving and the Integrity of Philippians', *NT* 12 (1970), 40–53.

Jonas, H., *Gnosis und spätantiker Geist*, I (Göttingen, 1954).

Judge, E. A., 'St. Paul and Classical Society', *Jahrbuch für Antike und Christentum* 15 (1972), 19–36.

Käsemann, E., 'A Primitive Christian Baptismal Liturgy', in *Essays on New Testament Themes* (London, 1964), pp. 149–68.

'Die Legitimität des Apostels', *ZNW* 41 (1942), 33–71; also in *Das Paulusbild in der neueren deutschen Forschung*, ed. K. H. Rengstorf (Darmstadt, 1969), pp. 475–521.

'Epheserbrief', in *Die Religion in Geschichte und Gegenwart*, II (Tübingen, 1958), pp. 517–20.

Jesus Means Freedom (London, 1969).

Leib und Leib Christi (Tübingen, 1933).

'On The Topic of Primitive Christian Apocalyptic', in *Apocalypticism*, ed. R. W. Funk, *JThCh* VI (New York, 1969), 99–133.

'The Beginnings of Christian Theology', *JThCh* VI (1969), 17–46.

Kee, A., *The Way of Transcendence: Christian Faith Without Belief in God* (Harmondsworth, 1971).

Kehl, N., *Der Christushymnus Kol. 1, 12–20* (Stuttgart, 1967).

'Erniedrigung und Erhöhung in Qumran und Kolossä', *ZKTh* 91 (1969), 364–94.

Kettler, F. H., 'Enderwartung und himmlischer Stufenbau im Kirchenbegriff des nachapostolischen Zeitalters', *TLZ* 79 (1954), 385–92.

Kirby, J. C., *Ephesians, Baptism and Pentecost* (London, 1968).

Klijn, A. F. J., 'Paul's Opponents in Philippians 3', *NT* 7 (1965), 278–84.

Klinzing, G., *Die Umdeutung des Kultus in der Qumrangemeinde und im Neuen Testament* (Göttingen, 1971).

Knox, W. L., *St. Paul and the Church of the Gentiles* (Cambridge, 1939).

Koch, K., *The Rediscovery of Apocalyptic* (London, 1972).

Koester, H., 'The Purpose of the Polemic of a Pauline Fragment', *NTS* 8 (1962), 317–32.

Kuhn, H.-W., *Enderwartung und gegenwärtiges Heil* (Göttingen, 1966).

Kuhn, K. G., 'πανοπλία', *TDNT* V, 298–300.
  'The Epistle to the Ephesians in the Light of the Qumran Texts', in *Paul and Qumran*, ed. J. Murphy-O'Connor (London, 1968), pp. 115–31.

Ladd, G. E., *The Pattern of New Testament Truth* (Grand Rapids, Michigan, 1968).

Lähnemann, J., *Der Kolosserbrief* (Gütersloh, 1971).

Lampe, G. W. H. and Woollcombe, K. J., *Essays on Typology* (London, 1957).

Lang, F. G., *2 Korinther 5, 1–10 in der neueren Forschung* (Tübingen, 1973).

Liddell, H. G. and Scott, R., *A Greek-English Lexicon* (revised by H. S. Jones) (Oxford 1948).

Lietzmann, H., *An die Galater* (Tübingen, 1923).

Lietzmann, H. and Kümmel, W., *An die Korinther I/II* (Tübingen, 1949).

Lightfoot, J. B., *St. Paul's Epistles to the Colossians and to Philemon* (London, 1892).
  The Epistle of St. Paul to the Galatians (London, 1890).

Lincoln, A. T., '"Paul the Visionary": The Setting and Significance of the Rapture to Paradise in II Corinthians XII. 1–10', *NTS* 25 (1979), 204–20.
  'A Re-Examination of "The Heavenlies" in Ephesians', *NTS* 19 (1973), 468–83.

Lindars, B., *New Testament Apologetic* (London, 1961).

Lindblom, J., *Gesichte und Offenbarungen* (Lund, 1968).

Lohfink, G., *Die Himmelfahrt Jesu* (München, 1971).

Lohmeyer, E., *Der Brief an die Philipper* (6th edn, Göttingen, 1964).
  Die Briefe an die Philipper, an die Kolosser und an Philemon (Göttingen, 1930).

Lohse, E., *Colossians and Philemon* (Philadelphia, 1971).
  'πεντηκοστή', *TDNT* VI, pp. 44–53.
  'Σιών, Ἰερουσαλήμ', *TDNT* VII, 319–38.

Longenecker, R., *Paul, Apostle of Liberty* (New York, 1964).
  The Christology of Early Jewish Christianity (London, 1970).

Lütgert, W., *Freiheitspredigt und Schwarmgeister in Korinth* (Gütersloh, 1908).
  Gesetz und Geist, eine Unteruschung zur Vorgeschichte des Galaterbriefes (Gütersloh, 1919).

Mackay, B. S., 'Further Thoughts on Philippians', *NTS* 7 (1960-1), 161-70.
Maier, J., 'Das Gefährdungsmotiv bei der Himmelsreise in der jüdischen Apokalyptik und "Gnosis"', *Kairos*, 5 (1963), 18-40.
Malinine, M., Puech, H.-C., Quispel, G. and Till, W., *De Resurrectione* (Zürich, 1963).
Manson, T. W., *Studies in the Gospels and Epistles* (Manchester, 1962).
The Teaching of Jesus (2nd edn, Cambridge, 1967).
Manson, W., *Jesus the Messiah* (London, 1943).
Martin, R. P., 'An Early Christian Hymn (Col. 1: 15-20)', *EQ* 36 (1964) 195-205.
'An Epistle in Search of a Life-Setting', *ET* 79 (1968), pp. 296-302.
Carmen Christi (Cambridge, 1967).
Colossians and Philemon (London, 1974).
Colossians: The Church's Lord and the Christian's Liberty (Exeter, 1972).
'Ephesians' in *Broadman Bible Commentary* (vol. 11) (London, 1971), pp. 125-77.
The Epistle of Paul to the Philippians (London, 1959).
New Testament Foundations (vol. 2) (Grand Rapids, Michigan, 1978).
Philippians (London, 1976).
eds. Marty, M. E. and Peerman, D. G., *New Theology, no. 7: The Recovery of Transcendence* (New York, 1970).
Masson, C., *L'Épître de Saint Paul aux Colossiens* (Neuchatel, 1950).
McKelvey, R. J., *The New Temple* (Oxford, 1969).
Meeks, W., *The Prophet-King* (Leiden, 1967).
Merk, O., 'Der Beginn der Paränese im Galaterbrief', *ZNW* 60 (1969), 83-104.
Metzger, B., *A Textual Commentary on the Greek New Testament* (London, 1971).
Minear, P., 'The Cosmology of the Apocalypse' in *Current Issues in New Testament Interpretation*, ed. W. Klassen and G. Snyder (New York, 1962), pp. 23-37.
Mitton, C. L., *Ephesians* (London, 1976).
The Epistle to the Ephesians (Oxford, 1951).
Moule, C. F. D., *An Idiom-Book of New Testament Greek* (Cambridge, 1968).
'"Fulness" and "Fill" in the New Testament', *SJT* 4 (1951), 79-86.
'St. Paul and Dualism', *NTS* 12 (1965-6), 106-23.
The Epistles of Paul the Apostle to the Colossians and to Philemon (Cambridge, 1957).
'The Influence of Circumstances on the Use of Eschatological Terms', *JTS* 15 (1964), 1-15.
Moulton, J. H., *A Grammar of New Testament Greek* (4 vols.) (Edinburgh, 1908-76).
Muirhead, I. A., 'The Bride of Christ', *SJT* 5 (1952), 175-87.
Munck, J., *Paul and the Salvation of Mankind* (London, 1959).
Mussner, F., *Christus, das All und die Kirche* (Trier, 1955).
'Contributions Made by Qumran to the Understanding of the Epistle to

the Ephesians', in *Paul and Qumran*, ed. J. Murphy-O'Connor (London, 1968), pp. 159–78.

Der Galaterbrief (Freiburg, 1974).

'Hagar, Sinai, Jerusalem – zum Text von Gal. 4, 25a', *TQ* 135 (1955), 56–60.

Neugebauer, F., 'Das Paulinische "in Christo"', *NTS* 4 (1957–8), 124–38.

Nickelsburg, G. W. E., *Resurrection, Immortality and Eternal Life in Inter-testamental Judaism* (Cambridge, 1972).

Nock, A. D., 'The Vocabulary of the New Testament', *JBL* 52 (1933), 131–9.

Odeberg, H., *The View of the Universe in the Epistle to the Ephesians*, Lund Universitets Arsskrift Bd. 29 nr. 6 (Lund, 1934).

Oepke, A., 'γυμνός κτλ.', *TDNT* I, 773–6.

Der Brief des Paulus an die Galater (2nd edn, Berlin, 1964).

Oostendorp, D. W., *Another Jesus: A Gospel of Jewish-Christian Superiority in II Corinthians* (Kampen, 1967).

Palmer, D. W., '"To die is gain" (Philippians 1. 21)', *NT* 17 (1975), 203–18.

Patte, D., *Early Jewish Hermeneutic in Palestine* (Missoula, Montana, 1975).

Pearson, B. A., *The Pneumatikos–Psychikos Terminology in 1 Corinthians*, Society of Biblical Literature (Dissertation Series 12, Missoula Montana, 1973).

Peel, M. L., 'Gnostic Eschatology and the New Testament', *NT* 12 (1970), 141–65.

The Epistle to Rheginos (London, 1969).

Percy, E., *Die Probleme der Kolosser- und Epheserbriefe* (Lund, 1946).

Peterson, E., 'Die Einholung des Kyrios', *ZST* 7 (1929–30), 682–702.

Plummer, A., *A Critical and Exegetical Commentary on the Second Epistle of St. Paul to the Corinthians* (Edinburgh, 1915).

Pollard, T. E., 'The Integrity of Philippians', *NTS* 13 (1966–7), 57–66.

Pope, R. M., 'Studies in Pauline Vocabulary: of the Heavenly Places', *ET* 23 (1912), 365–8.

Porter, C. H., 'The Descent of Christ: An Exegetical Study of Eph. 4: 7–11', in *One Faith*, ed. R. L. Simpson (Oklahoma, 1966), pp. 45–55.

Porter, F. C., *The Mind of Christ in Paul* (London, 1930).

'The Place of Apocalyptical Conceptions in the Thought of Paul', *JBL* 41 (1922), 183–204.

Preisker, H., 'ἐμβατεύω', *TDNT* II, 535, 536.

Procksch, O., 'ἅγιος', *TDNT* I, 100–15.

Ramsay, W. M., *The Teaching of Paul in Terms of the Present Day* (London, 1913).

Reitzenstein, R., *Die hellenistischen Mysterienreligionen* (Stuttgart, 1910) (reprinted Darmstadt, 1956). [ET – *Hellenistic Mystery-Religions*, Pittsburgh, 1978].

Richardson, P., *Israel in the Apostolic Church* (Cambridge, 1969).

Ridderbos, H., *The Epistle to the Galatians* (London, 1954).

Paul (Grand Rapids, Michigan, 1975).

Rissi, M., *Studien zum zweiten Korintherbrief* (Zürich, 1969).

Robertson, A. and Plummer, A., *A Critical and Exegetical Commentary on the First Epistle of St. Paul to the Corinthians* (Edinburgh, 1929).

Robinson, J. A., St. *Paul's Epistle to the Ephesians* (2nd edn, London, 1928).

Robinson, J. A. T., *The Body* (London, 1952).

Robinson, J. M., 'A Formal Analysis of Colossians 1: 15–20', *JBL* 76 (1957), 270–87.

ed. Robinson, J. M., *The Nag Hammadi Library* (New York, 1977).

Roels, E., *God's Mission: the Epistle to the Ephesians in Mission Perspective* (Franeker, 1962).

Rollins, W. G., 'The New Testament and Apocalyptic', *NTS* 17 (1971), 454–76.

van Roon, A., *The Authenticity of Ephesians* (Leiden, 1974).

Ropes, J. H., *The Singular Problem of the Epistle to the Galatians* (Harvard, 1929).

Roszak, T., *The Making of a Counter Culture* (New York, 1968).

Ruppel. W., 'Politeuma. Bedeutungsgeschichte eines staatsrechtlichen Terminus', *Philologus* 82 (1927), 268–312, 433–54.

Russell, D. S., *The Method and Message of Jewish Apocalyptic* (London, 1964).

Saake, H., 'Paulus als Ekstatiker', *NT* 15 (1973), 153–60.

Sanders, E. P., *Paul and Palestinian Judaism* (Philadelphia, 1977).

Sanders, J. T., 'Hymnic Elements in Ephesians 1–3', *ZNW* 56 (1965), 214–32.

The New Testament Christological Hymns (Cambridge, 1971).

Sasse, H., 'αἰών', *TDNT* I, 197–209.

'γῆ', *TDNT* I, 677–81.

Saunders, E. W., 'The Colossian Heresy and Qumran Theology' in *Studies in the History and Text of the New Testament*, ed. B. L. Daniels and M. J. Suggs (Salt Lake City, 1967), pp. 133–45.

Schille, G., 'Der Autor des Epheserbriefes', *TLZ* 82 (1957), 325–34.

Frühchristliche Hymnen (Berlin, 1965).

Schlatter, A., *Die korinthische Theologie* (Gütersloh, 1914).

Paulus, der Bote Jesu (4th edn, Stuttgart, 1969).

Schlier, H., *Christus und die Kirche im Epheserbrief* (Tübingen, 1930).

Der Brief an die Epheser (5th edn, Düsseldorf, 1965).

Der Brief an die Galater (3rd edn, Göttingen, 1962).

Schmidt, K. L., *Die Polis in Kirche und Welt* (Basel, 1939).

'Jerusalem als Urbild und Abbild', *Eranos Jahrbuch*, 18 (1950), 207–48.

Schmithals, W., *Gnosticism in Corinth* (Nashville, 1971).

'Die Häretiker in Galatien', *ZNW* 47 (1956), 26–67.

'Die Irrlehrer des Philipperbriefes', *ZThK* 54 (1957), 297–341.

Schnackenburg, R., *Baptism in the Thought of St. Paul* (Oxford, 1964).

'Christus, Geist und Gemeinde (Eph. 4: 1–16)', in *Christ and Spirit in the New Testament*, ed. B. Lindars and S. Smalley (Cambridge, 1973), pp. 279–96.

Schneider, J., 'ἀναβαίνω κτλ.', *TDNT* I, 518–23.

'μέρος', *TDNT* IV, 594–8.

Schniewind, J., 'Die Leugner der Auferstehung in Korinth', in *Nachgelassene Reden und Aufsätze* (Berlin, 1952), pp. 110-39.
Schoeps, H. J., *Paul* (London, 1961).
Scholem, G., *Jewish Gnosticism, Merkabah Mysticism and Talmudic Tradition* (New York, 1960).
Major Trends in Jewish Mysticism (London, 1955).
Schoonhoven, C., *The Wrath of Heaven* (Grand Rapids, Michigan, 1966).
Schrage, W., 'Die Stellung zur Welt bei Paulus, Epiktet und in der Apokalyptik: Ein Beitrag zu 1 Kor. 7, 29-31', *ZThK* 61 (1964), 125-54.
Schweitzer, A., *The Mysticism of Paul the Apostle* (London, 1931).
Schweizer, E., *Der Brief an die Kolosser* (Zürich, 1976).
'Christus und Geist im Kolosserbrief', in *Christ and Spirit in the New Testament*, ed. B. Lindars and S. Smalley (Cambridge, 1973), pp. 297-313.
'Die "Elemente der Welt" Gal. 4: 3, 9, Kol. 2: 8, 10', in *Verborum Veritas*, ed. O. Böcher and K. Haacker (Wuppertal, 1970), pp. 245-59.
Erniedrigung und Erhöhung bei Jesus und seinen Nachfolgern (Zürich, 1962).
Lordship and Discipleship (London, 1960).
'πνεῦμα', *TDNT* VI, 389-455.
'The Church as the Missionary Body of Christ', *NTS* 8 (1961-2), 1-11.
Scott, C. A. A., *Christianity According to St. Paul* (Cambridge, 1932).
Scroggs, R., 'The Exaltation of the Spirit by Some Early Christians', *JBL* 84 (1965), 359-73.
The Last Adam (Oxford, 1966).
Sevenster, J. N., 'Some Remarks on the ΓΥΜΝΟΣ in II Cor. V. 3', in *Studia Paulina in honorem J. de Zwaan*, ed. J. N. Sevenster and W. C. van Unnik (Haarlem, 1953), 202-14.
Sharpe, J. L., 'The Second Adam in the Apocalypse of Moses', *CBQ* 35 (1973), 35-46.
Sherwin-White, A. N., *Roman Society and Roman Law in the New Testament* (Oxford, 1963).
Siber, P., *Mit Christus leben* (Zürich, 1971).
Sider, R. J., 'The Pauline Conception of the Resurrection Body in 1 Corinthians XV. 35-54', *NTS* 21 (1975), 428-39.
Simon, U., *Heaven in the Christian Tradition* (London, 1958).
Smalley, S., 'The Theatre of Parousia', *SJT* 17 (1964), 406-13.
Smith, W., *The Biblical Doctrine of Heaven* (Chicago, 1968).
Soden, H. von, *Der Brief an die Epheser* (Freiburg, 1891).
'Sakrament und Ethik bei Paulus', in *Urchristentum und Geschichte*, 1 (Tübingen, 1951), pp. 239-75.
Spittler, R., 'The Limits of Ecstasy: An Exegesis of 2 Corinthians 12: 1-10' in *Current Issues in Biblical and Patristic Interpretation*, ed. G. F. Hawthorne (Grand Rapids, Michigan, 1975), pp. 259-66.
Spörlein, B., *Die Leugnung der Auferstehung* (Regensburg, 1971).
Stadelmann, L., *The Hebrew Conception of the World* (Rome, 1970).
Stagg, F., 'The Abused Aorist', *JBL* 91 (1972), 222-31.
Stauffer, E., *New Testament Theology* (London, 1955).

Stegmann, B. A., *Christ, the 'Man from Heaven'. A Study of 1 Corinthians 15: 45–47 in the Light of the Anthropology of Philo Judaeus* (Washington, 1927).

Steinmetz, F.-J., *Protologische Heilszuversicht: Die Strukturen des soteriologischen und christologischen Denkens im Kolosser- und Epheserbrief* (Frankfurt, 1969).

Strack, H. L. and Billerbeck, P., *Kommentar zum Neuen Testament aus Talmud und Midrasch* (Munich, 1926).

Strathmann, H., 'πόλις κτλ.', *TDNT* VI, 516–35.

Strecker, G., 'Redaktion und Tradition im Christushymnus Phil. 2', *ZNW* 55 (1964), 63–78.

Strugnell, J., 'The Angelic Liturgy at Qumran', in *Congress Volume* (Oxford, 1959), supplement to *Vetus Testamentum*, VII (Leiden, 1961), pp. 318–45.

Stuhlmacher, P., 'Erwägungen zum ontologischen Charakter der καινὴ κτίσις bei Paulus', *EvT* 27 (1967), 1–35.

'Erwägungen zum Problem von Gegenwart und Zukunft in der paulinischen Eschatologie', *ZThK* 64 (1967), 423–50.

Talbert, C. H., 'The Myth of a Descending-Ascending Redeemer in Mediterranean Antiquity', *NTS* 22 (1976), 418–40.

Tasker, R. V. G., *The Second Epistle of Paul to the Corinthians* (London, 1958).

Thiselton, A. C., 'Realized Eschatology at Corinth', *NTS* 24 (1978), 510–26.

Thompson, G. H. P., *The Letters of Paul to the Ephesians, to the Colossians and to Philemon* (Cambridge, 1967).

Thrall, M. E., *Greek Particles in the New Testament* (Leiden, 1962).

Torrance, T. F., *Space, Time and Resurrection* (Grand Rapids, 1976).

Traub, H., 'οὐρανός', *TDNT* V, 497–502, 509–43.

Tyson, J. B., 'Paul's Opponents at Philippi', *Perspectives in Religious Studies* 3 (1976), pp. 82–95.

Vaux, R. de, *Ancient Israel* (2 vols.) (New York, 1965).

Vawter, B., '"And He Shall Come Again With Glory": Paul and Christian Apocalyptic', in *Studiorum Paulinorum Congressus*, 1961 (Rome, 1963), pp. 143–50.

Vielhauer, P., *Oikodome* (Karlsruhe-Durlach, 1940).

Vincent, M. R., *A Critical and Exegetical Commentary on the Epistles to the Philippians and to Philemon* (Edinburgh, 1897).

Vogel, C. J. de, 'Reflections on Philipp. i 23–24', *NT* 19 (1977), 262–74.

Volz, P., *Die Eschatologie der jüdischen Gemeinde* (2nd edn, Hildesheim, 1966).

Vos, G., 'The Eschatological Aspect of the Pauline Conception of the Spirit', in *Biblical and Theological Studies* (New York, 1912), pp. 209–59.

The Pauline Eschatology (2nd edn, Grand Rapids, Michigan, 1961).

Wedderburn, A. J. M., 'Adam and Christ' (unpublished Ph.D. Thesis, Cambridge, 1970).

'The Body of Christ and Related Concepts in 1 Corinthians', *SJT* 24 (1971), 74–96.

'Philo's "Heavenly Man"', *NT* 15 (1973), 301–26.

Weiss, H., 'The Law in the Epistle to the Colossians', *CBQ* 34 (1972), 294–314.

Weiss, J., *Der erste Korintherbrief* (Göttingen, 1925).

Wernberg-Møller, P. C. H., *The Manual of Discipline* (Leiden, 1957).

Widengren, G., *The Ascension of the Apostle and the Heavenly Books*, Uppsala Universitets Arsskrift (Uppsala, 1950).

Wilcke, H. A., *Das Problem eines messianischen Zwischenreichs bei Paulus* (Zürich, 1967).

Wilckens, U., *Weisheit und Torheit. Eine exegetische-religionsgeschichtliche Untersuchung zu 1 Kor. 1 und 2* (Tübingen, 1959).

Wilder, A. N., *Theopoetic* (Philadelphia, 1976).

Williams, A. Lukyn, 'The Cult of the Angels at Colossae', *JTS* 10 (1909), 413–38.

Wilson, J. H. 'The Corinthians Who Say There is No Resurrection of the Dead', *ZNW* 59 (1968), 90–107.

Wilson, R. A. '"We" and "You" in the Epistle to the Ephesians', in *Studia Evangelica*, II, ed. F. L. Cross (Berlin, 1964), pp. 676–80.

Wilson, R. McL. 'How Gnostic Were the Corinthians?', *NTS* 19 (1972), 65–74.

'The Trimorphic Protennoia' in *Gnosis and Gnosticism*, ed. M. Krause (Leiden, 1977), 50–4.

Windisch, H., *Der Zweite Korintherbrief* (1924) (reprinted Göttingen, 1970).

Winter, M., *Pneumatiker und Psychiker in Korinth* (Marburg, 1975).

Yadin, Y., 'Some Notes on the Newly Published Pesharim of Isaiah', *IEJ* 9 (1959), 39–42.

Yamauchi, E., *Pre-Christian Gnosticism: A Survey of the Proposed Evidences* (London, 1973).

'Sectarian Parallels: Qumran and Colossae', *BS* 121 (1964), 141–52.

Yates, R., 'A Re-examination of Ephesians 1: 23', *ET* 83 (1972), 146–51.

Young, J. C. de, *Jerusalem in the New Testament* (Kampen, 1960).

Zeilinger, F., *Der Erstgeborene der Schöpfung* (Vienna, 1974).

INDEX OF PASSAGES CITED

INDEX OF AUTHORS